POLITICAL ECOLOGIES
OF MEAT

Edited by Jody Emel and Harvey Neo

Routledge
Taylor & Francis Group

LONDON AND NEW YORK

earthscan
from Routledge

First published 2015
by Routledge
2 Park Square, Milton Park, Abingdon, Oxon OX14 4RN
and by Routledge

711 Third Avenue, New York, NY 10017

Routledge is an imprint of the Taylor & Francis Group, an informa business

British Library Cataloguing-in-Publication Data
A catalogue record for this book is available from the British Library

Library of Congress Cataloging in Publication Data
A catalog record for this book has been requested

ISBN: 978-0-415-73694-7 (hbk)
ISBN: 978-0-415-73695-4 (pbk)
ISBN: 978-1-315-81828-3 (ebk)

Typeset in Bembo
by GreenGate Publishing Services, Tonbridge, Kent

POLITICAL ECOLOGIES OF MEAT

Livestock production worldwide is increasing rapidly, in part due to economic growth and demand for meat in industrializing countries. Yet there are many concerns about the sustainability of increased meat production and consumption, from perspectives including human health, animal welfare, climate change and environmental pollution.

This book tackles the key issues of contemporary meat production and consumption through a lens of political ecology, which emphasizes the power relations producing particular social, economic and cultural interactions with non-human nature. Three main topics are addressed: the political ecology of global livestock production trends; changes in production systems around the world and their implications for environmental justice; and existing and emerging governance strategies for meat production and consumption systems, and their implications.

Case studies of different systems at varying scales are included, drawn from Asia, Africa, the Americas and Europe. The book includes an editorial introduction to set the context and synthesize key messages.

Jody Emel is Professor of Geography at Clark University, USA.

Harvey Neo is an Assistant Professor in the Department of Geography at the National University of Singapore.

Routledge Studies in Political Ecology

The *Routledge Studies in Political Ecology* series provides a forum for original, innovative and vibrant research surrounding the diverse field of political ecology. This series promotes interdisciplinary scholarly work drawing on a wide range of subject areas such as geography, anthropology, sociology, politics and environmental history. Titles within the series reflect the wealth of research being undertaken within this diverse and exciting field.

Published:

Political Ecology of the State
The basis and the evolution of environmental statehood
Antonio Augusto Rossotto Ioris

Sustainability in Coffee Production
Creating shared value chains in Colombia
Andrea Biswas-Tortajada and Asit K. Biswas

Political Ecologies of Meat
Edited by Jody Emel and Harvey Neo

CONTENTS

LIST OF FIGURES

LIST OF TABLES

LIST OF CONTRIBUTORS

Emma R. M. Archer van Garderen, Chief Researcher, Council for Scientific and Industrial Research (CSIR) Natural Resources and the Environment, University of the Witwatersrand, South Africa

Kin Wing Chan, PhD Researcher in China's Environmental Governance and Policy, School of Planning and Geography, Cardiff University, UK

Annalisa Colombino, Assistant Professor, Institute of Geography, University of Graz, Austria

Mark H. Cooper, Doctoral Candidate, Department of Geography, University of Wisconsin-Madison, USA

Paula Daniels, Lecturer, Institute of the Environment and Sustainability, University of California Los Angeles, USA

Claire L. Davis, Researcher, CSIR Natural Resources and the Environment, South Africa

Jacque (Jody) Emel, Professor of Geography, Graduate School of Geography, Clark University, USA

Paolo Giaccaria, Ricercatore confermato (tenured Assistant Professor) in Economic and Political Geography, Dipartimento di Scienze EconomicoSociali e Matematico, Statistiche Università di Torino, Italy

Ryan Gunderson, Assistant Professor of social Justice Studies and Sociology, Miami University, USA

Lewis Holloway, Reader in Human Geography, University of Hull, UK

Pascale Joassart-Marcelli, Associate Professor of Geography, San Diego State University, USA

Adrienne Johnson, Doctoral Candidate, Graduate School of Geography, Clark University, USA

Connie Johnston, Visiting Assistant Professor of Geography, University of Oregon, USA

Keith C. L. Lee, Doctoral Candidate, Department of City and Regional Planning, University of California, Berkeley, USA

Julia Lenhardt, Technical GIS Analyst, Environmental Systems Research Institute (ESRI), USA

Ian MacLachlan, Professor, University of Lethbridge, Canada

Colleen McKinney, Policy Analyst, Los Angeles Food Policy Council, USA

Hug March, Senior Researcher, Universitat Oberta de Catalunya, Spain

Mara Miele, Reader, School of Planning and Geography, Cardiff University, UK

Harvey Neo, Assistant Professor of Geography, National University of Singapore, Singapore

Joshua P. Newell, Assistant Professor, School of Natural Resources and Environment, University of Michigan, USA

Yelena Ogneva-Himmelberger, Assistant Professor of Geographic Information Systems, Clark University, USA

Pablo Pacheco, Principal Scientist, Center for International Forestry Research (CIFOR), Indonesia

René Poccard-Chapuis, International Researcher, Centre International de Coopération en Recherche Agronomique pour le Développement (CIRAD), Brazil

Christopher Rosin, Honorary Research Fellow, Center for Integrated Agricultural Systems, University of Wisconsin, Madison, USA

Karolina Rucinska, PhD and Freelance Researcher, School of Planning and Geography, Cardiff University, UK

David Saurí, Professor of Geography and Environmental Sciences, Universitat Autònoma de Barcelona, Spain

Elisabeth (Lisa) A. Stoddard, Assistant Teaching Professor, Social Science and Policy Studies and Undergraduate Studies, Worcester Polytechnic Institute, USA

Mark A. Tadross, Technical Advisor, UNDP/Climate Systems Analysis Group, University of Cape Town, South Africa

Elizabeth Waithanji, Gender Consultant, International Livestock Research Institute (ILRI), Kenya

Jennifer R. Wolch, William W. Wurster Dean, Professor of City & Regional Planning, University of California Berkeley, USA

ACKNOWLEDGEMENTS

This book has been a long time coming. It began back in the 1970s with a public viewing of the first documentary on factory farming. Jody and her sister, Jan, hosted the film in the library of the University of Arizona. It gained momentum with a vegetarian meal in Los Angeles in the 1990s when Jennifer Wolch and Jody discovered a common interest in animals and wondered why it couldn't be possible to write about them theoretically and politically within the discipline of geography. This third wave of animal geographies, so coined by Julie Urbanik, was co-produced through works by Jennifer Wolch, Chris Philo, Sarah Whatmore, Chris Wilbert, Kay Anderson, William Lynn, Henry Buller, Mara Miele, and many others. Harvey's organization of several sessions over the years at the annual meeting of geographers was seminal in furthering the notion that there are indeed political ecologies of animal production and consumption that go beyond economy, culture and politics – emerging from and into social justice and social theories.

We are deeply indebted to all of the contributors, our supportive colleagues within the Clark Graduate School of Geography and the Department of Geography, National University of Singapore, as well as our families for encouraging this work. Jody is especially grateful to her sister Jan and her daughter Julia for their unmediated support for her political action (including writing) on animal rights (with all of the problems that language produces, there is still no better way to describe the objective of improving animal lives). Her 'animal students' have provided an unparalleled community of provocative, inquisitive and dynamic co-learners. Harvey has benefited much from the invigorating discussions and the generous intellectual space provided by the Politics, Economies and Space research group in the Department of Geography. Through the years, the hundreds of students who have taken his course, 'Nature and Society', taught him as much about nature, animals and society as he has tried to teach them. Their collective inspiration is duly acknowledged here.

Last, we would like to thank the many people on the planet who work against the grain to challenge and change the hyper-exploitative capitalist systems of animal production that threaten to engulf us all. Within this group, we especially want to thank the brilliant photographer, Meg Birnbaum, who allowed us to use her beautiful photographs for the cover (www.megbirnbaumphotography.com, from the collection 'Corn Dogs and Blue Ribbons').

FOREWORD

Praise goes to Jody Emel, Harvey Neo and the wealth of contributors whose scholarship and research forms the basis of *Political Ecologies of Meat*. They take us 'behind the curtain' of the livestock industry through an enriching fusion of political ecology with animal geography. They challenge us to consider the factory floors, breeding protocols, feed regimens, health standards, labour conditions, meat-eating norms, neoliberal policies, ecological impacts, and everyday practices that frame and condition the lives of millions of cows, pigs, goats, sheep, chickens, rabbits, and other animals. What Emel, Neo and the contributors expose – and what we find – is a messiness and complexity of political economic, social cultural, and ecological dynamics that manifest themselves across individual human and animal bodies, households and social groups, cities and their rural environs, nation states and the globe. Laid bare are the unsettling contradictions of animals (read humans) producing and consuming other animals (read nonhumans). These contradictions necessarily express themselves in terms of profit and exploitation, empowerment and disempowerment, haves and have-nots. 'Meat' is meant to feed and nourish people, nurture cultural traditions around dinner tables, generate jobs and income, and boost national economies. Yet 'meat' takes a serious and devastating toll on the animals, and many of the humans, whose lives are wrapped up with its production; it also severely compromises the natural environments and societal contexts in which we all live. As such, the animals that feature as 'meat' themselves endure genetic manipulation, prodding, containment, and slaughter as they move through intensive industrial livestock systems. The human labourers endure working conditions characterized by long hours, low pay, dust-laden and contaminant-filled spaces, and carcass butchering. The industry that prides itself on production of high-quality meats to line grocery store shelves and feature in family mealtimes relentlessly churns out nitrates and other waste that pollute spring water sources and vital waterways. And the cultural traditions wrapped up in meat production and consumption take on gender, class, and race-based connections that reinforce differences and inequalities among both human and animal social groups. *Political Ecologies of Meat* covers this wide range of issues across various perspectives, generating meticulous empirical details and provocative theoretical insights.

Exposing the livestock industry to this end aligns with my own research focused on poultry production in (peri-)urban Botswana over the past few decades. Early iterations of this work highlighted gender relations of power against a backdrop of chicken-based industrial farming in Greater Gaborone while subsequent iterations highlighted explicitly the lives of chickens within this sector. The research reveals differences and inequalities between male- and female-owned commercial operations generated by government promotion and support of entrepreneurship through poultry production. On the one hand, women entrepreneurs have empowered themselves by embracing chickens as 'women's work' and taking advantage of financial grants within a newly urbanized, commercial version of poultry-raising in Botswana; they have gained access to land, income, and social networks that offer them substantial opportunities. Chickens too have gained socio-economic and political status; they are valued more highly as a foodstuff and entrepreneurial activity (relative to the still-preferred cattle sector), and the poultry sector is seen as a 'success story' of national economic growth and self-sufficiency. On the other hand, the poultry industry reproduces substantial inequalities between men (who exert control as the largest producers at the top of this vertically integrated system) and women (who labour as contract growers for these male producers). The chickens themselves are exposed to manipulative breeding, crowded and dusty housing conditions, aggressive handling, and halaal slaughtering. As such, women's empowerment as successful chicken producers, as well as their disempowerment within a male-dominated poultry sector, pivots on the poor treatment and killing of hundreds of thousands of birds each year in Botswana. The intersectionality of women and chickens marginalizes them first, given that chickens are 'women's work' in Botswana society and not as valued or respected as cattle, which are 'men's domain'; it empowers them second, through government-supported opportunities within the commercial poultry sector; and it exploits them third, with women relatively disadvantaged within the poultry sector, and more and more chickens produced as 'meat'. The inhospitable working conditions within poultry farms, as well as the pollution generated in terms of contaminants and odours, reinforce further the contradictions of how a national 'success story' can undermine the labourers (both humans and chickens) and environment (water, soil, air) on which it fundamentally relies.

So now what? What happens when critical scholarship and scientific investigations reveal such unsettling and unacceptable circumstances, dynamics and outcomes of the political ecologies of meat? What happens when we allow ourselves to consider, let alone acknowledge, that 'meat' may have a standpoint and is owed ethical consideration on account of simply being 'animal'? Seeking empathetic understanding of animals, paying attention to their physical materiality and their embodied ecologies are a necessary next step to ensuring our theoretical and empirical insights move into ethical deliberations and policy responses. We must learn to be affected in ways that do not shy away from the daily experiences of animals (nonhuman and human) whose bodies, personalities, and fates are wrapped up in the industrial livestock complex. We must nurture an ethics of care by paying attention to the voices of these animals and engaging them responsibly and ethically within dinner table conversations and public arenas. Emel, Neo and contributors to the *Political Ecologies of Meat* encourage us to be affected by those whose lives and deaths are implicated in the livestock industry.

Alice J. Hovorka
Professor of Geography and Environmental Studies
Queen's University, Canada

1

INTRODUCTION

Jody Emel and Harvey Neo

> Species interdependence is a well-known fact – except when it comes to humans.
> (Tsing, 2012, p. 141)

The ever-expansive livestock industry

The tangle of livestock issues arising at the beginning of the 21st century promises to provide fodder for politics and policy for some time to come. Just as the sentience and subjectivities of domesticated animals are being researched and understood as never before, so is the intensification of livestock production fast rising throughout the world. The 'global meat complex' is dynamically shifting from north to south with longer supply chains and complicated trade arrangements influenced by disease, animal welfare, religion and taste. More than quadrupling in size since 1960, global meat production was around 312 million tons by 2013 (FAO, 2014). Governments are subsidizing livestock and feed production in many countries, notably China, India, Brazil, the US, Australia, and the European Union. In the US, feed grains are the biggest recipient of government agricultural subsidies. India prides itself on its recent 'pink revolution'. Who would have thought that the land of the holy cow would become the largest beef exporter in the world? How amazing is it that China's pig production (and consumption) constitutes half the world's supply (102 million metric tons of meat from nearly 660 million pigs) and that the country also imports more than half of the globally traded soy (Schneider, 2011)? China now consumes 60 per cent more meat than did the entire world population in 1950 (Ma, 2013), although Luxembourg, the US, Australia, and New Zealand are the biggest consumers per capita.

Also astonishing is the news from the Intergovernmental Panel on Climate Change (IPCC) and the United Nations Food and Agricultural Organization (FAO) that livestock production systems have generated more greenhouse gas (GHG) emissions than any other sector of the global economy. In fact, FAO claims livestock production is one of the top two or three 'most significant contributors to environmental problems, at every scale from local to global ... livestock's contribution to environmental problems is on a massive scale and its potential contribution to their solution is equally large' (Steinfeld et al., 2006, p. xx; also see Gunderson, 2013). Livestock production is one of the largest drivers of biodiversity destruction through genetic erosion, species loss and habitat conversion (UNEP, 2010). The sector uses one quarter of global land for pasture and one-third of global crop land for feed crops (Robinson et al., 2011). Thanks to imperialism and the European mission to colonize (and 'develop') as much territory as possible, indigenous ecologies have been vastly altered across much of the world. A number of researchers and authors have enumerated the ecological impacts of global livestock production/consumption. With the emergence of life cycle and footprint analyses, we can account for the magnitudes of water, pesticides, energy, and pollutants that are used or produced alongside animal flesh, hides, milk and eggs (see Weis, 2013 and Fairlie, 2010 for excellent and conflicting analyses).

The number of animal bodies – beings – involved is staggering. According to FAO (2014), 2012 saw the planetary slaughter of 1,394,489,497 pigs; 59,793,859,000 chickens; 2,546,236 camels; 1,206,844,000 rabbits; 2,939,796 ducks; 4,831,548 horses; 296,244,063 cattle; 439,998,718 goats; 706,329 geese and guinea fowl; and 535,752,859 sheep and lambs. These animals were turned into meat, animal feed (bone meal, meat meal, and blood meal), hides, feathers, wool, hair, wax, fat, fertilizer, fuel, pet food, and thousands of other products. How do we even comprehend these numbers of bodies that are given birth to, fed and killed? Sixty billion chickens? And global institutions like the FAO are forecasting the doubling of this production and slaughtering by 2050 (see MacLachlan, this volume).

Expectations of the doubling of livestock production are mind-boggling in terms of impact (see Gunderson, Saurí and Marchand, and Stoddard, this volume). Even if animals are intensively confined, thus limiting the grazing areas they require (and thereby reducing GHG emissions), they still have to be fed, slaughtered and processed. Non-ruminates (mostly confined pigs and birds) already consume 72 percent of all animal feed that is grown on arable land (Galloway et al., 2007). International institutions are calling for conflicting types of policy approaches, with FAO asking for more intensification to reduce the production of GHG emissions, and UNCTAD claiming less meat production and consumption is the way forward. FAO and others are also advocating livestock augmentation as a route to economic development and acceleration of improved livelihoods, particularly for poor women (see Waithanji, this volume). Yet much of the investment in livestock production is based on the intensification model and experience shows that it does not aid poor people in the intermediate to long term – but only those who can access the capital to make the necessary innovations in production facilities and processes (Neo, 2010). Furthermore, we are moving in the opposite direction (from intensification) in terms of social movements: many people are fighting for animals to be unconfined. Scientists, increasingly, are validating what many farmers, pastoralists, and sanctuary keepers already know: farmed and other 'domesticated' animals are intelligent. They have memories, they can tell people and each other apart, they bond with each other, they make mental maps, and they care about their offspring (Hatkoff, 2009). These animals have emotional lives; they get depressed and aggressive when their social patterns are thwarted.

Finally, there are issues with changing climate affecting existing livestock growers including pastoralists in some of the most vulnerable places of the world (see Archer van Garderen et al., Waithanji, and Rosin and Cooper, this volume). Existing and new diseases are also concerns, both those that affect only the domesticated animals but spread quickly with global trade, and those that cross species boundaries.

Just how the politics of livestock production are developing and will be shaped is an area of considerable importance for social scientists and the public. Will consumers lead the way or will new governance fora comprised of industry representatives, environmental non-governmental organizations (NGOs) and retailers (see Lee et al., and Johnson, this volume)? These are important questions that we will explore in this volume, but before we do that, it would be proper to rethink, more fundamentally, the relationship between human and the animals we consume.

Human–animal relations

Humans and animals have produced each other or co-evolved (Tsing, 2012; Shepard, 1997). As many writers have pointed out, 'human' is a relational term, only definable against an 'other' – a non-human animal or a machine (or perhaps a god or spirit) (Plumwood, 1993). As Donna Haraway wrote in *Companion Species Manifesto*, 'beings do not pre-exist their relatings' (2003, p. 6). Posthumanists like Braidotti (2013), Derrida (2008), Haraway (2008), and Wolfe (2010) have roundly dismissed the autonomy and disembodiment of the 'human', affirming the animalism and dependencies we share with other living beings. Posthumanism, although a contested term, 'expresses dissatisfactions with modes of philosophical, social and political thought and consequent action which have derived from Enlightenment presumptions about human sovereignty and primacy within the world order' (McNeil, 2010, p. 429). Assemblage thinking and monism have furthered relational thinking beyond the concept of hybridity, which Massumi (2014) argues still assumes separate domains. Also refusing to recognize firm boundaries between living beings, post-anthropocentrism, as explained by Braidotti, is an egalitarian recognition of *zoe*, 'the dynamic, self-organizing structure of life itself' (2013, p. 56). She argues: 'Zoe-centered egalitarianism, is for me, the core of the post-anthropocentric turn; it is a materialist, secular, grounded and unsentimental response to the opportunistic trans-species commodification of Life that is the logic of advanced capitalism' (ibid.).

Postcolonialism and post-anthropocentrism also afford glimpses of the multiplicities of human–animal relations beyond the assumption of free access to the bodies of others. Vivieros de Castro's (2012) anthropological findings that illustrate how many Amerindian myths reveal little differentiation between plants, animals and humans (they are all human) provide fuel for accepting the provincialism of the Eurocentric idea that animals are vastly different and lesser than humans. Descola's (2013) work on the multiple forms of human cultural identifying and relating to animals, which he labels as animism, totemism, analogism, and naturalism, testifies to the existence of ontological multiplicity regarding human–animal relations. He maintains that different cultures make 'ontological choices' about domestication; some choose not to domesticate even though there are potentially domesticable species available.

Whatever human relationships and identifications with animals, most groups of humans and particular non-humans have long, long coevolutionary histories. In fact it is amazing to think of the length of time over which humans and animals have been in relationship. As Vitebsky wrote, '[t]he reindeer (*Rangifer tarandus*) has been giving life to humans for hundreds of thousands of years over much of the northern hemisphere… One main migration route ran from Paris to Brussels, and another from the Massif Central to the coastal plains of Bordeaux' (2005, p. 18). Alongside the taming of the reindeer, the domestication of goats and sheep has been ongoing for thousands of years and is said to have pre-dated agriculture (Caras, 2002). Domestic animals have provided security for humans within a vast array of ecologies, and in the process, humans were also domesticated (Anderson, 1997).

Whether symbiotic, exploitative, parasitic, or a product of ecology, the process of domestication is still debated. It is widely believed that the type of animal and its fear of predators had much to do with which animals were tamed and which not. Budiansky (1992) argued that the animals themselves had contributed to the process by being opportunistic in finding food in human settlements, identifying that taming is not the same as domestication as of course many wild animals have been tamed but few domesticated. Clutton-Brock (2012) claimed that some species have similar social patterns as humans (e.g. wolves) that allow them to follow a leader or accept the dominance of a human. A lamb might have imprinted upon a person instead of its mother in an ecological relationship (Franklin, 2007). Ceremonial uses of animals may be another reason that particular animals were tamed and included in the household.

Domesticated thousands of years ago, in various places including Eurasia, Egypt, India and Southeast Asia, Africa and the Americas, contemporary meat, milk and egg animals still possess capacities they held in the wild (although domestication generally reduces the size of the brain). Domesticated animals can still breed with their wild counterparts although they generally do not because they are confined, yet some pastoralists do still depend upon this breeding practice. Domesticated animals can also become feral or wild again; wild cattle roamed Organ Pipe National Monument in the US just 30 years ago and persevere in the Alaskan Aleutian Islands. Thought to be a civilizing enterprise, one that pulled 'man' from barbarism into higher cultural forms, domestication and production of animals has received enormous scientific and technological attention over the past couple of centuries. The animal sciences are featured at all land grant schools in the United States and at universities in virtually every other country. Such an enlightenment impulse to improve, this application of science to breeding, has also permeated the human realm (through education, eugenics programs, medical screening), just as the impulse to domesticate became part and parcel of further humanizing the puta-tively less than human (Anderson, 1997).

The alteration of ecologies through domestication has produced tremendous change. Some have called it ecological cleansing because the original 'wildlife' (the term in the English language used to denote non-domesticated animals) were eliminated to make room for the domesticated animals (Emel, 1995). Just consider the American bison – Europeans found herds so vast they couldn't see past them for ten miles. One observer said it took five days for a herd to cross a particular location (Gard, 1959). But by the late 1880s, they were nearly gone and the cat-tle industry was booming. Imagine – animals domesticated some 20,000 years ago now constitute 65 per cent of all terrestrial vertebrates by weight (humans evolved from other apes some 200,000 years ago). Humans and their pets constitute most of the rest with wildlife a mere 3 per cent (Serpell, 2012, ix).

How does intensified animal production change the people and animals who live in societies which practice it? Bulliet (2005) distinguishes between what he calls 'postdomesticity' and domesticity. He claims that domesticity refers to the social, economic and intellectual dimensions of communities in which most mem-bers have daily contact with domestic animals (other than pets) and postdomesticity is a situation in which most people live far from the animals exploited for food, fiber and other goods, and they do not witness births, deaths, daily lives, and other practices utilized to intensively produce such animals. And while they continue to consume large quantities of these animals and their products, these people may experience feelings of guilt and discomfort from doing so, in part, because they have such close relationships with companion animals. He claims that this separa-tion produces different perspectives among people, illustrating his point with the example of children witnessing animal sexuality or reproduction during life on the farm, ranch or grassland. When the witnessing stops, people change; their fantasies, their interest in sex, and their protectiveness about visualizing sexual acts shift. Many people in urban areas fail to relate to the animals at all, but merely think of their meat as the packaged stuff in the grocery store. If they are aware of the life of the meat, there is little ethical concern and what exists is delegated to the meat retailer or the government; high welfare meat is a niche market (Schroder and McEachern, 2004; Vanhonacker and Verbeke, 2014; Neo, this volume). We would venture to guess that many Americans, at least, fail to realize that cows have to be birthing calves to provide milk, believing that cows, unlike humans, provide milk on demand. Within this postdomestic situation, the animals are not only lesser subjects than humans and therefore deemed worthy of complete domina-tion, but also objects – machines of production, bred for docility unless it clashes with other desirable attributes. There is even talk of producing animals with neural discontinuities such that they won't feel as much pain or depression in confinement. Postdomestic meat and milk animals have lost their biolegitimacy – they've become de-animalized, socially deprived, alienated from their own products and from the outdoors (Noske, 1997). Spatially removed and hidden from site, they are isolated and ignored by most of society unless there is a health scare (like BSE) (see Lee et al., this volume; Stuart et al., 2013). This is a far cry from earlier forms of domestication or from pastoralism where animals interact with each other and the outdoors, and maintain their natural reproduction cycles. We will come back to the importance of visualizing, not just sexual acts, births and deaths, but also animal lives day-to-day in the factory farms.

The livestock bioeconomy

What should be clear is that the livestock industry is a prime example of a bioeconomy – an extensive economy that explicitly deals with, and modifies lives. Many of us think of the bioeconomy – generally referring to clones, genetic engineering, organ transplants and other biotechnologies – as new. Yet the global meat industry, both old and new, is fundamentally a bioeconomy as Lewis Holloway so aptly illustrates in this volume (also see Twine, 2010). A bioeconomy is characterized by the capture of the latent value found in biological material, purportedly to achieve some version of sustainability (Birch and Tyfield, 2013). Animal bodies produce value; their bodily growth and reproduction is subsumed within capitalist social relations, especially under conditions of factory farming. Marx, in fact, argued that pastoralists might be considered among the first capitalists 'for the original meaning of the word capital is cattle' (1964, no pagination). He identified the appearance of capital in 16th-century England as occurring in 'not agriculture proper, but such branches of production as cattle-breeding, especially sheep-raising' (Capital, vol 3, chapter 47). In his brilliant study of reindeer pastoralism, Ingold (1995) argued that value derives not just from human labor, but from the animals themselves in pastoral economies. 'For if the "surplus" that accrues to the primitive accumulator is of live stock [sic], its formation depends ultimately on the productive labour of the animals themselves, rather than on the appropriative labor of their herdsmen … one species is treated by another as the natural condition of its own reproduction' (1995, p. 234). Catherine Waldby, in 2000, coined the term biovalue, 'generated wherever the generative and transformative productivity of living entities can be instrumentalized along lines which make them useful for human projects' (p. 33). This definition assuredly applies to meat as it is the result of the vitality of living entities 'transformed into technologies to aid the intensification of vitality for other living beings' (ibid., p. 19). While her intent was to apply this concept to newer human body-based biotechnologies, it fits the animal industry as well. Similarly, Sarah Franklin and Margaret Lock's use of the term 'biocapital' refers to 'reproductive technologies generative of surplus value' (Birch and Tyfield, 2013, p. 305). This application is quite similar to Harriet Ritvo's (1989) claims that labor accumulates in the bodies of reproducing animals. Take for example, bull semen: first sold for profit in 1938, it is now a booming global business. One Dutch bull, Sunny Boy, has 500,000 daughters within 22 countries; Black Star, residing in the US, has daughters in 50 countries. Miles McKee, a Hereford bull from the US named for a professor from Kansas State University, was sold for $600,000 (and valued at $800,000) in 2013, making him the most expensive bull in the world. He produces semen for the global meat and dairy economies.

Another way to think about the global meat economy is as one of Timothy Morton's 'hyperobjects'. A hyperobject 'refers to things that are massively distributed in time and space relative to humans' (2013, p. 1). Hyperobjects 'are viscous, which means that they "stick" to beings that are involved with them. They are nonlocal; in other words, any "local manifestation" of a hyperobject is not directly the hyperobject. They involve profoundly different temporalities than the human-scale ones we are used to' (ibid.). Indeed, the global meat industry – like Morton's other examples including climate change, the Lago Agrio oil field in Ecuador, or the Everglades – has many of the characteristics of a hyperobject. There are many times more farmed animals than people; New Zealand has 7.5 sheep per person, Uruguay has 3.7 cows per person, and Brunei has 40 chickens per person. The meat industry produces a relatively large amount of GHG emissions and those that were produced from deforestation and grassland destruction 20–100 years ago will have impacts far into the future. The hyperobject of the global meat industry is interconnected with other hyperobjects like climate change, deforestation, and biosecurity. It involves, among other things, the pharmaceutical industry, irrigation dams, soil salinity, nitrogen cycles, slaughterhouse union workers, the tanning industry, Pets R Us, Mongolian gers, electricity systems fueled with feathers and litter, domestication, artificial insemination, food pyramids, the eradication of Native Americans, multinational firms, and Hindu nationalism. Barad (2007) and other feminist theorists remind us that there is no gap between us and the 'object', in this case the global meat industry – there is rather embodied, interactive, scientifically and culturally mediated knowledge. The reindeer herder does not experience 'it' the same way an Iowan agricultural school animal scientist does. And clearly, nearly all of us are entangled with the animal bodies that move through the system – we swallow them, wear them, put them on our faces and limbs, shape and clean our hair with them, use them as medicines, walk on them. We are entangled with and stuck to the irrigation systems, soil erosion, industrial corn and soy production, diesel tractors, farm laborers, slaughterhouse workers, and reproducing sows, cows, and hens.

According to the Worldwatch Institute (2006) 74 percent of the world's poultry, 43 percent of beef, 50 percent of pork, and 68 percent of eggs were produced intensively or through factory farms (including feedlots). Undoubtedly, intensification has proceeded apace since 2006. And the truth is all intensified animal production is done via a capitalist process. Intensification means inputs – buildings, specific feeds, antibiotics, hormones, and waste treatment. Capital is required for these kinds of investments – particularly for the buildings and other infrastructure.

Loans of $500,000 are commonplace for buildings alone. And capital isn't particularly concerned with what is produced. As Morton writes: '[w]hat capitalism makes is some stuff called capital … It's no wonder industrial capitalism has turned the Earth into a dangerous desert. It doesn't really care what comes through the factory door, just as long as it generates more capital … Nature is the featureless remainder at either end of the process of production. Either it's exploitable stuff, or value-added stuff' (2013, p. 112).

Corporate control of industrial agriculture is not news in the so-called 'developed' world. It is common knowledge that 'big ag' controls most of the chicken and hog industries, increasingly the cattle industry, and most of the genetics. Hendrickson and Heffernan's 2002 illustration of the oligopolistic control of these industries made the point loud and clear, as did Boyd and Watts's (1997) seminal essay on the problems with contract chicken farming. More recently, Christopher Leonard, in *The Meat Racket* (2014), elaborated the practices of powerhouses Tyson and Smithfield and reported the failure of US administrative bodies to enact antitrust governance of the industry. The corporations that dominate the global meat industry operate all over the world. JBS SA is the world's largest (by sales) meat company in the world, processing factory beef, chicken and pork. Headquartered in Sao Paulo, Brazil, it operates in several countries and is the biggest beef processor in the United States. Shuanghui (the largest meat processor in China by value of company), recently bought Smithfield (located in the US), which is the world's largest pig producer (by sales). According to its SEC filings (which will come to an end as Shuanghui is not publicly traded), Smithfield is more than twice as large as its nearest US competitor and larger than the next three combined (based on per cent of breeding sows). Shuanghui owns nearly 900,000 breeding sows and eight slaughterhouses with an aggregate capacity of 113,000 pigs per day. Shuanghui will export more US pork to China for processing into packaged meats. The Chinese company has the capability to slaughter 15 million pigs per year but owns only 400,000 – thus the desire to buy pork or pigs from the American company. The great value added comes in the further processing and that's what the Shuanghui will capture, along with the value provided by American safety standards. US-based Tyson remains one of the world's largest poultry companies, competing with JBS's acquisitions in the poultry industry.

The global meat economy is continuously scrutinized by politicians and citizens, particularly in terms of food safety. Quite often, disease or particular drugs and other chemicals are used as real and efficacious reasons to prohibit imports or exports (see Stoddard, this volume); other times, the reason could be politically motivated. At the time of writing, Russia is banning all meat from the US, the EU, Norway, Canada, and Australia until August 2015 because of sanctions. Brazil, meanwhile, has doubled its exports to Russia to make up the supply. China prohibits US (and other countries') meat from pigs given ractopamine (a drug that produces rapid lean growth and behaves like an amphetamine) but China cannot export fresh pork or beef to the US because China still has outbreaks of foot and mouth disease, though processed foods like hams and sausages can be exported.

Over 80 percent of the tilapia (a farm-raised fish) sold in the US comes from China (see Daniels and McKinney, this volume) as does a significant amount of other seafood, although China has banned all US west coast shellfish. Japan refused US beef following the 'mad cow' fiasco, banning and unbanning it several times. The European Union banned 'meat glue', or 'pink slime' as it was called more recently, as well as, meat from animals given synthetic hormones.

Considerable political attention followed the Chinese purchase of Smithfield. Buying Smithfield gives Shuanghui access to more advanced production technology as well as to 460 farms that raise about 15.8 million hogs a year. Smithfield also promises brand reassurance after numerous Chinese food-safety scandals including the deaths of at least six infants in 2008 because of melamine-tainted milk and the discovery of more than 16,000 dead pigs illegally dumped into Shanghai's Huangpu River. A CCTV report announced that farmers in Henan province fed the additive to their pigs and then sold them to a Shuanghui slaughterhouse. The company had to apologize and promise better efforts at consumer protection in future. Pig meat is apparently crucial to political stability in China. Beijing has managed a strategic pork reserve, the only one of its kind in the world, since 2007 in order to keep the prices desirable. A live-hog reserve of a few million pigs is rotated every four months between 200 to 300 commercial farms; and a frozen-pork reserve of about 200,000 tons, is rotated every four months to ensure freshness and administered through domestic packing plants with pig facilities such as Shuanghui. The state-owned China National Cereals, Oils and Foodstuffs Corporation (COFCO) has control over the reserve. We know of no export or import policies explicitly based upon the welfare of animals, workers, or smallholders, although there are certainly millions of people who fight for justice for these groups. Some of the biggest political movements are involved in promoting the transparency of factory farms, in banning the live animal export trade, in protecting smallholders against corporate agriculture, and in unionizing slaughterhouse workers (Neo, and Johnston, this volume).

The Obama administration failed to stand up to the meat industry when it attempted to take on the industry by way of asking the Department of Justice to support the Grain Inspection, Packers and Stockyards Administration (GIPSA) in 2010. GIPSA is supposed to ensure fair and competitive trading practices for producers and consumers. Given the concentration (oligopoly) among processors in the industry and the price determination that went on at the hands of the integrators (in the poultry industry) or the processors in the pig industry, Obama administrators tried to strengthen (and even implement) the federal law to protect contract holders against the processors. The processors and their lobbying councils spent millions to defeat the attempt, going to Congress to ensure that nothing would get in the way of their continued profitability (see Leonard, 2014). The only new thing to come out of the attempt (which was a campaign pledge – Hillary Clinton was supported by the National Pork Producers Council) was a rule that allows chicken contractees to sue processors in actual courts (before they had to go to industry mitigation). During her 2008 campaign, Clinton created a Rural Americans for Hillary committee that was co-chaired by Joy Philippi, a Nebraska hog farmer who had been the immediate past president of the National Pork Producers Council (NPPC). The NPPC opposes rules on country of origin labeling for meat and stronger regulations on confined animal feeding operations. Obama came out for tougher Environmental Protection Agency rules and fines for CAFOs that polluted air and water supplies, but most of this has come to naught because of the power of the industry over Congress in the US.

The preceding section has shown that the livestock industry is a bioeconomy not simply because it trades in and exploits the lives and genetic materials of food animals; neither is it a bioeconomy simply because the ramifications of the live-stock industry are in part biological in nature (in the guise of zoonotic diseases and food safety lapses). Rather, the lives of people who work in the industry and who consume the products of this industry are also implicated in an economy rooted in cold calculations of costs and benefits. In this profit driven bioeconomy, intensifi-cation is the name of the game.

Intensification and gray goo

Ramping up the intensification of livestock production means a reduction in animal freedom, social life, reproductive relations and human-animal interaction in all of those locations that heretofore practiced a more domesticated or pastoral version of animal production. Once in the confined spaces, and once part of the flow of capital, the animals are just gray goo. They are not individuals or household members, or even recognizable as specific beings such as those who belong to smallholders and pastoralists. Despite the fact that we can never actually know the pigs, goats, chick-ens, geese, lambs, camels, and so forth that we put to death every day, we are learning ever more about them. Pigs have such a keen sense of smell that 'Experimenters have found that pigs who have nuzzled plastic cards can pick them out from a deck days later, even after the cards have been washed. Pigs' hearing, too, is excellent – with a frequency range that extends far above those of humans' (Montgomery, 2007, p. 53). All sorts of stories abound from both recognized scientific researchers and farmers or 'owners' (families) of farm animals suggesting how wide and deep are their reper-toires of sensory, emotional, social and other practices, skills, and desires. One of the best examples of this is the *Good Good Pig* by Sy Montgomery, providing something of a biography of Christopher Hogwood who lived out his fourteen years on her property. Christopher loved people, especially children, and recognized many of his visitors; he got along well with the chickens who lived in the same yard, and relished the 'slop' provided to him by his many admirers in the New Hampshire community of which he was an important member.

> Christopher Hogwood knew how to relish the juicy savor of this fragrant, abundant, sweet, green world. To show us this would have been gift enough. But he showed us another truth as well. That a pig did not become bacon but lived fourteen years, pampered and adored till the day he died peacefully in his

sleep – that's proof that we need not 'be practical' all the time. We need not accept the rules that our society or species, family or fate seem to have written for us. We can choose a new way. We have the power to transform a story of sorrow into a story of healing. We can choose life over death. We can let love lead us home.

(Montgomery, 2007, p. 225)

This quote brings into stark contrast the possibility of a Hogwood contra the featureless grey goo bodies that walk or are shoved into the slaughter line to become so many trillions of steaks, legs, breasts, thighs, loins, ground meat, shoes, and biofuels. For Foucault, the famous quote from Borges does a similar job of demonstrating 'the exotic charm of another system of thought' and the 'limitation of our own' (Foucault, 1970, xv). Borges cited 'a certain Chinese encyclopaedia' in which it is written that 'animals are divided into: (a) belonging to the Emperor, (b) embalmed, (c) tame, (d) sucking pigs, (e) sirens, (f) fabulous, (g) stray dogs, (h) included in the present classification, (i) frenzied, (j) innumerable, (k) drawn with a very fine camelhair brush, (l) et cetera, (m) having just broken the water pitcher, (n) that from a long way off look like flies'. Elaborating on the constructed taxonomy of Linnaeus, Londa Scheibinger (2004) illustrates how mammals got their breast-centered niche in a classification system developed by heterosexual white men of a particular time and place. Western taxonomies were based upon body types and functions it seems – not much concern was shown to behavior or desire. The focus was on the flesh and the skeleton rather than the mind and heart. Only 'reason' served as a distinction between humans and other primates. And now we know from cognitive ethologists and psychologists that many animals, including all of the so-called meat animals, also reason – a term that is itself highly contested as the Frankfurt critical theorists have brilliantly argued.

The political ecology of meat

First popularized in the biological sciences, 'ecology' is the study of the interactions between organisms and their environments. Political ecology, at its simplest, holds that ecology (both in terms of the academic discipline as well as the interactions between organisms and environment it refers to) is political. Hence, politics, defined broadly, is a key factor in the changing relationships between organisms and other organisms, as well as with their larger milieu. Politics also fundamentally influences how we approach the study of these changing relationships. For example, for the longest time, political ecology as a field of study was anthropocentric, in that it was especially concerned with human lives who were marginalized or impoverished by capital accumulation processes. Any consideration of animals was incidental. However, with 'the question of animal' gaining prominence in popular consciousness, it is inevitable that the concerns for animals and their environments have filtered into policies and politics. Indeed, political ecological research has since expanded to include ever more amorphous subjects such as climate change.

As a loose assemblage of theories and analytics, the oeuvre of political ecology has traditionally problematized the mainstream and given power-laden explanations for environmental degradation, environmental crisis, or solutions to such problems. Along with postcolonialists and decolonists, political ecologists question big science and its suppression of alternative understandings and explanations, especially arising from diverse and/or local perspectives. It has always concerned itself with justice and its many interpretations and intangibilities. Perhaps more importantly, it is a body of theory that questions the distribution of resources and ecological access, and the economic, technological, and social systems and institutions that produce inequality. Thus, research by political ecologists 'tends to reveal winners and losers, hidden costs, and the differential power that produces social and environmental outcomes' (Robbins, 2004, p. 11). In pursuing such research goals, there needs to be an awareness of the numerous variables that are nestled in various spatial scales, rooted in diverse 'bodies'. Such bodies would include individuals or groups of individuals (e.g. humans, non-human animals and microorganisms), regulatory institutions, activist networks and private commercial interests.

The political ecology of meat builds upon the core concerns of political ecology and extends it further. Instead of a preoccupation with the marginalization of rural communities (in especially developing areas), it identifies marginalization in multiple places and in multiple subjects. As with mainstream political ecology, it traces the root of marginalization in political-economic institutions of varying spatial scales. A political ecology of meat bears witness to the ramifications of these institutions (and the policies and discourse that arose from them) for people, animals and places. The peoples identified in this book are diverse and run the gamut of livestock farmers, scientists, regulators, animal activists and consumers. The animals highlighted represent a wide spectrum of meat protein, including cattle, poultry, pigs and even fish. Finally, the places implicated hail from almost all parts of the world (the Americas, Europe, Africa, Asia and the Oceanic countries). In these places, we focus on different sites and institutions, including farms, governmental agencies, homes, restaurants, and laboratories.

By way of concluding this introductory chapter, we will elaborate on the key themes in the book.

Sustaining power structures and knowledges of the global meat trade

We look at the power structures of the global meat trade and the accumulation therein. The starting point of this enquiry is that power does not rest exclusively in one site. We look at the contract farming that results in some segments and its 'traveling' to newer places and farmers. We look at the ecological impacts of meat production/consumption, and the governance of practices that produce or restrain them. In short, we posit that insofar as the global meat trade is fundamentally and explicitly dealing with the lives and deaths of animals, it is essentially a bioeconomy that draws on science, knowledge and technology to rationalize and normalize the fast growing industry.

Specifically, in Part I ('The "Livestock Revolution": Geographies and Implications'), a political ecology of meat entails a focus on the political, economic and cultural structures that support animal production and consumption, along with studies of the implications for the poor, for women, for the dispossessed, and the natural environment (including non-human animals). Indeed, only recently, with the emergence of critical animal geographies and other critical animal studies, has political ecology begun to embrace the implications of global economic structures on non-human others. As the preceding sections have alluded to, the spatial structures of the meat sector are dense, complex and almost too overwhelming to grasp. The four chapters in Part I look at the morphing of the livestock industry as a key developmentalist strategy. Since the advent of the livestock revolution, producing food animals has been perennially heralded as one way to uplift the marginalized in developing countries. MacLachlan traces the evolution of the revolution while the three chapters that follow critically analyze the developmental potential and ramifications of the livestock industries in South America and Africa.

In Part III, we take the argument further to include the way in which knowledges about food animals are produced, reproduced and sustained. The five chapters in Part III show that producer and consumer understandings about pertinent issues along the meat production chain are neither straightforward nor entirely objective. Rather, they arise out of politicization (both covert and overt) between different actors in the production/consumption food chain. For example, Colombino and Giaccaria show how the production of an allegedly gourmet meat is an outcome of decades of cultural politics and scientific intervention. Similarly, how issues such as climate change (Lee et al.), genetic modification (Holloway), animal welfare standards (Johnston) and meat avoidance (Neo) are understood illuminates a highly contested bioeconomy which is far from the alleged neutrality and (scientific) infallibility of an apolitical economy assumed by many.

Implications of meat production and consumption

Beyond a critical analysis of the development of the (global) livestock industry and its associated knowledges, we are interested in the direct ramifications of such an industry on human and non-human lives as well as the broader environment. In Part II, we look at how climate and water are impacted negatively by the production of meat and the novel ways these impacts are mitigated through policy and political and technological interventions. We also examine the sufferings of communities, animals and humans in sustaining the modern political ecology of meat production. Undergirding the four chapters in Part II is the valorization of environmental justice – itself a perennial focus of political ecology. These chapters are specifically interested in the negative impacts of intensified livestock production. How and why we should address and redress the injustices wrought onto diverse actors and places are questions which the chapters in Part IV attempt to answer.

The five chapters in this last part of the book explore the question of governance in the food animal industry. Focusing on issues as diverse as halal food certification

(Miele and Rucinska), green regulation of the livestock industry (Johnson and Rosin and Cooper), governance and control of urban livestock farming and food fish (Chan, and Daniels and McKinney), the chapters are empirically drawn from diverse places, including Europe, America, Asia, and New Zealand. Broadly, these chapters demonstrate how governance is wrought with difficulties and complexities. The latter could be the result of different and contested ideology, ineffectual enforcement, disputed knowledges and institutional/political interventions.

Conclusion

Through these chapters, we hope to show how biopolitics sustain particular forms and practices of meat production, resulting in a particular form of bioeconomy. This is seen in Chan's chapter on how the restructuring and eventual demise of the Hong Kong pig industry is the result of political imperative and control over marginalized farmers, through the promulgation of 'authoritative knowledges' about livestock farming. In general, livestock has been hailed as a route to pro-poor development by multiple international and regional institutions, following on the 'livestock revolution' discourse first promoted by Delgado et al. (1999). Yet, how will livestock be a path to development when intensification actually crowds out smallholders and non-specialists? Furthermore, the experience of industry and university-based sciences promoting genetic modification, hybridization, cloning and other biotechnologies has not favored the smallholder but rather accelerated the treadmill of production (Cochrane, 1979) that has served to concentrate the industry in the US, Australia, Brazil, and EU (see Holloway, and Pacheco and Poccard-Chapuis, this volume). Biopower is at the moment in the hands almost entirely of global biotechnological companies and meat packing companies with countervailing voices muted and incapable of breaking through. We see then a crying need for policies that point in the direction of more farmers, support for small to medium scale organic farms, an agroecological approach, 'livelier livelihoods' for farm animals (Emel et al., forthcoming) and more land and other resources for farming. Organizations (to name just a few) like the United Nations Conference on Trade and Development (see particularly UNCTAD, 2013), the Center for Rural Affairs and La Via Campesina provide some significant templates.

In assembling this collection of research, we have strived to represent the broad contours of the contemporary livestock industry in diverse locales, focusing on as many issues associated with this industry as we can. Despite the obvious thematic and areal differences in these chapters, we unearth significant commonalities. We can see how science, diverse knowledges and, most importantly, political power differentials between institutions and peoples have resulted in an exploitative system of meat production that marginalizes, trivializes and degrades workers, consumers, animals and the environment. As many of the following chapters will show, in a world where the demand for meat will grow exponentially, this is surely an increasingly untenable system.

References

Anderson, K. (1997) 'A walk on the wild side: A critical geography of domestication', *Progress in Human Geography*, vol 21, no 4, pp. 463–485

Barad, K. (2007) *Meeting the Universe Halfway: Quantum Physics and the Entanglement of Matter and Meaning*, Duke University Press, Durham, NC and London

Birch, K. and Tyfield, D. (2013) 'Theorizing the bioeconomy: Biovalue, biocapital, bioeconomics or what?', *Science, Technology and Human Values*, vol 38, no 3, pp. 299–327

Boyd, W. and Watts M. J. (1997) 'Agro-industrial just-in-time: the chicken industry and postwar American capitalism', in D. Goodman and M. J. Watts (eds), *Globalising Food: Agrarian Questions and Global Restructuring*, Routledge, London

Braidotti, R. (2013) *The Posthuman*, Polity, Cambridge

Budiansky, S. (1992) *The Covenant of the Wild: Why Animals Choose Domestication*, William Morrow and Co., New York

Bulliet, R. (2005) *Hunters, Herders and Hamburgers: The Past and Future of Human-Animal Relationships*, Columbia University Press, New York

Caras, R. A. (2002) *A Perfect Harmony: The Intertwining Lives of Animals and Humans throughout History*, Purdue University Press, West Lafayette, IN

Clutton-Brock, J. (2012) *Animals as Domesticates: A Worldview through History*, Michigan State University Press, East Lansing

Cochrane, W. W. (1979) *The Development of American Agriculture: A Historical Analysis*, University of Minnesota Press, Minneapolis

Delgado, C., Rosegrant, M., Steinfeld, H., Ehui, S. and Courbois, C. (1999) *Livestock to 2020: The Next Food Revolution. Food, Agriculture, and the Environment*. Discussion Paper 28. International Food Policy Research Institute, Washington, DC

Derrida, J. (2008) *The Animal That Therefore I Am*, Fordham University Press, New York

Descola, P. (2013) *The Ecology of Others*, Prickly Paradigm Press, Chicago

Emel, J. (1995) 'Are you man enough, big and bad enough?: Ecofeminism and wolf eradication in the U.S.', *Society and Space*, vol 13, no 6, pp. 707–734

Emel, J., Johnston, C. and Stoddard, E. (forthcoming) 'Livelier livelihoods: Animal and human partnership on the farm', in K. Gillespie and R. Collard (eds), *Critical Animal Geographies*, Routledge, London

Fairlie, S. (2010) *Meat: A Benign Extravagance*, Chelsea Green Publishing, White River Junction, VT

FAO (2014) 'FAOSTAT Primary Livestock', http://faostat.fao.org/site/569/default.aspx#ancor, accessed 23 October 2014

Foucault, M. (1970) *The Order of Things*, Pantheon, New York

Franklin, S. (2007) *Dolly Mixtures: The Remaking of Genealogy*, Duke University Press, Durham, NC and London

Galloway, J., Galloway, N., Burke, M., Bradford, G. E., Naylor, R., Falcon, W., Chapagain, A. K., Gaskell, J. C., McCullough, E., Mooney, H. A., Oleson, K. L. L., Steinfeld, H., Wassenaar, T. and Smil, V. (2007), 'International trade in meat: The tip of the pork chop', *Ambio*, vol 36, no 8, pp. 622–629

Gard, W. (1959) *The Great Buffalo Hunt*, Alfred A. Knopf, New York

Gunderson, R. (2013) 'From cattle to capital: Exchange value, animal commodification, and barbarism', *Critical Sociology*, vol 39, no 2, pp. 259–275

Haraway, D. (2003) *The Companion Species Manifesto: Dogs, People, and Significant Otherness*, Prickly Paradigm Press, Chicago

Haraway, D. (2008) *When Species Meet*, University of Minnesota Press, Minneapolis and London

Hatkoff, A. (2009) *The Inner World of Farm Animals*, Steward, Tabori and Chang, New York

Hendrickson, M. and Heffernan, W. (2002) *Concentration of Agricultural Markets*, Table prepared for National Farmers Union, Washington DC

Ingold, T. (1995) *Hunters, Pastoralists and Ranchers*, Cambridge University Press, Cambridge, London and Melbourne

Leonard, C. (2014) *The Meat Racket: the Secret Takeover of America's Food Business*, Simon and Schuster, New York

Ma, D. (2013) 'China's changing appetites', The Paulson Institute US-China Investment Program, Spring 2013 Newsletter, Chicago

Marx, K. (1964) Pre-capitalist Economic Formations, www.marxists.org/archive/marx/works/1857/precapitalist/ch02.htm; last accessed January 27, 2015

Massumi, B. (2014) *What Animals Teach Us about Politics*, Duke University Press, Durham, NC and London

McNeil, M. (2010) 'Post-millennial feminist theory: Encounters with humanism, materialism, critique, nature, biology and Darwin', *Journal for Cultural Research*, vol 14, no 4, pp. 427–438

Montgomery, S. (2007) *The Good Good Pig: The Extraordinary Life of Christopher Hogwood*, Ballantine Books, New York

Morton, T. (2013) *Hyperobjects: Philosophy and Ecology after the End of the World*, University of Minnesota Press, Minneapolis and London

Neo, H. (2010) 'Geographies of subcontracting', *Geography Compass*, vol 4, no 8, pp. 1013–1024.

Noske, B. (1997) *Beyond Boundaries: Humans and Animals*, Black Rose Books, Montreal

Plumwood, V. (1993) *Feminism and the Mastery of Nature*, Routledge, London

Ritvo, H. (1989) *The Animal Estate: The English and Other Creatures in the Victorian Age*, Harvard University Press, Cambridge, MA

Robbins, P. (2004) *Political Ecology: A Critical Introduction*, Wiley, London.

Robinson, T. P., Thornton, P. K., Franceschini, G., Kruska, R. L., Chiozza, F., Notenbaert, A., Cecchi, G., Herrero, M., Epprecht, M., Fritz, S., You, L., Conchedda, G. and See, L. (2011), *Global Livestock Production Systems*, Food and Agriculture Organization of the United Nations (FAO) and International Livestock Research Institute, Rome

Scheibinger, L. (2004) *Nature's Body: Gender in the Making of Modern Science* (2nd edition), Rutger's University Press, New Brunswick, NJ

Schneider, M. (2011) *Feeding China's Pigs: Implications for the Environment, China's Smallholder Farmers and Food Security*, Institute for Agriculture and Trade Policy, Minneapolis

Schroder, M. and McEachern, M. (2004) 'Consumer value conflicts surrounding ethical food purchase decisions: A focus on animal welfare', *International Journal of Consumer Studies*, vol 28, no 2, pp. 168–177

Serpell, J. (2012) 'Foreword', in J. Clutton-Brock, *Animals as Domesticates: A World View through History*, Michigan State University Press, East Lansing

Shepard, P. (1997) *The Others: How Animals Made Us Human*, Island Press, Washington, DC

Steinfeld, H., Gerber, P., Wassenaar, T. D., Castel, V. and de Haan, C. (2006), *Livestock's Long Shadow: Environmental Issues and Options*, United Nations Food and Agriculture Organization, Rome

Stuart, D., Schewe, R. and Gunderson, R. (2013) 'Extending social theory to farm animals: Addressing alienation in the dairy industry', *Sociologia Ruralis*, vol 53, no 2, pp. 201–222

Tsing, A. (2012) Unruly edges: Mushrooms as companion species, *Environmental Humanities*, vol 1, pp. 141–154

Twine, R. (2010) *Animals as Biotechnology: Ethics, Sustainability and Critical Animal Studies*, Earthscan, London

UNCTAD (2013) 'Trade and environment review: wake up before it is too late', http://unctad.org/en/publicationslibrary/ditcted2012d3_en.pdf, accessed 30 March 2015

UNEP (2010) 'Assessing the Environmental Impacts of Consumption and Production', www.greeningtheblue.org/sites/default/files/Assessing%20the%20environmental%20impacts%20of%20consumption%20and%20production.pdf, accessed 30 March 2015

Vanhonacker, F. and Verbeke, W. (2014) 'Public and consumer policies for higher welfare food products: Challenges and opportunities', *Journal of Agricultural and Environmental Ethics*, vol 27, no 1, pp. 153–171

Vitebsky, P. (2005) *Reindeer People: Living with Animals and Spirits in Siberia*, Houghton-Mifflin, Boston

Vivieros de Castro, E. (2012) *Radical Dualism: 100 Notes, 100 Thoughts*, Hatje Cantz, Berlin

Waldby, C. (2000) *The Visible Human Project: Informatic Bodies and Posthuman Medicine*, Routledge, Oxford and New York

Weis, T. (2013) *The Ecological Hoofprint: The Global Burden of Industrial Livestock*, Zed Books, London and New York

Wolfe, C. (2010) *What Is Posthumanism?* University of Minnesota Press, Minneapolis and London

Worldwatch Institute (2006) 'Livestock and climate change', www.worldwatch.org/files/pdf/Livestock%20and%20Climate%20Change.pdf, accessed 24 October 2014

PART I

The 'livestock revolution'

Geographies and implications

2

EVOLUTION OF A REVOLUTION

Meat consumption and livestock production in the developing world

Ian MacLachlan

In 1999, an International Food Policy Research Institute (IFPRI) team of researchers led by Christopher Delgado, Mark Rosegrant and Henning Steinfeld (1999a, b) identified a structural shift in the diets of developing countries. Per capita human consumption of livestock source foods (LSF), in the form of meat, eggs and milk, was growing much more rapidly in developing countries than in developed countries (Rosegrant et al., 2001).[1] For example, between 1983 and 1993, the annual per capita consumption of meat in developing countries rose from 14 to 21 kilograms, an increase of 50 percent. By contrast, per capita meat consumption in the global north increased from 74 to 76 kilograms (3 percent) over the same period (Delgado et al., 1999b, p6). Mirroring this gradual shift in meat consumption, livestock production was also growing faster in developing countries and by 1995, the volume of meat produced in the global south exceeded the global north, shifting the centre of gravity of the world's livestock from the temperate zones of the globe's most highly developed countries to the subtropical latitudes of less developed regions (Steinfeld and Chilonda, 2006, p3).

The goal of this chapter is to contextualize the livestock revolution concept as it was first described in 1999. It begins with a review of the emerging debate about the significance and implications of the livestock revolution, and goes on to pose four more specific but intertwined questions:

1   Is it appropriate to use the term 'revolution' to describe global–scale changes in meat consumption? Have these trends continued into the new millennium?
2   Are the observed dietary changes the outcome of changes in demand for LSF by autonomous consumers?
3   Has the regional distribution of global livestock production been evenly distributed? What are the ecological implications of the growth in different livestock species and different regions?

4   Will increased livestock production provide income growth and development
      opportunities in rural regions of developing countries?

The paper concludes with a case study of meat consumption and livestock production in China as the prototype of the livestock revolution to exemplify and
illustrate the answers to each of these questions.

The livestock revolution and its critics

The livestock revolution is a convenient shorthand for an empirical observation
together with its implications. No one argues seriously with the validity or the
importance of the empirical evidence that points to rapid growth in global stocks
of food animals; however, a number of authors have taken issue with some of
its alleged causes and implications and two camps seem to be emerging. On the
one hand, the 'dominant paradigm' (Pica-Ciamarra and Otte, 2009, p1) is represented by researchers and policy analysts connected with the FAO, IFPRI, and the
International Livestock Research Institute (ILRI):

> Population growth, urbanization, and income growth in developing countries
> are fueling a massive global increase in demand for food of animal origin. The
> resulting demand comes from changes in the diets of billions of people and
> could provide income growth opportunities for many rural poor. It is not
> inappropriate to use the term 'livestock revolution' to describe the course of
> these events in world agriculture over the next 20 years.
>
> (Delgado et al., 1999b, p1)

Assertions such as this have been reiterated with a conviction verging on dogma
(ILRI, 2000; Rosegrant et al., 2001; Steinfeld et al., 2006a), yet as will be shown,
many of these causes are open to a more carefully nuanced explanation. Another
more heterogeneous group of researchers is considering the causes and implications of
a growing dependency on LSF and livestock production in a more critical light, especially under intensive industrial conditions (Fritz, 2014; Mathias, 2012; Pica-Ciamarra
and Otte, 2011; Schneider, 2011; Sumberg and Thompson, 2013; Weis, 2013).

First, a considerable portion of the absolute growth in human consumption of
LSF is due simply to the growth of the human population. For example, the incre-
mental increase in population in a sample of 88 developing countries accounted
for an average of 77 percent of the increase in aggregate consumption of meat over
the period from 1980 to 2003. This finding would seem to downplay the effect of
increases in real per capita income and urbanization in most developing countries
(Pica-Ciamarra and Otte, 2011, p9).

Second, assertions that people in developing countries have fundamentally
changed their diets must be tempered by recognizing the heterogeneity among
countries and that, *on average*, meat and milk consumption within national food
baskets have not changed significantly (ibid., 2011, p10). The most striking

geographical feature of the livestock revolution is that it is not a global phenomenon so much as it is a regionally specific outcome of massive change in livestock production in a handful of extremely large developing countries.

Third, and contradicting assertions that per capita consumption of LSF is growing rapidly, the *average* per capita consumption growth rate by country was only 0.93 percent for meat and −0.14 percent for milk from 1980 to 2003, the period in which the revolution in dietary habits was alleged to have occurred (Pica-Ciamarra and Otte, 2011, pp10–11). The solution to this apparent paradox is, once again, that a large number of small countries changed little while a handful of very large countries are experiencing truly revolutionary changes in diets and livestock production.

Fourth, assertions that the livestock revolution is leading to a global scale convergence in diets overlook the fact that per capita consumption of LSF in the developed world is vastly greater and growing in absolute increments considerably higher than in the developing countries. The median consumer in a sample of developing countries will experience an annual dietary increase equivalent to 'one small piece of meat accompanied by a sip of milk' (Pica-Ciamarra and Otte, 2011, p12). The geography of meat consumption is still characterized by a sharp north-south divide, most notable in the case of Africa and South Asia (Delgado et al., 1999b, p5; Fritz, 2014, p4). Growth in livestock production has been similarly dominated by a small number of countries that are shifting to industrial scale production in confined animal feeding operations (CAFOs) with integrated marketing systems (Mathias, 2012, p6). Since CAFOs are more dependent on commercial inputs than are backyard producers, there is concern that global grain supplies will be diverted from human consumption to animal consumption. In the 2012–2013 crop year, about one-third of global cereal grain production (largely corn, wheat, and barley) was dedicated to livestock consumption, contributing to the rising global price of cereal grains for human consumption (Erb et al., 2012, pp34–35; Fritz, 2014, pp5–6, 9; Steinfeld et al., 2006b, p32).

Is the livestock revolution still in progress?

The livestock revolution refers to changes in human diets over a period of some 50 years based on average per capita consumption of a variety of LSF types. The standard source for global trends in food consumption is FAOSTAT (FAO, 2014), a database that estimates annual food supply using a balance sheet methodology on a national basis. Different LSF types include meat of different species (cattle, buffalo, pigs, sheep, goats, poultry and others); edible offal such as organ meats; animal fats; dairy products; eggs and a variety of marine and aquatic products. While rapid growth in the consumption of all LSF types has been observed, notably as the 'white revolution' in small-scale dairy production in India (Bellur et al., 1990; Kumar et al., 2013; Nair, 1985), this analysis will focus on meat. FAOSTAT also provides estimates of the 'stocks' of different types of food animals, calculated in an accounting framework for different years and countries (FAO, 2001).

The global sea change in LSF consumption trends in the 1980s and 1990s appeared just as suddenly, with impacts just as profound, as the 'green revolution' in the 1960s and 1970s. Conceding that the term 'revolution' was a simplistic label describing a complex set of changes, Delgado et al. (1999b, p59) argued that 'the "revolutionary" aspect comes from the participation of developing countries on a large scale in transformations that had previously occurred mostly in the temperate zones of developed countries.' Between the 1970s and the 1990s, the market value of LSF consumption in developing countries increased by approximately US$155 billion, more than twice the market value of increased cereals consumption under the green revolution (Delgado, 2003, p3907S). According to Simon Ehui of the ILRI (2000, p3), 'We call it a revolution to draw people's attention to the fact that the change is happening rapidly and on a massive scale.' Beyond questions of their suddenness and scale, the idea of a revolution, especially an agricultural revolution, conveys a vivid image of progress and betterment yet revolutions may also imply a threatening future and in any case, the outcomes of revolutions are almost always contested. The livestock revolution is no different (Sumberg and Thompson, 2013, pp5–6). Whether these reservations and futures are couched in terms of livestock's 'long shadow' (Steinfeld et al., 2006b), its 'ecological hoofprint' (Weis, 2013), its impact on human welfare, or its impact on animal welfare, the role, impact and dynamics of the global population of food animals is becoming a critical global issue.

Since the 'revolutionary' aspect stems from the *rate of change* in the consumption of LSF in different regions, meat consumption in kilograms per capita is portrayed on a logarithmic axis over the fifty-year period ending in 2011 for selected world regions (Figure 2.1). North America is emblematic of meat consumption in the global north; it is higher than any other world region but the trend is relatively flat with fluctuations showing the influence of economic cycles on consumer spending. Average annual meat consumption in South America and Central America have both doubled, while East Asia, led by China, has increased by a factor of ten. All of these regions have grown to exceed the global average. On the other hand, India and Africa display much slower rates of increase in meat consumption over the same fifty-year period. What impact is this growing per capita consumption of LSF likely to have on aggregate consumption?

Table 2.1 compares total and per capita meat consumption for selected countries and world regions between 1991 and 2001 (approximating the last decade observed by Delgado et al. 1999b) and then adds the next and most recent available decade, bringing the series up to 2011 to see whether revolutionary change has persisted. Representative of developed countries, the United States has levels of aggregate consumption far higher than any other entry, and the absolute consumption of meat is still increasing even though meat consumption per capita actually decreased between 2001 and 2011. Focusing on the period since the livestock revolution was first identified, global scale per capita meat consumption has increased by five kilograms per person or 13 percent in just ten years, propelled in significant

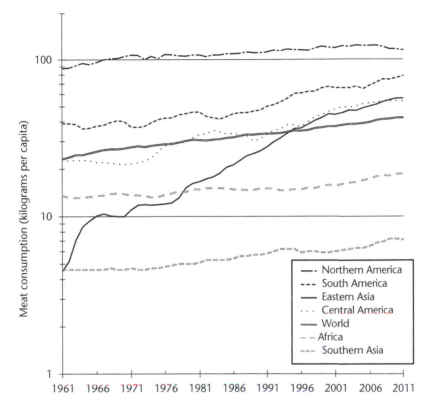

FIGURE 2.1 Per capita meat consumption in selected world regions.

Source: Raw data from FAO (2014), Food supply, Livestock and fish primary equivalent

measure by enormous increases in Brazil, China and Southeast Asia. The impact of these increases in per capita consumption is levered sharply upwards by population growth in all three regions. In tonnage terms, Brazil and China increased by more than one-third, while Southeast Asia grew by over three-quarters in just the ten years between 2001 and 2011. Annual rates of change in both total consumption and consumption per capita of meat between 2001 and 2011 are slightly higher than the trend from 1991 to 2001 and in some cases (notably Southeast Asia), consumption is actually increasing more rapidly than in the previous decade.

In general, Table 2.1 shows that the trend described as the livestock revolution in 1999 shows every indication that it is continuing into the new millennium. The enormity of such dietary changes coupled with rapid population growth in the regions experiencing the largest changes has implications for the entire supply chain for meat, from the reproduction of live animals to the domestic refrigerator. If consumption of LSF is increasing, it follows that global stocks of food animals must also have grown rapidly over the past five decades. For that reason, we turn from human consumption of LSF to food animal production.

TABLE 2.1 Meat Consumption for Selected Regions, 1991, 2001, and 2011.

Total consumption	Meat consumption (kilotonnes)			Average annual growth rate (%)	
	1991	2001	2011	1991–2001	2001–2011
Brazil	8,009	13,516	18,309	6.9	3.5
China	32,092	58,977	80,421	8.4	3.6
India	3,747	4,266	5,156	1.4	2.1
USA	29,378	34,768	37,037	1.8	0.7
Central America	3,958	6,783	8,788	7.1	3.0
South America	15,087	23,191	31,259	5.4	3.5
Southeast Asia	6,519	9,800	17,460	5.0	7.8
Africa	9,079	11,916	18,105	3.1	5.2
World	179,384	227,562	290,649	2.7	2.8

Per capita consumption	Meat consumption per capita (kilograms)			Average annual growth rate (%)	
	1991	2001	2011	1991–2001	2001–2011
Brazil	52.6	76.4	93	4.5	2.2
China	26.5	44.8	57.5	6.9	2.8
India	4.2	4	4.2	−0.5	0.5
USA	114.3	120.9	117.6	0.6	−0.3
Central America	33.7	47.9	54	4.2	1.3
South America	50.1	65.7	78.5	3.1	1.9
Southeast Asia	14.5	18.6	29.1	2.8	5.6
Africa	15	15.6	18.6	0.4	1.9
World	33.5	37.2	42.2	1.1	1.3

Source: Raw data from FAO (2014), Food supply, Livestock and fish primary equivalent

Is the livestock revolution truly demand driven?

The oft-noted contrast between the supply-driven green revolution and the demand-driven livestock revolution (ILRI, 2000, p3; Steinfeld and Gerber, 2010, p18,237) is open to challenge. As Sumberg and Thompson (2013, p8) observe,

> The language of 'demand-driven production systems' looms large in the story of the Livestock Revolution ... This distinction between a supply (Green) and a demand (Livestock) driven agricultural revolution has often

been repeated and is now inextricably linked to debates and discourse around the Livestock Revolution.

The green revolution was prompted by the development of new high-yielding cereal grains adapted to low-latitude environments (Johnson, 1972; King, 1973; Yapa, 1979). It was conceived as a process of modernization in which technology was actively transferred by aid agencies and multinational agricultural suppliers in the expectation that developing countries would participate in an agrarian transition and dietary transformation similar to the more developed countries (Parayil, 2003). In contrast to these supply-side changes, the livestock revolution was putatively caused by demand-side changes in the size of the market (population growth); individual and family purchasing power (real income growth); and a consumer meat preference associated with urbanization and a growing middle class. Tony Weis describes the 'meatification' of diets as an indicator of modernization:

> the climb up the 'animal protein ladder' is part and parcel of the climb up the 'development ladder,' and patterns of rising meat consumption at the national scale have been very tightly linked to patterns of rising affluence, with industrialized countries consuming meat at vastly higher levels and the world's poorest regions at the bottom of the meat consumption spectrum.
>
> (Weis, 2013, p71)

Dietary meatification has long been viewed as 'a goal and measure of development and a marker of class ascension' (Fritz, 2014, p15). For example: 'we know meat-eating races have been and are leaders in the progress made by mankind in its upward struggle through the ages' (Hinman and Harris, 1939, p1).

In essence, the doctrine of consumer sovereignty has become an integral part of the dominant livestock revolution paradigm, assuming that all initiative for food consumption decisions lies with the consumer. The consumer's demand function is given and producers comply with market signals. This presumption of consumer sovereignty in market economies was called into question by J. K. Galbraith (1971, p211; Waller, 2008, pp17–18) in an industrial context in which corporate power extends into the commercial culture and politics of food production, allowing firms to shape consumers' attitudes and food preferences. Galbraith's theory of the 'revised sequence' argues that consumers are responding to the marketing blandishments of a corporate technostructure dedicated to the creation of wants and needs where none existed before and a *dirigiste* state that regulates purchasing power through trade, fiscal and monetary policy instruments. While consumers may be sovereign in preindustrial economies, industrial state policy incites a belief that a diet rich in meat is desirable and an appropriate means of expressing one's status.

What are the ecological implications of the livestock revolution?

To appreciate the magnitude of the increase in the stocks of food animals of different kinds and magnitudes (e.g. to compare billions of chickens to millions of cattle on the same scale), the global change in food animal stocks since 1961 has been transformed into index numbers that are evaluated in relation to human population change over that same period (Figure 2.2).[2] Global stocks of chickens and goats have grown at rates well in excess of the human population over the 50 years ending in 2012, with no evidence of abatement in the ten years after the livestock revolution was first observed (Delgado et al., 1999b). The ongoing revolution in meat consumption is sustained by an ongoing revolution in animal production. Over a time period in which the human population more than doubled, the world's chicken stocks increased more than fivefold, while goat stocks nearly trebled. By contrast, the number of cattle and sheep increased at rates significantly less than human population growth. In the case of each of the food animal species graphed in Figure 2.2, China accounts for the largest growth in these livestock types both as a proportion of the total growth and in

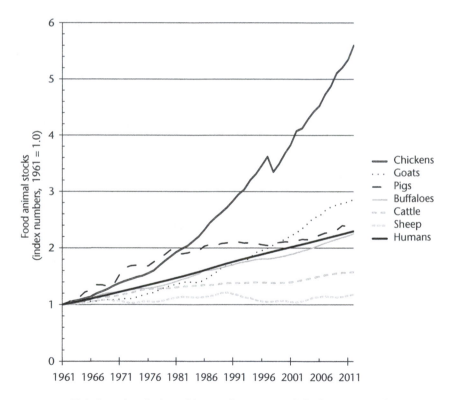

FIGURE 2.2 Global stocks of selected livestock species and the human population presented as index numbers.

Source: Raw data from FAO (2014), Production, Live animals and United Nations (2013)

absolute numbers. China now accounts for 24 percent of the world's chickens and 48 percent of its pigs. Cattle stocks declined in countries such as the United States, Canada, France and the United Kingdom between 2005 and 2012, a cyclical decline in contrast to global-scale cattle stocks, which have been growing, albeit below the rates experienced by any other of the principal food animals.

Global scale growth in animal production raises the risk of pandemic animal diseases, some with zoonotic potential, due to the growing numbers of animals housed at high densities and the long-distance trade in livestock that is necessary to match animal supplies with meat demand (Hall et al., 2004, pp429–432; Liverani et al., 2013; McLeod et al., 2010). The environmental impact of these food animals is one element of the 'ecological footprint' (Wackernagel and Rees, 1998), an indicator of the global resources appropriated by humans over a unit of time – typically one year. Based simply on global rates of growth in total stocks shown in Figure 2.2, it is tempting to believe that chickens, goats and pigs are key to understanding the growing environmental impact of the livestock revolution considered in detail by Henning Steinfeld et al. (2006b) in *Livestock's Long Shadow* and by Tony Weis (2013) in *The Ecological Hoofprint*. However, the growth trend of livestock numbers does not give a valid impression of their environmental impact. Different food animal species, from chickens to cattle, have different average metabolic weights thus they have varying environmental impacts (e.g. consumption of water and biomass, soil compaction and erosion, and excretion).

The simplest estimate of this differential environmental loading would be to weight the stocks of different types of food animals in terms of 'tropical livestock units' (TLU) (for details see FAO, 2003, p34, Njuki et al., 2011, p12).[3] Livestock units are used to establish maximum stocking rates per unit area for different types of livestock. Using the example of TLU, one cow has an environmental impact on grazing land equivalent to seven goats (FAO, 2003, p33). Figure 2.3 provides a graphical comparison of global scale TLUs, reflecting the smaller size of grazing cattle in tropical regions; thus it is more conservative than it would be if the animal units used in temperate latitudes were the weighting factors.[4] Notwithstanding the spectacular growth records of chickens, goats and pigs shown in Figure 2.2, the environmental impact of livestock on the landscape is dominated by cattle, not small stock or poultry.

It has been well established that the livestock revolution has been remarkably uneven in the food animal species and world regions involved (Fritz, 2014, p3). The most rapid growth in absolute numbers of food animals has involved chickens in China and the United States; pigs in China; goats in South Asia, China and Africa; and cattle in India, Brazil and China (FAO, 2014). Yet for all that growth, Figure 2.3 suggests that it is the sheer mass of cattle that is imposing the largest burden on global environmental capacity. And for this reason, it is not just consumption that ranges widely, it is not just production that ranges widely, it is the environmental impact that ranges widely among world regions and species.

The global-scale comparison of TLUs displayed in Figure 2.3 makes no allowance for the sharp regional differences in livestock housing, whether they are

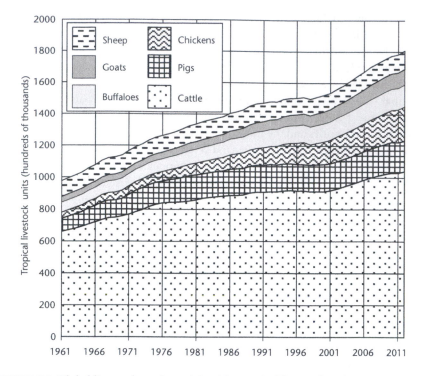

FIGURE 2.3 Global livestock stocks weighted by tropical livestock units.

Source: Raw data from FAO (2014), Production, Live animals

free-ranging or housed intensively in barns. Low-intensity impacts caused by overgrazing and ensuing degradation of pastoral resources feature in the environmental history of the rangelands of the American west (Sayre, 1999, pp248–250). Soil erosion continues as one of the most pervasive manifestations of globalization in countries such as Botswana that remain dependent on extensive grazing (Darkoh and Mbaiwa, 2002). To these extensive livestock land uses may be added the 'high-intensity' impacts of confined animal feeding operations (CAFOs) that include contamination of riparian habitat and urban water sources by high volumes of manure. The ecological impact of livestock is a function of their sheer numbers, their metabolic weighting in animal units, and the regionally variable blend of intensive and extensive livestock husbandry.

The ecological impact of livestock is exacerbated by a significant transformation in land use at a global scale as livestock numbers have grown. The areal extent of arable land (land suitable for the cultivation of annual or perennial crops) and grazing land (land that is managed to support livestock grazing without cultivation) have both expanded considerably since the 1960s (Steinfeld et al., 2006c). Typically it is forest land that is being converted to pasture or cropland and this has been most widely observed in the Amazon basin. Much of the new cropland is given over to soybean production in regions such as Brazil's vast *cerrado* and the cultivation of millet and sorghum for animal consumption overseas. Indeed, developing countries now account for over one-third (36 percent) of the cereal grains used to feed animals (Delgado, 2005; Thornton, 2010, p2856).

Delgado et al. (1999b, p1) were not wrong when they described 'a massive global increase in demand for food of animal origin' but this has deflected some of the debate away from the key regions and species that have the greatest influence on global rates of change and the greatest potential environmental impact. For example, some analysts have argued that the world's livestock and associated land-use changes contribute an estimated 18 percent of the world's greenhouse gas emissions (Garnett, 2010, pp37–39; Steinfeld et al., 2006b, p112). And for those reasons, 'reining in the global livestock sector should be considered a key leverage point for averting irreversible ecological change' (Pelletier and Tyedmers, 2010, p18373). The stock response to this concern is that countervailing trends such as the shift from ruminant livestock to monogastric species[5] with their much higher daily rates of gain, their greater feed conversion ratios, and yield gains in the production of feed grain crops are liable to mitigate these livestock impacts.

> Calling for reining in livestock sector growth as a priority in environmental policy also carries the risk that all such efforts target those countries and population segments that currently have low levels of consumption and where food intakes need to grow as opposed to those countries where they are currently high and where a reduction may also be desirable from a nutritional perspective.
>
> (Steinfeld and Gerber, 2010, p18238)

This admonition leads us to the question of the benefits of livestock production in developing countries.

The livestock revolution and rural development

From the earliest identification of the livestock revolution, human welfare implications were recognized as an issue of balance between the negative effects of rising competition for cereal grains between humans and livestock and opportunities for income growth among small-scale animal producers (Delgado et al., 1999b, pp40–42). This led to the launch in 2001 of the 'Pro-Poor Livestock Policy Initiative' by the FAO (Otte et al., 2012, pix). In this view, the negative impact of rising cereal grain prices on the food security of the rural poor would be compensated by the positive impacts of enhanced livestock production on the incomes and welfare of rural small-holders in developing countries.

The key strategic goal of the International Livestock Research Institute is to improve food security and reduce poverty in developing countries through research into the most efficient, safe and sustainable use of livestock, believing that 'to acquire livestock is to set foot on the first rung of the ladder out of poverty' (ILRI, 2000, p3). Livestock are appreciating assets that provide an opportunity for the landless and unbanked poor to accumulate wealth in a relatively secure form, to hedge against inflation, reduce vulnerability to natural and economic shocks, and create a living insurance instrument for times of crisis (Heffernan, 2004; Randolph et al., 2007, p2789). Livestock provide a regular source of income in the case of eggs and dairy products, buffering seasonal fluctuations in income from cash crops. Livestock are an efficient way of managing crop residues and domestic waste, a source of fertilizer and of motive power. Ruminants can graze on public pastoral resources such as open range land, roadside verges and vacant land in urban areas thus the opportunity cost for their sustenance is small (Janzen, 2011, p787). Livestock husbandry allows labour spreading outside of the planting and harvest periods, smoothing family labour across seasons, genders and generations (Otte et al., 2012, pp37–39). The care, feeding and milking of livestock and livestock products is often sharply gendered, and while women seldom hold property rights to land, they often own livestock, which makes an important contribution to women's income, wealth and status (Otte et al., 2012, pp48–49).

In a developing world characterized by enormous income inequality, livestock ownership tends to be more prevalent and more equitable than land ownership. While livestock are kept across all household income classes, households in the bottom expenditure quintile are more likely to have livestock in their asset portfolios than wealthier households. Thus, 'livestock are often more equally distributed across wealth groups than land' as even the poorest households are able to keep a few animals. Increasing livestock productivity confers greater welfare benefits on the poorest rural income groups than corresponding increases in land productivity (Otte et al., 2012, pp34–35). The poorest households of the developing world are likely to suffer some level of malnutrition and have the most to gain in nutritional terms from the high-quality proteins and micronutrients available through animal source foods (Garnett, 2010, pp39–40; Neumann et al., 2002, p195). Finally, livestock production has economic spin-offs in rural employment and increased spending that generate additional trade with local suppliers. As a result, the livestock sector may be responsible for a circular and cumulative process of economic growth and development.

However, there is another, sceptical, school of thought about the supposed benefits of livestock production to the smallholders of the developing world (Fritz, 2014, pp13–14). In the very sectors with the fastest growing consumption and the fastest growing production (pork and poultry), the global tendency in most regions has favoured larger-scale CAFOs at the expense of smallholders. By 2000, 77–79 percent of the world's total pork, poultry meat and egg production were produced in intensive industrial facilities (cf. Bruinsma, 2003, p166; Herrero et al., 2013, p20889).

Global growth in livestock production is made especially complex by changing production technologies in different world regions which have important environmental implications. On the one hand extensive grazing is still the only economic land use for the world's grasslands, and at sustainable stocking densities it can actually contribute to carbon sequestration (Garnett, 2010, p40). Grazing covers a larger area than any other land use. However, grasslands are becoming seriously degraded, especially during drought conditions and when stocking densities exceed carrying capacity. On the other hand, a growing proportion of the globe's food animals are raised in CAFOs. In such cases livestock production is shifting geographically from rural to peri-urban areas in an effort to locate closer to urban meat markets; to sources of feed from industrial by-products such as soybean cake, dried distillers grains and fruit pomace; or to transportation hubs as sources of feed grain. And there is also a shift of species in favour of monogastrics and dairy cattle which are increasingly housed in CAFOs. Ruminants for meat production (cattle, sheep and goats) graze on grass and stover in rural areas for a considerable portion of their lives although they are typically grain-finished in CAFOs in North America and parts of western Europe (Herrero et al., 2013, p20889 and supporting data p9; Steinfeld et al., 2006b, pp xx, 31–33).

The diversion of cereal grains from human to animal consumption in CAFOs will cause the price of staple food grain to increase, imposing a burden on the poorest people that far exceeds any benefit received by the shrinking number of small-scale livestock producers. Smallholders are further disadvantaged relative to industrial-scale producers as the urban demand for livestock products grows and food quality standards become more stringent (Hall et al., 2004, pp431–432). Urban food markets are being increasingly supplied by larger-scale, more intensive and technologically sophisticated producers, and in some cases imports and smallholders are struggling to supply these markets (Narrod et al., 2010, pp275–280). The supermarket revolution in developing countries is becoming an influential power at the head of buyer-driven supply chains (Gereffi and Lee, 2012; Humphrey, 2007; Randolph et al., 2007, pp2796–2797; Reardon et al., 2012).

Turning from supply chain governance to rural labour markets, evidence suggests that when alternate employment opportunities arise in occupations such as urban construction, manufacturing or service sectors, small-scale livestock keepers tend to exit the sector in favour of better paid and less risky urban employment opportunities. Thus as Dijkman (2009, p2) argues, 'it appears that the "livestock ladder" – the process by which small-scale traditional livestock keepers could gradually intensify and scale up their production, and, in doing, so use livestock as "pathways out of poverty" – is largely a myth'. There seems to be a growing gulf between traditional small-scale livestock producers who serve a largely local and rural clientele, and the intensive large-scale sector that serves the larger processing plants of urban markets (Dijkman, 2009, p3).

Case study: China's livestock revolution

With its massive human and livestock population, China has experienced the livestock revolution more rapidly and more intensively than any other world region. Thus, it is the obvious candidate for a detailed case study; however, it is not at all representative. Using a global food demand, supply and trade model, Rosegrant et al. (2001, p65) forecasted a 57 per cent increase in global meat demand from

1997 to 2020 with China alone accounting for 43 per cent of the global total. With rising real incomes and rapid urbanization in the post-reform period, pork consumption increased rapidly from 8.9 kilos in 1978 (the start of Deng Xiaoping's Open Door Policy) to 35.9 kilos by 2010 (303 per cent), while chicken consumption increased from 1.6 to 12.9 kilos or 706 per cent over the same period (FAO, 2014; Rae, 2008, p285). Thus meat consumption in China has increased at rates far above any other developing country. While the market power of status-conscious middle-income earners at the vanguard of meat consumption and their role as a 'catalyst class' driving changes in attitudes, behaviours and values should not be gainsaid (Bonnefond and Clément, 2014, p23), this case study illustrates the key role played by the state in encouraging meat consumption and livestock production in China.

Until 1978, livestock production in China was based on traditional small-scale 'backyard feeding,' raising fewer than five pigs a year, a handful of chickens, or a single dairy cow (Huajiao et al., 2008, p251; Speedy, 2003, p4049S). Comparatively small numbers of pigs and poultry consumed a varied diet of domestic waste products and crop residues, while on-farm lagoons were commonly used to recycle plant nutrients and generate bioenergy. Pork and chicken played a peripheral role in the Chinese diet; meat was only consumed on festive occasions and pigs were generally worth more alive than dead as means of domestic waste disposal and manure production for small-scale agriculture (Schneider and Sharma, 2014, p12). With the reforms and opening up of the Chinese economy, import tariffs on livestock feed commodities such as soybeans were reduced, making large-scale pig farming feasible. Meat and dairy consumption in China was encouraged by liberal trade policies facilitating the import of feed grain and LSF such as edible offal, chicken wings and feet, and other low value animal by-products (Wang et al., 1998, p129).[6] Among the most worrisome outcomes of dietary change on such a scale is the growing problem of obesity observed in China which has become the prototype of the nutritional transition (Bonnefond and Clément, 2014; Du et al., 2014; Popkin, 2014).

CAFOs were first introduced to China in 1979 and by the 1990s, they accounted for 15 per cent of pigs, 25 per cent of eggs, 40 per cent of broiler chickens and 50 per cent of milk (Huajiao et al., 2008, p250). By 2010, an estimated 66 per cent of pork production was based in CAFOs (Herrero et al., 2013, p20889, supporting information, p43). While it may be argued that the advantage of intensive pig production is its high daily rate of gain, it is often overlooked that high rates of gain are based on the use of commercially obtained high-concentrate feeds that divert grain away from the human food supply while small-scale farms tend to rely on foraging as the main source of swine feed, albeit with lower rates of gain (Chin, 2014, p154).

When an epizootic reproductive and respiratory disease drove domestic pork prices up in 2006, the Chinese government brought in a package of subsidies to encourage large-scale pig farms to address food safety concerns and stabilize food prices (Schneider and Sharma, 2014, p13). This policy appears to be supported by consumer preferences.

From a Chinese consumer's perspective, the industrial approach seems to represent values such as achievement and evolution, as well as quality and safety, since pig production is moving away from low-cost, low-quality, and low-safety family-scale systems.

(de Barcellos et al., 2013, p443)

After a widely reported infant formula adulteration scandal in 2008, Chinese consumers lost confidence in the safety of domestic dairy products, inducing the Chinese government to encourage consolidation of the dairy industry. The result of all this has been a massive shift away from traditional, small-scale dispersed livestock production to large-scale, concentrated and standardized farms (Sharma and Rou, 2014, pp14–15).

Thus, primary livestock production in China is an industry in the midst of a restructuring process that varies with longitude. Dispersed smallholders and backyard production are still common in the western interior while intensive industrial-scale CAFOs have completely replaced traditional livestock raising systems in the eastern coastal regions (Bingsheng, 2010, pp96–97). Specialist producers tend to be located on the margins of major metropolitan regions of the southeast close to slaughter and processing facilities (Schneider and Sharma, 2014, pp18–20; Webber, 2012, pp23–36). The poultry sector has also consolidated. In the twenty years ending in 2005, some 70 million small-scale poultry farmers withdrew from the industry and in the fifteen years ending in 2011, the number of broiler farms in China had decreased by 75 per cent.

Outside of China's largest metropolitan centres, livestock logistics are still informal and the cold chain for meat is fragmented and unreliable. Thus, traditional wet markets continue their role as the main distribution channel for meat (Pi et al., 2014, p16). However, the supermarket revolution has arrived in urban China (Mei and Shao, 2011) and there is growing integration of the value chain all the way from livestock feed importers to meat retailers, coordinated by the 'dragon head' agribusiness companies (Pi et al., 2014, pp22–23; Schneider and Sharma, 2014, pp23–26; Sharma, 2014, p17). For example, Shuanghui (often described as 'Shineway Group' by English-speakers) has become China's largest meat processor and in 2013 it acquired Smithfield Foods, America's largest pork producer in a deal worth about $4.7 billion. This was the largest-ever acquisition by a Chinese company of a US asset and upon being renamed WH Group, it became the world's biggest producer of pork. Notwithstanding Chinese government rhetoric that encourages cooperative and contractual arrangements as a means of integrating small producers with the dragon heads, barriers to entry such as unattainable market standards and the high cost of contractual relationships tend to discriminate against small-scale pig producers (Schneider and Sharma, 2014, pp17, 29).

Between China's Ministry of Health that is promoting milk as an essential dietary ingredient, and the Ministry of Agriculture's conviction that food quality standards are best served by large-scale processing plants integrated with CAFOs, state policy is an important explanatory factor in the growth of meat and dairy production. The Chinese agro-food system is modernizing along the same lines as advanced western economies (Schneider and Sharma, 2014, p21) as CAFOs make intensive use of commercial feed sources, far beyond China's capacity to supply. Thus, China has become a major importer of soybean cake and fishmeal, largely from South America. Yet another challenge of applying the CAFO model in a Chinese context is the management of livestock manure that in sheer volume exceeds the pollution problem from all other urban and industrial sources (Huajiao et al., 2008, p250).

Conclusions

This chapter outlines some of the key issues raised by the livestock revolution. First, the changes in human consumption of LSF have continued since they were first observed. These dietary changes are far from uniform, proceeding extremely rapidly in parts of East and Southeast Asia and in Latin America and scarcely at all in many parts of Africa and West Asia. By measuring production in TLUs, the chapter shows that the fastest growing livestock species (chickens, goats and pigs) are unlikely to have the environmental impact of cattle, which will be felt most strongly in just three countries: China, India and Brazil.

Assertions that the livestock revolution is significantly different from the green revolution need to be more carefully qualified, indeed the comparison may obscure more than it illuminates. Complex changes that come under the revolutionary rubric have none of the suddenness that is characteristic of a true agricultural revolution. Instead, the data suggest that the growth in the global livestock population is revealing itself as a gradual evolutionary process.

In the absence of effective policies to foster small-scale livestock production, an opportunity to create a more equal distribution of income in rural areas appears to have been lost. Intensive industrial-scale livestock production is making rapid inroads in parts of East and Southeast Asia and in Latin America, while global scale agribusiness firms are tightening their grasp on the grain-livestock-meat supply chain, often to the detriment of traditional small-scale producers and their local markets. Thus, the agro-industrial model based on economies of scale and the integrated industrial grain–oilseed–livestock complex of the developed western countries is gradually finding its way into the most rapidly developing countries of the global south.

Increasing meat consumption reflects a positive income elasticity of demand for luxury foodstuffs and the rising real incomes of a new urban middle class. However, the Galbraithian 'revised sequence' and manifest evidence of state policy that has favoured large-scale livestock producers is a reminder of the importance of corporate and government regulation of markets in 'new industrial states' such as China.

Acknowledgments

Bibliographic assistance from Alison Butler and Leona Jacobs, advice from Ugo Pica-Ciamarra and constructive commentary by Diane Clark, Glenn Coulter and Jody Emel are gratefully acknowledged.

Notes

1 Following the convention generally accepted in this research area, the developed countries comprise Australia, Canada, Europe, Israel, Japan, New Zealand, Russian Federation, South Africa and the United States, while the remainder are classified as developing.
2 FAOSTAT provides data on other livestock species such as camelids, horses, asses and mules, rodents, rabbits and a variety of poultry types, however, none of these is exploited to the same degree as the food animals included in Figure 2.2.
3 Animal unit measures vary considerably in the literature and can only be considered as approximations. For present purposes, TLU are assigned as follows: cattle and water buffalo (0.7), pigs (0.2), sheep and goats (0.1), and chickens (0.01). In a North American context, cattle would be assessed at 1.0 animal units while pigs would have a value of 0.25, reflecting the larger size, weight and metabolic requirements of cattle and pigs in Canada and the United States. Thus TLU is a relatively conservative weighting.
4 TLU are normally used to establish grazing capacity in extensive rangeland environments; however a large and growing proportion of the world's livestock are housed in CAFOs with a highly localized but much more intensive environmental impact. Irrespective of how animals are housed, TLUs provide a crude estimate of the relative impacts of livestock of different species.
5 Ruminants have four stomachs in the digestive system and the most common food animals include cattle, goats, sheep and buffalo. Monogastrics have a single stomach and include pigs and poultry.
6 In contrast to North American consumer preferences, Chinese consumers favour bone-in chicken feet and 'white organ meats', which command a price equal to or greater than the muscle cuts preferred by North American shoppers.

References

Bellur, V. V., Singh, S. P., Chaganti, R. and Chaganti, R. (1990) 'The white revolution: How Amul brought milk to India', *Long Range Planning*, vol 23, no 6, pp. 71–79

Bingsheng, K. (2010) 'China', *Livestock in a Changing Landscape: Experiences and Regional Perspectives*, Island Press, Washington, DC

Bonnefond, C. and Clément, M. (2014) 'Social class and body weight among Chinese urban adults: The role of the middle classes in the nutrition transition', *Social Science & Medicine*, vol 112, pp. 22–29

Bruinsma, J. (2003) 'Livestock production', in J. Bruinsma (ed.), *World Agriculture: Towards 2015/2030: An FAO Perspective*, Earthscan, London

Chin, V. (2014) 'Understanding the growth and the decline of small-farm production in the swine industry of Guangdong Province and in China from 1980 to 2010', in L. Augustin-Jean and B. Alpermann (eds), *The Political Economy of Agro-Food Markets in China: The Social Construction of the Markets in an Era of Globalization*, Palgrave Macmillan, Basingstoke

Darkoh, M. B. K. and Mbaiwa, J. E. (2002) 'Globalisation and the livestock industry in Botswana', *Singapore Journal of Tropical Geography*, vol 23, no 2, pp. 149–166 de Barcellos, M. D., Grunert, K. G., Zhou, Y., Verbeke, W., Perez-Cueto, F. J. and Krystallis, A. (2013) 'Consumer attitudes to different pig production systems: A study from mainland China', *Agriculture and Human Values*, vol 30, no 3, pp. 443–455

Delgado, C. L. (2003) 'Rising consumption of meat and milk in developing countries has created a new food revolution', *The Journal of Nutrition*, vol 133, no 11, pp. 3907S-3910S

Delgado, C. L. (2005) 'Rising demand for meat and milk in developing countries: Implications for grassland-based livestock production', in D. A. Mcgilloway (ed.), *Grassland: a Global Resource*, Waginingen, Academic Publishers, Waginingen, The Netherlands

Delgado, C. L., Rosegrant, M., Steinfeld, H., Ehui, S. and Courbois, C. (1999a) 'The coming livestock revolution', *Choices*, pp. 40–44, Agricultural and Applied Economics Association, Washington, DC

Delgado, C. L., Rosegrant, M., Steinfeld, H., Ehui, S. and Courbois, C. (1999b) 'Livestock to 2020: The next food revolution', International Food Policy Research Institute, Washington, DC

Dijkman, J. (2009) 'Innovation capacity and the elusive livestock revolution', *Link News Bulletin*, United Nations University-MERIT

Du, S. F., Wang, H. J., Zhang, B., Zhai, F. Y. and Popkin, B. M. (2014) 'China in the period of transition from scarcity and extensive undernutrition to emerging nutrition-related non-communicable diseases, 1949–1992', *Obesity Reviews*, vol 15 no Suppl 1, pp. 8–15

Erb, K.-H., Mayer, A., Kastner, T., Sallet, K.-E. and Haberl, H. (2012) *The Impact of Industrial Grain Fed Livestock Production on Food Security: An Extended Literature Review*, Compassion in World Farming, The Tubney Charitable Trust and World Society for the Protection of Animals, Alpen Adria University Klagenfurt-Vienna-Graz, Austria.

FAO (2001) *Food Balance Sheets: A Handbook*, Food and Agriculture Organization of the United Nations, Rome

FAO (2003) 'Compendium of Agricultural – Environmental Indicators, 1989–91 to 2000', Food and Agriculture Organization of the United Nations Rome

FAO (2014) 'FAOSTAT', Food and Agricultural Organization of the United Nations, Rome

Fritz, T. (2014) 'The illusory promise of the livestock revolution: Meatification of diets, industrial animal farms and global food security', FDCL-Verlag, Berlin

Galbraith, J. K. (1971) *The New Industrial State*, Houghton-Mifflin, New York

Garnett, T. (2010) 'Livestock and Climate Change', in J. D'Silva and J. Webster (eds), *The Meat Crisis: Developing More Sustainable Production and Consumption*, Earthscan, London

Gereffi, G. and Lee, J. (2012) 'Why the world suddenly cares about global supply chains', *Journal of Supply Chain Management*, vol 48, no 3, pp. 24–32

Hall, D. C., Ehui, S. and Delgado, C. (2004) 'The livestock revolution, food safety, and small-scale farmers: Why they matter to us all', *Journal of Agricultural and Environmental Ethics*, vol 17, pp. 425–444

Heffernan, C. (2004) 'Livestock and the poor: Issues in poverty-focused livestock development', in E. Owen, T. Smith, M. A. Steele, S. Anderson, A. J. Duncan, M. Herrero, J. D. Leaver, C. K. Reynolds, J. I. Richards and J. C. Ku-Vera (eds), *Responding to the Livestock Revolution: The Role of Globalisation and Implications for Poverty Alleviation*, British Society of Animal Science

Herrero, M., Havlík, P., Valin, H., Notenbaert, A., Rufino, M. C., Thornton, P. K., Blümmel, M., Weiss, F., Grace, D. and Obersteiner, M. (2013) 'Biomass use, production, feed efficiencies, and greenhouse gas emissions from global livestock systems', *Proceedings of the National Academy of Sciences*, vol 110, no 52, pp. 20888–20893

Hinman, R. B. and Harris, R. B. (1939) *The Story of Meat*, Swift and Company, Chicago

Huajiao, Q., Zhang, F., Wanbin, Z., Haibin, W. and Xu, C. (2008) 'Reorientation of China's agriculture over the next two decades', *Outlook on Agriculture*, vol 37, no 4, pp. 247–254

Humphrey, J. (2007) 'The supermarket revolution in developing countries: tidal wave or tough competitive struggle?', *Journal of Economic Geography*, vol 7, no 4, pp. 433–450

ILRI (2000) 'ILRI annual report 1999: Making the livestock revolution work for the poor', International Livestock Research Institute, Nairobi

Janzen, H. H. (2011) 'What place for livestock on a re-greening earth?', *Animal Feed Science and Technology*, vol 166–167, pp. 783–796

Johnson, S. (1972) *The Green Revolution*, Harper & Row, New York

King, R. (1973) 'Geographical perspectives on the green revolution', *Tijdschrift voor economische en sociale geografie*, vol 64, no 4, pp. 237–244

Kumar, A., Parappurathu, S. and Jee, S. (2013) 'Do Dairy co-operatives enhance milk production, productivity and quality? Evidences from the Indo-Gangetic Plain of India', *Indian Journal of Agricultural Economics*, vol 68, no 3, pp. 457–468

Liverani, M., Waage, J., Barnett, T., Pfeiffer, D. U., Rushton, J., Rudge, J. W., Loevinsohn, M. E., Scoones, I., Smith, R. D., Cooper, B. S., White, L. J., Goh, S., Horby, P., Wren, B., Gundogdu, O., Woods, A. and Coker, R. J. (2013) 'Understanding and managing zoonotic risk in the new livestock industries', *Environmental Health Perspectives*, vol 121, no 8, pp. 873–877

Mathias, E. (2012) 'Livestock out of balance: From asset to liability in the course of the livestock revolution', League for Pastoral Peoples and Endogenous Livestock Development, Ober-Ramstadt, Germany

McLeod, A., Honhold, N., Steinfeld, H., Mooney, H., Schneider, F. and Neville, L. (2010) 'Responses on emerging livestock diseases', in H. Steinfeld, H. A. Mooney, F. Schneider and L. E. Neville (eds), *Livestock in a Changing Landscape, Volume 1: Drivers, Consequences, and Responses*, Island Press, Washington, DC

Mei, L. and Shao, D. (2011) 'Too cheap hurt farmers, too expensive hurt customers: The changing impacts of supermarkets on Chinese agro-food markets', *Millennial Asia*, vol 2, no 1, pp. 43–64

Nair, K. N. (1985) 'White revolution in India: Facts and issues', *Economic and Political Weekly*, vol 20, no 25/26, pp. A89–A95

Narrod, C., Tiongco, M. and Delgado, C. (2010) 'Socioeconomic implications of the livestock industrialization process: how will smallholders fare?', in H. Steinfeld, H. A. Mooney, F. Schneider and L. E. Neville (eds), *Livestock in a Changing Landscape, Volume 1: Drivers, Consequences, and Responses*, Island Press, Washington, DC

Neumann, C., Harris, D. M. and Rogers, L. M. (2002) 'Contribution of animal source foods in improving diet quality and function in children in the developing world', *Nutrition Research*, vol 22, no 1–2, pp. 193–220

Njuki, J., Poole, J., Johnson, N., Baltenweck, I., Pali, P., Lokman, Z. and Mburu, S. (2011) 'Gender, livestock and livelihood indicators', International Livestock Research Institute, Nairobi

Otte, J., Costales, A., Dijkman, J., Pica-Ciamarra, U., Robinson, T., Ahuja, V., Ly, C. and Roland-Holst, D. (2012) *Livestock Sector Development for Poverty Reduction: An Economic and Policy Perspective –Livestock's Many Virtues*, Food And Agriculture Organization of the United Nations, Rome

Parayil, G. (2003) 'Mapping technological trajectories of the Green Revolution and the Gene Revolution from modernization to globalization', *Research Policy*, vol 32, no 6, pp. 971–990

Pelletier, N. and Tyedmers, P. (2010) 'Forecasting potential global environmental costs of livestock production 2000–2050', *Proceedings of the National Academy of Sciences*, vol 107, no 43, pp. 18371–18374

Pi, C., Rou, Z. and Horowitz, S. (2014) 'Fair or fowl? Industrialization of poultry production in China', in S. Sharma and B. Lilliston (eds), Institute for Agriculture and Trade Policy

Pica-Ciamarra, U. and Otte, J. (2009) 'The "livestock revolution": Rhetoric and reality', Pro-Poor Livestock Policy Initiative, FAO

Pica-Ciamarra, U. and Otte, J. (2011) 'The "livestock revolution": Rhetoric and reality', *Outlook on Agriculture*, vol 40, no 1, pp. 7–19

Popkin, B. M. (2014) 'Synthesis and implications: China's nutrition transition in the context of changes across other low- and middle-income countries', *Obesity Reviews*, vol 15, no Suppl 1, pp. 60–67

Rae, A. (2008) 'China's agriculture, smallholders and trade: Driven by the livestock revolution?', *Australian Journal of Agricultural and Resource Economics*, vol 52, no 3, pp. 283–302

Randolph, T. F., Schelling, E., Grace, D., Nicholson, C. F., Leroy, J. L., Cole, D. C., Demment, M. W., Omore, A., Zinsstag, J. and Ruel, M. (2007) 'Invited Review: Role of livestock in human nutrition and health for poverty reduction in developing countries', *Journal of Animal Science*, vol 85, no 11, pp. 2788–2800

Reardon, T., Timmer, C. P. and Minten, B. (2012) 'Supermarket revolution in Asia and emerging development strategies to include small farmers', *Proceedings of the National Academy of Sciences*, vol 109, no 31, pp. 12332–12337

Rosegrant, M., Paisner, M. S., Meijer, S. and Witcover, J. (2001) *Global Food Projections to 2020*, International Food Policy Research Institute, Washington, DC

Sayre, N. F. (1999) 'The cattle boom in southern Arizona: Towards a critical political ecology', *Journal of the Southwest*, vol 41, no 2, pp. 239–271

Schneider, M. (2011) 'Feeding China's pigs: Implications for the environment, China's smallholder farmers and food security', Institute for Agriculture and Trade Policy

Schneider, M. and Sharma, S. (2014) 'China's pork miracle? Agribusiness and development in China's pork industry', Institute for Agriculture and Trade Policy

Sharma, S. (2014) 'The need for feed: China's demand for industrialized meat and its impacts', Institute for Agriculture and Trade Policy

Sharma, S. and Rou, Z. (2014) 'China's dairy dilemma: The evolution and future trends of China's dairy industry', Institute for Agriculture and Trade Policy

Speedy, A. W. (2003) 'Global production and consumption of animal source foods', *The Journal of Nutrition*, vol 133, no 11, pp. 4048S–4053S

Steinfeld, H. and Chilonda, P. (2006) 'Old players, new players', in H. Steinfeld, A. Costales, J. Rushton, B. Scharfe, T. Bennett and D. C. Hall (eds), *Livestock Report*, FAO, Rome

Steinfeld, H., Costales, A., Rushton, J., Scharfe, B., Bennett, T. and Hall, D. C. (2006a) 'Livestock Report', FAO, Rome

Steinfeld, H., Gerber, P., Wassenaar, T., Castel, V., Rosales, M. and de Haan, C. (2006b) 'Livestock's long shadow: Environmental issues and options', FAO, Rome

Steinfeld, H., Wassenaar, T. and Jutzi, S. (2006c) 'Livestock production systems in developing countries: Status, drivers, trends', *Scientific and Technical Review of the Office International des Epizooties*, vol 25, no 2, pp. 505–516

Steinfeld, H. and Gerber, P. (2010) 'Livestock production and the global environment: Consume less or produce better?', *Proceedings of the National Academy of Sciences*, vol 107, no 43, pp. 18237–18238

Sumberg, J. and Thompson, J. (2013) 'Revolution reconsidered: Evolving perspectives on livestock production and consumption', STEPS Centre, Institute of Development Studies, University of Sussex, Brighton

Thornton, P. K. (2010) 'Livestock production: recent trends, future prospects', *Philosophical Transactions of the Royal Society of London. Series B: Biological Sciences*, vol 365, no 1554, pp. 2853–2867

United Nations (2013) World Population Prospects The 2012 Revision, New York: Population Division, Department of Economic and Social Affairs, http://esa.un.org/wpp/index.htm, accessed 30 March 2015

Wackernagel, M. and Rees, W. (1998) *Our Ecological Footprint: Reducing Human Impact on the Earth*, New Society Publishers, Gabriola Island, BC

Waller, W. (2008) 'John Kenneth Galbraith: Cultural Theorist of Consumption and Power', *Journal of Economic Issues*, vol 42, no 1, pp. 13–24

Wang, Q., Fuller, D., Hayes, D. and Halbrendt, C. (1998) 'Chinese consumer demand for animal products and implications for U.S. pork and poultry exports', *Journal of Agricultural and Applied Economics*, vol 30, no 1, pp. 127–140

Webber, M. J. (2012) *Making Capitalism in Rural China*, Edward Elgar Publishing, Cheltenham, UK

Weis, T. (2013) *The Ecological Hoofprint: The Global Burden of Industrial Livestock*, Zed Books, London

Yapa, S. L. (1979) 'Ecopolitical economy of the green revolution', *The Professional Geographer*, vol 31, no 4, pp. 371–376

3

CATTLE RANCHING DEVELOPMENT IN THE BRAZILIAN AMAZON

Looking at long-term trends to explore the transition towards sustainable beef cattle production

Pablo Pacheco and René Poccard-Chapuis

Introduction

This chapter looks at the main trends of cattle ranching development in the Brazilian Amazon, which is the main activity supporting landholders' production strategies. Cattle ranching has significant implications not only for economic development but also land-use change since it has led to important forest conversion to agriculture, with associated impacts on biodiversity and climate change.[1] This analysis is placed in the context of current interests from multiple stakeholders in Brazil and in the international arena – including national and subnational governments, producer associations, and international and national development and environmental organizations – to transition towards more sustainable beef cattle production to respond to broader concerns on sustainable development and climate change. The arguments provided here are linked to a process of collaborative research undertaken by the Center for International Forestry Research (CIFOR) and the French agricultural research organization (CIRAD) to understand the main drivers, processes and implications of ranching development in the Amazon for people's livelihoods, regional development and landscape change. This research is undertaken in the context of the CGIAR Research Program on Forests, Trees and Agroforestry (CRP-FTA).[2]

Frontier development in the Brazilian Amazon is inextricably linked to the evolution of cattle ranching, which has contributed in a significant way to shape rural society and landscape change. Cattle ranching has provided important economic benefits to a large number of medium- and large-scale landholders as well as livelihoods for a numerous group of smallholders. Nonetheless, it has also led to the removal of forest for pasture expansion with critical implications for biodiversity conservation, and associated impacts on local and global environmental change (Margulis, 2004). The role of cattle ranching in regional development has become increasingly complex through time due to the fact that disparate social groups depend on cattle ranching as a main income stream, there is increasing competition from other land uses for food and feed production, and low-emissions agriculture is emerging as a priority goal for the mitigation of climate change agenda (Nepstad et al., 2013). As a result, state and civil society actors, including a growing involvement of the beef industry and retailers, are looking for options to reduce the environmental footprint of cattle ranching, and supporting the transition to low-emission cattle ranching development (Cohn et al., 2014).

Understanding the factors and conditions shaping cattle ranching development is crucial for critically assessing the policy responses emerging to manage the trade-offs between development and forest conservation, and aimed at advancing towards a low-emission cattle ranching. Public policies and markets have played a fundamental role in shaping cattle ranching in the Brazilian Amazon with important shifts in priorities over time, which to a large extent have shaped the long-term trends of cattle ranching development in the region. Five interacting trends can be observed, as suggested by Pacheco and Poccard-Chapuis (2012), which are:

1   the establishment of the beef and dairy industry closer to production zones, contributing to the expansion of market value chains;
2   gradual improvements in pasture and herd management systems that have led to gains in productivity, although extensive ranching tends to persist;
3   shifts in tenure with large-scale landholdings decreasing in size, probably to achieve more efficient production scales, while simultaneously land concentration taking place in areas dominated by smallholders; and
4   cattle raising, for either beef or milk production, expanding its importance in small-scale farming systems that are strongly articulated to local value chains organized by the beef industry.

These trends are currently reshaped by a more stringent institutional environment driven by greater enforcement and beef industry commitments that have led to reduced deforestation.

Some of the trends mentioned above have already been explored in the literature, but they have been analyzed in isolation from each other. This chapter offers a comprehensive review of the magnitude of these trends by adopting a wide regional approach. Our main objective with this analysis is to improve the understanding of the evolving dynamics of cattle ranching expansion in the Brazilian Amazon as influenced by changes in environmental law and emerging public-private arrangements, and by market constraints associated with growing climate-change concerns. In this context, we revisit current strategies put in place by state agencies, NGO coalitions and the beef industry to support more sustainable beef production in the context of government commitments to reduce deforestation. The main current policy goals are reducing the pressures of cattle ranching on deforestation, transitioning towards more intensive beef cattle production, and building the necessary institutional mechanisms to ensure 'clean' beef supply chains.

This chapter is organized in five parts, including this introduction. The second part reviews the main factors explaining the expansion of cattle ranching in the Brazilian Amazon, according to different perspectives. The third part describes the four main long-term trends that can be observed when looking at ranching development in this region. The fourth part describes contemporary policy, and institutional and economic development taking place in the Amazon aimed at reducing the expansion of ranching over forestlands, and assesses implications not only for land-use change but also for economic benefit sharing. The fifth part discusses the implications of the recent trends on development and conservation, and highlights emerging policy and institutional challenges to address climate-change mitigation while simultaneously making possible the transition towards low-emission ranching development with equity.

Main factors shaping cattle ranching expansion in the Amazon

Significant efforts have been spent, using approaches from different disciplinary perspectives, to explain the drivers of cattle sector expansion and their impacts on regional development and forest conservation. These include political economy perspectives (Hecht, 1982, 1985), neoclassical economic views focused on cost–benefit analysis (Mattos and Uhl, 1994; Arima and Uhl, 1997), agronomic perspectives looking at livestock and pasture management practices (Serrão and Toledo, 1992), spatial analyses focused on the influence that biophysical factors and infrastructure have on pasture expansion and land-use change (Chomitz and Thomas, 2001; Mertens et al., 2002; Alves, 2003), and value chain analyses of beef and dairy markets (Poccard-Chapuis et al., 2003; Poccard-Chapuis, 2004). Each of these different perspectives, however, offers only a partial explanation for cattle expansion processes in the Brazilian Amazon.

Previous research, undertaken mainly from 1970 to 1990, claimed that the main factors encouraging livestock expansion and deforestation in the Amazon were associated with policy incentives and institutional rents linked to land speculation (Hecht, 1993; Schneider, 1993; Alston et al., 1999). Since the early 2000s, however, it has been more commonly argued that market-driven forces constitute the most important trigger for ranching development (Margulis, 2004; Pacheco, 2005; Nepstad et al., 2006). In this view, market forces associated with growing urban demand for beef in the domestic market, along with more developed value chains linked to growing investment of the beef industry closer to production zones, have had marked effects on the growth of cattle herds and pasture expansion, with a cattle sector gradually increasing its articulation to global beef markets (Kaimowitz et al., 2004).

In addition, despite a growing body of literature acknowledging the interactions between local and regional cattle ranching dynamics on the one hand and global market changes on the other (Kaimowitz et al., 2004; Nepstad et al., 2006; Walker et al., 2009), there has been little effort to disentangle their differentiated effects on cattle production, especially those effects associated with changes in production systems, land tenure, and actor types across landscapes. Only a few researchers have adopted integrated perspectives to elucidate the multiple interactions shaping economic and landscape change (Faminow, 1998; Margulis, 2004).

Cattle ranching expansion takes place in medium- and large-scale landholdings, mainly through specialized livestock production systems, as well as integration to more diversified production systems in small-scale landholding. In tropical regions, cattle production constitutes an attractive option. This is because of: the availability of relatively cheap land that facilitates extensive beef production coupled with low labor and supervision requirements; the easier transportability and limited risk compared with agricultural activities; the minimal use of purchased inputs; the biological and economic flexibility; low costs of production and banking services; and indirect financial benefits, such as wealth maintenance and secure cash flow (Hecht, 1993; Kaimowitz, 1995; Sunderlin and Rodríguez, 1996; Walker et al., 2000; Pacheco, 2009a). In addition, cattle ranching can assist producers in slowing spontaneous forest regeneration after slash-and-burn agriculture, which leaves smallholders with large areas of cleared land that is suitable only for cattle (Vosti et al., 2000). Pacheco (2012) suggests that in spite of the broad growing trend of pasture expansion for adoption of cattle ranching as the main land use in the Brazilian Amazon, some differences persist across actor types since, in comparative terms, smallholders tend to maintain higher cattle stocking rates than medium- and large-scale landholders, which tend to adopt extensive systems of cattle production, but it varies across frontier types.

Large-scale landholders view cattle as a financial investment, and thus base their decisions on financial returns, profit margins, land-value increases, eventual subsidies, and tax benefits, among other factors (Hecht, 1993; Kaimowitz, 1995; Faminow, 1998). Ranching offers further advantages because the productivity of labor is generally higher than that in crop cultivation, the risk of product loss is low, transport and commercialization are simple, and the sale price of animals usually tracks inflation (Hecht, 1993; Arima and Uhl, 1997). In contexts in which returns from cattle are lower than cash crop production, ranchers may still prefer to invest in cattle ranching because of risk considerations, or merely because they typically have few alternative investment options (Kaimowitz and Angelsen, 1998). In addition, ranchers expand pasture, often encroaching onto public lands, because demonstrating the land being used serves as a cheap and effective way of justifying land ownership, thus helping landholders to defend their land possession (Alston et al., 1999; Lele et al., 2000; Fearnside, 2001).

Smallholder decisions to invest in cattle consider returns from beef and dairy production as well as integration of livestock into a diversified system of production, which allows producers to obtain more secure returns (Tourrand et al., 1995). Smallholders produce a diversified portfolio of agricultural products depending on price variations (Faminow et al., 1999). Those who are risk averse often prefer to develop dual-purpose livestock systems (milk and meat). Some producers, however, choose to specialize in milk production because the payoff from the investment in cattle is steadier and occurs much sooner, and the returns can be higher (Faminow, 1998). Usually farmers focus on milk when they have accessible, guaranteed milk markets. Income from the sale of calves has the advantage of being relatively concentrated in one period of the year, allowing investments in property, whereas milk income is better suited for covering daily domestic expenses (da Veiga et al., 2001). Smallholders who can accumulate capital prefer to invest it in livestock because it is less risky, easier to market, and requires less labor than annual crops (Kaimowitz, 1995). Cattle production also serves an important function in wealth accumulation, because it helps owners endure economic shocks (Pacheco, 2009a).

Different production systems may coexist in frontier areas.[3] While some ranchers adapt their systems of production according to changing conditions, others are not in a position to adopt new technologies, particularly smallholder farmers and cattle ranchers with little access to investment capital. In most cases, adoption of improved technologies, which could include more fences, recovery of degraded pastures, and the purchase of more productive animals, leads to the development of semi-intensive systems of range fattening or specialized systems of calf production (Arima and Uhl, 1997; Faminow, 1998). Smallholders who adopt these livestock production technologies tend to transition from low-productivity range fattening to more profitable semi-intensive systems of dairy production (da Veiga et al., 2001). The different ways in which these processes have played out in the Brazilian Amazon are described in next section.

A look at four long-term trends in cattle ranching development

Four of the long-term trends that have shaped cattle ranching development in the Brazilian Amazon are described in this section. This analysis considers information generated by the Municipal Livestock Survey produced by the Brazilian Institute of Geography and Statistics (IBGE), as well as data generated by IBGE through the agricultural census in 1995/96 and 2006, for the region known as Brazilian Legal Amazon (BLA).[4] Data from the National Institute for Spatial Research (INPE) is used to assess impacts of ranching on deforestation.

Investments and development in the cattle industry

Brazil holds one of the largest cattle herds in the world. According to IBGE (2014), the total cattle herd was about 198 million head in 2012, of which 79 million head were located in the Amazonian states (Table 3.1, Figure 3.1). Cattle herds have primarily been located in southern Brazil, an area that has experienced significant intensification of livestock production through improved herd and pasture management with growing feedlot systems. For more than a decade, however, the cattle population in the south has stagnated, mainly because of the lack of available land. Pressures from cattle industry growth have therefore been displaced to west-central and northern Brazil. As a result, the annual rate of growth of the cattle population in Brazil as a whole was 1.88 percent in the period 2000–2012, while for the Brazilian Amazon was equivalent to 4.35 percent, and for the south and southern states it was about 0.5 percent.

The dramatic growth in Brazil's cattle population has been accompanied by the expansion of the downstream cattle industry during the past two decades. The federal government has certified 300 slaughterhouses across the country, and states and municipalities have certified 1,500 small-scale abattoirs (Franco, 2004). Most of Brazil's cattle industry is now located in the southeast and west-central regions of the country (IEL/CNA/SEBRAE, 2000). Thirty-one of the 95 slaughterhouses in the Brazilian Amazon were established in the 1990s, with a further 45 slaughter-houses set up in the 2000s, and six more in the last four years (Table 3.2). Hence, the Amazon's meat-processing capacity has expanded enormously since the 1990s, matching the increase in cattle population.

A two-way interaction exists between the increase in processing capacity and cattle sector expansion. On the one hand, slaughterhouses were set up in areas with a relatively sizeable local supply of beef cattle, and on the other hand, landholders are attracted to areas with processing capacities already in place, since that indicates a more secure local demand for live cattle, which also reduces costs linked to trans-portation. With changes in beef supply from live cattle to packed meat enabling industrial producers to reach more distant markets, some of the largest Brazilian beef industries played a significant role in the expansion of the Amazon's meat-processing capacity. Nine groups in the beef sector in Brazil, taken together, own about 40 percent of the slaughterhouses established in the region (Smeraldi and May, 2009).[5]

TABLE 3.1 Profile of the livestock sector in Brazil for six years between 1970 and 2012.

	1970	1980	1990	2000	2010	2012
Population of Brazil (thousands)[a]	95,991	121,618	149,527	174,167	195,153	198,700
Cattle in Brazil (thousand head)[b]	75,447	118,971	147,102	169,876	209,541	211,279
Cattle in the Brazilian Legal Amazon (BLA) (thousand head)[b]	n/a	14,568	25,921	47,224	77,434	79,619
Beef production (thousand tons)[c]	1,845	2,850	4,115	6,580	9,115	9,307
Beef exports (thousand tons)[d]	116	80	123	316	951	945
Milk production (thousand tons)[e]	7,353	11,956	14,933	20,380	30,715	32,304
Milk exports (thousand tons)[e]	–	1	0	19	113	81

Notes: (a) CEPALSTAT, www.eclac.org/estadisticas/. (b) Data are from IBGE municipal livestock surveys from 1961 to 2012. (c) Based on FAOSTAT (http://apps.fao.org). (d) Based on COMTRADE (www.trademap.org/), includes cattle meat, meat dried, meat extracts, meat of beef, meat cattle bone-less and preparations of beef meat. (e) Based on COMTRADE (www.trademap.org/), comprises butter, butter oil, fresh milk, and skim milk, all from cows.

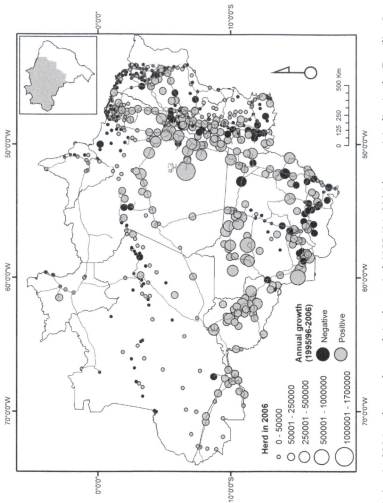

FIGURE 3.1 Cattle population in 2006 and annual growth in the period 1995/96–2006 by municipality in the Brazilian Legal Amazon.

Authors' elaboration based on data from the Agricultural Censuses 1995/96 and 2006, National Institute of Geography and Statistics (IBGE). Modified based on Pacheco and Poccard–Chapuis (2012).

TABLE 3.2 Number of slaughterhouses and dairy processing plants in the Brazilian Amazon states by industrial capacity and year established.

Industrial capacity	Year established				Total
	Until 1990	1991–2000	2001–2010	2011–2014	
Slaughterhouses (capacity in cattle/hour)					
<20	2	3	11	1	17
20–40	3	11	16	1	31
40–80	4	11	13	4	32
>80	4	6	5	0	15
Total	13	31	45	6	95
Dairy plants (capacity thousand of liters)					
<5	1	24	11	4	40
5–10	1	6	23	6	36
10–50	2	10	12	4	28
>50	0	2	0	0	2
Total	4	42	46	14	106

Source: Elaborated by authors based on data by 2014 from the Federal Inspection Service (SIF), Ministry of Agriculture, www.agricultura.gov.br/portal/page/portal/Internet-MAPA/pagina-inicial/servicos-e-sistemas/sistemas/sif

Poccard-Chapuis (2004) identifies three types of meat commercialization circuits: meat supply to local markets; meat supply to meet demand from proximate urban centers; and circuits that supply beef to more distant markets, often located in other states of Brazil. A large proportion of the meat produced in the Brazilian Amazon reaches markets in the main cities in the northeast states, and much of the Mato Grosso production is sold in Brazil's southern cities (Arima et al., 2005). A small proportion of meat is exported directly from the slaughterhouses in the Amazon, yet this proportion has tended to grow over time, and there are some exports of live cattle. Industrial producers benefit from lower transportation costs to the Atlantic seaports. Exports of live cattle, originating in Pará, to Venezuela, Egypt, and Lebanon began in 2005, although this relatively recent trend accounts for only a small fraction of total beef exports and it is not clear whether it will continue to future (IDESP, 2010).[6]

The situation for investments in milk production is slightly different. Brazil has 828 dairy-processing plants, most of which are small and heavily concentrated in urban centers in the country's southeast. Since the Plano Real, a process of concentration has been under way in the dairy sector (Jank et al., 1999). In this context, the Amazon region emerged as a reserve for potential milk producers seeking to grow their operations, some of which were companies with headquarters in southern Brazil aiming to expand their operations across the country (da Veiga et al., 2001). From 1990 to 2014, more than 100 new plants were installed in the Amazon region, mostly of low processing capacity and mainly in the states of Mato Grosso, Pará, and Rondônia, following the expansion of their main urban centers (Table 3.2). The expansion of a network of dairy-processing plants close to production areas in Rondônia and southern Pará, similar to the trends noted for the beef industry, has allowed industrial milk producers to reach distant markets, particularly in the northeast (Poccard-Chapuis et al., 2003). Much of these investments originate in the dairy industry from northeastern and southern Brazil that was interested to expand their sources of supply in areas with lower production costs.

Improvements in cattle herds and management systems

The growth in cattle herds in the Brazilian Amazon has been explosive, particularly since the mid-1970s: the cattle population in the northern states was about three times larger in the late 1980s than in the mid-1970s, and it had doubled again by the early 2000s. In absolute numbers, the cattle population in the Amazon reached 35 million head in 1995/1996, and nearly 56 million head in 2006 (Table 3.3). The proportion of cattle in the Amazon relative to the cattle herds in Brazil grew from 23 percent in 1995/1996 to 33 percent in 2006. Growth was particularly significant in southern Pará, around the Trans-Amazon highway in Pará, in northwest Mato Grosso, and in Rondônia (Figure 3.1). Overall, the cattle population on the margins of the Amazon region has decreased; this could be associated with agricultural expansion that tends to make use of degraded pastures, the analysis of which is beyond the scope of this chapter.

According to IBGE data, cattle raising has augmented in the Brazilian Amazon, particularly in older frontier areas better connected to infrastructure, but through increasing stocking rates, this is a higher number of animals per unit of land. Although the increase in the cattle herd is partly due to the expansion of cultivated pastures at the expense of forestland, a larger part is the result of higher stocking rates. The stocking ratio (the number of head per hectare of pasture) in the region grew from 0.7 in 1995/1996 to 1.0 in 2006 (Table 3.3, Figure 3.2), a trend observed across Brazil as a whole. Nevertheless, the extent of pasture grew from 50.4 million to 53.4 million ha during the same period. Without the increase in stocking ratios, an additional 20 million ha of pasture would have been needed to raise the same number of cattle.

Most indicators of herd management have improved over time, which are reflected in increased calving rates, reduced mortality rates, reduction of the age of first conception or improvement in the precocity of cows' first conception, younger weaning age, and reduced slaughter age of calves with a higher weight. Pasture productivity has also improved over time. Furthermore, pasture life and productivity continue for longer than in the past due to more careful pasture management. Yet, in recent years, a fungus that affects *Brachiaria* pasture grasses

TABLE 3.3 Comparison of growth in cattle production and pasture by landholding size in the Brazilian Legal Amazon, between 1995/1996 and 2006.

Landholding size (ha)	Number of landholdings (thousands)	Average size (ha)	Pasture (thousand ha)	Head of cattle (thousands)	Stocking ratio (head/ha)
In 1995/96					
Less than 50	534	11.4	1,645	2,866	1.7
50 to 100	109	65.6	2,502	2,946	1.2
100 to 500	112	182.4	9,288	8,509	0.9
500 to 1,000	15	674.4	5,239	3,811	0.7
More than 1,000	18	4,190.3	31,796	16,986	0.5
Total	*788*	*150.1*	*50,469*	*35,117*	*0.7*
In 2006					
Less than 50	451	14.8	3,472	6,325	1.8
50 to 100	121	65.6	4,082	5,796	1.4
100 to 500	109	189.0	11,322	14,060	1.2
500 to 1,000	15	659.9	5,550	5,984	1.1
More than 1,000	18	3,372.5	29,016	23,277	0.8
Landless	77	–	–	108	–
Total	*792*	*134.7*	*53,443*	*55,550*	*1.0*
Growth in % (1995/96–2006)	0.1	(1.1)	0.6	4.6	4.0

Notes: The estimate corresponding to IBGE Agricultural Census in 2006 is lower than the one provided by IBGE Municipal Livestock Survey (Portuguese abbreviation: PPM). The PPM estimates indicate that the total cattle herd in Brazil in 2006 was 205.8 million head – 35.9 million head more than the figure in the 2006 agricultural census. The PPM estimates indicate that the cattle herd in the Amazon was equivalent to 73.3 million head – 17.7 million more than the figure provided by the 2006 agricultural census. The current work considers the agricultural census to be a more reliable source than the PPM. Taken from Pacheco and Poccard-Chapuis (2012), based on agricultural censuses of 1995/96 and 2006, National Institute of Geography and Statistics (IBGE).

has spread, and many landholders had to resow their pasture areas (Pacheco and Poccard-Chapuis, 2012). Improved management has contributed to increase the profitability of ranching. Margulis (2004), drawing on data taken from Camargo et al. (2002), estimates a relatively high internal rate of return (IRR) of 9–14 percent, disregarding land prices. Pacheco (2005), drawing on estimates from a diverse range of cattle ranching systems in Uruará and Redenção (i.e. self-reproducing herds, calf production, and range fattening), estimates the IRR in a range of 2.5–9.7 percent, without considering increments in land prices, suggesting a wide range

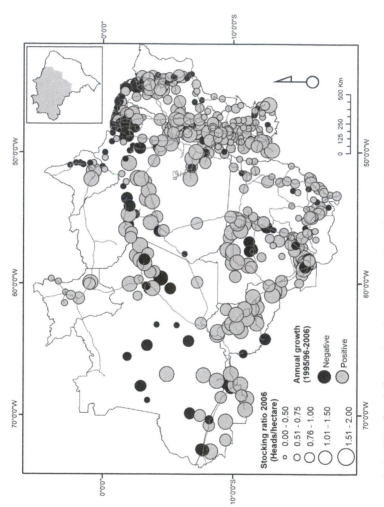

FIGURE 3.2 Cattle stocking ratio in 2006 (head /hectare) and annual growth in the period 1995/96–2006 by municipality in the Brazilian Legal Amazon.

Authors' elaboration based on data from the agricultural censuses of 1995/96 and 2006, National Institute of Geography and Statistics (IBGE). Modified based on Pacheco and Poccard-Chapuis (2012).

of situations in which modernized cattle ranching is much more profitable than traditional ranching systems. Issues of scale also matter. Barreto and Silva (2009), based on information corresponding to the period from 2002–2008, suggest that large-scale ranching operations (with about 5,000 head) tend to obtain greater benefits compared with operations with no more than 500 head.

Two simultaneous processes of land tenure change

Land distribution in the Brazilian Amazon is skewed: most landholders own a small portion of the land, and most land is owned by a few large-scale landholders. According to the 1995/1996 IBGE agricultural census, 81.2 percent of the total number of agricultural establishments were smallholdings of less than 100 ha. These smallholders accounted for only 11.2 percent of total land in landholdings. By contrast, 2.3 percent of the total number of establishments larger than 1,000 ha accounted for 63.2 percent of all land. In the past decade, however, this situation has changed slightly. According to 2006 IBGE agricultural census, large-scale landholders controlled 57.5 percent of all land. While the average size of small-scale landholdings has not changed significantly, the average size of medium-scale landholdings is increasing slowly, and that of large-scale landholdings has shrunk (Table 3.3). The latter results from two land tenure changes taking place in the region. The first is related to fragmentation of large-scale landholdings in areas with previously notable land concentration for extensive cattle ranching. The second is land concentration that is linked to persistent encroachment of public lands in remote areas, though it is evident in already consolidated frontiers with a greater presence of smallholders (Figure 3.3).

The processes of tenure change have been documented at the local scale in some locations in the Amazon region (Browder et al., 2004; Pacheco, 2005; Aldrich et al., 2006). Fragmentation of large-scale landholdings is evident to the extent that these landholdings are becoming smaller over time, which is associated with the abovementioned trend toward intensification. The latter is also partly due to increasing land values, which tend to be higher in the more consolidated frontiers closer to roads, particularly in eastern and west-central Mato Grosso and southern Pará. Land fragmentation mostly takes place through transactions in the land market, which is relatively vigorous. As suggested by Pacheco (2009b) in assessing the development of cattle ranching in southern Pará, the fragmentation of landholdings is largely associated with more developed markets for beef production, which tend to stimulate improvements in pasture productivity as a way of increasing profits from beef production. This leads to increased land values, thus fostering the fragmentation of large-scale landholdings.

Many farmers operating at a large and extensive scale do not have enough capital to make improvements in pasture maintenance because of agronomic pasture degradation processes, and are thus prevented from competing in a market that demands higher quality and productivity. Many large-scale landholders built and maintained extensive properties as a form of financial saving activity and to build

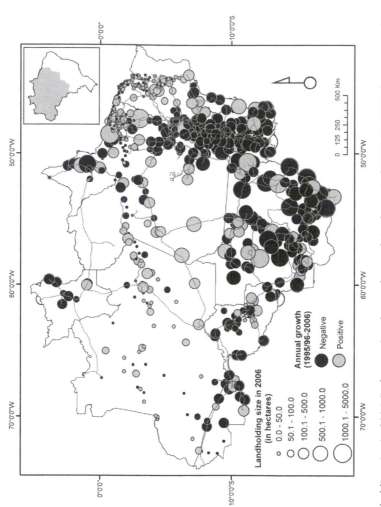

FIGURE 3.3 Average landholding size in 2006 (in hectares) and annual growth in the period 1995/96–2006 by municipality in the Brazilian Legal Amazon.

Authors' elaboration based on data from the agricultural censuses of 1995/96 and 2006, National Institute of Geography and Statistics (IBGE). Modified based on Pacheco and Poccard-Chapuis (2012).

a heritage, rather than as a means of creating an economically efficient business (Hecht, 1993). Nowadays, in a context of increasing land values, selling part of the land tends to be a solution for reforming the pasture and improving productivity. Intergenerational transmission can promote land fragmentation between heirs and could provide rents to finance nonagricultural projects. Additional research is required for more in-depth understanding of this dynamic. In some cases, fragmentation of large-scale landholdings is due to the encroachment of these landholdings by landless people as a way to put pressure the Federal Land Reform Agency (INCRA) for the creation of agrarian reform settlements. This process has been analyzed in some detail elsewhere (see Pacheco, 2009c; Simmons et al., 2010).

With regard to land concentration, some large-scale landholders are concentrating land in more remote areas, particularly in northeast and central portions in the state of Mato Grosso, along the BR-163 highway in Pará, and in the eastern part of the state of Amazonas. This is likely the result of persistent land speculation aimed at reaping profits from expected increases in land prices (Carrero and Fearnside, 2011). Assessing the rationales behind land speculation is beyond the scope of this article; for an analysis, see Alston et al. (1999). A different process of land concentration takes place when better-off farmers purchase additional tracts of land to expand cattle production in locales where small-scale agriculture has been consolidated and ranching is widely adopted as a source of income (Pacheco, 2005; Aldrich et al., 2006). The latter process is evident along the Trans-Amazon highway and in the eastern part of the state of Maranhão.

Increased adoption of cattle production in small-scale farming systems

Smallholders in the Amazon are increasingly adopting cattle ranching, a trend related to smallholders' occupation of frontier land. Hence, smallholders are allocating more of their plots to pasture, thus stimulating land concentration, as discussed above. Increasing cattle production in areas dominated by smallholders has been documented in the Trans-Amazon (Tourrand et al., 1995; da Veiga et al., 1996; Castellanet et al., 1998), Acre (Vosti et al., 2003), and Rondônia (Browder et al., 2004). Data from the two most recent IBGE agricultural censuses (1995/1996 and 2006) reveal that cattle herds expanded significantly in small-scale landholdings during that 10-year period. The cattle population increased by about 20 million head during that decade, with a third of that increase (6.5 million head) taking place in landholdings smaller than 100 hectares (Table 3.3). In 1995/1996, smallholders owned about 16.5 percent of the total cattle herd. This proportion had increased to 21.8 percent by 2006. Smallholders were encouraged to take up ranching by the availability of financial subsidies, as mentioned above (Arima, 2000; Arima et al., 2005). In addition, smallholders tend to benefit from expanding markets and networks largely developed by traders, large-scale ranchers, and industry (Poccard-Chapuis et al., 2005).

Furthermore, smallholdings are often characterized by higher stocking ratios. There is an inverse relationship between the density of cattle head per hectare and landholding size: stocking ratios on small-scale landholdings are almost double those on large-scale landholdings. This evidence is consistent with the precept about farming systems that land scarcity induces more intensive production practices. As smallholders grow to depend on cattle production, raising cattle is becoming an important livelihood strategy for people living on the Amazonian forest frontiers. This trend has important implications for policies aiming to reduce deforestation.

Policies and arrangements to support sustainable beef production

Cattle ranching development, with the consequent pasture expansion, has been the main proximate cause of deforestation in the Brazilian Amazon (Hecht, 1982; Faminow, 1998; Kaimowitz et al., 2004; Margulis, 2004). However, where and when the deforestation occurs has shifted over time, and uncertainties remain with regard to its eventual stabilization. Margulis (2004), drawing on data from the IBGE 1995/1996 agricultural census, indicates that 70 percent of total forest conversion by that time was devoted to planted pasture. Pacheco and Poccard-Chapuis (2012), based on the IBGE 2006 agricultural census, confirm that, by 2006, pasture accounted for 75 percent of total accumulated deforestation. It is noteworthy that these estimates include only the area comprised by landholdings accounted for in the censuses. The remaining forest conversion is associated with subsistence agriculture and soybean cultivation.

The Brazilian Agricultural Research Agency (EMBRAPA) and the National Institute for Space Research (INPE), through a project labeled Terra Class, have estimated the land uses that emerged as result of forest clearing, and currently two assessments are available for 2008 and 2010 (Terra Class, 2013). As of 2010, the assessment, which covers 73.9 million hectares, suggests that a relatively low portion (3.9 million hectares, 5.4 percent) out of the total area was converted to annual crops, and that 62.1 percent (45.9 million hectares) was under pasture. When considering only the total pasture lands, 74 percent are clean pastures, which correspond to areas with grass species predominance in adequate condition (33.9 million hectares), 12.3 percent (5.6 million hectares) are degraded pastures, and 13.7 percent (6.3 million hectares) are regenerated pasture. It is noteworthy that the areas under secondary forest regrowth are relatively important, accounting for about 22.2 percent of the total deforested area (16.5 million hectares) by 2010.

It is noteworthy that deforestation in the Brazilian Legal Amazon (BLA) driven by frontier expansion, increased continuously until 2004, when it peaked at 2.7 million hectares in the year. Since then, deforestation has tended to decrease until 2012 when it reached 457,100 hectares. However, a slight increase of 28 percent in the rate of deforestation was reported in 2013 with regard to 2012. In the last five years, deforestation annual rates have stabilized in a range between 500–700 thousand hectares (INPE, 2014). Extensive research has been conducted to explain deforestation trends. Deforestation is assumed to be linked to fluctuations in commodity markets, especially for beef and soybeans (see Kaimowitz et al.,

2004; Nepstad et al., 2006). The expansion of deforestation in the mid-2000s has likely responded to increases in prices and demand from global markets in a context of weak enforcement of environmental regulations (Alencar et al., 2004). Deforestation decline in the last period was also affected by the global economic downturn in 2008. In addition, this decline was also influenced by conservation policies aimed at expanding forest areas under protection as well as strengthening – at the federal and state level – government enforcement of environmental regulations through improved monitoring and sanctioning systems (Astill, 2010; Barreto and Silva, 2010; Godar et al. 2014). The latter policies were part of a wider effort to mainstream climate change goals in the government agenda and mainly related to supporting mitigation actions (La Rovere et al., 2014).

In this regard, some policies adopted by the Brazilian government have been determinant for the slowdown of deforestation in the Brazilian Amazon, and have placed important constraints on cattle ranching expansion due to the closure of the agricultural frontier. A cornerstone in the policies to reduce deforestation was the Action Plan for Preventing and Controlling Deforestation in the Legal Amazon (PPCDAM) approved in 2004. This was a very comprehensive plan comprising three main components at the federal level (i.e. land tenure and planning, environmental monitoring and control, and fostering sustainable production). A major action undertaken under this plan was the establishment of a mosaic of conservation units as a way to halt the expansion of cattle ranching on the frontier. This was complemented with the implementation of a system to monitoring deforestation in real time by INPE, labeled DETER aimed at alerting forest clearing in the most active areas of frontier expansion. The combination of all these measures led to a notable reduction in deforestation since 2005 (Hecht, 2012).

In 2008, the operation Arco de Fogo was initiated, a major effort to combat deforestation using more repressive mechanisms against landholders clearing forests for pasture expansion beyond the limits allowed by the Forest Code (FC). Approved in 1965, the FC was transformed during the 1990s into a de facto environmental law via a series of presidential decrees. As of 2001, the FC required landholders in the Amazon to convert 20 percent of their landholdings to agricultural uses, and set aside 80 percent as Legal Reserve (LR).[7] The proportion of legal reserve in other biomes was set at 20 percent (Soares-Filho et al., 2014). Land use regulations included in the FC were difficult to enforce in practice, and most deforestation occurred in areas beyond the allowed limit of 20 percent, thus affecting forests within the LRs. In addition, legislation passed at the state level, such as in the state of Pará, indicated that the LR could be reduced to 50 percent but only on those lands that were classified in the state's Land Use Zoning Plan as lands for agricultural consolidation and expansion.[8] In this context, the development of economic and ecological zoning constitute another key instrument for guiding the state actions for the development of infrastructure, tenure and other associated policies.

Additional measures to combat deforestation were issued in 2009 with the approval of Presidential Decree No. 7029 that established a program for the environmental regularization of rural landholdings (Programa Mais Ambiente) in order to encourage landholders to comply with environmental laws by maintaining or restoring Areas of Permanent Preservation (APP) and the LRs. As part of the program, the government environmental agency developed the 'Terms of Accession and Commitment' (TAC). Landholders that subscribed to a TAC had to register in the Rural Environmental Cadastre (CAR) and, from the date of subscription, were immune from sanctions applying to damaging forests or natural vegetation but had to commit to the restoration of APPs and LRs affected. In 2012, the Brazilian House of Representatives approved a new version of the FC. The main relevant points of the reform are that it condones areas deforested illegally before July 2008 by forgiving the LR debt of 'small' properties, ranging in size from 20 hectares in southern Brazil to 440 hectares in the Amazon. Under these new rules, 90 percent of Brazilian rural properties qualify for amnesty (Soares-Filho et al., 2014). Yet, what is important is that the FC ratified the need to restore and maintain APPs and LRs for other properties and sanctions for the areas deforested after July 2008. This is still a controversial issue.

Besides changes in the regulatory framework, two major events that imposed constraints in the cattle ranching sector to reduce pressures on forests have been, on the one side, market constraints originating in the supermarkets in southern Brazil and, on the other side, the involvement of the Federal Public Ministry. In regards to the first event, three largest supermarket chains operating in southern Brazil's main cities (i.e. Wal-Mart, Carrefour and Pão de Açúcar) agreed in 2009 to suspend contracts with suppliers found to be involved in Amazon deforestation, as a result of environmental campaigns to prevent beef markets from driving illegal deforestation in the Amazon. This decision was linked with the policies that allow only cattle ranchers who prove to be complying with environmental laws to sell their product to the beef industry. With regards to the second event, the Public Prosecutor's Office committed to support 'legal beef'. In 2010, it supported a program with the beef industry to certify 'legal beef' bought from landholders with a signed TAC in 2010. By 2013, about 100 processors had signed a TAC, through which they committed to not purchase beef originating from areas illegally cleared.[9]

Associated with livestock-related regulations are the programs for the eradication of foot and mouth disease (FMD), which date from 1965 in southern Brazil. International cooperation supported other such programs in the 1980s, but it was not until 1992 that the government implemented a program aimed at eradicating this disease from the entire country. In 1995, this state-run program was consolidated in partnership with the private sector and in the mid-1990s, these national programs began to be implemented in the Amazon region. Such programs involve delimitation of livestock circuits, which impedes herd transportation from FMD-infected zones to disease-free zones, and forbids the exchange of animals (except for deboned meat which is permitted to cross the zone boundaries). In 2001, all the southern states including Mato Grosso and Tocantins were declared FMD-free zones. Rondônia was included as an FMD-free zone in 2003, Acre in 2005, and the south-central region of the state of Pará in 2007 (PNEFA, 2009).

In addition, the federal government has introduced measures to improve the efficiency of monitoring systems of slaughterhouses and meatpacking plants. In 1989, some monitoring functions were transferred to state and municipal governments, with the federal government retaining oversight of large slaughterhouses. The standards in the municipal systems of control are lower than in the state and federal systems. In 1996, a ministerial decree established standards for beef cattle commercialization in terms of temperature, packing, and labeling, forcing the expansion of the refrigerated beef supply. Furthermore, in 1998, another decree standardized sanitary regulations for the livestock sector across the entire country, thus requiring all slaughterhouses and meatpacking plants, independent of their processing capacity, to comply with the same sanitary rules. These regulations have largely favored large-scale beef companies to the detriment of local slaughterhouses (Poccard-Chapuis et al., 2001; Poccard-Chapuis, 2004).

Growing constraints on cattle ranchers to reduce pressures on forests and increasing concerns for improving quality and productivity have led NGOs, research and extension state agencies, and the agribusiness sector, to develop initiatives aimed at supporting the adoption of good practices for sustainable beef cattle production, as part of the approach towards ranching intensification. For example, The Nature Conservancy (TNC) and the Amazon Institute of People and the Environment (IMAZON) have supported farmers in the elaboration of their CARs as part of a broader initiative to put in place the Green Municipality scheme in municipalities in eastern Pará. Some of the major beef industry groups (e.g. JBS) have also supported the state initiatives towards sustainable beef production by signing terms of accession and commitment with the Public Prosecutor's Office, and helping their major supplier in the elaboration of CARs, motivating them to improve their production practices.[10] The state agricultural research agency (EMBRAPA) is also investing resources in order to produce recommendations on more sustainable beef cattle production systems able to achieve higher productivities and lower greenhouse gasses emissions in comparison to conventional ranching systems.[11] In addition, the Brazilian Roundtable on Sustainable Livestock (BRSL) was created in 2007, and formally constituted in 2009 (see Johnson, this volume). It comprises representatives of industries and industry organizations, associations of farmers, retailers, banks, civil society organizations, research centers and universities. The main goal of the BRSL is to discuss and formulate, in a participative way, principles, standards and common practices to be adopted in the sector.

Discussion and conclusions

Important transformations have been taking place in the Amazon region, mainly related to changes under way in the beef cattle sector. The main long-term trends are the growing investments for processing capacity closer to the production zones; a slow improvement in cattle herd and pasture management, which has improved the productivity and profitability of cattle ranching over time, associated with simultaneous processes of land concentration and fragmentation; and the increasing presence of smallholders in the beef cattle sector. The latter implies that changes taking place in this sector are going to have substantial implications not only for local development but also for local people's livelihoods and benefit sharing. The cattle sector has also had significant impacts on deforestation over time, yet these impacts have decreased in the last few years, not necessarily due to endogenous forces, but due to external factors that have placed important constraints limiting the expansion of ranching into new frontier lands, as was typical in the past. These factors are related, on the one side, to increased attempts to enforce environmental regulations, and on the other side, to growing pressures from retailers. There is a significant agronomic potential in the Amazon region for livestock production, and adoption of improved practices could lead to substantial increase in productivity.

The institutional and market constraints limiting the possibility of ranching to expand to new frontier lands, has placed at the center the importance of making progress towards the adoption of sustainable beef production. The concept of sustainability in the beef cattle sector entails different dimensions, which comprise legal, economic, and ecological aspects. From a legal standpoint, sustainable beef production should comply with existing environmental regulations, which entails that ranching should be exclusively developed into the allowed areas for agricultural expansion. Sustainable beef, from an economic perspective, implies the adoption of more productive ranching system that increase productivity under improved herd and pasture management systems. Furthermore, from an ecological point of view, sustainable beef should reduce the environmental footprint of beef production, mainly through reduced greenhouse gas emissions. The combination of these different dimensions of sustainability should improve the contribution of cattle ranching to low-emission development strategies. It is not realistic to foresee a reduction in cattle production in the Brazilian Amazon since it constitutes a major source of economic growth and supports a large number of people's livelihoods.

The efforts undertaken by the state in enforcing environmental regulations, as well as from other actors in society, including NGOs and the beef industry, have no doubt triggered actions leading to identifying supply chains in which it is possible to distinguish beef originating from illegally deforested lands. The latter may likely reach only a few ranchers, specifically the segment of large-scale landholders with more ability to adapt to changes in the regulatory framework, and to comply with the requests adopted by the beef industry. It seems likely that a large number of medium- and small-scale ranchers, while mandated to comply with the environmental regulations, might not be able to make the transformations in their production systems in order to increase their productivity while reducing the pressure on forest conversion. This implies that there is still a lack of production alternatives for local ranchers, and for most medium-scale ranchers that depend on relatively extensive systems due to the lack of financial resources to intensify. In this light, to move beyond a policy framework based on repressive actions against deforestation will be difficult, since there are still not institutional capacities to move towards a framework that actively promotes sustainable beef cattle through improved access to financial resources, incentive systems and access to markets that reward for the adoption of good practices.

In this light, there are promising institutional arrangements in Brazil to keep moving along the track towards sustainable beef production, yet economic incentives to support this transition are still needed. Cattle ranching is entering into a new phase of development in the Amazon where it is no longer possible to keep developing low productive and extensive ranching, yet the transition towards a more sustainable and low-emission sector will depend on continued coordination among the different actors to make this transition possible. Additional conditions required are investments in improving infrastructure, and developing value chains, along with logistics for processing and commercialization. Nonetheless, a major issue of concern is that efforts towards sustainability should come along with equity considerations. The latter entails ensuring that small- and medium-scale ranchers are able to adapt their production practices to the new regulatory and economic conditions. Only actions that explicitly manage the trade-offs between efficiency and equity can pave the way to sustainable beef cattle production that contributes to long-term regional development and poverty alleviation in the Amazon.

Notes

1 Part of the material presented in this chapter was originally published in Pacheco and Poccard-Chapuis (2012) 'The complex evolution of cattle ranching development amid market integration and policy shifts in the Brazilian Amazon' *Annals of the Association of American Geographers*, vol 102, no 6, pp. 1366–1390; doi:10.1080/00045608.2012.6780 40

2 Additional details on the CRP-FTA program can be found at http://foreststreesagroforestry.org.

3 There is a diverse range of cattle ranching systems in the Amazon. Extensive systems are normally based on free ranging while semi-intensive systems adopt a subdivision of large pastures into smaller paddocks to facilitate more uniform grazing patterns and pasture rotation, along with an improved use of mineral supplements, vaccination and artificial insemination. More traditional systems consist of self-reproducing herds while others specialize in cow-calf production. Heifer calves may be retained for herd expansion or sold to other operators who specialize in calf production and finish them for slaughter. These different systems can be dedicated only to beef production, or to comprise both beef and dairy production.

4 The Brazilian Legal Amazon was defined by government decree in 1953; it covers an area of 5,000,000 km² encompassing six 'northern' states (Acre, Amapá, Amazonas, Pará, Roraima, and Rondônia), plus part of three others (Tocantins, north of the 130 parallel; Mato Grosso, north of the 160 parallel; and Maranhão, west of the 440 meridian). The entire state of Mato Grosso was included in the BLA by the complementary Law no. 31 issued in October 1977 (art. 45).

5 The main economic groups operating in the beef sector in Brazil are Bertin, Independência, JBS Friboi, Marfrig, Margen, Minerva, Perdigão, Quatro Marcos, and Sadia.

6 The relative increase in exports of live cattle is likely occurring because of growing constraints on selling cattle originating from unauthorized deforested lands to the beef industry.

7 This mechanism was adopted in the 1934 Forest Code, which stipulated that one-quarter of each property's forest area had to be conserved. Under the 1965 version

of the Forest Code, half the area of each property in the northern region could be converted to agricultural uses, with the other half to be maintained as legal forest reserve. In 1996, the proportion of legal forest reserves was set to be not less than 80 percent of an establishment's total area, allowing for forest conversion in the remaining 20 percent.

8 Presidential Decree No. 7130, issued 11 March 2010, applies only to lands classified as productive areas in ecological and economic zoning in the area of influence of the BR-163 highway (Cuiabá–Santarém) and the western zone of the BR-230 highway (Trans-Amazon).

9 See www.cnmp.mp.br/premio/premiados/10:1-lugar-carne-legal.

10 In this regard, see the audit to the purchases from JBS during 2013, which looks at 12,135 transactions representing 15 percent out of the total transactions conducted by JBS in the Amazon region: www.jbs.com.br/sites/jbs.com.br/files/relatorio_publico_jbs_greenpeace_2014.pdf.

11 See www.cppse.embrapa.br/redepecus.

References

Aldrich, S. P., Walker, R. T., Arima, E. Y., Caldas, M. M., Browder, J. O. and Perz, S. (2006) 'Land-cover and land-use change in the Brazilian Amazon: Smallholders, ranchers, and frontier stratification'. *Economic Geography*, vol 82, no 3, pp. 265–88

Alencar, A., Moutinho, P., Nepstad, D., Vera, M. C., Pacheco, P., McGrath, D. and Ramos, C. (2004) *Desmatamento na Amazônia: Indo alem da emergência crônica [Deforestation in the Amazon: Going Beyond the Chronic Emergency]*, Instituto de Pesquisa Ambiental da Amazônia (IPAM), Woods Hole Research Center (WHRC), Belém, Brazil

Alston, L. J., Libecap, G. D. and Mueller, B. (1999). *Titles, Conflict, and Land Use: The Development of Property Rights and Land Reform on the Brazilian Amazon Frontier*, University of Michigan Press, Ann Arbor, MI

Alves, D. (2003) 'An analysis of the geographical patterns of deforestation in Brazilian Amazônia in the 1991–1996 period', in C. Wood and R. Porro (eds), *Patterns and Processes of Land Use and Forest Change in the Amazon*, University of Florida Press, Gainesville, FL

Arima, E. (2000) *Incentivos fiscais e de crédito para pecuária na Amazônia Legal [Fiscal and credit incentives for livestock in the Legal Amazon]*, Instituto do Homem e Meio Ambiente na Amazônia, Belém, Brazil

Arima, E., Barreto, P. and Brito, M. (2005) *Pecuária na Amazônia: Tendências e implicações para a conservação ambiental [Livestock in the Amazon: Trends and Implications for Environmental Conservation]*. Instituto do Homem e Meio Ambiente na Amazônia, Belém, Brazil

Arima, E. and Uhl, C. (1997) 'Ranching in the Brazilian Amazon in a national context: Economics, policy, and practice', *Society and Natural Resources*, vol 10, no 5, pp. 433–51

Astill, J. (2010) 'A special report on forests: Seeing the wood', *The Economist*, 23 September, www.economist.com/node/17062713, accessed 27 September 2014

Barreto, P. and Silva, D. (2009) *Os desafios para uma pecuária mais sustentável na Amazônia. [Challenges for More Sustainable Cattle Ranching in the Amazon]*, Instituto do Homem e Meio Ambiente na Amazônia, Belém, Brazil

Barreto, P. and Silva, D. (2010) 'Will cattle ranching continue to drive deforestation in the Brazilian Amazon?', Paper read at the conference Environment and Natural Resources Management in Developing and Transition Economies, 18–19 November, Clermont-Ferrand, France

Browder, J. O., Pedlowski, M. and Summers, P. M. (2004) 'Land use patterns in the Brazilian Amazon: Comparative farm-level evidence from Rondônia', *Human Ecology*, vol 32, no 2, pp. 197–224

Camargo, G. S., Zen, S. D., Ishihara, S. M. and Osaaki, M. (2002) *Economia da pecuária de corte e o processo de ocupação da Amazônia* [*Economy of Beef Production and the Process of Occupation in the Amazon*], Centro de Estudos Avançados em Economia Aplicada, University of São Paolo, Piracicaba, Brazil

Carrero, G. C. and Fearnside, P. M. (2011) 'Forest clearing dynamics and the expansion of landholdings in Apuí, a deforestation hotspot on Brazil's Transamazon Highway', *Ecology and Society*, vol 16, no 2, pp. 26

Castellanet, C., Simões, A. and Filho, P. C. (1998). *Diagnóstico preliminar da agricultura familiar na Transamazônica: Indicações para pesquisa e desenvolvimento* [*Diagnostic of Smallholder Agriculture in the Transamazon: Guidance for Research and Development*], Empresa Brasileira de Pesquisa Agropecuária, Belém, Brazil

Chomitz, K. M. and Thomas, T. S. (2001) *Geographic Patterns of Land Use and Intensity in the Brazilian Amazon*, World Bank, Development Research Group, Infrastructure and Environment, Washington, DC

Cohn, A. S., Mosnier, A., Havlík, P., Valin, H., Herrero, M., Schmid, E., O'Hare, M. and Obersteiner, M. (2014) 'Cattle ranching intensification in Brazil can reduce global greenhouse gas emissions by sparing land from deforestation', *Proceedings of the National Academy of Sciences*, vol 111, no 20, pp. 7236–7241

da Veiga, J. B., Poccard-Chapuis, R., Piketty, M. G. and Tourrand, J. F. (2001) *Milk Production, Regional Development and Sustainability in the Eastern Amazon*, Agricultural Research for Development, Empresa Brasileira de Pesquisa Agropecuária, Belém, Brazil

da Veiga, J. B., Tourrand, J. F. and Quanz, D. (1996) *A pecuária na fronteira agrícola da Amazônia: O caso de município de Uruará, PA, na região da Transamazônica* [*Cattle Production in the Amazon Agricultural Frontier: The Case of the Municipality of Uruará, PA in the Transamazon*], Empresa Brasileira de Pesquisa Agropecuária, Belém, Brazil

Faminow, M. D. (1998) *Cattle, Deforestation, and Development in the Amazon: An Economic, Agronomic, and Environmental Perspective*, CAB International, New York

Faminow, M. D., Dahl, C., Vosti, S., Witcover, J. and Oliveira, S. (1999) *Smallholder Risk, Cattle and Deforestation in the Western Brazilian Amazon*, International Development Research Center, International Food Policy Research Institute, Empresa Brasileira de Pesquisa Agropecuária, Washington, DC

Fearnside, P. M. (2001) 'Land-tenure issues as factors in environmental destruction in Brazilian Amazonia: The case of southern Pará', *World Development*, vol 29, no 8, pp. 1361–72

Franco, M. (2004) 'Da marginalidade à carne com griffe' [From marginalized to trademarked beef], *DBO*, September 2004

Godar, J., Gardner, T. A., Tizado, E. J. and Pacheco, P. (2014) 'Actor-specific contributions to the deforestation slowdown in the Brazilian Amazon', *Proceedings of the National Academy of Sciences,* doi:10.1073/pnas.1322825111

Hecht, S. (1982) 'Cattle ranching development in the eastern Amazon: Evaluation of development strategy', Ph.D. thesis, University of California at Berkeley, CA

Hecht, S. (1985) 'Environment, development and politics: Capital accumulation and the livestock sector in eastern Amazonia', *World Development*, vol 13, no 6, pp. 663–84

Hecht, S. (1993) 'The logic of livestock and deforestation in Amazonia', *Bioscience*, vol 43, no 10, pp. 687–95

Hecht, S. (2012) 'From eco-catastrophe to zero deforestation? Interdisciplinarities, politics, environmentalisms and reduced clearing in Amazonia', *Environmental Conservation*, vol 39, pp. 4–19

IBGE (2014) 'Livestock Municipal Survey', www.sidra.ibge.gov.br/bda/pesquisas/ppm/, accessed 26 September 2014

IDESP (2010) 'Tendências e perspectivas da pecuária de corte no Pará. Boletim de conjuntura' [Trends and perspectives of the beef livestock sector], Belém, Brazil

IEL/CNA/SEBRAE (2000) *Estudo sobre a eficiência econômica e competitividade da cadeia agroindustrial da pecuária de corte no Brasil* [*Study on the economic efficiency and competitiveness of agroindustrial beef production in Brazil*], IEL/CNA/SEBRAE, Brasília, Brazil

INPE (2014) 'Monitoramento da floresta Amazônica Brasileira por satélite', Instituto Nacional de Pesquisas Espaciais, São José dos Campos, Brazil www.obt.inpe.br/prodes/prodes_1988_2013.htm, accessed 26 September 2014

Jank, M. S., Farina, E. Q. and Galan, V. B. (1999) 'O agribusinees do leite no Brasil' [Agribusiness in the milk sector in Brazil], USP/FIA/PENSA/IPEA, São Paulo, Brazil

Kaimowitz, D. (1995) *Livestock and Deforestation in Central America in the 1980s and 1990s: A Policy Perspective.* Washington, DC: International Food Policy Research Institute, Inter-American Institute for Cooperation on Agriculture.

Kaimowitz, D. and Angelsen, A. (1998) *Economic Models of Tropical Deforestation: A Review.* Center for International Forestry Research, Bogor, Indonesia

Kaimowitz, D., Mertens, B., Wunder, S. and Pacheco, P. (2004) 'Hamburger connection fuels Amazon destruction: Cattle ranching and deforestation in Brazil's Amazon', Center for International Forestry Research, Bogor, Indonesia

La Rovere, E. L., Pereira, A. O., Dubeux, C. B. S. and Wills, W. (2014) 'Climate change mitigation actions in Brazil', *Climate and Development*, vol. 6, pp. 25–33.

Lele, U., Verissimo, V. M. V., Vosti, S., Perkins, K. and Husain, S. A. (2000) 'Brazil, forests in the balance: Challenges of conservation with development' World Bank, Washington, DC

Margulis, S. (2004) 'Causes of deforestation of the Brazilian Amazon', Report No. 22, 107. World Bank, Washington, DC

Mattos, M. M. and Uhl, C. (1994) 'Economic and ecological perspectives on ranching in the Eastern Amazon', *World Development*, vol 22, no 2, pp. 145–58

Mertens, B. R., Poccard-Chapuis, M.-G. Piketty, A.-E. Lacques, and A. Venturieri (2002) 'Crossing spatial analyses and livestock economics to understand deforestation processes in the Brazilian Amazon: The case of Sao Felix do Xingu in South Pará', *Agricultural Economics*, vol 27, no 3, pp. 269–94

Nepstad, D., Boyd, W., Stickler, C., Bezerra, T. and Azevedo, A. (2013) 'Responding to climate change and the global land crisis: REDD+, market transformation and low-emissions rural development', *Philosophical Transactions of the Royal Society B*, vol 368, no 1619, pp. 20120167

Nepstad, D., Stickler, C. and Almeida, O. (2006) 'Globalization of the Amazon soy and beef industries: Opportunities for conservation', *Conservation Biology*, vol 20, no 6, pp. 1595–603

Pacheco, P. (2005) 'Populist and capitalist frontiers in the Amazon: Dynamics of agrarian and land-use change', Ph.D. thesis, Graduate School of Geography at Clark University, Worcester, MA.

Pacheco, P. (2009a) 'Smallholder livelihoods, wealth and deforestation in Eastern Amazon', *Human Ecology*, vol 37, no 1, pp. 27–41

Pacheco, P. (2009b) 'Agrarian change, cattle ranching and deforestation: Assessing their linkages in southern Para', *Environment and History*, vol 15, no 4, pp. 493–520

Pacheco, P. (2009c) 'Agrarian reform in the Brazilian Amazon: Its implications for land distribution and deforestation', *World Development*, vol 37, no 8, pp. 1337–47

Pacheco, P. (2012) 'Actor and frontier types in the Brazilian Amazon: Assessing interactions and outcomes associated with frontier expansion', *GeoForum*, vol 43, no 4, pp. 864–874

Pacheco, P. and Poccard-Chapuis, R. (2012) 'The complex evolution of cattle ranching development amid market integration and policy shifts in the Brazilian Amazon', *Annals of the Association of American Geographers*, vol 102, no 6, pp. 1366–1390

PNEFA (2009) 'Evolução geográfica do processo de implantação de zona livre de febre aftosa no Brasil' [Geographic evolution of the implementation process for achieving a foot-and-mouth disease-free zone], PNEFA, Belém, Brazil

Poccard-Chapuis, R. (2004) 'Les réseaux de la conquête filière bovine et structuration de l'espace sur les fronts pionniers d'Amazonie oriental Brésilienne' [Livestock evolution and spatial structuring of the pioneer frontiers in the Brazilian western Amazon], Department de Geography, University of Paris X, Nanterre, France.

Poccard-Chapuis, R., da Veiga, J., Piketty, M. G., Morelly, C. and Tourrand, J. F. (2003). 'A cadeia produtiva da leite: Alternativa para consolidar a agricultura familiar nas frentes pioneiras da Amazônia' [The milk value chain: Alternative to consolidate family agriculture in the pioneer frontiers in the Amazon], Embrapa Amazônia Oriental, Belém, Brazil

Poccard-Chapuis, R., Thales, M., Venturieri, A., Piketty, M. G., Mertens, B. da Veiga, J. and Tourrand, J. F. (2005) 'Cadeia produtiva da carne: Uma ferramenta para monitorar as dinamicas nas frentes pioneiras na Amazônia brasileira' [The beef value chain: A tool for monitoring the dynamics in pioneer frontiers in the Brazilian Amazon], *Cadernos de Ciencia & Tecnologia*, vol 22, no 1, pp. 125–38

Poccard-Chapuis, R., Tourrand, J. F., Piketty, M. G. and da Veiga, J. (2001) 'Cadeia produtiva de gado de corte e pecuarização da agricultura familiar na Transamazônica' [Livestock value chain and small-scale cattle ranching in the Transamazon], Documentos No. 106, Empresa Brasileira de Pesquisa Agropecuaria, Belém, Brazil

Schneider, R. 1993. 'Land abandonment, property rights, and agricultural sustainability in the Amazon', Dissemination Note No. 3, World Bank, Washington, DC

Serrão, A. and Toledo, J. M. (1992) 'Sustainable pasture-based production system in the humid tropics', in T. E. Downing, S. B. Hecht, H. A. Pearson, and C. Garcia-Downing (eds), *Development or Destruction: The Conversion of Tropical Forest to Pasture in Latin America*, Westview Press, Boulder, CO

Simmons, C., Walker, R., Perz, S., Aldrich, M., Caldas, Pereira, R., Leite, F. and Arima, E. (2010) 'Doing it for themselves: Direct action land reform in the Brazilian Amazon', *World Development*, vol 38, no 3, pp. 429–44

Smeraldi, R. and May, P. (2009) 'A hora da conta: Pecuária, Amazônia e conjuntura' [Time to pay the bill: Livestock, Amazonia and conjuncture], Amigos da Terra, São Paulo, Brazil

Soares-Filho, B., Rajão, R., Macedo, M., Carneiro, A., Costa, W., Coe, M., Rodrigues H. and Alencar, A. (2014) 'Cracking Brazil's Forest Code', *Science*, vol 344, pp. 363–364

Sunderlin, W. D. and Rodríguez, J. A. (1996) 'Cattle, broadleaf forests and the agricultural modernization law of Honduras', Center for International Forestry Research, Bogor, Indonesia

Terra Class (2013) 'Levantamento de informacoes de uso e cobertura de terra na Amazonia – 2010' [Land use assessment in the Amazon - 2010], INPE, EMBRAPA, Brasilia, Brazil

Tourrand, J. F., da Veiga, J. B., Guia, A. P. O. M., Carvalho, S. A. and Pessoa, R. O. (1995) 'Stratégies et pratiques d'élevage en Amazonie Brésilienne: Dynamisme e diversité dans l'agriculture familiale' [Strategies and practices of cattle production in the Brazilian Amazon: Dynamics and diversity of smallholder agriculture], Agricultural Research for Development, Montpellier, France

Vosti, S., Carpentier, C. L., Witcover, J. and Valentim, J. F. (2000) 'Intensified small-scale livestock systems in the western Brazilian Amazon', in A. Angelsen and D. Kaimowitz (eds), *Agricultural Technologies and Tropical Deforestation*, CABI Publishing, Center for International Forestry Research, New York

Vosti, S., Witcover, J. and Carpentier, C. L. (2003) *Agricultural Intensification by Smallholders in the Western Brazilian Amazon: From Deforestation to Sustainable Land Use*. International Food Policy Research Institute, Washington, DC

Walker, R., Browder, J., Arima, E., Simmons, C., Pereira R., Caldas, M., Shirota, R. and de Zen, S. (2009) 'Ranching and the new global range: Amazônia in the 21st century', *Geoforum*, vol 40, no 5, pp. 732–45

Walker, R., Moran, E. and Anselin, L. (2000) 'Deforestation and cattle ranching in the Brazilian Amazon: External capital and household processes', *World Development*, vol 28, no 4, pp. 683–99

4

THE POLITICAL ECOLOGY OF FACTORY FARMING IN EAST AFRICA

Elizabeth Waithanji

Each one of us, especially those in the high income brackets, should feel unhappy and uncomfortable when those around are poor and hungry. The lot is not an ordained state. It could be the result of injustice, just as the existing international economic order is unjust to poor nations. Any society which loses that feeling has lost the essential morality, which alone can guarantee its stability and continued development.

Philip Ndegwa (1985: 126)

Introduction

The discipline of political ecology is based on the fact that change in human behaviour begets ecological change and that ecological change begets change in human behaviour. Political ecology combines the concerns of ecology and political economy to represent the dynamic tension between ecological and human change as well as between diverse groups of society at multiple scales constituted by a plethora of actors ranging from the local to the global and from individuals to organizations and institutions (Peterson, 2000) and with complex and overlapping identities, affinities and interests (Rocheleau, 2008).

The literature review presented in this chapter is intended to demonstrate how the actors – including institutions and the state – in the livestock industry in Africa interact with each other and the ecosystem, and how these interactions have created and maintained inequalities among actors in the meat industry. The review is conducted in a space characterized by unequal economic capabilities and capacities of actors, and governments that are 'non-responsive' to these inequalities. Simultaneously, the governments appear to stifle attempts of weaker actors to thrive by imposing high tariffs and failing to build the much-needed infrastructure to facilitate trade.

Understanding the African political setting in which the political ecology of meat, presented in this chapter, takes place is a necessary prerequisite to the understanding of this subject matter. The author uses Levitsky and Way's (2002) theory of 'competitive authoritarianism' together with Fligstein's (1996) theory of 'markets as politics' to explain the unique trends and processes observed by scholars of this subject in Africa. Briefly, after the end of the cold war in the 1990s, governance of most developing countries was intended, by the western hegemons, to shift from authoritarian to democratic.[1] Most, if not all, African, Latin American and Eastern European countries did not reach the democratic end of the continuum, but stopped somewhere in between and formed hybrid regimes. Labels used to describe these hybrid regimes include competitive authoritarianism, semidemocracy, virtual democracy, electoral democracy, pseudodemocracy, illiberal democracy, semi-authoritarianism, electoral authoritarianism and Freedom House's 'Partly Free' (Levitsky and Way, 2002, p. 52). Kenya and some other African governments fall in the category of competitive authoritarianism whereby the governing executives violate rules of democracy using tools such as bribery, subtle persecution such as the use of tax authorities, compliant judiciaries and other state agencies to legally harass, persecute or extort cooperative behaviour from critics (Levitsky and Way, 2002).

(Competitive) authoritarian governments may coexist indefinitely with meaningful democratic institutions while subduing tensions arising from opposition using bribery, co-optation and various forms of legal persecution without provoking massive protest or international repudiation. This potentially explosive tension has occasionally resulted in uprising with three possible outcomes: they may lose power (e.g. Nicaragua, Zambia and Mexico); they may become weakened and eventually fall (e.g. Peru and Serbia); and they may crack down and the regime digs in deeper (e.g. Kenya, Malaysia, Russia and Ukraine). In addition, removal of autocratic elites creates an important opportunity for regime change and even democratization, but does not ensure such an outcome (Levitsky and Way, 2002). In some cases, the elite executive class is so well entrenched that its members recycle leadership from among their lot, entrenching themselves deeper in the system and protecting each other. They own successful businesses that thrive in incredibly difficult economic environments. The ownership of these companies is also often undisclosed.

In Fligstein's (1996) 'markets as politics' metaphor, social institutions that establish and develop markets try to create stable worlds and find social solutions to unfair competition. In addition, markets and states are intimately linked. Politics in markets work during market formation, stability and transformation. At the formation of markets stage, actors in firms try to create a status hierarchy that enforces non-competitive forms of competition. The processes of political action at market formation resemble the processes at social movements' formation. In stable markets, incumbent firms defend their positions against challengers and invaders, whereas during market transformation, invaders can reintroduce more fluid social-movement-like conditions that then transform the market (Fligstein, 1996). Drawing on examples from Kenya, the two theories have been used in the analysis of the meat industry in Eastern Africa to aid in the understanding of the effect of unequal relations of power among actors in an evolving complex social, economic, environmental and political context, spanning the historical epoch of the immediate postcolonial to the current period.

The chapter is divided into five broad sections. It starts with a background section that situates Africa's agriculture and meat industry in the context of the global industry, pointing out how Africa differs from developed and other developing areas and countries. Second, it looks at the status of meat production, trade and consumption in East Africa, while citing data from other sub-Saharan countries where available. Third, the chapter looks at the challenges experienced by various actors on livestock, and more specifically the meat industry. Finally the paper concludes with some explanations of phenomena and proposes some recommendations that would improve meat production and trade in sub-Saharan Africa.

Background information

Historically, the demand for livestock production, globally, was largely driven by growth in human population, income and urbanization. For the most part, the increase in livestock production was due to the increase in livestock numbers. Over time, the feasibility of enhancing production by increasing the animal numbers became less and less promising because of competition of livestock, wildlife and humans for natural resources, land and water in particular, between humans and livestock for food and feed and the need to operate production-enhancing interventions in a complex landscape whose governance was becoming increasingly influenced by environmental and social justice (Thornton, 2010; Godfray et al., 2010). The challenge posed by increasing livestock numbers has been addressed to a small extent by developing the technology for breeding bigger but fewer animals and confining these animals in small spaces where food is delivered to them. Breeding technology is, however, fairly limited and it eventually narrows down to selection of suitable animals within the herd by culling less desirable ones. In economies that are able to confine livestock, conditions of production are changing. Attributes barely recognized as necessary for responsible production a few decades ago, such as product quality, animal welfare (with the recognition of animal sentience), augmented disease resistance and reduced environmental impact, now receive attention in the politics and economics of production (Thornton, 2010).

Most discussants of the subject of 'livestock revolution' (Delgado et al., 1999) tend not to separate the developing world into its different economies, creating an impression that the developing world is a homogenous place.[2] The different economic blocks of the developing world have fairly distinctive trends with East Asia being very advanced in the revolution and sub-Saharan Africa being the least advanced. The countries/regions where statistics have been collected include China, India, other South Asia, Southeast Asia, Latin America, Western Asia and

North Africa (WANA) and sub-Saharan Africa (Delgado, 2005). A paucity of discussion on the trends of the revolution in for example sub-Saharan Africa (SSA) is evident. Nevertheless, the general consensus is that owing to the economic development status of SSA, the revolution is unlikely to be of the magnitude of East Asian and Latin American countries (Bruinsma, 2003; Delgado, 2005; Thornton, 2010). In spite of the complexity of the social and economic factors that influence food industrialization, and in spite of its problems, food industrialization is likely to continue and the current problems facing developed countries are likely to be experienced, ultimately, by all developing countries (Lang, 2004).

Land-use intensity has increased in some places like East Asia where cereal yields have trebled in the last 20 years, whereas in sub-Saharan Africa, yields have not increased at all. At least 75 per cent of total livestock production growth to 2030 will be in confined systems in developing countries such as East Asia. In contrast, there will be much less growth of confined livestock production systems in Africa because the current domination by few integrated large-scale commercial operations are likely to continue displacing small-scale livestock farmers – especially under the current policies that do not support smallholder farmer competitiveness, and intensification would just put greater pressure on the already fragile extensive pastoral areas and the densely populated high-potential areas close to urban centres (Bruinsma, 2003). Unlike crops, where production is mainly enhanced by increasing yield, livestock production in developing countries will increase because of increased livestock numbers, particularly of ruminants (Thornton, 2010).

Climate change will impact livestock in mixed production smallholder systems in developing countries where people are already highly vulnerable (Lang, 2004). For example, the easy to grow highly prolific Napier grass, *Pennisetum purpurium*, which is a very popular fodder grown and utilized by more than half of all smallholder producers in Kenya, may potentially meet the anticipated fodder demand in the event of expansion of beef cattle production. It is, however, threatened by Napier headsmut, which may cause a reduction in yield by 50–90 per cent (Mwangi et al., 2005). Napier may, therefore, require supplementation with another equally prolific product to avoid significant feed deficits. Stover, a by-product of sorghum, maize and other cereals may be a promising feed supplement alternative, but competition for land and water may render production of alternative animal feeds through irrigation untenable especially for more intensive livestock crop systems (Herrero et al., 2009). Most of the world's livestock, therefore, shall most likely continue to suffer from seasonal nutrient deficits owing to the inability of farmers to sustain enhanced feed production (Bruinsma, 2003). To enhance livestock production in extensive pastoral production systems of Africa, integrating existing technology such as dissemination of information from early warning systems and drought prediction may be the most feasible option because it will enable the pastoralists to plan their production around these climatic events (Thornton, 2010). Considering the unique position of sub-Saharan Africa's slow economic growth, the demand for meat is unlikely to increase substantially beyond what it is currently. It, therefore, appears unlikely that factory farming will grow in SSA as it has in the rapidly growing economies of East Asia and some Latin American countries.

Other challenges constraining Kenya and similar economies' development include lack of foreign exchange, a stagnating agricultural sector, rapid population growth, massive unemployment, inability to compete in the world markets and dependence on borrowing from the development world for economic growth (Clayson, 1980). Kenya and similar economies also differ from developed economies in that Kenya substitutes labour for capital whereas developing countries substitute capital for labour (ibid.) – what most foreign development critiques call a bloated labour force. And, because much of the production in smallholder farming relies on family labour, gendered division of labour is crucial and productivity is often determined by cooperation between men and women within the household. In Kenya, therefore, the bulk of smallholder farm labour is typically provided by women as part of their reproductive obligations. With commercialization of production, women continue to provide labour to produce for profit and men control the income owing to the land tenure and other sociocultural characteristics of this patriarchal society that favours men (Waithanji et al., 2013). If men deny women benefits from the income, women have been known to cripple the production process. One example where women have transformed the gender landscape is in tea contract farming through persistent resistance from producing without being paid (Von Bulow and Sorensen, 1993). It appears likely that if factory farms will thrive in Kenya, they will have to develop through contract farming. For them to be successful, they will have to pay attention to the needs of women who, although they do not control land, control labour, which is crucial in the labour-intensive contract-farming process. Furthermore, most chicken contract farmers in Kenya are women.

Current status of meat production, trade and consumption in East Africa

Over 90 per cent of livestock production in East Africa takes place in small-scale tropical livestock systems (Upton, 2000). These systems are predominantly located in rural areas; exploit the natural environment; are mainly family enterprises whereby decisions on production, consumption and marketing are interdependent; they utilize family rather than hired labor; face large environmental risks to droughts, floods, pests and diseases and considerable market risk owing to their partial integration to mainstream markets because they are rural; are strongly risk averse owing to their low subsistence on income and in kind while rarely aiming at maximizing income or profit; and have strong social support systems that enable them to cope with challenges (Sumberg, 1998; Upton, 2000). For pastoralists whose entire livelihood is based on livestock, a household needs about 20 head of cattle and about 100 head of sheep and goats to survive (Dahl and Hjort, 1976). In the strictly pastoral communities, human and subsequent livestock population growth increases pressure on the physical environment that they draw upon for their survival, resulting in migration as a key coping strategy. In less austere environments, although population growth puts pressure on the land, application of new technology enhances production of the same land (Boserup 1965) without necessitating migration. The small-scale livestock production systems consist of a combination of pure pastoral and agropastoral production systems that use migration and use of technology as the two main coping/ adaptive strategies (Swallow, 1994; Juul, 1996; Niamir-Fuller, 1998).

A proportion of the agropastoral production systems are located in peri-urban areas and have better access to markets and might prosper at the expense of opportunities to improve productivity for more remote rural areas (Upton, 2000). The intensive urban poultry market often owned by wives of middle-class urban residents (reported to have emerged in Dar es Salaam) constitute a significant proportion of intensive small-scale producers of broilers and eggs (Upton, 2000). Women-dominated commercial poultry (broiler) enterprises have also been documented in Gaberone, Botswana, but the women hailed from diverse social and economic status (such as wives, widows, divorced women, etc.; Hovorka, 2006). Urban poultry and dairy production is now well established and constitutes big business in Kenya and probably other African countries and can no longer be classified as a middle-class wives' preserve. It is now a market in its own right whereby men and women participate according to how much money they have and their market share. In Kenya, some urban poultry farmers are still contracted by Kenchic. Contract farming notwithstanding, poultry business in Kenya is still fraught with market challenges characterized by business booms and busts associated with changes in supply and demand.

Livestock and meat production

Livestock production systems in Eastern Africa are predominantly traditional and extensive with minimal intensification mainly in the dairy, poultry, pig and aquatic production systems. Generally, domestic meat consumption is low in eastern Africa, which makes livestock production an enterprise for trade rather than subsistence. Sudan's livestock population estimate in 2006 was 41 million head of cattle, 50.1 million sheep, 42.1 million goats and 4 million camels (el Dirani et al., 2009). Ethiopia's cattle population is 41 million while that of sheep and goats is 50 million (Nell, 2006). In Kenya, pastoralists maintain about 70 per cent of the national ruminant herd and provide about 67 per cent of the red meat produced in Kenya. The 70 per cent is estimated to be constituted by about 9.7 million beef cattle, 9.6 million goats, 8.3 million sheep, and 0.8 million camels (EPZA, 2005). Red meat, comprising of beef, mutton, goat and camel meat, accounts for over 80 per cent of all the meat consumed locally (ibid.). Nineteen per cent of the meat produced is white – poultry and pork. Farmers Choice rears around half the pigs it produces and buys about 50,000 pigs per year from contract farmers. Kenchic produces about 300,000 broilers a week, of which 70 per cent are sold to contract farmers – a total of 65.5 per cent of whom are women – and the rest to other non-contracted farmers. Kenchic then buys grown chickens from contract farmers, processes and sells about 85 per cent to the local market and exports the rest to wider East Africa (Keskin et al., 2008). In 2008, Kenchic sold about 15.6 million birds, a paltry number when compared with India's 800 million bird output in 2003 (Lang, 2004). Kenchic is owned by the Kenyan based NAS Holdings Ltd (Tlc partnership, 2014) whereas Farmer's Choice Limited is owned by the Aga Khan Fund for Economic Development (a for-profit company based in Geneva). Unofficial sources purport that NAS Holdings Ltd is owned by members of Kenya's ruling class just like the dairy industry and some beef ranches. These companies are monopolies and monopolies typically have excessive profit margins (House, 1973). Nevertheless, Kenchic and Farmers' Choice have worked against great odds and in innovative ways in order to stay afloat in a non-supportive policy environment fraught with challenges (Keskin et al., 2008). One per cent of the meat consumed in Kenya originates from game, but the government restricts marketing and export of game meat in fear that legalizing it could stimulate demand for illegal bush meat and poaching. There are, however, a few licensed game meat dealers, hotels and restaurants (EPZA, 2005).

From a livestock census conducted in Tanzania in 1984, the livestock numbers, more than 90 per cent of which are indigenous, were documented to be 12.5 million cattle, 3.1 million sheep, 6.4 million goats and 280,000 pigs. The population is projected to have grown to about 18.5 million cattle, 13.1 million goats, 3.6 million sheep, 1.2 million pigs and 53 million poultry based on data obtained from 2002/2003 National Sample Census (Njombe and Msanga, 2010). Annual meat production in Tanzania in 2005 was documented at 378,500 tons, but this quantity declined to 370,566 tons in 2007 after the 2005–2007 Rift Valley fever outbreak (ibid.). According to the Uganda Investment Authority (UIA, undated) the cattle population in 2008 was 11.4 million and annual per capita beef consumption was estimated at 6kg. Chicken population was estimated at 23.5 million of which 84.2 per cent were indigenous. In 2006, 44,000 tons of broiler meat was produced in Uganda and 80 per cent of this was consumed locally. The annual per capita poultry production is 2kg (ibid.).

From the foregoing, and based on the proposal by UIA (undated), the report by EPZA (2005), and articles by other authors cited in this section, livestock production for the market is still basic, and production at the factory farming magnitude is yet to be realized.

Livestock and meat trade

Livestock contributes up to 3.3 per cent of Kenya's national GDP, a figure that is obtained from calculating 10 per cent of agriculture's contribution, which is about 33 per cent of the national economy. Calculated in a similar manner, livestock constitute 2.1 per cent of the national GDP in Ethiopia and 8.4 per cent in Sudan (Aklilu, 2003). Livestock contribution to GDP is 3.2 per cent in Uganda (IGAD, 2013) and 5–6 per cent in Tanzania (Covarrubias et al., 2012).

Government contribution of the national budget towards livestock is dismal in most eastern African countries with Ethiopia allocating less than 0.3 per cent of its recurrent budget on livestock and Kenya allocating 0.75 per cent to livestock and 0.47 per cent to animal health. Although data on Sudan was not available, Sudan was reported to have allocated more funds to livestock than Ethiopia and Kenya (Aklilu, 2003).

In Eastern Africa, Sudan has outdone Kenya and Ethiopia in its livestock export because of its long-term relationship with the Gulf States and its well established quarantine system. In Sudan, livestock and livestock products export is the second most important foreign exchange commodity after oil, with exports predominantly to Saudi Arabia. Of the Arab livestock import market, Sudan's livestock account for about 70 per cent of cattle, 31 per cent of sheep, 49 per cent of goats and 25 per cent of camels (el Dirani et al., 2009). Ethiopia exports 8301 metric tonnes (MT) of meat to Saudi Arabia, Dubai, Yemen, Congo Brazzaville and South Africa. Of this, 93 per cent is constituted by chilled sheep and goat meat, 6 per cent by beef and one per cent by offal (Nell, 2006). Ethiopia's export potential is hindered by the fact that it is land-locked and has to export through other countries (Aklilu, 2003). Up to 1987, Kenya was a net exporter of all main livestock products, but from 1997 it became a net importer of beef, sheep and goat meat, and eggs, whereas poultry exports had declined to almost zero and pig meat was the only export commodity (Upton, 2000). By 2000 Kenya's meat export trade was restricted to about 1500 tons of chilled frozen pork, and a little beef (ibid.). Locally, meat in Kenya is mainly retailed from strategically located roadside butcheries (Oyaro et al., 2007).

Livestock and livestock products constituted a small portion of Uganda's official export trade, in the period from 2006 to 2010, never amounting to more than 1.5 per cent of all exports by value (IGAD, 2013). Trade in livestock and livestock products, in Tanzania, is still minimal with official exports of live animals to the Comoros Islands and Burundi in 2006/07 totalling 2,542 cattle and 1,852 goats valued at 1.03 billion Tanzanian shillings (TZS) and 92 tonnes of meat (goat, sheep and cattle) worth TZS 352 million exported to Kuwait, Oman and United Arab Emirates (Dubai).[3] In addition, approximately 300,000 heads of cattle are reported to cross to Kenya, undocumented, annually (Njombe and Msanga, 2010).

Proposals and offers to foreign companies for foreign direct investments (FDI) by Kenya and Uganda, as seen in the proposal by UIA (undated), and report by EPZA (2005) suggest that FDI can be an option to enhance livestock production for trade. Foreign direct investment is only likely to thrive in an environment where the market experiences healthy competition and the role of the state as a regulator and facilitator of terms of trade is clear. In an ideal democracy with healthy competitive markets and a functional state engagement, the state is supposed to play an important role in the construction of market institutions by making and enforcing the rules governing economic interaction in a given geographical area (Krasner, 1988). As part of state building as development, the state is supposed to govern the state economies while providing stable and reliable conditions under which firms organize, compete, cooperate and exchange (Fligstein, 1996). From such a state's intervention, some firms are likely to benefit more than others, but the state should also restrict unhealthy (e.g. predatory) competition by restricting entry through trade barriers (ibid.). Other than taxation, the role of the African states in meat trade is quite unclear. Indeed, in Kenya, the state appears to undermine the meat market by not supporting the market infrastructure and not protecting markets from predatory competition and through multiple (punitive) taxations. Only Farmer's Choice and Kenchic appear to make some business progress in Kenya. The meat market in Kenya, therefore, does not follow the economic principles of market formation, stability and trans-formation described by Fligstein (1996). In spite of their dominance in the market, Farmer's Choice and Kenchic's accounts of struggles to attain their current economic growth have demonstrated that a certain extent of investment by the government is required (Keskin et al., 2008). This investment is lacking in Kenya (ibid.) and other eastern African countries (Aklilu, 2003). Kenchic and Farmers' Choice have pros-pered against great odds owing to their own efforts rather than because of being in a investment-conducive environment (Keskin et al., 2008).

In a healthy market environment, FDI has a positive role in industrial develop-ment through spillover benefits (Gachino, 2009). For example, spillover of superior technologies and managerial practices may occur as a result of employees from mul-tinational corporations (MCs) interacting with employees from local firms who adopt these technologies. As they interact, employees from MCs learn about local consumers from employees from local firms and local company employees learn about efficiency-enhancing technologies used by the MCs from the MC employees. Positive spillover effects are more likely to happen if the investing foreign company is jointly owned by foreign and local partners, whereas unfair competition is likely to occur if the investing company is owned entirely by foreigners (Konings, 2001; Javorcik, 2004). The chances for success for FDI in Kenya and similar economies are low because of the unhealthy market environment. Calls for FDI in the meat indus-try in Kenya, and similar quasi-democracies, are, therefore, naive.

Domestic meat consumption

Per capita annual meat consumption for Uganda is about 11kg, which is much less than that of Kenya (41kg) and Sudan (15kg) (IGAD, 2013). The annual per capita meat consumption for Tanzania in 2007 was documented at 11kg (Njombe and Msanga, 2010) whereas that for Ethiopia in 2005 was the lowest at 4.6kg (Tafere and Worku, 2012) (Table 4.1). The Food and Agriculture Organization of the United Nations (FAO) recommends an annual per capita meat consumption of 50kg for any given country (UIA, undated). Per capita meat consumption for the United States is about 202.8 lbs (92kg) (NCC, 2014).

Kenya consumes more livestock products per capita than the average for the whole of sub-Saharan Africa (Upton, 2000). For example, annual per capita con-sumption of milk was estimated to be 81kg in Kenya against only 30.4kg for all sub-Saharan Africa; calories derived from livestock products at 240.7 compared to 143.1; and the daily protein intake at 15.6g compared to 10.4g for the whole

TABLE 4.1 Annual meat consumption in Eastern African Countries.

Country	Annual per capita meat consumption (kg)	Population in 2014	Population* annual per capita meat consumption	Total meat consumed annually in thousand MT
Uganda	11	36,345,860	399,804,460	399.8
Kenya	41	43,178,141	1,770,303,781	1770.3
Tanzania	11	47,783,107	525,614,177	525.6
Ethiopia	4.6	91,728,849	421,952,705.4	422
Sudan	15	37,195,349	557,930,235	557.9

Source: Author

subcontinent (Upton, 2000). The high consumption pattern in Kenya could be explained, in part, by Kenya's unique economic development history. Kenya underwent a comparatively rapid transition to capitalist relations of production due, in large part, to the political strength of an indigenous class of capital, with the state playing an important role in subsidizing and guaranteeing the process of industrial expansion by foreign capital (Leys et al., 1980), which may have been defined less in other African countries. Colonial business enterprises were sustained post-independence and Kenya's hegemonic economic and ruling class established similar enterprises and sustained them by building old and new infrastructure, while securing financing to expand businesses (ibid.). Some of these businesses included dairy farms and beef ranches.

Challenges experienced in livestock and meat production and trade in Eastern Africa

Using a political ecology lens to look at multiple perspectives of livestock and meat production and trade in Eastern Africa, this review has demonstrated that the position of a state in the authoritarian–democracy continuum can help inform the type of markets, institutions, property rights and structures that govern them. This study has demonstrated that in Kenya, and possibly other eastern African countries, characterized by competitive authoritarianism, the livestock and meat markets have been ignored by the state, which provides minimal budgetary and infrastructure support, and which promotes predatory meat businesses such as the private beef ranches. The link between a state's lack of democracy and its inaction with regard to markets has been demonstrated in this study. The converse, whereby a democratic state is likely to support competitive markets while discouraging predation by more powerful firms is likely to be true. Democracy, therefore, is a prerequisite to functional markets, and without it, no intervention can fix the problem of dysfunctional markets. In addition to addressing the democracy problem, this study has identified the following challenges that need to be addressed as well.

Once the democracy challenge is addressed, policymakers should invest in establishing meat production and market models that work best for the multiple eastern African contexts rather than, for example, trying to replace pastoralism with a livestock sector based on western models of animal husbandry or alternative land use systems (Sumberg, 1998; Hesse and MacGregor, 2006). Pastoral production systems are, however, dynamic and poorly understood with uncertainty as to whether they are overall beneficial or harmful. A review by Aklilu (2003) identified factors that impact livestock trade in Kenya, Ethiopia and Sudan, and include lack of livestock data (also identified by Baker et al., 2011 and Nakweya, 2013) that can inform production and marketing strategies; low prioritization of funding of livestock related interventions; absent or dilapidated livestock holding grounds that lack necessary equipment such as feed and water troughs, livestock scales, loading ramps and crushes, but still charge revenues for use; high transit and point of sale livestock taxes; cartels by middlemen and butchers; and value addition is very expensive with value added meat products being inaccessible to most of the population. For example, Farmers' Choice products reach only 2 per cent of the Kenyan population. A study on butchery operators in Meru, Kenya on factors influencing the decision to add value, demonstrated that credit availability, management's level of education and age significantly influenced the decision to engage in value addition (Ngore et al., 2011).

Poor access to forex services in Ethiopia more than Kenya, Somalia and Sudan interferes with the growth potential of the meat export business (Aklilu, 2003). In Ethiopia, all foreign currency transactions must be approved by Ethiopia's central bank, the National Bank of Ethiopia (NBE) and the local currency (Birr) is not freely convertible (Aklilu, 2003; USDS, 2013).

Climate change entails changes in temperature, rainfall, humidity, and extreme weather events (McMichael et al., 2007). Among the challenges associated with climate change include low rainfall, high temperature and high evapotranspiration rates especially in the arid and semi-arid lands (ASALs). The subsequent negative water balance is inadequate for food crop growing and pasture for livestock production (Ngaira, 2009). Climate change carries a special importance in agriculture because the agricultural sector accounts for 70 per cent water use (Thornton et al., 2009). In addition, agricultural activity worldwide, especially livestock production, accounts for about a fifth of total greenhouse-gas (GHG) emissions, which contribute to climate change and cause a threat to food yields in many regions. Efforts to reduce the intensity of these emissions must, therefore, be made (McMichael et al., 2007). Overall, the subject of climate change is still not clearly understood and less is known about climate change and livestock than climate change and crops (Thornton et al., 2009).

Some of the most important impacts of global climate change will be felt among the 'subsistence' or 'smallholder' farmers from developing countries (Morton, 2007). Smallholder farmers include crop-only farmers, livestock-only farmers (pastoralists) and livestock and crop farmers (agropastoralists). The impact of climate change on livestock includes the quality and quantity of feeds; heat stress; livestock diseases and disease vectors; biodiversity; systems and livelihoods; and indirect impacts (for details see Thornton et al., 2009). According to the Fourth Assessment Report of the Intergovernmental Panel on Climate Change (IPCC), by 2020, rain-fed agricultural output could drop by 50 per cent in some African countries (IPCC, 2007).

Box 4.1 Facts on Impact of Climate change in Kenya (Ngaira, 2009)

Drought

Lake Baringo (1990–1992)

- Surface area: 1988 – 144km^2; 1992 – 112km^2
- Fish catch: 1990 – 380MT; 1992 – 37MT

Northern Kenya (1990–1992)

- All livestock of 70% pastoralists of Mandera, Wajir and West pokot wiped out

La Nina drought (1998–2001)

- Artificial powdered milk introduced in Kenya because drought caused cattle mortality

2005–2006 drought

- 80% livestock died in Turkana, Wajir and Karamoja (Uganda)
- Migration leading to environmental refugees and conflict
- Human death due to starvation and water and pasture related conflicts in Mandera and Wajir

Floods

1997/98 El Nino

- Livestock drowned and died
- Livestock died in mudslides in the highlands
- Outbreaks of diseases (contagious bovine pleuropneumonia (CBPP) and Rift Valley fever (RVF) in the ASALs and East Coast fever (ECF) in the highlands)

Affected communities deal with the effects of climate change through adaptation to it or by mitigating practices (Thornton et al., 2009). They can adapt through technological innovations, for example using drought resistant crops; change in behaviour, such as by eating what is available; managerial, for example supplementation of animals with hay; and policy interventions such as planning regulation and infrastructure development. They mitigate through agricultural practices such as collectively contributing to increasing soil carbon sinks and reducing emission of greenhouse gases such as methane.

Discussion and conclusion

The livestock revolution of the magnitude of East Asia and Latin America is unlikely to happen in Africa, south of Sahara (SSA) owing to its development status (Bruinsma, 2003; Delgado, 2005; Thornton, 2010). Some of the factors associated with SSA's underdevelopment include the fact that crop yields have not increased and therefore, confined livestock production is unlikely to happen (Bruinsma, 2003). Increased production will be mainly due to increase in numbers of ruminants (Thornton, 2010). Because of competition between humans and livestock, large irrigation projects for fodder for the ruminants are untenable (Herrero et al., 2009) and as a result, most developing countries' livestock are already suffering from seasonal nutrient deficits (Bruinsma, 2003) and may continue doing so at a larger scale. In SSA, therefore, livestock production among the pastoral communities may only be enhanced by providing pastoralists with information on early warnings and predictions of droughts (Thornton et al., 2009). It might also be time for a shift in the current producer–exploitative paradigm whereby producers are expected to bear the burden of year-round sustained production to one where the marketers and processors absorb products at bumper harvest, while paying reasonable prices for them, and taking the responsibility of sustaining supply to the consumers.

Urban livestock production, on the other hand, is thriving owing to the accessibility of communication infrastructure and markets by the urban farmers. These enterprises may not have an impact on the export trade because the spaces where most businesses are conducted are small backyards in residential areas. Further, these production systems are a public health hazard because waste disposal facilities are inadequate, and sometimes inappropriate, because they were not factored in during urban planning.

Although consumption patterns of animal source foods have demonstrated that livestock in SSA is produced for trade more than for subsistence (Aklilu, 2003), a plethora of mutually reinforcing political and market-based challenges to trade in livestock and meat have been documented in this study. With some countries being more affected than others, the main issue is the type of regime (authoritarian/democracy hybrid) governing the country. For example, in some competitive authoritarian countries, the governing elite may own predatory meat businesses that are protected by the state. In this case, all other competition is likely to fail unless democracy is attained. Other issues, in no specific order of importance, include unfair local and international terms of trade in terms of cartels by middlemen all over eastern Africa – and butchers in Kenya; culture, which is more socialistic than capitalistic whereby a portion of surplus produce is shared among kith and kin while being produced by family labour in which efficiency is hard to enforce; lack of accurate baseline knowledge on production, which compromises planning and developing of targets of production for the market; and lack of market intelligence, which, for the purpose of this study, is the information relevant to a producer's or producer country's markets, gathered and analysed specifically for the purpose of accurate and confident decision-making in determining market opportunity, market penetration strategy, and market development metrics.

Further, available data on livestock is obtained for different purposes and different historical periods using diverse methods, ranging from censuses to estimates, making collaboration with potential country partners impossible. Political rivalry and contestations for supremacy – and hence hegemony among neighboring countries leads to undercutting each other's efforts, which works against all the actors.

To enhance the production and marketing potential of the eastern African countries, and countries with similar political dispositions, these nations need to shift towards the democratic end of the authoritarian-democracy continuum. This is especially difficult for countries where the competitive authoritarian regime is entrenched and systemic and the state machinery undermines healthy competition by facilitating predatory competition through inaction with regard to making and enforcing rules that govern healthy competition. Addressing other challenges without dealing with the political disposition will yield no lasting results.

Notes

1 According to Fligstein 1996, markets refer to situations where a good or service is sold to customers for a price; institutions refer to shared rules that can be laws or collective understandings, held in place by custom, explicit or tacit agreements; property rights are social relations that define who has claims on the profit of firms; and governance structures refer to the general rules in society that define relations of competition, cooperation and market specific definitions of how firms should be organized.
2 The term Livestock Revolution was coined by Delgado et al. (1999) and highlights accelerated growth in demand for livestock products in parts of the developing world, tied to human population growth, rising incomes, continuing urbanisation and changing food preferences. The Livestock Revolution – with its promise of diet diversity, better nutrition and health, and also economic opportunities for small-scale producers – is one of the most powerful ideas to emerge in the areas of food, nutrition and agricultural development over the last decade (Sumberg and Thompson 2013).
3 1 USD = 1623 TZS (Tanzania shillings) on 10 March 2014.

References

Aklilu Y. (2003) 'Critical issues impacting livestock trade in Kenya, Ethiopia and Sudan', Proceedings of the 10th annual conference of the Ethiopian Society of Animal Production (ESAP) held in Addis Ababa, Ethiopia, 21–23 August 2003 (a summary version of this publication available at: ftp://ftp.cgiar.org/ilri/ICT/Theme%203/Aklilu%20Marketing%20vol%20II.pdf, accessed 12 March 2014)

Baker, D., Ahmed, I. and Pica-Ciamarra, U. (2011) 'Livestock data in sub Saharan Africa: Availability and Issues', 12th Interagency donor group meeting, Nairobi, www.slideshare.net/ILRI/livestock-data-in-sub-saharan-africaavailability-and-issues, accessed 20 March 2014

Boserup, E. (1965) *The Conditions of Agricultural Growth: the Economics of Agrarian Change under Population Pressure*, Allen & Unwin, London (republished 1993, Earthscan, London)

Bruinsma, J. (2003) *World Agriculture: Towards 2015/2030, an FAO Perspective*, Earthscan/FAO, Rome,

Clayson, E. J. (1980) 'How relevant is operational research to development? The case of Kenyan industry', *Journal of the Operational Research Society*, vol 31, no 4, pp. 293–299.

Covarrubias, K., Nsiima, L. and Zezza, A. (2012), 'Livestock and livelihoods in rural Tanzania: A descriptive analysis of the 2009 National Panel Survey', www.africalivestockdata. org/sites/africalivestockdata.org/files/PAP_LIV_TZ_LSMS-ISA_July_!2.pdf, accessed 10 March 2014

Dahl, G. and Hjort, A. (1976) *Having Herds: Pastoral Herd Growth and Household Economy*, Department of Social Anthropology, University of Stockholm, Stockholm

Delgado, C. (2005) 'Rising demand for meat and milk in developing countries: Implications for grasslands-based livestock production', In D. A. McGilloway (ed.), *Grassland: A Global Resource*, pp. 29–39, Wageningen Academic Publishers, Wageningen

Delgado, C., Rosegrant, M., Steinfeld, H., Ehui, S. and Courbois, C. (1999). 'Livestock to 2020: The next food revolution', IFPRI Food, Agriculture, and the Environment Discussion Paper 28, IFPRI, Washington, DC

el Dirani, O. H., Jabbar, M. A. and Babiker, I. B. (2009) 'Constraints in the market chains for export of Sudanese sheep and sheep meat to the Middle East', Research Report 16, Department of Agricultural Economics, University of Khartoum, Khartoum, and ILRI (International Livestock Research Institute), Nairobi, http://ageconsearch.umn. edu/bitstream/99128/2/2009-Sudan%20sheep%20market%20ILRIRR16.pdf, accessed 10 March 2014

EPZA (2005) 'Meat production in Kenya 2005', Export Processing Zone Authority (EPZA), www.epzakenya.com/UserFiles/files/MeatIndustry%20sector%20profile.pdf, accessed 10 March 2014

Fligstein, N. (1996) 'Markets as politics : A political-cultural approach to market institutions', *American Sociological Review*, vol 61, no 4, pp. 656–673

Gachino, G. (2009) 'Industrial policy, institutions and foreign direct investment: The Kenyan context', *African Journal of Marketing Management*, vol 1, no 6, pp. 140–160, www.academicjournals.org/ajmm, accessed 27 July 2013

Godfray, C. H., Beddington, J., Crute, J. R., Haddad, I. R., Lawrence D. R., Muir, J. F., Pretty, J., Robinson, S., Thomas, S. M. and Toulmin, C. (2010), 'Food security: The challenge of feeding 9 billion people'. *Science*, vol 327, pp 812–818; doi:10.1126/science. 1185383

Herrero, M., Thornton P. K., Notenbaert, A., Msangi, S., Wood, S., Kruska R., Bossio, D., Van de Steeg, J., Freeman, H. A., Li, X., Sere, C., McDermott, J., Peters, M. and Rao, P. P. (2009) 'Drivers of change in crop–livestock systems and their potential impacts on agro-ecosystems services and human well-being to 2030', study commissioned by the CGIAR Systemwide Livestock Programme (SLP), ILRI, Nairobi, www.slideshare.net/ILRI/drivers-of-change-in-croplivestock-systems-and-their-potential-impacts-on-agroecosystems-services-and-human-wellbeing-to-2030, accessed 14 March 2014

Hesse, C. and MacGregor, J. (2006), 'Pastoralism: Drylands' invisible asset? Developing a framework for assessing the value of pastoralism in East Africa', IIED issue paper no 142, http://pubs.iied.org/pdfs/12534IIED.pdf, accessed 5 March 2014

House, J. W. (1973) 'Market structure and industry performance: The case of Kenya', *Oxford Economic Papers*, New Series vol 25, no 3, pp. 405–419

Hovorka, A. J. (2006). 'The no. 1 ladies' poultry farm: A feminist political ecology of urban agriculture in Botswana', *Gender, Place and Culture: A Journal of Feminist Geography*, vol 13, no 3, pp. 207–225; doi:10.1080/09663690600700956

IGAD (2013) 'The contribution of livestock to the Ugandan economy', IGAD Center for Pastoral Areas & Livestock Development (ICPALD), Policy Brief No: ICPALD 7/CLE/8/2013, http://igad.int/attachments/714_The%20Contribution%20of%20Livestock%20to%20 the%20Ugandan%20Economy.pdf, accessed 10 March 2014

IPCC (2007) 'Climate change 2007: impacts, adaptation and vulnerability', Report of Working Group II. IPCC, Geneva

Javorcik, B. S. (2004) 'Does foreign direct investment increase the productivity of domestic firms? In search of spillovers through backward linkages', *American Economic Review*, vol 94, no 3, pp. 605–627

Juul, K. (1996) 'Post drought migration and technological innovation among Fulani herders in Senegal: The triumph of the tube', IIED discussion paper no 64.

Keskin, E., Mirjam, S., Dijkman, J. and Hall A. (2008) 'Private capacity and public failure: Contours of livestock innovation response capacity in Kenya'. Working Paper Series No 2008-068.

Konings, J. (2001) 'The effects of foreign direct investment on domestic firms', *Economics of Transition*, vol 9, no 3, pp. 619–633.

Krasner, S. (1988) 'Sovereignty: An institutional perspective', *Comparative Political Studies*, vol 21, pp. 66–94.

Lang T., (2004) 'Food industrialisation and food power: Implications for food governance', *Gatekeeper Series*, no 114, IIED

Levitsky, S. and Way, L. (2002). 'The Case of Competitive Authoritarianism', *Journal of Democracy*, vol 13, no 2, pp. 51 - 65

Leys, C., Borges, J. and Gold, H. (1980) 'State capital in Kenya: A research note', *Canadian Journal of Africa Studies/Reveu Canadienne des Études Afrcaines*, vol 14, no 2, pp. 307–317

McMichael, A. J., Powles, J. W., Butler, C. D. and Uauy, R. (2007) 'Food, livestock production, energy, climate change, and health', *Lancet*, vol 370, no 9594, pp. 1253–1263

Morton, J. F. (2007) 'The impact of climate change on smallholder and subsistence agriculture', *Proceedings of the National Academy of Sciences*, vol 104, no 50, pp. 19680–19685

Mwangi, D. M., Romney, D., Staal, S., Baltenweck, I. and Mwendia, S. W. (2005) 'Improved livelihoods from grasslands: The case of Napier grass in smallholder dairy farms in Kenya', in D. A. McGilloway (ed.), *Grassland: A Global Resource*, pp. 347–350, Wageningen Academic Publishers, Wageningen

Nakweya, G. (2013) 'African countries must improve livestock data', Sci Dev Net, May 2013, www.scidev.net/global/farming/news/african-countries-must-improve-livestock-data.html, accessed 10 March 2014

NCC (2014) 'Per capita consumption of poultry and livestock, 1965 to estimated 2014, in pounds', National Chicken Council (NCC). www.nationalchickencouncil.org/about-the-industry/statistics/per-capita-consumption-of-poultry-and-livestock-1965-to-estimated-2012-in-pounds, accessed 15 August 2014

Ndegwa, P. (1985) *Africa's Development Crisis and related International Issues.* Heinemann Kenya, Nairobi.

Nell, A. J. (2006) 'Quick scan of the livestock and meat sector in Ethiopia: Issues and opportunities', Wageningen International, Wageningen, http://library.wur.nl/way/bestanden/clc/1885725.pdf, accessed 10 March 2014

Ngaira, J. K. (2009) 'Challenges of water resource management and food production in a changing climate in Kenya', *Journal of Geography and Regional Planning*, vol 2, no 4, pp. 97–103

Ngore, P. M., Mshenga, P. M., Owuor, G. and Mutai, B. K. (2011) 'Socioeconomic factors influencing meat value addition by rural agribusinesses in Kenya', *Current Research Journal of Social Sciences*, vol 3, no 6, pp. 453–464

Niamir-Fuller, M. (1998) 'The resilience of pastoral herding in Sahelian Africa', in F. Berkes and C. Folke (eds), *Linking Social and Ecological Systems: Management Practices and Social Mechanisms for Building Resilience*, pp. 250–284, Cambridge University Press, Cambridge

Njombe, A. P. and Msanga, Y. N. (2010) 'Livestock and Dairy Industry Development in Tanzania', Ministry of Livestock Development and Fisheries, no 17, Dar es Salaam, www.mifugo.go.tz/documents_storage/LIVESTOCK%20INDUSTRY%20DAIRY%20 DEVELOPMENT%20IN%20TANZANIA%20-%20LATEST3.pdf, accessed 10 March 2014

Oyaro, N., Ogendi, J., Murago E. N. and Gitonga, E. (2007) 'The contents of Pb, Cu, Zn and Cd in meat in Nairobi, Kenya', *Journal of Food, Agriculture & Environment*, vol 5, nos 3 and 4, pp. 119–121

Peterson, G. (2000) 'The human actor in ecological-political ecology and ecological resilience : An integration of human and ecological dynamics', *Ecological Economics*, vol 35, pp. 323–336.

Rocheleau, D. E. (2008) 'Political ecology in the key of policy: From chains of explanation to webs of relation', *Geoforum*, vol 39, no 2, pp. 716–727; doi:10.1016/j. geoforum.2007.02.005

Sumberg, J. (1998) 'Mixed farming in Africa: The search for order, the search for sustainability', *Land Use Policy*, vol 15, no 4, pp. 293–317

Sumberg, J. and Thompson, J. (2013) 'Revolution reconsidered: Evolving perspectives on livestock production and consumption', STEPS Working Paper, no 52, STEPS Centre, Brighton, http://steps-centre.org/publication/revolution-reconsidered-evolving-perspectives-on-livestock-production-and-consumption/, accessed 10 March 2014

Swallow B. (1994) 'The role of mobility within the risk management strategies of pastoralists and agro-pastoralists', *Gatekeeper Series*, no 47, IIED, http://pubs.iied.org/pdfs/6061IIED.pdf, accessed 10 March 2014

Tafere, K. and Worku, I. (2012) 'Consumption patterns of livestock products in Ethiopia: Elasticity estimates using HICES (2004/05) data', ESSP II Working Paper no 38, International Food Policy Research Institute / Ethiopia Strategy Support Program II, Addis Ababa, www.ifpri.org/sites/default/files/publications/esspwp38.pdf, accessed on 10 March 2014

Thornton, P. K. (2010) 'Livestock production: Recent trends, future prospects', *Philosophical Transactions B*, vol 365, pp. 2853–2867; doi:10.1098/rstb.2010.0134

Thornton, P. K., Van de Steeg, J., Notenbaert, A. and Herrero, M. (2009) 'The impacts of climate change on livestock and livestock systems in developing countries: A review of what we know and what we need to know', *Agricultural Systems*, vol 101, no 3, pp. 113–127.

Tlc partnership, the (2014) 'NAS Holdings Ltd – Nairobi Kenya (NAS Airport Services, Kenchic Ltd, ABM, Chloride Exide, Ennsvalley Bakers)', www.thetlcpartnership.com. au/testimonials/nas-holdings-ltd---nairobi-kenya/, accessed 23 July 2014

UIA (undated) 'Invest in Uganda's meat sector', An investment proposal by the Uganda Investment Authority (UIA), www.ugandainvest.go.ug/index.php/unique-selling-prepositions/39-usp-meat/file, accessed 10 March 2014

Upton, M. (2000) 'The "livestock revolution" – implications for smallholder agriculture: A case study of milk and poultry production In Kenya', Livestock Policy Discussion Paper, no 1, Food and Agriculture Organization, Livestock Information and Policy Branch, AGAL

USDS (2013) '2013 investment climate statement – Ethiopia', Report of Bureau of Economic and Business Affairs, April 2013, US Department of State (USDS), www.state.gov/e/eb/rls/othr/ics/2013/204639.htm, accessed 12 March 2014

Von Bulow, D. and Sorensen, A. (1993) 'Gender and contract farming: Tea outgrower schemes in Kenya', *Review of African Political Economy*, vol 20, no 56, pp. 38–52

Waithanji, E., Njuki, J. and Bagalwa, N. (2013) 'Gendered participation in livestock markets', in J. Njuki and P. Sanginga (eds), *Women, Livestock Ownership and Markets: Bridging the Gender Gap in Eastern and Southern Africa*, pp. 39–59, Routledge, New York

5

A CHANGING ENVIRONMENT FOR LIVESTOCK IN SOUTH AFRICA

Emma R. M. Archer van Garderen, Claire L. Davis and Mark A. Tadross

Introduction

This chapter focuses on the livestock sector in South Africa, and the changing environment (in all senses) in which it finds itself. We begin by detailing key trends in livestock production in South Africa, first describing a (brief) history of the agricultural sector, followed by post-1994 trends in consumption and livestock figures. The latest findings regarding climate change projections for South and southern Africa are then discussed, followed by what is currently known regarding the implication of such projections for the livestock sector, with preliminary observations regarding current and planned research. As we mention later in the chapter, although the livestock sector comprises a key component of South Africa's agricultural economy, it has traditionally received less attention in research and development than, for example, staple crops. In order to improve its resilience, given current and ongoing internal and external changes and their effects, we need to increasingly engage in efforts to understand its current and projected characteristics.

Key trends in livestock production in South Africa

The political economy of agriculture in South Africa under apartheid has been described as a 'dual agriculture' (Vink and Kirsten, 2003), where white large-scale agriculture effectively accounted for 80 per cent of agricultural production, versus black small-scale or subsistence agriculture (Brand et al., 1991). White farming dominated the sector in terms of production and economic activity, despite the fact that only one-third of white-owned farms in the 1980s were commercially viable (Cooper, 1988). Such a situation was enabled through a distinctive support system designed by the apartheid government – comprising direct and indirect support through a range of institutions, including government, quasi-governmental and commercial banking (Brand et al., 1991; Bundy, 1979; Cell, 1982; Lemon, 1987). Political and economic interests of white commercial agriculture were regarded as essential to ruling National Party interests, hence the design of such a system (Archer, 2004).

Key areas of support included extensive credit (in the form of finance and equipment subsidies), loans with subsidized interest rates and land policies in favour of white land owners (Brand et al., 1991; Cooper, 1983; Cooper, 1988; Land and Agriculture Policy Centre, 1993; Levin and Weiner, 1997; Lipton, 1977; Mabin, 1991; van Zyl and van Rooyen, 1991; Vink and Kassier, 1991; Vink and Kirsten, 2003). Researchers argue that such a support system had two important results. First, one argument proposes that such support made farmers less responsive to price input changes, and thus less concerned with ecologically sustainable practice (Fernandez et al., 2002; Vogel, 1994; Wilson, 1991). Second, and of significance to our discussion below, is the argument that such a system buffered farmers from market and climate stresses, perhaps discouraging them again from engaging in adaptive strategies (Fernandez et al., 2002). The situation of political economic stress, or 'squeeze', within which farmers now find themselves post-1994 is described in more detail below.

Post 1994, the commercial and emerging agriculture sectors have undergone substantive changes, many of which are critical to the livestock sector. Beginning in the 1980s, the system of support for commercial farming described previously began to undergo large-scale revision. Such a revision was accelerated in the 1990s and post-1994 as part of a major push by the government to redirect support to small-scale agriculture, and to make commercial farming more viable and efficient (Van Zyl et al., 1996; Vink and Kirsten, 2000).

The 1995 White Paper on Agriculture was formulated with specific reference to Reconstruction and Development Programme (RDP) principles on agriculture. It is thus compatible with all concrete policy suggestions made in the RDP document with regard to the transformation of the agricultural sector away from the dominance of the old groups and old institutions. Since agriculture in post-apartheid South Africa is constituted as a provincial function, the document was developed as a mission statement and set of principles to be interpreted by provincial administrations within certain constraints (Republic of South Africa, 1995). Two source documents provided the basis for the White Paper: the Land and Agricultural Policy Center (LAPC) 1994 Draft Agricultural Policy Paper 13, and the 1993 Department of Agriculture's document on agricultural policy.

The White Paper acknowledges the past ability of South African agriculture to 'produce, under adverse weather, physical and biological conditions, in excess of domestic needs[,] a phenomenon unknown on the African continent' (Republic of South Africa, 1995). It further ascribes all weaknesses of the sector to state intervention and subsidization, and calls for a new vision of South African agriculture comprising:

> A highly efficient and economically viable market-directed farming sector, characterized by a wide range of farm sizes, which will be regarded as the economic and social pivot of rural South African and which will influence the rest of the economy and society.
>
> (Republic of South Africa, 1995)

TABLE 5.1 Critical Agricultural Goals for the Republic of South Africa circa 1995.

1. Develop a new order of economically viable market-directed commercial farmers, with the family farm as the basis
2. Support increased access to agricultural land via land reform
3. Financial systems focus on resource-poor and beginner farmers
4. Trade in and marketing of agricultural products to reflect market tendencies
5. To be based on sustainable use of natural agricultural and water resources
6. Develop agriculture's key role in the regional development of South African and other countries

Source: RSA (1995)

Table 5.1 shows the central goals of the sector envisaged to comprise this 'new agricultural paradigm'.

To this end, the paper calls for a regulatory framework for agriculture that is scale-neutral and encourages new farming. It also notes that 'social subsidy programs should not jeopardize the realization of the economic viability of the agricultural sector' (Republic of South Africa, 1995). In reference, for example, to drought aid, the paper proposes that '[t]he Government should not support measures that soften the negative impact on farm incomes caused by poor risk management as this will cause farmers to use high-risk methods which could endanger resource conservation' (ibid.). Most direct subsidization schemes have been curtailed, including drought aid, although the 'developing agriculture' sector has variable (and frequently critiqued) access to state support.

Macroeconomic stress external to South Africa is argued to have further complicated the effects of such support system revision (van Zyl et al., 1996; Vink and Kirsten, 2000). The most important factors here include changes in carcass prices, declining terms of international trade, and increased interest and input price rates in the 1980s and 1990s (DEA, 2000). Such coupled stress in the political economic sector placed meat producers, for example, under increasing pressure to produce higher yields and/or to diversify their production mix.

Independent of climate stress and the role of stocking patterns, for example, the entire pre-apartheid system has been transformed in a way that appears to be have changed the 'calculus' of livestock production and strategy choice (Archer, 2004). Government subsidies and other mechanisms available to farmers to provide a buffer from market and environmental vagaries have largely been removed. More recently, key policy initiatives have seen the effects of legislation in land reform and land restitution on the agricultural sector, including the recent proposal that 50 per cent ownership of farms is ceded to farm labour, incorporating years of service as a determinant of shareholding, while 50 per cent ownership is retained by the owner (Hall and du Toit, 2014).

Other key trends in legislation include further changes in security of tenure for farmworkers (which should be viewed against a background of increasing insecurity of farmworker tenure, in certain agricultural industries); changes in credit access, and changes in input prices (including steep increases in the costs of electricity and fuel). For example, the landscape of agricultural credit has changed dramatically, with most farmers with debt in the commercial sector now depend-ent on commercial bank overdrafts, rather than Land Bank loans (as many were able to be in the past). Many commercial farming sectors have, as a result, been increasingly exposed to the interest rate component of the macroeconomic stress described above. In addition, costs of key inputs such as electricity and fuel have increased – electricity tariffs alone (of significance to particular agribusinesses) have increased markedly since 1994, due to a range of factors.

At the same time, the 20 years post-1994 in South Africa have seen interesting trends in meat consumption, further affecting farmer choice and production mix. For example, as living standards have improved in most sectors of the population, and affluence has increased, choices in food consumption have similarly changed, and continue to do so. Effectively, consumption of meat and eggs has increased significantly (in line with the animal products consumption trends noted globally in other chapters in this volume) (Holmes, 2013).

First, the consumption of white meat has increased, increasing 48 per cent from 1992 to 2004, and increasing by another 54 per cent by 2012 (ibid.). Egg consumption, in the meantime, has effectively more than doubled in the past 20 years. Finally consumption of red meat, of key importance here, has also increased, although it is of interest to note that the growth has been at a more moderate pace than has the growth of white meat (ibid.) with suggestions that price may be a limiting factor.

Taljaard et al. (2006) note, however, in their analysis of meat consumption trends in South Africa that the most striking changes in meat consumption have been between the various meat categories. It would appear that as meat consump-tion rises (and, presumably, as affluence and disposable income rise), non-economic factors start to play a more significant role in determining which meat consumers choose to purchase. The authors certainly find this to be the case in South Africa, where the aforementioned substantial increase in white meat demand has been observed; and taste changes in red meat consumption are evident. As a result, consumer taste, attitudes and preferences have become increasingly significant in determining consumption, and a key trend affecting producers is the recommenda-tion that they increasingly need to take taste, attitudes and preferences into account both in terms of what they produce, and in how they produce it (ibid.). Such a recommendation remains as relevant to the emerging agricultural sector as to the large-scale commercial sector, and is further relevant to the meat supply chain.

Further clues to choices and trends in livestock production are provided by the latest livestock figures for South Africa nationally and provincially, provided by the Department of Agriculture, Forestry and Fisheries (DAFF) in November 2013. Livestock figures are provided for cattle, sheep, pigs and goats, measured quarterly, in a time series running from November 1996 through to November 2013 (with measurement continuing). It should immediately be noted that any livestock figures on the national and provincial scale are likely to be flawed, but such limitations are taken (and continue to be taken) into account in analysis and

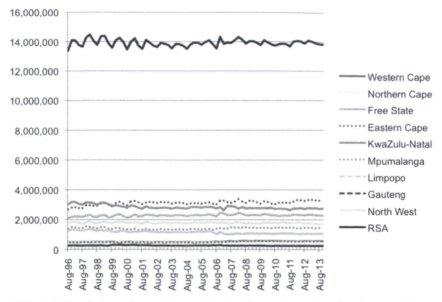

FIGURE 5.1 Trends in cattle numbers in South Africa at the national and provincial scale.

Source: DAFF (2013)

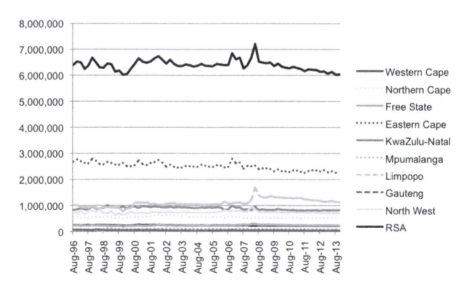

FIGURE 5.2 Trends in goat numbers at the national and provincial scale.

Source: DAFF (2013)

interpretation. Research described below is currently being undertaken to analyse trends and possible drivers of change, but a few characteristics of interest are immediately evident. We will limit our discussion here to cattle and goats, but future publications will deal with all four datasets.

A first clear point to make is that at the provincial scale, the Eastern Cape overtook KwaZulu-Natal in terms of cattle production around mid-1999, a trend that agricultural researchers are still trying to understand (one argument may be for the role of former homeland areas, and the changing nature of agricultural production, but this needs substantive further investigation). National figures show a gradual recovery after a small dip in the early to mid-2000s, a trend that may be related to production choices and costs, although further verification is required. As mentioned below, possible seasonal climate drivers of cattle number changes at the national and provincial level are currently in analysis.

Goat numbers at the national scale showed an initial decline in the latter 1990s, followed by a recovery, with a peak in production nationally and in the Eastern Cape (with consistently the highest goat stock numbers) in November 2006. A further peak in production is seen nationally and in Limpopo Province (the province with the second highest goat stock numbers) in May 2008. In the case of goat production, climatic factors are being particularly carefully considered, since goat production is often (although not always) not associated with supplemental feeding, and could be closely correlated with forage availability.

A critical and unfortunate omission in the database is game numbers, a rising industry in South Africa and a key feature of the livestock industry in recent years. A significant aspect of the worldwide trend in rising demand for meat is the increasing demand for meat products associated with health and so-called 'natural' origins (D'Amato et al., 2013; van Schalkwyk et al., 2011), as well as those produced from farming methods with lower levels of inputs, such as 'organic' meats (van Schalkwyk et al., 2011). Consumption of game meat has markedly increased in South Africa, and D'Amato et al., (2013), among others, observe that the same trend as that observed globally is evident here, where game meat is often viewed as a healthier substitute for beef (primarily due to generally lower levels of saturated fat and cholesterol), generally (but not exclusively – see analyses to follow) the domain of higher income consumers. Consumers are further increasingly including, as mentioned earlier, non-economic factors in their choice of meat products, including health concerns, and desire for meat from natural sources. Some of the work by the Green Trust and Conservation International in South Africa, for example, is starting to focus on the nature of sustainable and 'green' branding for meat products, clearly reflecting (in certain geographic areas and economic sectors) consumer tastes and preferences in flux.

As a result, game ranching and production has increased significantly in South Africa. In 1964, game ranches constituted approximately 600,000 in numbers, while in 2007, numbers stood at 18.6 million, with 80 per cent of game production undertaken on private land (D'Amato et al., 2013). As at 2013, the authors indicate that over 10,000 commercial wildlife ranching farms constitute 2.5 million head of game, comprising 20.5 million ha of (generally) marginal agricultural land (ibid.). This trend is by no means limited to South Africa. In Namibia, for example, van Schalkwyk et al. (2011) observe that wildlife commercial production represents effectively the only animal production system actually expanding. Many of these ranches are of substantial size, and fairly large production scale, including a mix of income-producing activities. To date, the vast majority of such game ranches are white owned, although change is becoming evident in this regard (including consortium-owned ranches). Due to concerns regarding taste and preservation, demand tends to be more in the direction of dried and processed meats, including dried sausage and other dried meat products, which are regarded as delicacies throughout the subcontinent (ibid.), concerns regarding local standards and inspection for local markets notwithstanding (see, for example, Bekker et al., 2011; van der Merwe et al., 2011).

Climate change in South Africa, and implications for livestock

In this section, we present recently projected climate changes for southern Africa, using a range of different methods, to identify where they agree on changes, including those likely to affect agriculture and livestock. We then analyse selected latest findings regarding the implications of these climate changes for livestock production. We conclude by discussing current and future research in this area, including key gaps in both operational and research communities in South Africa and in the SADC region more broadly.

The climate projections from both dynamical (Engelbrecht et al., 2009, 2013) and statistical (Hewitson and Crane, 2006) downscaling techniques presented here are drawn from Chapter 3 of the SADC Climate Change Handbook, titled 'Regional scenarios of future climate change over southern Africa' (Tadross et al., 2011). A multi-model ensemble approach is taken in here in order to describe the range of uncertainty associated with climate change projections. All the models assume an A2 SRES emissions scenario and are for the 2036–2065 period relative to the 1961–2000 period.

Global climate models (GCMs), statistical downscalings and dynamical downscalings[1] all agree on an overall increase in minimum, average and maximum temperatures throughout the southern African region. Within and between these projected scenarios, there are clear regional differences, with greater increases in the central regions (particularly towards the south-west) of the subcontinent compared to the coastal regions (Figures 5.3 and 5.4). Projected increases in maximum temperatures range (10th and 90th percentile) between 1.2 and 3.4°C in the central regions, and between 1.0 and 2.6°C in the coastal areas (depending on location). An increase in very hot days (>35°C) is further projected for the region – a significant finding in the light of findings regarding implications of heat stress for livestock detailed below, for example.

Figures 5.5 and 5.6 show the median simulated change in the multi-model ensemble of ten statistically downscaled GCMs (Figure 5.5) and six dynamically downscaled GCMs (Figure 5.6). The median represents the tendency of the model ensemble to be either wetter or drier in the future, but should not be misinterpreted as precluding the possibility that the opposite will occur. In this sense it indicates the most likely scenario, but absolute simulated changes in rainfall (in mm) are conservative.

The statistically downscaled model ensemble (Figure 5.5) indicates a tendency for increases in rainfall in several areas (though this tendency is small, and in many cases less than expected increases in evapotranspiration due to increasing temperatures). The tendency for higher rainfall is strongest in south-eastern South Africa (particularly during September to November) and in the tropics (northern Mozambique and Angola). Decreases in rainfall over Zambia and Zimbabwe are apparent during early and mid-summer (September to February).

The dynamically downscaled ensemble indicates a tendency for drying over a wider region of southern Africa than does the statistically downscaled ensemble. It also indicates, however, a tendency for wetting over south-eastern South Africa during summer, and over central/northern Mozambique during December to May.

The difference in rainfall projections between the statistical and dynamical downscaling methods may be attributed to the manner in which they relate surface rainfall to the physical changes in the overlying atmosphere and, in the case of the dynamical downscaling, the simulated change in the overlying atmosphere. Despite the differences between the projected changes in rainfall derived from the statistical and dynamical downscaling methods, there are still regions where the ensembles agree (Figure 5.5 and 5.6): namely, increases in rainfall over south-east South Africa and northern Mozambique, decreases in rainfall over southern Zambia and Zimbabwe during summer (December–February), and decreases in rainfall over central Zambia and western Mozambique (Tete) during spring (September–November).

Finally, the Long Term Adaptation Scenarios (LTAS) process developed by the majority of the community of scientists in South Africa working on climate change for the South African National Biodiversity Institute and the Department of Environmental Affairs in South Africa (the UNFCCC focal point), further detailed in relation to agriculture and livestock in the following section, has taken the latest climate change downscaled scenarios for South Africa, choosing emission scenarios based on high and low emission pathways (specifically, Regional Concentration Pathways 8.5 and 4.5 Wm^{-2}) (DEA, 2013a). The choice of RCPs were undertaken to allow comparison with the Intergovernmental Panel on Climate Change (IPCC) AR4 A2 and B2 emissions scenarios, since the latter have provided the basis for much climate scenarios work in South Africa (ibid.); and the challenges facing the climate impacts and modelling community include, among others, comparability of findings.

The LTAS Technical Working Group on Climate Scenarios effectively came up with four sets of projected climate futures for South Africa (DEA, 2013a: 18), namely:

1   Warmer/wetter
2   Warmer/drier
3   Hotter/wetter
4   Hotter/drier

'Warmer' is considered to be less than 3°C above the 1961–2000 reference period, while 'hotter' is considered to be more than 3°C above the same reference period. Scenario 1 includes a higher frequency of extreme rainfall events, while Scenario 2 includes a somewhat higher frequency of such events and an increased frequency of drought events. Scenario 3 includes the projection of a 'substantially' (DEA, 2013a: 18) higher frequency of extreme rainfall events, while Scenario 4 includes both the Scenario 3 projection, as well as an additional 'substantial' increased frequency of drought events.

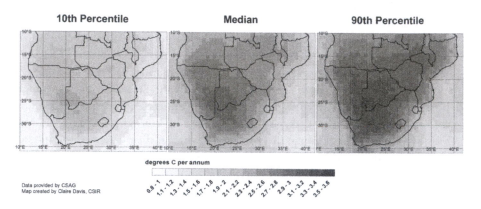

FIGURE 5.3 Projected changes in maximum temperature (°C) by 2036–2065 relative to the 1961–2000 period based on the 10th percentile, median and 90th percentile of the 10 statistically downscaled GCMs.

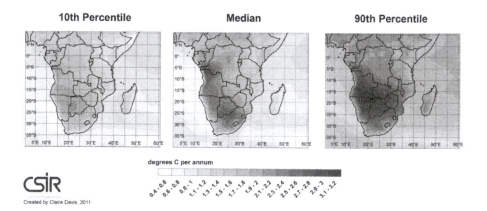

FIGURE 5.4 Projected changes in maximum temperature (°C) by 2036–2065 relative to the 1961–2000 period based on the 10th percentile, median and 90th percentile of six dynamically downscaled GCMs.

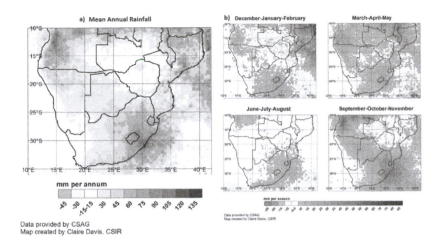

Data provided by CSAG
Map created by Claire Davis, CSIR

FIGURE 5.5 Projected changes in mean summer (DJF), autumn (MAM), winter (JJA) and spring (SON) rainfall (by 2036–2065, relative to 1961–2000) expressed as the change per season (millimetres) and based on the median change of 10 statistical downscaled GCMs.

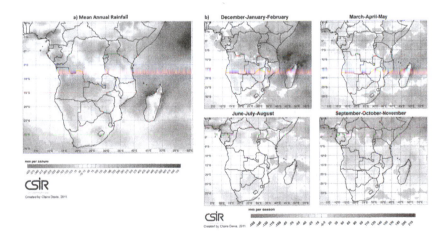

FIGURE 5.6 Projected changes in mean summer (DJF), autumn (MAM), winter (JJA) and spring (SON) rainfall (by 2036–2065, relative to 1961–2000) expressed as the change per season (millimetres) and based on the median change of six dynamically downscaled GCMs.

Although there has been some debate on the utility of the four scenarios, they comprise a substantive contribution to the availability of usable projected climate working messages for South Africa, and essentially form the base for the consolidation of findings regarding impacts on key sectors described in other LTAS reports, and (partly) drawn upon below in the case of livestock.

The most recent consolidation of findings regarding implications of climate change for the agriculture and livestock sector in South Africa may also be found in the aforementioned LTAS reports, at least until the release of South Africa's Third National Communication to the UNFCCC (due in late 2015). In particular, the sectoral report titled *Climate Change Implications for the Agriculture and Forestry Sectors in South Africa* (DEA, 2013b) provides at least an initial attempt to develop actionable messages for the sector, using, in part, the four sets of futures described above, based on the aforementioned attempt to develop working climate futures actionable messages from the (selected) full set of downscaled climate projections available for South Africa at the time.

Effectively, the report details generally adverse impacts on agriculture in South Africa over the next few decades (ibid.: 10); with specific findings for livestock provided. The report firstly considers the effects of heat stress directly on livestock, as well as implications of climate change for forage. In all these cases, research is under way to improve and advance findings with more specificity, and this will be detailed further in the conclusion of the section.

All four of the projected climate futures described in LTAS (see above) indicate higher projected temperatures (and current work in progress by the author on an updated set of dynamical downscalings shows similar findings). We measure heat stress for livestock in a number of ways, but a common methodology is to use the Temperature Humidity Index (THI), effectively combining heat stress and humidity in a way that represents real discomfort to livestock (as well as humans) (Archer van Garderen, 2011; Nesamvuni et al., 2012; Sirohi and Michaelowa, 2007). In a literature review considering the range of critical thresholds for livestock, Archer van Garderen (2011) found that 72 THI constitutes the comfort threshold for certain types of cattle breeds (in particular, US Holsteins – see Sanchez et al., 2009; Ravagnolo et al., 2000; and Freitas et al., 2006, for example), while at 28°C ambient temperature and high humidity, heat stress begins to affect most breeds (Archer van Garderen, 2011; Agricultural Information Centre, Government of Alberta, personal communication); 32°C constitutes a generally recognized comfort threshold for most cattle breeds, while 78 THI represents a 'critical limit for every kind of livestock' (DEA, 2013b: 30; Archer van Garderen, 2011).

Work by Nesamvuni et al. (2012) and Archer van Garderen (2011) shows the likelihood of exceeding THI thresholds and ambient temperature heat stress thresholds in the future for the full range of climate scenarios, and the four sets of climate futures in LTAS are particularly concerning in this regard, as mentioned earlier. For example, Archer van Garderen (2011) shows areas newly exceeding a 30°C threshold drawn from the published literature, using older Regional Climate Model projections, in particular the Northern Cape Province of South Africa, bordering Namibia – a key area for livestock production. It should be noted, as noted in previous sections, that much of this area (although not all), is in the process of transitioning, or has transitioned to game production. Many species critical for game meat are also sensitive to heat stress, however, and work currently in progress at the University of the Witwatersrand should produce useful thresholds in this regard, given the aforementioned growing centrality of the sector in livestock production in South Africa and SADC. Thresholds for sheep and goats are less well understood (notwithstanding recent studies on angora, for example; Hetem et al., 2011); but a series of studies are currently under way to measure real effects of changes in temperature and precipitation on liveweight, reproduction and feeding patterns.

DEA (2013b) detail further findings for other livestock sectors, including critical impacts of heat stress for broilers (for example, increased in energy consumption for additional ventilation, constituting a significant change in input costs for the industry) and for pigs (with impacts on growth rates, and some recommendations for adaptation; ibid.: 32).

Finally, in the case of forage, a small working group are currently working to develop a revised carrying capacity map for South Africa and the SADC region (drawing on earlier work in this regard), with a renewed focus on climate relationships with forage availability in the form of dry matter productivity (DMP). Preliminary findings (Maluleke, 2014) show the November–December– January–February–March (NDJFM) period of rainfall as the best predictor in certain areas tested for Limpopo of DMP; and further predictive modelling is now being undertaken. DMP would generally be converted to the general measurement of carrying capacity, livestock standard unit per hectare (DEA, 2013b: 31; Maluleke, 2014).

The intention here is to both understand longer term implications of climate change for carrying capacity (drawing on the substantive previous work already undertaken in this area) and to develop a tailored forecast suite for livestock, including predictions of carrying capacity changes on a seasonal timescale (Maluleke, 2014). It is of interest to note that, although tailored forecasting for staple crops, as well as understanding of longer term climate change for staple crops, is fairly well developed, the livestock sector has been somewhat underserved in this regard. Although a predictive forage product was available for the livestock sector until a few years ago, for a variety of reasons it has not, for example, been available in recent years, and research described here comprises one attempt to redress this, in both a research and operational sense.

In conclusion, all above changes are likely to impact more severely on South Africa's emerging agriculture sector, due to (among other issues) fewer resources to adapt, including access to information and advisory services, as well as generally fewer options to diversify (into, for example, game production). In South Africa's Second National Communication reporting to the UNFCCC, the emerging agricultural sector was regarded as a priority area of concern, with an accordant call on planners and policymakers to ensure that any (sorely needed) improvements to extension and advisory services include capacity building around climate change and risk, and to focus on emerging agriculture. South Africa is, at the time of writing, starting the process of planning for their Third National Communication, and this recommendation is only expected to be made more strongly.

Managing a fragile future

In this chapter, we have shown how livestock production in South Africa finds itself within a changing environment, both in terms of external changes experienced (particularly in the last 20 years, post-apartheid) and in terms of a changing climate. Further, key trends within the livestock sector itself, such as the continued rise of game production and changes in tastes in meat consumption, place the sector at a particularly critical and interesting point in developing adaptive capacity in responding to external changes. A detailed assessment of the adaption options recommended for the livestock sector is beyond the scope of the chapter, but will be detailed in future (and ongoing) work.

Briefly, however, government and the private sector have focused on how to improve advice to and market access for the emerging agricultural sector, improving, for example, both climatic and market information available to emerging livestock farmers to allow for more resilient decision-making. Further work has focused on balancing the need for high productivity in species selection with the need for increased resilience to climatic and associated pest/pathogen changes; given some of the environmental changes detailed here. Lastly, the rise of wildlife ranches and the game meat industry provides both challenges and opportunities for the livestock sector, not least in terms of uneven knowledge regarding appropriate game and ranching techniques for sustainable farming (both in terms of economic and environmental sustainability). As consumption and markets change, and the industry experiences increasing levels of climate risk, accessible and usable knowledge that may further improve this sector's resilience will become increasingly necessary.

Note

1 Downscaling techniques effectively translate changes in large-scale atmospheric circulation (such as those typically better captured by Global Climate Models) to finer spatial scales (Tadross et al., 2011: 28).

References

Archer, E. R. M. (2004) 'Beyond the "climate versus grazing" impasse: Using remote sensing to investigate the effects of grazing system choice on vegetation cover in the eastern Karoo', *Journal of Arid Environments*, vol 57, no 3, pp. 381–408

Archer van Garderen, E. R. M. (2011) '(Re) considering cattle farming in southern Africa under a changing climate', *Weather, Climate, and Society*, vol 3, no 4, pp. 249–253.

Bekker, J. L., Hoffman, L. C. and Jooste, P. J. (2011) 'Knowledge of stakeholders in the game meat industry and its effect on compliance with food safety standards', *International Journal of Environmental Health Research*, vol 21, no 5, pp. 341–363

Brand, S. S., Christodoulou, N. T., Van Rooyen, C. J. and Vink, N. (1991) *Agriculture and distribution: A growth with equity approach*, Development Bank of South Africa unpublished paper, Halfway House, Midrand

Bundy, C. (1979) *The Rise and Fall of the South African Peasantry*, University of California Press, Berkeley, CA

Cell, J. W. (1982) *The Highest Stage of White Supremacy: The Origins of Segregation in South Africa and in the American South*, Cambridge University Press, Cambridge

Cooper, D. (1983) 'Looking at development projects', *Work in Progress*, no 26, pp 29–37

Cooper, D. (1988) *Working the Land: A Review of Agriculture in South Africa*, Environmental and Development Agency, Westro Productions, Johannesburg

D'Amato, M. E., Alechine, E., Cloete, K. W., Davison, S. and Corach, D. (2013) 'Where is the game? Wild meat products authentication in South Africa: A case study', *Investigative Genetics*, vol 4, no 1, pp. 1–13

DAFF (2013) www.nda.agric.za/publications/publications.asp?category=Statistical+information

DEA (2000) *Abstract of Agricultural Statistics*. Government Printer, Pretoria

DEA (2013a) *Long Term Adaptation Scenarios Flagship Research Programme (LTAS) for South Africa: Climate Trends and Scenarios for South Africa*, Department of Environmental Affairs, Pretoria

DEA (2013b) *Long Term Adaptation Scenarios Flagship Research Programme (LTAS) for South Africa: Climate Change Implications for the Agriculture and Forestry Sectors in South Africa*, Department of Environmental Affairs, Pretoria

Engelbrecht, C., Engelbrecht, F. and Dyson, L. (2013) 'High-resolution model-projected changes in mid-tropospheric closed-lows and extreme rainfall events over southern Africa', *International Journal of Climatology*, vol 33, no 1, pp. 173–187

Engelbrecht, F., McGregor, J. and Engelbrecht, C. (2009) 'Dynamics of the conformal–cubic atmospheric model projected climate-change signal over southern Africa', *International Journal of Climatology*, vol 29, no 7, pp. 1013–1033

Fernandez, R. J., Archer, E. R. M., Ash, A. J., Dowlatabadi, H., Hiernaux, P. H. Y., Reynolds, J. F., Vogel, C. H., Walker, B. H. and Wiegand, T. (2002) 'Degradation and recovery in socio-ecological systems: a view from the household/farm level', in J. F. Reynolds and D. M. Stafford Smith (eds), *Global Desertification: Do Humans Cause Deserts?*, pp. 297–323, Dahlem University Press, Berlin

Freitas, M. S., Misztal, I., Bohmanova, J. and West, J. (2006) 'Utility of on- and off-farm weather records for studies in genetics of heat tolerance' *Livestock Science*, vol 105, pp. 223–228

Hall, R. and Du Toit, A. 2014. 'Smoke and mirrors in government's farm worker policy', 15 April 2014, PLAAS, www.plaas.org.za/blog/smoke-and-mirrors-government%E2%80%99s-farm-worker-policy, accessed July 2014

Hetem, R. S., de Witt, B. A., Fick, L. G., Fuller, A., Maloney, S. K., Meyer, L. C. R., Mitchell, D. and Kerley, G. I. H. (2011) 'Effects of desertification on the body temperature, activity and water turnover of Angora goats', *Journal of Arid Environments*, vol 75, no 1, pp. 20–28

Hewitson, B. and Crane, R (2006) 'Consensus between GCM climate change projections with empirical downscaling: precipitation downscaling over South Africa', *International Journal of Climatology*, vol 26, no 10, pp. 1315–1337.

Holmes, T. (2013) 'Growing wealth helps SA make both ends "meat"', *Mail and Guardian*, 13 September 2013; www.mg.co.za, accessed July 2014

Land and Agriculture Policy Centre (1993) 'Debt relief and the South African drought relief programme: An overview', unpublished policy paper # 1, LAPC, Johannesburg

Lemon, A. (1987) *Apartheid in Transition*, Westview Press. Boulder CO

Levin, R. and Weiner, D. (eds) (1997) *No More Tears: Struggles for Land in Mpumalanga, South Africa*, Africa World Press, Trenton, Asmara

Lipton, M. (1977) 'South Africa: Two Agricultures?', in D. Hendrie, A. Kooy and F. Wilson (eds), *Farm Labour in South Africa*, David Phillip, Cape Town

Mabin, A. (1991) 'The impact of apartheid on rural areas of South Africa', *Antipode*, no 23, pp. 33–47

Maluleke, P. (2014) 'Using seasonal forecasts and remote sensing products to estimate a dynamically adjusted carrying capacity output for Limpopo Province', Presentation at Agricultural Research Council PDP Conference, 27 June 2014, Agricultural Research Council, Pretoria

Nesamvuni, E., Lekalakala, R., Norris, D. and Ngambi, J. W. (2012) 'Effects of climate change on dairy cattle, South Africa', *African Journal of Agricultural Research*, vol 7, no 26, pp. 3867–3872.

Ravagnolo, O., Misztal, I. and Hoogenboom, G. (2000) 'Genetic component of heat stress in dairy cattle, development of heat index function', *Journal of Dairy Science*, vol 83, no 9, pp. 2120–2125

Republic of South Africa. (1995) *White Paper on Agriculture*, Government Printer, Pretoria

Sanchez, J. P., Miztal, I., Aguilar, I., Zumbach, B. and Rekaya, R. (2009) 'Genetic determination of the onset of heat stress on daily milk production in US Holstein cattle', *Journal of Dairy Science*, vol 92, no 8, pp. 4035–4045

Sirohi, S. and Michaelowa, A. (2007) 'Sufferer and cause: Indian livestock and climate change', *Climatic Change*, vol 85, nos 3–4, pp. 285–298

Tadross, M., Davis, C., Engelbrecht, F., Joubert, A. and Archer van Garderen, E. (2011) 'Regional scenarios of future climate change over southern Africa' in C. Davis (ed.), *Climate Risk and Vulnerability: a handbook for Southern Africa*, CSIR, Pretoria

Taljaard, P. R., Jooste, A. and Asfaha, T. A. (2006) 'Towards a broader understanding of South African consumer spending on meat', *Agrekon*, vol 45, no 2, pp. 214–224

Van der Merwe, M., Jooste, P. J. and Hoffman, L. C. (2011) 'Application of European standards for health and quality control of game meat on game ranches in South Africa', *Journal of the South African Veterinary Association*, vol 82, no 3, pp. 170–175

Van Schalkwyk, D. L., McMillin, K. W., Booyse, M., Witthuhn, R. C. and Hoffman, L. C. (2011) 'Physico-chemical, microbiological, textural and sensory attributes of matured game salami produced from springbok (Antidorcas marsupialis), gemsbok (Oryx gazella), kudu (Tragelaphus strepsiceros) and zebra (Equus burchelli) harvested in Namibia', *Meat Science*, vol 88, no 1, pp. 36–44

Van Zyl, J. and Van Rooyen, J. (1991) 'Agricultural production in South Africa', chapter 9 in M. de Klerk (ed.), *A Harvest of Discontent: The Land Question in South Africa*, Institute for a Democratic Alternative for South Africa (IDASA), Cape Town

Van Zyl, J., Biswanger, H. P. and Kirsten, J. F. (eds) (1996) *Agricultural Land Reform in South Africa: Policies, Markets and Mechanisms*, Oxford University Press, Oxford

Vink, N. and Kassier, E. (1991) 'Agricultural policy and the South African state', chapter 10 in M. de Klerk (ed.), *A Harvest of Discontent: The Land Question in South Africa*, Institute for a Democratic Alternative for South Africa (IDASA), Cape Town

Vink, N. and Kirsten, J. (2000) *Deregulation of Agricultural Marketing in South Africa: Lessons Learned*, Free Market Foundation Monograph 25, Free Market Foundation of Southern Africa, Sandton

Vink, N. and Kirsten, J. (2003) 'Agriculture in the national economy', chapter 1 in L. Nieuwoudt and J. Groenewald (eds), *The Challenge of Change: Agriculture, Land and the South African Economy*, University of Natal Press, Scottsville

Vogel, C. H. (1994) 'Consequences of droughts in southern Africa (1960–1992)', PhD thesis, University of the Witwatersrand, Johannesburg

Wilson, F. (1991) 'A land out of balance', in M. Ramphele and C. McDowell (eds), *Restoring the Land: environment and change in post-apartheid Africa*, pp. 27–38, Panos Institute, London

PART II

Environmental justice and meat production/ consumption

6

MEAT AND INEQUALITY

Environmental health consequences of livestock agribusiness

Ryan Gunderson

Introduction

Large-scale, intensive, industrial, corporate livestock production ('factory farming') has increased steadily in all livestock sectors in the last half-century (MacDonald and McBride, 2009). The shift toward concentrated animal feeding operations (CAFOs) is a global trend expected to increase in both developed and developing regions (FAO, 2006). Today, in the United States, the great majority of animal products and by-products derive from huge feedlots. These have raised various ethical, social, and environmental concerns.

In addition to the barbarous treatment experienced by animals, contemporary livestock rearing practices have been shown to lead to various physical, social, and mental human health problems. Many of the health consequences are an outcome of CAFO and abattoir environmental pollutants. However, the global poor, workers, and marginalized rural communities disproportionately endure the environmental and general public health consequences of livestock agribusiness. This chapter demonstrates that the public health consequences of livestock agribusiness span environmental and social justice concerns. The movement for a sustainable and just food system necessitates communication and teamwork between environmental and social justice advocates.

Grain and the global poor

With the rise of corporate livestock production, global meat consumption has also steadily risen in developed and developing regions (Cunningham et al., 2005). However, the rise in consumption is uneven across regions and classes. As meat consumption increased in the United States it became 'identified with "the American way of life",' resulting in a 'dietary modernization' for the wealthy of developing countries (i.e. a shift from grain-based diets to meat-based diets) (McMichael, 2008, p74). The global poor are dependent on cereal grains for sustenance. Thus, the global redistribution of cropland use from human food to the animal feed needed to support intensive, grain-based feedlots reallocates food from the poor to the rich. Walker et al. (2005) have illustrated the most glaring health contradiction of this global shift in diet: one billion people are overweight or obese largely due to increased meat consumption (as animal products are the primary source of saturated fats) while one billion people are malnourished due to reduced crop availability to sustain increased meat consumption for the wealthy.

The general, though unequally distributed, global increase in meat consumption has had dramatic effects on global human health for both the global poor (decreased food crop availability) and the more prosperous (increased saturated fat consumption). Further, increased meat production perpetuates corporate livestock production as it 'provides artificially cheap meat for the consumer, and the consumer demand in turn fuels the IAP [industrial animal production] system' (Walker et al., 2005, p354). This association preserves and deepens the environmentally unsustainable practices of corporate livestock production (FAO, 2006) and, in turn, generates further consequences for human health (see Figure 6.1).

Feed production, nitrogen, and pesticides

The amount of nitrogen needed to grow feedstuffs has increased dramatically with intensive corporate farming practices. For instance, half of the grain produced in the United States is fed to livestock (Howarth et al., 2002). These demands are supplied largely by synthetic chemical fertilizer production. Much of the synthetic nitrogen created is inefficiently absorbed by feed crops and animals and ends up in the air and water through leaching, misapplication of manure to the land, runoff, and manure lagoon overflows and leaks (Burkholder et al., 2007). Concentrations of nitrogen oxides in the air are linked to reactive airways disease, coughs, asthma, reductions in lung function, chronic respiratory disease, and respiratory tract

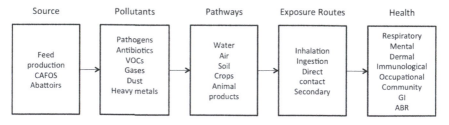

FIGURE 6.1 Livestock production's environmental health impact.

VOCs: volatile organic compounds. GI: gastrointestinal disorder. ABR: antibiotic-resistant organisms.

Source: Adapted from Walker et al. (2005)

inflammation (Chameides et al., 1994; Townsend et al., 2003). The nitrate that ends up in groundwater down the 'nitrogen cascade' (Galloway, 1998) can lead to reproductive problems, methemoglobinemia (especially in infants, i.e. 'blue-baby' syndrome), and various cancers (Townsend et al., 2003). Further, more pesticides are needed for increased feed production (FAO, 2006). Pesticides harm human health by increasing the risks of poisoning, cancer, and immune, reproductive, and nervous system damage through direct contact or through food and water contamination (Walker et al., 2005).

Water, food, and feces

Nitrate is only one of the many hazards found in the 133 million tons of livestock manure excreted every year in the US (13 times more than that produced by humans) (United States Environmental Protection Agency, 1998). Animal manure contains various zoonotic bacterial and viral pathogens that can be ingested by humans via animal products and contaminated drinking water. Zoonotic pathogens are highly correlated with the cramped and unsanitary conditions in CAFOs and abattoirs that operate at very high, deregulated speeds (Horrigan et al., 2002).

Because *Escherichia coli* O157:H7 (*E. coli*) infections are so deadly, *E. coli* is one of the more well-known pathogens related to livestock production, though it is not common (62,000 US illnesses a year) (Mead et al., 1999). *E. coli* can cause bloody diarrhea, irritable bowel syndrome, seizures, comas, high blood pressure, severe kidney damage, and death. Usually originating from cattle manure, *E. coli* can contaminate drinking water via runoff or end up in food. Collecting over 1,000 food samples from various retail markets, Minnesota medical researchers found that almost 70 percent of the pork and beef samples and over 90 percent of the poultry samples were contaminated with fecal matter (Johnson et al., 2005). More worryingly, *E. coli* bacteria were found in almost half of the poultry samples. Cargill Meat Solutions (one of the largest beef cattle firms) was recently forced to recall thousands of pounds of beef (Neuman, 2010a).

Salmonella and *Campylobacter* illnesses are much more common than *E. coli*, with 3 million US foodborne illnesses a year (Mead et al., 1999). *Salmonella* and *Campylobacter*, originating from chickens, can contaminate food through feces, leading to diarrhea, stomach pains, and, less commonly, death. Just recently, Wright County Egg (a huge firm with multiple CAFO units) was forced to recall millions of eggs due to *Salmonella* contamination (Neuman, 2010b).

Bovine spongiform encephalopathy (BSE) ('mad cow disease') (Creutzfeldt-Jakob disease in human form) and H1N1 ('swine flu') recently infected thousands and scared millions. BSE was created by making cattle into cannibals via meat and bone meal – a practice originating from intensive operations to cut costs (UCS, 2006). Schmidt (2009) has speculated that the H1N1 outbreak evolved due to factory farming and may have originated from a Mexican factory farm, but there is still not enough conclusive evidence showing where the strain developed.

Heavy metals, phosphorus, hormones, and pharmaceuticals have all been found in drinking and recreational water due to CAFOs (Barker and Zublena, 1995; Boxall et al., 2003; Raman et al., 2004; FAO, 2006). Heavy metals are used as growth promoters in feedstuffs and are not absorbed well by livestock. Copper, zinc, arsenic, cobalt, iron, manganese, cadmium, and selenium are commonly added to livestock feed, accumulate in their waste, and can cause various dermal, nervous, and immune disorders when ingested and accumulated by humans (FAO, 2006). Next to pathogens and nitrate, the mass amounts of veterinary pharmaceuticals used for animals in intensive operations are one of the leading concerns of livestock production-related public health issues.

The (mis)use of pharmaceuticals

It is estimated that over 70 percent of all antibiotics manufactured in the United States are used for producing livestock (UCS, 2001). The massive amount of veterinary pharmaceuticals used in intensive livestock production is to keep food animals 'healthy' in the extremely crowded and filthy conditions where they grow (therapeutic use) and to promote rapid tissue growth (nontherapeutic use) (Gaskins et al., 2002). The great majority of antibiotics used in livestock production are for nontherapeutic purposes (UCS, 2001). Because many of the antibiotics used for livestock are related to antibiotics used to treat humans, scientists and the United Nations are growing increasingly concerned about more quickly developing and more diverse antibiotic-resistant strains of bacteria (World Health Organization, 1997; UCS, 2001; Bonfoh et al., 2010); however more research is needed to determine the long-term impacts of exposure (Burkholder et al., 2007).

Workers and the surrounding community

Livestock agribusiness has consistently shown to negatively affect rural community well-being: firms avoid local taxes, reduce housing market prices, and shut down operations when markets are bad, leaving contract farmers with overhead costs (Lobao and Meyer, 2001). Further, CAFOs are usually unwanted by rural communities and are disproportionately placed in low-income areas with less political influence (Donham et al., 2007). Thus, poor communities penetrated by CAFOs further suffer economically through lessened property values and the 'proletarianization' of small farmers through unbalanced and unjust contractual agreements (Lewontin, 2000). These communities have been shown to be at greater risks for various physical, mental, and social health problems due to neighboring CAFOs (Donham et al., 2007). In North Carolina, physical health problems associated with high-density livestock production include respiratory problems due to increased exposure to air pollution (Reynolds et al., 1997; Thu et al., 1997). Increased rates of post-traumatic stress disorder, anxiety, and depression have been linked to the economic stressors and declining quality of life caused by neighboring CAFOs

(Schiffman et al., 1995; Bullers, 2005). The leading social health impact associated with high-density livestock production areas is the impact on quality of life due to the foul and far-ranging odors emitted by CAFOs (Donham et al., 2007). Communities that once depended on outdoor activities for identity formation and networking must now take cover indoors due to the overwhelming smell. As Donham et al. (2007, p318) stated, '[h]omes are no longer an extension of or a means for enjoying the outdoors. Rather, homes become a barrier against the outdoors that must be escaped.'

CAFO workers, most without adequate or any health care, experience a vile work environment of manure gases (including ammonia), odors, bacteria, and dust (Osterberg and Wallinga, 2002). Due to these unsanitary conditions, up to 30 percent of CAFO workers suffer from respiratory diseases (Horrigan et al., 2002). The conditions for slaughterhouse workers have not fundamentally improved since Upton Sinclair's (1906/1981) century-old critique. To increase profits, slaughterhouses operate at dangerously quick tempos without suitable protective equipment and workers experience high rates of injury and repetitive motion syndrome (Eisnitz, 2007).

Toward a healthy food and social system

As this chapter has shown, the environmental health problems created by livestock production are unequally distributed due to, and perpetuated by, social stratification. Thus, to achieve the goal of a sustainable agriculture – sustainable for the environment, humans, and animals – would also mean confronting the unjust social formation that preserves these environmental health impacts. A growing body of literature shows that a truly sustainable food system may need to eliminate the production of meat altogether (Fox, 1999; Leitzmann, 2003; Stănescu, 2010). In opposition to the growing global thirst for meat, these scholars have claimed that a healthy and ecologically sound agriculture would include universal vegetarianism as a consumptive counterpart. Indeed, a recent United Nations Environmental Programme (2010) report has concluded that the current patterns of production and consumption of meat are simply unsustainable and advises a shift from animal-based diets to plant-based diets.

Social and environmental justice advocates must struggle to remove corporate livestock production from the food system. This potential may lie outside the limits of a socioeconomic system that values profit-maximization more than health. Thus, the push for a healthy, plant-based, and sustainable food system is fastened to the push for a healthy and *just* social system. As the critical theorist Max Horkheimer (1947, p177) declared over 60 years ago, '[t]he subjugation of nature will revert to the subjugation of man, and vice versa, as long as man does not understand his own reason and the basic process by which he has created and is maintaining the antagonism that is about to destroy him.'

Conclusions

The public health consequences of corporate livestock production are substantial. Increased meat consumption increases saturated fat consumption, which is linked to heart problems, diabetes, stroke, and cancer. The mass amount of feed grain demanded by intensive livestock production not only further contributes to the health risks associated with nitrate and pesticide leaching and contamination, but also robs food grain from the poorest people in world. The filthy conditions at CAFO sites due to the concentration of animal manure are related to various waterborne and foodborne zoonotic pathogens. The massive use of veterinary pharmaceuticals, utilized mostly for growth promotion, is associated with antibiotic-resistant pathogens. The rural communities with CAFOs are at increased risk for various physical, social, and mental health problems. CAFO and livestock processing workers are subjected to filthy and unsafe working conditions with low pay and few health benefits.

The health consequences of factory farming require attention from public health researchers, policymakers, and social and environmental justice advocates. The negative health consequences associated with corporate livestock production extend across environmental and social justice concerns. As the public health consequences are experienced disproportionately by marginalized communities, social justice advocates must collaborate with environmental justice advocates in promoting and creating a more just and sustainable food system founded around meeting the needs of both humans and the rest of the biosphere.

References

Barker, J. C. and Zublena, J. P. (1995) 'Livestock manure nutrient assessment in North Carolina', North Carolina Agricultural Extension Service, https://www.bae.ncsu.edu/bae/extension/ext-publications/waste/animal/ebae-170-93-livestock-ass-nc.pdf, accessed 24 October 2014

Bonfoh, B., Schwabenbauer, K., Wallinga, D., Hartung, J., Schelling, E., Zinsstag, J., Meslin, F., Tschopp, R., Akakpo, J. A. and Tanner, M. (2010) 'Human health hazards associated with livestock production', in H. Steinfeld, H. A. Mooney, F. Schneider and L. E. Neville (eds), *Livestock in a Changing Landscape*, vol 1, Island Press, Washington, DC

Boxall, A. B., Kolpin, D. W., Halling-Sørensen, B. and Tolls, J. (2003) 'Are veterinarian medicines causing environmental risks?', *Environmental Science & Technology*, vol 37, no 15, pp. 286A–294A

Bullers, S. (2005) 'Environmental stressors, perceived control, and health: The case of residents near large-scale hog farms in eastern North Carolina', *Human Ecology*, vol 33, no 1, pp. 1–16

Burkholder, J., Libra, B., Weyer, P., Heahcote, S., Kolpin, D., Thorne, P. S. and Wichman, M. (2007) 'Impacts of waste from concentrated animal feeding operations on water quality', *Environmental Health Perspectives*, vol 115, no 2, pp. 308–312

Chameides, W. L., Kasibhatla, P. S., Yienger, J. and Levy II, H. (1994) 'Growth of continental-scale metro-agro-plexes, regional ozone pollution, and world food production', *Science*, vol 264, pp. 74–77

Cunningham, M., Latour, M. A. and Acker, D. (2005) *Animal Science and Industry*, Pearson Prentice Hall, Upper Saddle River, NJ

Donham, K. J., Wing, S., Osterberg, D., Flora, J. L., Hodne, C., Thu, K. M. and Thorne, P. S. (2007) 'Community health and socioeconomic issues surrounding concentrated animal feeding operations', *Environmental Health Perspectives*, vol 115, no 2, pp. 317–320

Eisnitz, G. (2007) *Slaughterhouse: The Shocking Story of Greed, Neglect, and Inhumane Treatment Inside the U.S. Meat Industry*, Prometheus Books, Amherst, NY

FAO (2006) *Livestock's Long Shadow: Environmental Issues and Options*, FAO, Rome

Fox, M. A. (1999) 'The contribution of vegetarianism to ecosystem health', *Ecosystem Health*, vol 5, no 2, pp. 70–74

Galloway, J. N. (1998) 'The global nitrogen cycle: Changes and consequences', *Environmental Pollution*, vol 102, pp. 15–24

Gaskins, H. R., Collier, C. T. and Anderson, D. B. (2002) 'Antibiotics as growth promoters: Mode of action', *Animal Biotechnology*, vol 13, pp. 29–42

Horkheimer, M. (1947) *Eclipse of Reason*, Continuum, New York

Horrigan, L., Lawrence, R. S. and Walker, P. (2002) 'How sustainable agriculture can address the environmental and human health harms of industrial agriculture', *Environmental Health Perspectives*, vol 110, no 5, pp. 445–456

Howarth, R. W., Boyer, E. W., Pabich, W. J. and Galloway, J. N. (2002) 'Nitrogen use in the United States from 1961–2000 and potential future trends', *Ambio*, vol 31, no 2, pp. 88–96

Johnson, J. R., Kuskowski, M. A., Smith, K., O'Bryan, T. T. and Tatini, S. (2005) 'Antimicrobial-resistant and extraintestinal pathogenic *Escherichia coli* in retail foods', *The Journal of Infectious Diseases*, vol 191, pp. 1040–1049

Leitzmann, C. (2003) 'Nutrition ecology: The contribution of vegetarian diets', *The American Journal of Clinical Nutrition*, vol 78, no 3, pp. 657S–659S

Lewontin, R. C. (2000) 'The maturing of capitalist agriculture. Farmer as proletarian', in F. Magdoff, J. B. Foster, and F. H. Buttel (eds), *Hungry for Profit: The Agribusiness Threat to Farmers, Food, and the Environment*, Monthly Review Press, New York

Lobao, L. and Meyer, K. (2001) 'The great agricultural transition: Crisis, change, and social consequences of twentieth century US farming', *Annual Review of Sociology*, vol 27, pp. 103–124

MacDonald, J. M. and McBride, W. D. (2009) 'The transformation of U.S. livestock agriculture: Scale, efficiency, and risks', United States Department of Agriculture, Economic Research Service, EIB-43

McMichael, P. (2008) *Development and Social Change: A Global Perspective*, Pine Forge Press, Los Angeles, CA

Mead, P. S., Slutsker, L., Dietz, V., McCaig, L. F., Bresee, J. S., Shapiro, C., Griffin, P. M. and Tauxe, R. V. (1999) 'Food-related illness and death in the United States', *Emerging Infectious Diseases*, vol 5, no 5, pp. 607–625

Neuman, W. (2010a) 'Beef recall heats up fight to tighten rules', *New York Times*, 2 September, www.nytimes.com/2010/09/03/business/03beef.html?_r=0, accessed 24 October 2014

Neuman, W. (2010b) 'Egg recall expanded after salmonella outbreak', *New York Times*, 18 August, www.nytimes.com/2010/08/19/business/19eggs.html, accessed 24 October 2014

Osterberg, D. and Wallinga, D. (2002) 'Addressing externalities from swine production to reduce public health and environmental impacts', *American Journal of Public Health*, vol 94, no 10, pp. 1703–1708

Raman, D. R., Williams, E. L., Layton, A. C., Burns, R. T., Easter, J. P., Daugherty, A. S., Mullen, M. D. and Sayler, G. S. (2004) 'Estrogen content of dairy and swine wastes', *Environmental Science & Technology*, vol 38, no 13, pp. 3567–3573

Reynolds, S. J., Donham, K. J., Stookesberry, J., Thorne, P. S., Subramanian, P., Thu, K. and Whitten, M. S. (1997) 'Air quality assessments in the vicinity of swine production facilities', *Journal of Agromedicine*, vol 4, nos 1 and 2, pp. 37–45

Schiffman, S. S., Sattely Miller, E. A., Suggs, M. S. and Graham, B. G. (1995) 'The effect of environmental odors emanating from commercial swine operations on the mood of nearby residents', *Brain Research Bulletin*, vol 37, no 4, pp. 369–375

Schmidt, C. W. (2009) 'Swine CAFOs & novel H1N1 flu: Separating facts from fears', *Environmental Health Perspectives*, vol 117, no 9, A394–A401

Sinclair, U. (1906/1981) *The Jungle*, Bantam Books, New York

Stănescu, V. (2010). '"Green" eggs and ham? The myth of sustainable agriculture', *Journal for Critical Animal Studies*, vol 8, no 1/2, 8–32

Thu, K. K., Ziegenhorn, D. R., Reynolds, S., Thorne, P. S., Subramanian, P., Whitten, P. and Stookesberry, J. (1997) 'A control study of the physical and mental health of residents living near a large-scale swine operation', *Journal of Agricultural Safety and Health*, vol 3, no 1, pp. 13–26

Townsend, A. R., Howarth, R. W., Bazzaz, F. A., Booth, M. S., Cleveland, C. C., Collinge, S. K., Dobson, A. P., Epstein, P. R., Holland, E. A., Keeney, D. R., Mallin, M. A., Rogers, C. A., Wayne, P. and Wolfe, A. H. (2003) 'Human health effects of a changing global nitrogen cycle', *Frontiers in Ecology and the Environment*, vol 1, no 5, 240–246

UCS (2001) 'Hogging it! Estimates of antimicrobial abuse in livestock', www.ucsusa. org/sites/default/files/legacy/assets/documents/food_and_agriculture/hog_front.pdf, accessed 24 October 2014

UCS (2006) 'They eat what? The reality of feed at animal factories', www.ucsusa.org/ food_and_agriculture/science_and_impacts/impacts_industrial_agriculture/they-eat-what-the-reality-of.html, accessed 2 July 2011

United Nations Environmental Programme (2010) 'Energy and agriculture top resource panel's priority list for sustainable 21st century', www.unep.org/Documents. Multilingual/Default.asp?DocumentID=628&ArticleID=6595&l=en&t=long, accessed 24 October 2014

United States Environmental Protection Agency (1998) 'Environmental impacts of animal feeding operations', 1998, www.epa.gov/waterscience/guide/feedlots/envimpct.pdf, accessed 2 July 2011

Walker, P. P., Rhubart-Berg, P., McKenzie, S., Kelling, K. and Lawrence, R. S. (2005) 'Public health implications of meat production and consumption', *Public Health Nutrition*, vol 8, no 4, pp. 348–356

World Health Organization(1997) 'Antibiotic use in food-producing animals must be curtailed to prevent increased resistance in humans', Press Release, *WHO/73*, WHO, Geneva

7

CAN'T GO TO THE FOUNTAIN NO MORE

Pigs, nitrates and spring water pollution in Catalonia

David Saurí and Hug March

Introduction: Nature and culture of public springs in Catalonia

Images of people carrying containers of all sorts and sizes full with spring water back to their car before returning to the city stand among some of the more common memories of Catalan weekenders of the last decades. That 'water from the fountain' was to be used during the week for drinking purposes in the metropolitan households as heavily chlorinated tap water, although suitable for human consumption according to health standards, smelled and tasted unpleasant. The following weekend, long lines along the most reputed (and accessible by car) fountains and springs would be formed again so this popular appropriation of 'natural water' would continue one week more. Water from these springs was highly appreciated for its properties (including above all taste), most notably in fountains and springs flowing from aquifers in fractured crystalline formations, preferred to the 'harder' waters coming from calcareous formations.

Going to the fountain with containers to store water was, however, just the more recent example of the long-standing tradition of the relationship between Catalans and one of their most cherished environments. Because of the quantity and purity of their watercourses, springs and, especially emblematic fountains, were also spaces of religious and secular celebrations, such as the so-called *Aplecs* (literally 'gatherings') or public festivals celebrating local patron saints or virgins. In this way, fountains became part of the natural and cultural heritage and in some cases decorated fountains and their environs produced remarkable works of artistic landscaping.

The busy Sunday afternoons at the fountains accessible by car began to wane somehow as cheap bottled water (sometimes of dubious quality) slowly substituted for spring water beginning in the 1980s. Later in the decade and especially during the 1990s and 2000s a more dramatic problem drastically reduced the number of fountain users. Many fountains, especially in central Catalonia, began to carry warning signs stating that the water was not suitable for drinking anymore. Even renowned fountains ancestrally used by people of certain towns (such as the 'Fountain of the Virgin' in the town of Manlleu; see Figure 7.1) would no longer provide drinking water to the citizens as they had done for hundreds of years. The reason for such a failure lay in the discovery of abnormally high concentrations of nitrates in the water, many times above the maximum level of 50 mg/l mandated in European water quality regulations. Subsequently, many fountains were closed down and lost their status as privileged sources of drinking water. Occasionally this led to paradoxical situations such as that of the 'Fountain of the Virgin' in the town of Manlleu cited above. In this case, the traditional fountain (lower picture, Figure 7.1) carries the warning sign of 'non-potable water' while a brass tap releases water coming from the municipal network and therefore 'drinkable' (upper picture, Figure 7.1).

Soon it was discovered that the source of nitrate pollution of groundwater in many areas of central Catalonia was pig manure spread in agricultural or pasture fields and infiltrating with rainwater into soils and aquifers. The tremendous growth in the number and size of pig farms since the 1980s had created a typical externality problem of a gigantic accumulation of pig waste which was deposited on agricultural fields and pastures with no previous treatment. Nitrogen present in pig waste mutates in water into the form of nitrate, which, at certain concentrations, has been associated with several health problems such as methemoglobinemia (or 'blue baby' syndrome) in infants or even stomach cancer (Prat et al., 2011). Hence the strict regulation of admissible concentrations of nitrates in drinking water by health authorities in the European Union and other developed countries. As in other examples, public policies regarding the nitrate problem showed the asymmetry of environmental risk management under neoliberal systems of governance (see Prudham, 2004). Thus by prohibiting the consumption of water from these fountains, regulations were put 'at the end of the pipe' (affecting most people), instead of directly dealing with the origins and causes of the issue (the number of farms and pigs) where they would be seen as a barrier to economic growth, employment, exports, and more specifically local and regional development.

In this chapter the political ecology of water will intersect with the political ecology (and economy) of food production. We will present and characterize one of the many socioenvironmental impacts of intensive meat production such as the pollution of groundwater by nitrates originating in pig manure and their subsequent effects on fountains and springs. Our study area will be Catalonia (northeastern Spain), which is one of the largest producers of pig meat not only of Spain but of Europe as well. More specifically we will illustrate our arguments through the case of Osona County, in central Catalonia, where the issue of aquifer contamination due to pig farming has been especially problematic. The chapter is organized as follows. After this introduction, the next section focuses on the production of pig meat and related products as one of

FIGURE 7.1 The fountain of the Virgin in Manlleu (Osona County, Catalonia).

Source: Daniel Salas and David Saurí

the key components of the Catalan food-processing industry. The third section describes the failure of pig manure management and the subsequent contamination of groundwater especially in the areas with a larger concentration of pig farms. Fourth, we focus specifically on the high levels of nitrate concentration in public fountains in central Catalonia as perhaps the most significant impact, at least in symbolic terms, of this pollution. Fifth, reactions to nitrate pollution by water and agricultural authorities but also by social and environmental groups will also be presented with the aim of showing different ways of dealing with what for many is an intractable problem. Finally, in the concluding section we will attempt to draw some lessons from our case study that might be relevant for an international audience.

Pig meat production as a key component of Catalan food processing industries

According to FAO data, pig meat tops the world production of meat with 109 million tons or over 40 percent of the total in 2010 (FAO, 2012). Asia leads the ranking followed by Europe and North America. At the country level, the most important producers are China (47 percent of the total world production of pig meat in 2010), the United States, Germany and Spain (see Table 7.1).

TABLE 7.1 Production of pork meat by the 10 highest producers in the European Union, 2002–2012 (in thousands tons).

Country	2002	2004	2006	2008	2010	2011	2012	Change 2002–2012 (%)
Germany	4,110	4,308	4,662	5,114	5,443	5,564	5,459	32.82
Spain	3,070	3,076	3,235	3,484	3,369	3,479	3,515	14.51
France	2,350	2,311	2,263	2,277	2,010	1,998	1,957	−16.72
Poland	2,023	1,923	2,071	1,888	1,741	1,811	1,695	−16.22
Denmark	1,759	1,809	1,749	1,707	1,666	1,718	1,603	−8.89
Italy	1,536	1,590	1,556	1,606	1,633	1,570	1,621	5.52
Holland	1,377	1,287	1,265	1,318	1,288	1,347	1,313	−4.62
Belgium	1,044	1,032	1,006	1,056	1,124	1,108	1,110	6.34
United Kingdom	795	720	697	740	774	806	825	3.69
Austria	511	516	505	526	542	544	530	3.57
EU-27	–	–	21,948	22,574	22,011	22,354	21,859	–

Source: own elaboration from data of the Grup de Gestió Porcina (2013a, 2013b)

In the European Union, while the total number of pigs decreased between 2008 and 2010, the production of pig meat continues to grow (some 22 percent between 2001 and 2011) because of the large proportion of fattening pigs within the total pig livestock. Pressures from environmental groups have reduced the pig stock of Holland, Denmark, and other Northern European countries, while in countries such as Spain the number of pigs has increased steadily.

As mentioned above, Spain is the second largest producer of pork meat in Europe after Germany. In 2009 meat products represented over 20 percent of the total added value of food-processing industries in Spain, and half of this 20 percent belonged to the pork sector (Teruel and Uclés, 2011). A small but growing proportion of this figure included Iberian pig breeds, raised in semi-captivity with traditional feed and reputed for the quality of their meat (*Jamón Ibérico*).

With over 6.6 million pigs (see Table 7.2), most of them for fattening in large and capital-intensive farms, Catalonia stands as the most important pig breeder in Spain. In 2012 Catalonia produced some 1.5 million tons of pork meat with an economic value of 1.5 billion euros (IDESCAT, 2012), accounting for almost half (42.5 percent) of the total Spanish pork meat production (MAGRAMA, 2013) as well as representing 70 percent of Spanish pork meat exports (Grup de Gestió Porcina, 2013a). The economic value of pork meat represented 56 percent of the total value of livestock production and almost 35 percent of the total value of the Catalan agricultural sector in the same year (IDESCAT, 2012). Meat and especially pork meat constitute also over one-third of the total value added of the food-processing sector, which is the second largest industrial sector in Catalonia and one of the few that has escaped the devastating crisis and restructuring processes affecting the Catalan industrial sector since 2008. Moreover, food-processing industries have tended to be spatially decentralized in many small and medium firms thus providing an important economic resource for many areas of Catalonia.

In Figure 7.2 we can observe the evolution in the number of pigs as well as the number of pig farms, both in Catalonia, and in the county of Osona, where the impact of pig breeding on water supply and fountains has been more notorious. Over three-quarters of these farms belonged to the so-called 'vertical integrated networks', including from genetic research to distribution to the final consumers,

TABLE 7.2 Composition of the pig livestock, Catalonia, 2012.

Type	Number	Percentage
Piglets (>20 kg)	1,889,548	28.5
Pigs (20–50 kg)	1,667,635	25
Fattening Pigs (>50 kg)	2,569,171	39
Breeding sows	497,792	7.5
Total	6,624,146	100

Source: own elaboration from data of Grup de Gestió Porcina (2013a)

and increasingly concentrated in fewer and fewer firms (Reimer, 2006; Teira Esmatges, 2007). In Catalonia we note a steady increase in the number of pigs since the early 1980s, while in Osona the increase rate was sharper between the 1980s and 1990s but then decreased slightly to around 800,000 pigs. In both cases, and

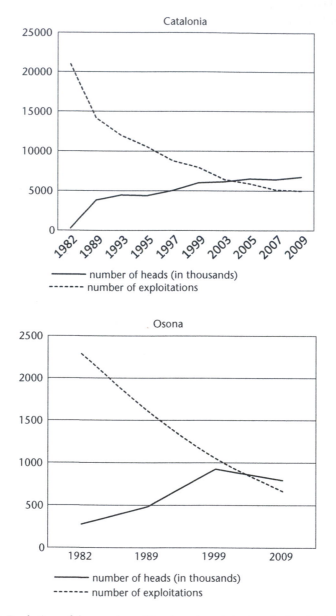

FIGURE 7.2 Evolution of the number of heads and exploitations in Catalonia and Osona, 1982–2009.

Source: own elaboration from data of Institut d'Estadística de Catalunya.

well within European trends, there is a decrease in the number of farms, leading to a concentration of the activity in large and capital-intensive units. In fact, and according to the environmentalist group Grup de Defensa del Ter (GDT) (2014), in the last decade family-run pig farms have decreased some 37 percent, and have been substituted by mega-farms with capacities over 4,000 pigs, very intensive in technology and requiring fewer workers. This process explains, according to GDT, the strong reduction in the labor force working in pig farms (over 40 percent between 2001 and 2010).

The side effects: the failure of pig manure management and the contamination of groundwater

Pig manure in farms stands as probably the most important environmental externality associated with the vertical integration model of pork meat production. The particular type of animal excrement, mostly in liquid form, results from the feed provided, which is high in protein and energy content. Pig manure can be used as fertilizer. However and compared to other livestock, it is poor in organic matter and the C/N relationship is also low. Both factors limit therefore the mineralization process and the subsequent takeover by plant roots. Moreover, if left in the ground for long periods of time, pig manure may also produce ammonia (NH_3) known for its impacts in the acidification of surface waters and its role as greenhouse effect gas (Álvarez-Rodríguez et al., 2013).

On average in Catalonia about 12.5 million cubic meters of pig excrement are produced every year. Before the construction of six cogeneration power plants to dry the manure and hence reduce its amount, almost 97 percent of waste was spread out on agricultural soil without any previous treatment. These cogeneration plants could absorb over 5 percent of the residue generated each year and the rest had to be applied to a relatively small and shrinking agricultural area (about 900,000 hectares) with different aptitudes to recycle waste as fertilizer (see above).

All in all, pig manure has been and still is one of the most important drivers behind the contamination of groundwater (and also surface water) with nitrates. This pollution has become an important public health issue. For instance, in 2002, it was reported that up to 100,000 people in Catalonia were being supplied drinking water with nitrate concentrations above 50 mg/l (Avui, 2002).

To tackle such impacts, the Council Directive 91/676/EEC of the European Union concerning the protection of waters against pollution caused by nitrates from agricultural sources obliged European states, among other things, to identify vulnerable zones as well as to draw up action programs to cut nitrate pollution (European Union, 2010). This Directive was incorporated into Spanish national law by means of the Real Decreto 261/1996 (Ministerio de la Presidencia, 1996). Abiding by European and Spanish legislation, in 1998 the Catalan government drafted an executive order to establish vulnerable zones by farming nitrate contamination in Catalonia (Presidència de la Generalitat, 1998). Later, in 2004 and 2009, new vulnerable zones were declared (Departament de la Presidència, 2004;

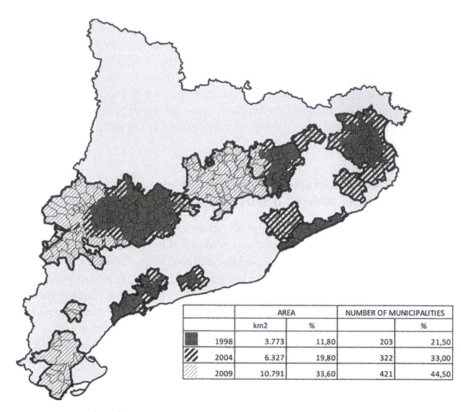

		AREA		NUMBER OF MUNICIPALITIES	
		km2	%		%
■	1998	3.773	11,80	203	21,50
▨	2004	6.327	19,80	322	33,00
▨	2009	10.791	33,60	421	44,50

FIGURE 7.3 Vulnerable zones to nitrate pollution by farming activities in Catalonia, including declared zones in 1998, 2004 and 2005.

Source: redrawn from map provided by Agència Catalana de l'Aigua.

Generalitat de Catalunya, 2009a) (see Figure 7.3). In Osona, our study area, 27 out of its 51 municipalities were included in the first draft of vulnerable zones in 1998. Five additional municipalities were added in 2004. In the last update of 2009, six new municipalities were included, up to a total of 38 municipalities.

The results obtained in the control points in the vulnerable zones reveal that there are no signs of improvement of nitrate concentration in water bodies. In Table 7.3 we can observe the percentage of control points for the vulnerable zones established in 1998, 2004 and 2009. Clearly, the zones that are doing worst are the vulnerable zones declared in 1998, notwithstanding the fact that these are precisely the only zones observing a slight improvement in their average concentrations in the recent years.

If we focus more specifically in the last period with available data (2008–2011) we note that, within vulnerable zones, control points showing average values in nitrate concentration above the drinking water standards threshold stand around 43 percent of the total (Table 7.4). We can observe also a large gap between nitrate contamination in the designated vulnerable zones and in non-vulnerable zones.

TABLE 7.3 Control points in different vulnerable zones.

	VZ 1998			VZ 2004		VZ 2009
% of control points with	2000– 2003	2004– 2007	2008– 2011	2004– 2007	2008– 2011	2008– 2011
Maximum value NO$_3$ over 50 mg/l	60.9%	68.4%	65.9%	42.0%	50.0%	42.9%
Average value NO$_3$ over 50 mg/l	45.9%	55.7%	51.1%	30.2%	31.4%	39.3%

Source: own elaboration from data provided by Agència Catalana de l'Aigua.
Note: VZ stands for vulnerable zone.

TABLE 7.4 Control points in vulnerable zones and non-vulnerable zones, 2008–2011.

% of control points with	Vulnerable zones	Non-vulnerable zones	All Catalonia
Maximum value NO$_3$ over 50 mg/l	56.2%	15.7%	44.9%
Average value NO$_3$ over 50 mg/l	43.1%	10.5%	34.0%

Source: own elaboration from data provided by Agència Catalana de l'Aigua.

Therefore, groundwater pollution by nitrates has somehow stabilized but not improved and the situation is serious enough to foresee that the Catalonia river basin district will be unable to meet the requirements of water quality of the European Water Framework Directive set for 2017.

The reasons behind the persistence of nitrates in the aquifers of central Catalonia have been extensively researched. To a large extent, this persistence can be attributed to complex hydrogeological conditions with distinct hydrogeological units and flow systems (Menció et al., 2011a) but also and perhaps more significantly to the effects of years of groundwater pumping in wells not cased adequately. Periods of abundant rainfall trigger the process with nitrates accumulating first in the sand and gravel aquifers located near the surface. From here, the low permeability of the geological formations would prevent in principle migration to the deeper aquifers. However, if wells are not well cased, groundwater from distinct aquifer types gets mixed more easily so that nitrate concentrations are higher than would be the case if the origin of the water had been in the deeper, relatively nitrate-free formations (Menció et al., 2011b). In a recent study it was found that the higher concentrations of nitrates (300 mg/liter or more) in Osona were common in the unconfined formations in the central areas where most of the agriculture and livestock is located. Values tended to decrease towards the more forested periphery and in deeper aquifers as well (in all these areas below 50 mg/l). However, nitrate concentrations up to 200 mg/l were found also in confined aquifers in the central areas again probably as a consequence of overpumping and deficiencies in the construction of wells (Boy-Roura et al., 2013).

In sum, the ubiquity of nitrate presence in groundwater located at different depths and the low permeability associated with the confined hydrogeological layers in Osona and elsewhere in Catalonia make extraordinarily difficult to foresee a control of nitrate pollution anytime soon. In fact, nitrate pollution continues to be perhaps the most important concern for many aquifers not only of Catalonia or Spain but of the European Union.

Devastated water landscapes: nitrate contamination of public fountains and springs in Osona

Groundwater contamination by nitrates is especially evident in the public fountains supplying water directly from natural springs. In Osona, half of such public fountains do not currently provide water with adequate drinking quality standards. Responding to a rising concern among the population of the area, since 2000 GDT has been periodically sampling and analyzing the presence of nitrates in public fountains and wells in the Ter river basin, which includes the county of Osona. Since 2004 this analysis has been explicitly focused on public fountains (Table 7.5), with the numbers of fountains analyzed fluctuating on a year-to-year basis. In 2004, 71 out of 157 public fountains in Osona had nitrates levels above 50 mg/liter, with 16 cases exceeding 200 mg/l (GDT, 2004). In 2005 and 2006 the percentage of fountains with concentrations above 50 mg/liter was similar, while in 2007 it presented a slight decrease (however, the number of samples was lower). In 2008 and 2009 the GDT reduced the number of samples (probably because of the severe drought affecting Catalonia in 2008 and its effects on the drying up of many fountains and springs). At any rate, 2009 registered the highest number of fountains contaminated, surpassing half of the analyzed sample. That year also registered the record of nitrate concentration in a public fountain in Osona, with values above 450 mg/l or nine times the maximum allowable level. This record did not pass unnoticed, and Catalan media echoed the news (La Vanguardia, 2009). In 2010 the sample was enlarged again. Since 2010, the percentage of public fountains of Osona not complying with drinking water quality standards oscillates between 40 and 45 percent of the sample.

Despite fluctuations in samplings, there is steady data since 2002 for 36 of the fountains. In Table 7.6 we observe that the percentage of fountains with concentrations above 50 mg/l as well as the average and maximum nitrate concentration in these fountains have actually increased during the period 2002–2012.

TABLE 7.5 Nitrate pollution in public fountains of Osona.

Year	Public fountains analyzed	>50 mg/l	% >50mg/l	>200 mg/l	Max. Concentration (mg/l)	Comments
2000	109	52	47.7	3	540 (Pou Cornellas); 217.1 (Font dels Enamorats)	Including wells and other sources of water
2002	246	89	36.2	17	303.3 (La Gatutxa); 300.5 (Font de Mas Xiquet)	Including wells and other sources of water
2004	157	71	45.2	16	366 (Font de Sant Miquel)	–
2005	145	63	43.4	10	466.4 (Font dels Enamorats)	–
2006	156	74	47.4	14	398 (Font de Cassanell)	–
2007	123	54	43.9	9	274.1 (Font de la Teula)	Not including 10 fountains that were dry
2008	103	42	40.8	5	292.2 (Font dels Enamorats)	Not including 16 fountains that were dry
2009	117	62	53.0	7	452.3 (Font de Casanell)	Not including 3 fountains that were dry
2010	152	75	49.3	15	358.9 (Font de Casanell)	Not including 2 fountains that were dry
2011	159	74	46.5	13	398.6 (Font Salada)	Not including 5 fountains that were dry
2012	142	67	47.2	17	420.40 (Font Salada)	Not including 2 fountains that were dry
2013	144	63	43.8	9	407.5 (Font de Gallisans)	Not including 13 fountains that were dry

Sources: own elaboration from GDT (2004–2012).

TABLE 7.6 Evolution of nitrate pollution in 36 fountains with data from 2002 to 2012.

	Fountains >50 mg/l	% Fountains >50 mg/l	Average nitrate concentration	Maximum nitrate concentration
2002	18	50.0	78.01	241.6
2004	22	61.1	104.51	354.5
2005	19	52.8	91.87	276.1
2006	21	58.3	97.68	329.2
2007	19	52.8	86.93	283.1
2008	16	44.4	68.8	258.6
2009	22	61.1	103.19	390.2
2010	19	52.8	94.51	353.3
2011	22	61.1	98.94	398.6
2012	21	58.3	108.28	420.4

Source: own elaboration from Nació Digital.cat (2012).

Resistances and policy reactions towards nitrate pollution

In Osona, the GDT has been one of the most active groups denouncing nitrate contamination in the area. The group was founded in 1989 and since then focused most of its attention on the impacts of livestock manure in Osona. The scope of its actions has been principally local and regional, but it has been also active at the European level. In what concerns the latter, the group has taken to the European Parliament on several occasions during the 1990s and 2000s the issue of livestock manure and nitrate contamination of water supplies in central Catalonia. As a response, in 2001 the European Commission requested information to the Consell Comarcal (the county authority) of Osona about the quality of drinking water in the area. In 2005, the European Court of Justice ruled against the Catalan government for not complying with the European Directive on Drinking Water supply and forced the elaboration of environmental impact assessments of livestock farms. In 2007 the GDT insisted again on the gravity of the problem and the urgency to take measures against a scenario of increasing production of manure and inadequate (in their opinion) or even lack of treatment for a very important part of pig excrement (some 120,000 cubic meters per year). At the local/regional level, as we have reported in the previous section, the group has performed a key task of monitoring periodically the nitrate contamination of public fountains in Osona since 2004 (GDT, 2005).

Beyond establishing nitrate vulnerable zones, European and Spanish law obliged Spanish regions to draw up action plans in these zones to eliminate or minimize water contamination by nitrates. Thus, in 1998 the Catalan Government drafted a code of good farming practices related to nitrogen (Departament d'Agricultura,

Ramaderia i Pesca, 1998) to be enforced in all vulnerable zones. Beyond other issues such as fertilizer use or irrigation practices, the code focused on adequate livestock manure management, including recommendations for sufficient and adequate manure storage design and construction, reduction of the volume of manure and also reduction of the nitrogen in manure. Two years later, in 2000, the Catalan Government approved an action program to cut nitrate contamination (Departament de Medi Ambient, 2000) abiding by European and Spanish legislation and in the lines of the aforementioned code of good practices. In 2001 the Catalan government made compulsory plans for manure management (including transportation) for livestock breeding farms, both at the individual and collective levels (if manure was managed collectively) (Presidència de la Generalitat, 2001). Five years later, it created the consortium for the management of farming fertilization (Consorci per la Gestió de la Fertilització Agrària, GESFER) (Agroactivitat, 2006). The incorporation of new vulnerable zones implied the periodical revision of the Catalan action program to cut nitrate contamination, with the last version approved in 2009 (Generalitat de Catalunya, 2009b). In Osona, a plan for manure management has existed since 2000, with the objective of recovering groundwater quality and reaching equilibrium between stockbreeding and the local environment. In 2008, a commission for the management of manure production (Comissió Comarcal de Gestió de Dejeccions Ramaderes a la comarca d'Osona) was created with participation of the public administrations and business and professional organizations as well as farmers' cooperatives. This commission had to promote new solutions to manure treatment and help to adapt farmers to new legal schemes particularly in what concerns the valorization of manure. In 2013 this plan was revised in order to make it compatible with the 2009 Catalan revision of the action program on manure management.

While the direct spreading of manure as a fertilizer in agricultural land has been one of the pillars of manure management, the other cornerstone action promoted by the public administration to solve the excess manure production issue has been the authorization to build in the late 1990s several energy cogeneration plants that burn natural gas to produce electricity and use the residual heat produced along the process to dry pig manure. Hence, through this process, the volume of manure is reduced and the resulting product could be used as a safer organic fertilizer rich in ammonium sulfate. Two of the six plants built in Catalonia were located in Osona and had a combined capacity of some 200,000 cubic meters of pig manure coming from over 150 farms of the county (El9nou.cat, 2013).

The installation of these plants has been, nonetheless, riddled with problems, and has faced the opposition of environmental groups. The same GDT opposed the operation of a livestock manure cogeneration treatment plant in the north of Osona in 2002 while, in parallel, three citizens sued against the construction of the plant. In 2006 the Higher Court of Catalonia ruled that the plant was illegal and had to be demolished. However, this proved problematic, because, beyond the economic compensations to be paid by the public administration, many pig farms were legalized under the condition that waste generated could be treated in the plant. The process underwent several appeals, but eventually in 2011, the Higher Court reversed its previous decision to demolish the plant. The GDT has been very critical of this model of centralized treatment, arguing that it does not reduce nitrate contamination and that it perpetuates an unsustainable intensive farming model (GDT, 2013). For the GDT, therefore, the real question was not to close the plant or leave it open, but the urgent need to reconvert the current intensive model, 'which condemns farmers ... and citizens to mortgage the land and that enslaves farmers to an industrial chain that does not take care of waste production and that reduces farming land to a mere sponge for the application of manure' (GDT, 2006, our translation). In this sense the group called for reducing pig numbers and rethinking the stockbreeding model (GDT, 2007) towards one more respectful with people, animals, the environment and social stability, and one able to internalize environmental and social costs (GDT, 2009).

In any case and due to changes proposed in energy subsidies by the Spanish government, the two manure treatment cogeneration plants in Osona have been (temporarily) closed down in February 2014. If the executive order by the Spanish government drastically cutting subsidies to cogeneration is made effective, costs to treat manure will increase from 6 to 50 euros/m^3 (Nació Digital.cat, 2014). The GDT (2014) argues that treatment plants were not oriented to solve a problem but to make a business out of it while capturing public subsidies paid with taxpayer's money. The immediate question that the group raises is the fate of the some 600,000 cubic meters of manure accumulated in the county. Up to 80 percent of manure production of some farms was treated in the cogeneration plants and the storage capacity of these farms only spans a few months. For the group, this critical situation, however, represents an opportunity to rethink the business model of pig breeding as well as to implement more sustainable solutions to manure treatment, such as biogas production, in the line of what has been included in the last Catalan plan to mitigate climate change emissions (Generalitat de Catalunya, 2008). One of the actions included in the plan foresees the promotion of anaerobic biodigestion of manure and the use of the resulting biogas. In this context, the Catalan government (including the Waste and Energy Catalan public agencies) and the consortium GESFER have promoted the 'Plan to promote pig manure biodigestion in Catalonia (2008–2012)' (PROBIOPUR) (GESFER, 2009), while both the Spanish and Catalan governments approved packages of public subsidies to promote manure biodigestion. In 2011 the Catalan government created an interdepartmental commission on nitrates and manure biodigestion to address in a comprehensive way the problem of nitrogen excess in vulnerable zones.

Other management options are also being explored. One is the reduction of 18 percent in the nitrogen content of pig feed which is increasingly applied by farms. The other, perhaps much more complex (and expensive) is denitrification. Some experiments with the support of EU LIFE Program have been carried out with certain success although its application at a large scale remains uncertain (Iglèsias, pers. comm., 2014).

Conclusions

This chapter has attempted to show how a particular model of pork meat production has created, among many other socio-environmental ills, the loss of valuable natural and cultural resources such as public springs and fountains, the water of which is no longer drinkable because of excessive concentrations of nitrates. Using Catalonia and specifically the Osona county case as an example, we have traced first the origins of nitrate production in groundwater to the high nitrogen content of pig waste spread on to agricultural fields and pastures with little control. Second, we have summarized the complex ways by which nitrates pollute not only shallow but also deep aquifers despite relatively low permeability. Third, we have pointed out some of the causes that make this type of pollution one of the most intractable water pollution problems not only of Osona and Catalonia but of the whole European Union.

Management of nitrate pollution is not an easy task. The reduction of nitrogen content in pig feed, denitrification processes or the reduction of waste in cogeneration plants have all shown their limitations. The alternative of producing biogas appears more promising although the massive curtailment in subsidies for renewable energy currently happening in Spain makes this alternative quite bleak. Still, one more fundamental option is to change drastically the model of pork meat production, as proposed by the most active NGO in the area, the Grup de Defensa del Ter, and step back towards less intensive, more sustainable pork meat production practices. This alternative has to acknowledge the formidable hurdle represented by the relevance of pig farming for the Catalan agrarian sector (more than one-third of the total economic value) and for the Catalan food-processing industries.

Nitrates, characterized by long residence periods in groundwater, are to remain in high concentrations in many of the Osona fountains. An additional problem is that, given the economic crisis currently affecting Catalonia and the increases in prices and taxes of municipal waters, some people have gone back to the fountains to provide water for themselves and thus save on the water bill. However, and as argued in the chapter, many fountains are no longer able to supply safe water and are being abandoned. With this abandonment and deterioration comes the loss of what used to be unique and little-studied socio-ecosystems of great historical, cultural and artistic values. Through the lenses of political economy and political ecology, typical externality problems such as the one presented in this chapter are no more than examples of the contradictions of the capitalist mode of production, particularly in what concerns the so-called 'transformation of nature' (O'Connor, 1994). Likewise and as Martínez-Alier (2003) has sharply argued, environmental externalities of the nature examined in this chapter are also no more than cost-shifting success stories for the private sphere, which remains unaffected by the hazard created and in this case is even able to avoid one of the classical solutions of modernization theory to environmental risks which is the 'polluter pays' principle. The loss of the public fountains because of the impacts of intensive pig meat production in large industrial farms could also be read as a case of 'accumulation by dispossession' (Harvey, 2003), where the pollution resulting from private economic activity results in the dispossession of a collective resource.

Voluntaristic views argue that polluted groundwater can still be used for non-potable functions such as the irrigation of gardens and orchards; street and sewer cleaning or in certain industrial processes. Other proposals include the mixing up of this groundwater with public supply water in order to reduce nitrate concentrations to levels apt for drinking. Notwithstanding the potential interest of these alternatives, the reality is that people in Osona and other parts of rural Catalonia 'won't be going to the fountain no more', at least for a long time.

Acknowledgements

The authors would like to thank Mireia Iglesias and Antoni Munné (Catalan Water Agency) for providing us with data and their helpful advice, and Anna Roca (Agrarian Chamber of Girona) for useful information regarding the situation of the pig sector in Spain and Catalonia. Hug March acknowledges funding from the Ministry of Economy and Competitiveness of Spain (JCI-2011-10709) (2012–2014).

References

Agroactivitat (2006) 'En marxa GESFER, un consorci per a la gestió dels purins', (GESFER created a consortium for pig waste management), *Agroactivitat*, vol 24, pp. 12–13

Álvarez-Rodríguez, J., Forcada, F., Guillén, R., Balcells, J. and Babot, D. (2013) 'El purín porcino: ¿un recurso agronómico o un residuo medioambiental?' (Pig manure: Agronomical resource or environmental waste?), *SUIS*, vol 102, pp. 20–29

Avui (2002) 'Unes 100.000 persones reben aigua contaminada pels purins' (100,000 people have their water polluted by pig manure), *Avui*, 3 May, p. 22

Boy-Roura, M., Nolan, B. T., Menció, A. and Mas-Pla, J. (2013.) 'Regression model for aquifer vulnerability assessment of nitrate pollution in the Osona region (NE Spain)', *Journal of Hydrology*, vol 505, pp. 150–162

Departament d'Agricultura, Ramaderia i Pesca (1998) 'Ordre de 22 d'octubre de 1998, del Codi de Bones Pràctiques Agràries en relació amb el nitrogen' (Executive Order of 22 October 1998, Protocol of Good Agricultural Practices regarding nitrogen), *Diari Oficial de la Generalitat de Catalunya*, no 2,761, pp. 13,751–13,756

Departament de la Presidència (2004) 'Decret 476/2004, de 28 de desembre, pel qual es designen noves zones vulnerables en relació amb la contaminació de nitrats procedents de fonts agràries' (Executive Order 476/2004 of 28 December on the declaration of new vulnerable zones regarding nitrate pollution from agrarian sources), *Diari Oficial de la Generalitat de Catalunya*, no 4,292, pp. 27,067–27,070

Departament de Medi Ambient (2000) 'Decret 205/2000, de 13 de juny, d'aprovació del programa de mesures agronòmiques aplicables a les zones vulnerables en relació amb la contaminació de nitrats procedents de fonts agràries' (Executive Order 205/2000 of 13 June on the approval of a program of agronomical measures applicable to vulnerable zones regarding nitrate pollution from agrarian sources), *Diari Oficial de la Generalitat de Catalunya*, no 3,168, pp. 8,278–8,280

El9nou.cat (2013) 'Els ramaders tenen coll avall que tancaran les dues plantes de purins d'Osona' (Pig farmers convinced that two pig manure treatment plants will close down in Osona), *El9nou.cat*, 24 January. www.el9nou.cat/noticies_o_0/34148/els_ramaders_tenen_coll_avall_que_tancaran_les, accessed 14 March 2014

European Union (2010) *The EU Nitrates Directive*. European Commission, Brussels

FAO (2012) *FAO Statistical Yearbook*. Food and Agriculture Organization, Rome

GDT (2004–2012) *Concentració de nitrats a l'aigua de les fonts de la comarca d'Osona (Nitrate Concentration in the Water of Fountains of Osona)*, annual reports, Grup de Defensa del Ter, Manlleu, Spain

GDT (2005) *Les fonts que tenim. Osona i el Lluçanés (Our Fountains: Osona and Lluçanés)*. Eumo Editorial, Barcelona

GDT (2006) 'Comunicat del Grup de Defensa del Ter sobre la sentència contra la planta de purins de l'Esquirol' (Statement by the Grup de Defensa del Ter on the court ruling against the pig waste plant of Esquirol), press release GDT, 25 April, Manlleu

GDT (2007) 'Consideracions i documentació' (Considerations and Documentation), press release GDT, 28 August, Manlleu

GDT (2009) 'Nota de premsa sobre purins al Mercat del Ram' (Press release on pig waste in the Mercat del Ram), press release GDT, Manlleu

GDT (2013) 'Crònica d'una mort anunciada' (Chronicle of a death foretold), press release GDT,12 April, Manlleu, Spain

GDT (2014) 'Les plantes de purins, d'un fracàs a una gran oportunitat' (Pig waste plats: from failure to opportunity), press release GDT, 20 February, Manlleu

Generalitat de Catalunya (2008) *Pla marc de mitigació del canvi climàtic a Catalunya (2008–2012) (Plan for Climate Change Mitigation in Catalonia 2008–2012)*. Generalitat de Catalunya, Barcelona

Generalitat de Catalunya (2009a) 'Acord GOV/128/2009, de 28 de juliol, de revisió i designació de noves zones vulnerables en relació amb la contaminació per nitrats procedents de fonts agràries' (Agreement GOV/128/2009 of 28 July on the revision and designation of new vulnerable zones regarding nitrate pollution from agrarian sources), *Diari Oficial de la Generalitat de Catalunya*, no 5,435, pp. 61,692–61,695

Generalitat de Catalunya (2009b) 'Decret 136/2009, d'1 de setembre, d'aprovació del programa d'actuació aplicable a les zones vulnerables en relació amb la contaminació de nitrats que procedeixen de fonts agràries i de gestió de les dejeccions ramaderes' (Executive Order 136/2009 of 1 September approving the program applicable to vulnerable zones concerning nitrate pollution from agrarian sources and the management of livestock waste), *Diari Oficial de la Generalitat de Catalunya*, no 5,457, pp. 65,858–65,902

GESFER (2009) *Gestió de la Fertilització Agrària de Catalunya (Management of Agricultural Fertilization in Catalonia)*, Consorci de gestió de la fertilització agrària de Catalunya, Lleida

Grup de Gestió Porcina (2013a) *Informe del Sector Porcí. Exercici 2012* (Report on the Pig Sector 2012), DARP, Generalitat de Catalunya, Barcelona

Grup de Gestió Porcina (2013b) *Observatori del Porcí* (Observatory of the Pig Sector), DARP, Generalitat de Catalunya, Barcelona

Harvey, D. (2003) *The New Imperialism*, Oxford University Press, Oxford

IDESCAT. (2012) *Anuari Estadístic de Catalunya 2012* (Statistical Yearbook of Catalonia 2012), IDESCAT, Generalitat de Catalunya, Barcelona

Iglèsias, M. (2014) Personal communication with the head of the groundwater division of the Catalan Water Agency, 7 February, Barcelona

La Vanguardia (2009) 'Contaminadas la mitad de las fuentes de Osona por purines' (Half the public fountains of Osona polluted by manure), *La Vanguardia, Vivir*, 7 April, p. 7

MAGRAMA (Ministerio de Agricultura, Alimentación y Medio Ambiente) (2013) *Caracterización del Sector Porcino Español* (*Assessment of the Spanish Pig Sector*), MAGRAMA, Madrid

Martínez-Alier, J. (2003) *Environmentalism of the Poor*. Edward Elgar, Cheltenham

Menció, A., Boy, M. and Mas-Pla, J. (2011a) 'Analysis of vulnerability factors that control nitrate occurrence in natural springs (Osona Region, NE Spain)', *Science of the Total Environment*, vol 409, pp. 3,049–3,058

Menció, A. Mas-Pla, J., Otero, N. and Soler, A. (2011b) 'Nitrate as a tracer of groundwater flow in a fractured multilayered aquifer', *Hydrological Sciences Journal – Journal des Sciences Hydrologiques*, vol 56, no 1, pp. 108–122

Ministerio de la Presidencia (1996) 'Real Decreto 261/1996, de 16 de febrero, sobre protección de las aguas contra la contaminación producida por los nitratos procedentes de fuentes agrarias' (Executive order 261/1996 of 16 February on the protection of water against nitrate pollution from agricultural sources), *Boletín Oficial del Estado*, no 61, pp. 9,734–9,737

Nació Digital.cat (2012) 'La contaminació de les fonts per nitrats no afluixa (Nitrate Pollution does not back down)', *Nació Digital.cat*, 27 March, www.naciodigital.cat/osona/noticia/31056/contaminacio/fonts/nitrats/no/afluixa, accessed 11 March 2014

Nació Digital.cat (2014) 'Les dues plantes de purins tanquen de manera provisional' (Two pig manure plants closed temporarily), *Nació Digital.cat*, 17 February, www.naciodigital.cat/osona/noticia/40456/dues/plantes/purins/tanquen/manera/provisional, accessed 11 March 2014

O'Connor, M. (ed.) (1994) *Is Capitalism Sustainable? Political Economy and the Politics of Ecology*, Guilford, New York

Prat, F. Oliveras, J. and Torresacana, E. (2011) 'Evolució dels nitrats analitzats a l'aigua de 87 fonts situades en 28 municipis de la comarca d'Osona' (Evolution of nitrate concentrations in 87 fountains of 28 municipalities in Osona County), *AUSA*, vol 25, no 168, pp. 250–280

Presidència de la Generalitat (1998) 'Decret 283/1998, de 21 d'octubre, de designació de les zones vulnerables en relació amb la contaminació de nitrats procedents de fonts agràries' (Executive Order 283/1998 of 21 October on the designation of vulnerable zones regarding nitrate pollution from agricultural sources), *Diari Oficial de la Generalitat de Catalunya*, no 2,760, pp. 13,677–13,680

Presidència de la Generalitat (2001) 'Decret 220/2001, d'1 d'agost, de gestió de les dejeccions ramaderes' (Order 220/2001 of 1 August regarding management of pig manure), *Diari Oficial de la Generalitat de Catalunya*, no 3,447, pp. 12,409–12,411

Prudham, S. (2004) 'Poisoning the well: Neoliberalism and the contamination of municipal water in Walkerton, Ontario', *Geoforum*, vol 35, no 3, pp. 343–359

Reimer, J. J. (2006) 'Vertical Integration in the Pork Industry', *American Journal of Agricultural Economics*, vol 88, no 1, pp. 234–248

Teira Esmatges, M. R. (2007) *Informe per a la millora de la gestió dels purins porcins a Catalunya* (*Report on the Improvement of Pig Manure Management in Catalonia*), CADS, Generalitat de Catalunya, Barcelona

Teruel, M. and Uclés, D. (2011) *El Sector del Porcino en España* (*The Pig Sector in Spain*), Colección Estudio y Monografías 32, Fundación Cajamar, El Ejido, Almería

8

ENVIRONMENTAL INJUSTICE IN THE SPATIAL DISTRIBUTION OF CONCENTRATED ANIMAL FEEDING OPERATIONS

A case study from Ohio, USA

Julia Lenhardt and Yelena Ogneva-Himmelberger

Introduction

In the last 50 years, the livestock industry has grown substantially in almost all countries due to economic growth and technological advancements (Steinfeld et al., 2006). Consequently, the importance of ecological conditions and resource availability as drivers for the siting of livestock operations has been replaced by opportunity cost of land and access to markets. Additionally, economic incentives and a growing competition for land use has resulted in a decrease in the number of livestock operations and an increase in the number of animals per farm through-out the United States (Donham et al., 2007; Thorne, 2007). There are fewer, but larger operations on cheap land in rural America – a trend that has significant environmental impacts (Imhoff, 2010).

Concentrated animal feeding operations (CAFOs) are animal feeding operations of at least 1,000 animal units (for example, 2,500 large pigs or 100,000 chickens), where animals are confined indoors for at least 45 days during a growing season in an area that does not produce vegetation (Osterberg and Wallinga, 2004). In 2011, CAFOs produced more than 500 million tons of manure in the United States, resulting in substantial air and water pollution (Imhoff, 2010). Workers and neigh-bors of CAFOs experience high levels of respiratory problems, and poorly treated waste may result in contamination of nearby surface waters with dangerous levels of bacteria, fungi, viruses, and nutrients (Pew Commission, 2008).

Even more concerning, studies have shown that CAFOs often have a dispro-portionate impact on low-income and nonwhite populations (Wing et al., 2000). In North Carolina, studies have found that hog operations tend to be dispropor-tionately located near poor, African-American communities (ibid.; Edwards and Ladd, 2010). Similarly, Wilson et al. (2002) found that swine CAFOs in Mississippi cause inequitable health and socioeconomic impacts on African-American and low-income communities. In Iowa, a study by Merchant et al. (2005) suggests that children living on or near swine-producing farms have higher rates of asthma compared to other children. Although the rapid rise in CAFOs impacts rural development and community health in almost every state, little research has looked beyond the highest meat-producing states.

This study explores the spatial distribution of CAFOs in the state of Ohio, one of the largest egg-producing states in 2007 and a state that experienced a 6.5 percent decrease in the number of livestock-producing farms and a 28 percent increase in the number of animals per farm from 2000 to 2007 (USDA NASS, 2008). Rural areas with high densities of CAFOs are compared to other rural areas to determine whether minority, low-income, and vulnerable populations (children and elderly) are unequally exposed to CAFOs. The study was completed using a Geographic Information System (GIS), incorporating spatial statistical analysis of populations at the census tract level.

Methods

Ohio CAFOs data were provided by the Ohio Environmental Protection Agency (EPA) and updated to 2010. Data included facility names, permit status, geographic coordinates, and the type and number of animals at each of the original 212 documented Ohio CAFO facilities. Ten CAFOs were removed because they were marked as either 'not built', 'no longer permitted', or 'empty', leaving 98 poultry facilities, 52 swine facilities, 41 dairy facilities, 8 beef facilities and 3 horse facilities. To avoid redundancy in spatial information, all facilities producing more than one type of animal were counted only once in overall spatial cluster analysis, but each facility location was counted for in a cluster analysis of individual animal types. Ten CAFOs produced more than one type of animal, resulting in 191 individual CAFO locations. The study was conducted at the census tract level due to the homogeneity of tract population (Liu, 2001) and because the census tract strongly reflects the structure of local communities (Bogue, 1985). Additionally, environmental hazards caused by CAFOs are likely experienced beyond the boundary of smaller units such as block or block groups. Select demographic characteristics (using nomenclature employed) from the 2010 US Census included percent African American, percent Hispanic, percent Asian populations, percent elderly (over 65), and percent children. In this study, children are defined as those 15 and younger, following EPA's standard where women of child-bearing age are considered to be between the ages of 16 and 49 years (EPA, 2012). This study aggregated population statistics for all age groups 15 and younger, so as not to include the EPA's 16-year minimum age of child-bearing women. Median household income in 2011 inflation-adjusted dollars was collected from the 2007–2011 American Community Survey (ACS) 5-year estimates. The coefficient of variation (CV), a data reliability measure, for ACS data yielded 2,091 tracts (71.2 percent) with median household income

estimates that are highly reliable (CV ≤ 12), 812 tracts (27.6 percent) with estimates of medium reliability (12 < CV ≤ 40), and 34 tracts (1.2 percent) with
low reliability (CV > 40); reliability thresholds were suggested by Environmental
Systems Research Institute (ESRI) (2011).

It has long been observed throughout the United States that rural communities
have lower wages, lower median incomes, and higher poverty rates than metropolitan
areas (Kumar, 2002; Maantay et al., 2010). Therefore, all census tracts within designated urban areas (as defined by the US Census Bureau Urban Areas data layer) were
removed from the analysis, resulting in the exclusion of 50.7 percent of Ohio census
tracts, 4.1 percent of the land area in Ohio, and one CAFO location. Furthermore,
the number of CAFOs per tract was normalized according to census tract size and
converted to the density of CAFOs, or the number of CAFOs per square kilometer.
Finally, beef- and horse-producing CAFOs were eliminated from the study because
of their low numbers.

Spatial autocorrelation of CAFO facilities

The global Moran's I statistic tested for spatial autocorrelation of CAFO densities
in Ohio. The Getis Ord Gi★ statistic then located clusters or 'hot spots' of high
CAFO densities. Additionally, the data were broken up according to the type of
animal being produced (poultry, pork, or dairy) to test for clustering of particular
livestock operations. An inverse distance function defined the neighborhood following the logic that high-density CAFO areas are more impactful on health and
environment when close together than when spaced farther apart.

Environmental justice analysis

Once spatial clustering was confirmed and located, a basic assessment of the demog-
raphy of those census tracts exhibiting clustering of CAFO density was completed,
using the following six socioeconomic variables: percent Black, percent Hispanic,
percent Asian, percent elderly, percent children, and median household income.
All census tracts with Z-scores ≥ 1.96 in the Getis Ord Gi★ results (indicating
significant clustering with 95 percent confidence) were extracted and their socioeconomic variables were compared to the averages for rural census tracts with
Z-scores <1.96. For each variable and within each animal-production group, a
two-sampled Welch's t-test was calculated to determine whether the populations
living in clusters of census tracts with high CAFO density are significantly different from those in rural census tracts outside of these clusters. The Welch's (1947)
t-test is an adaptation of the Student's t-test to account for samples with unequal
variances, and is computed as follows:

$$t = \frac{X_C - X_N}{\sqrt{\dfrac{var_C^2}{n_C} + \dfrac{var_N^2}{n_X}}}$$

where X_C is the mean of a socioeconomic variable in CAFO density hot spots, X_N is the mean of a variable in Ohio Census tracts that are not CAFO density hot spots, var_C is the variance of a variable in CAFO density hot spots, var_N is the variance of a variable in tracts that are not CAFO density hot spots, and n is the number of tracts in each category. If the probability of obtaining the calculated t-statistic is less than 0.05, the demographic means of the two samples are significantly different at the 95 percent confidence level, indicating unequal exposure to CAFOs.

Local indicators of spatial autocorrelation

For those variables that exhibited a positive statistically significant Z-score ($Z \geq 1.96$) in the demographic t-test, a Bivariate Local Indicator of Spatial Autocorrelation (LISA) analysis was performed using GeoDa open source GIS software in order to locate regions demonstrating the relationships between CAFO density and socio-economic variables described by the t-test analysis. An inverse distance function defined the spatial neighborhood of analysis. Each variable was paired with the CAFO density in each census tract, and the following clusters were extracted:

*   High–High (HH): Clusters with high values of a given socioeconomic variable and a high CAFO density
*   Low–Low (LL): Clusters with low values of a given socioeconomic variable and a low/zero CAFO density
*   High–Low (HL): Clusters with high values of a given socioeconomic variable and a low/zero CAFO density
*   Low–High (LH): Clusters with low values of a given socioeconomic variable and a high CAFO density.

Results

Spatial autocorrelation of CAFO facilities

The Moran's I analysis indicates that census tracts with all types of CAFOs, except for those with dairy facilities, are clustered at 99 percent confidence level (Table 8.1).

Hot Spot Analysis (Getis–Ord Gi*) identifies the spatial location of census tract clusters with densities of CAFOs that are higher than one would expect by random chance. This analysis revealed that the most consistent pattern is several tracts with high densities of CAFOs along the western border of Ohio. In particular, Wyandot, Putnam, Van Wert, Shelby and Hardin Counties are all impacted by CAFO placement due to the large area taken up by CAFO-dense census tracts in these counties. Despite showing a random distribution in the global Moran's I analysis, dairy facilities with Z-scores greater than 1.96 (95 percent confidence) in the Gi* analysis are located in the northwest corner of the state, primarily impacting Williams, Mercer, Van Wert and Defiance Counties. The number of

TABLE 8.1 Results of Global Moran's I analysis for census tracts, for all CAFOs and each type of CAFO.

CAFO density (number of facilities/km²)	Moran's Index	Z-score	P-value	Distribution
All CAFOS	0.03	3.04	0	Clustered
Dairy	0.01	1.02	0.31	Random
Poultry	0.06	6.3	0	Clustered
Swine	0.03	2.47	0.01	Clustered

poultry facilities exceeds that of dairy and swine facilities combined, yet the poultry CAFO-dense census tracts are clustered in fewer locations throughout the state. Mercer County and Darke County, on the western border of the state, contain eight hot spot census tracts with Z-scores ranging from 2.05 to 21.66, indicating significant clustering of high-density poultry CAFOs. Mercer County is also impacted by swine facilities, with Gi★ Z-scores in census tracts ranging between 2.60 and 11.62. Paulding, Crawford, Darke and Shelby Counties also contain hot spots of swine facilities (Z-scores between 2.02 and 14.17), and Pickaway County, Madison County, and Fairfield County, three counties immediately south of heavily populated Columbus, exhibit hot spots of swine CAFOs (Z-scores ranging from 2.44 to 3.51).

Environmental justice analysis

The t-values and p-values associated with the mean differences between hot spots of CAFO-dense census tracts and non-hot spots census tracts for minority, elderly and child populations, and median household incomes are listed in Table 8.2. The African-American population living in CAFO-dense census tracts is significantly smaller than in census tracts without CAFOs, regardless of the species produced. Similar results are found for Asian populations, although the statistical difference between population means is greater in magnitude. No significant relationship exists for median household income or elderly. Hispanic populations are higher in census tracts with high densities of all CAFOs, dairy CAFOs, and swine CAFOs, although the relationships are only significant at the $p < 0.1$ confidence and are therefore less certain. The number of children under 15 years of age is significantly higher ($p < 0.05$) in CAFO-dense census tracts, for all animal species excluding poultry.

A bivariate LISA analysis was performed using the percent children under 15 years of age measured against CAFO density due to the level of significance in the assessment-test results (Figure 8.1).

Percent Hispanic population was also included in a bivariate LISA for additional analysis because it shows higher values in census tracts with all CAFOs, dairy

TABLE 8.2 T-test results indicating the statistical difference between populations in CAFO-dense census tracts and non-CAFO dense tracts; values significant at the 95 percent confidence level are marked by a ⋆.

	Median HH income	% Black population	% Hispanic population	% Asian population	% Under 15 years of age	% Over 65 years of age
All CAFOs	−5.62 E-05	−1.31⋆	2.56	−8.34⋆	1.51⋆	−1.25
Dairy	−1.37 E-04	−1.17⋆	2.78	−9.09⋆	0.99⋆	−0.95
Poultry	4.68 E-05	−1.39⋆	−19.33	−8.92⋆	0.48	−0.07
Swine	4.57 E-05	−1.36⋆	0.32	−5.89⋆	1.25⋆	−0.29

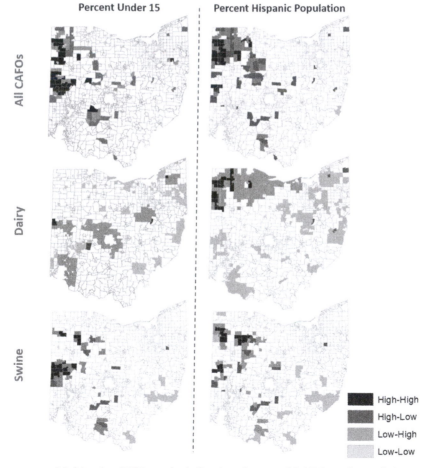

FIGURE 8.1 Multivariate LISA results indicating clusters of CAFOs and population percentages.

CAFOs and swine CAFOs, although it is not significant at the $p < 0.05$ level, and because Hispanic population has previously been highlighted as a concern in environmental justice issues. For all animal species types, areas of densely located CAFOs correspond to census tracts with high populations of children under age 15 primarily along the western border of the state. In particular, Mercer, Darke and Defiance Counties contain census tracts designated as High-High clusters, where high densities of CAFOs correspond to high percentages of children. A similar pattern is observed for Hispanic populations, although the concentration of High-High clusters dominates in Defiance County. Dairy CAFOs do not exhibit a dominant spatial pattern for percent children, and High-High clusters are few and spread across the northern portion of the State. Hispanic populations, however, show a clear cluster of high densities of Dairy CAFOs in the northwest corner of Ohio, in Defiance and Fulton Counties. High densities of swine CAFOs exist in census tracts with high percentages of children in a tight cluster of tracts in central-west Ohio, namely in Mercer and Darke Counties, and while Hispanic population shows clustering in the northwest corner of Ohio, there is not a dominant pattern of clustering.

Discussion

This study suggests that there is environmental discrimination with respect to the concentration of CAFOs and Hispanic populations and children. We used GIS and spatial statistics to examine the distribution of CAFOs in Ohio and their relationship to socioeconomic population groups in an environmental justice analysis. Poultry CAFOs are primarily clustered along the western border of the state, while dairy and swine CAFOs tend to be located in the northwestern corner. We find that, at the census tract level, there are higher proportions of children and Hispanic populations in regions with high densities of dairy and swine CAFOs. African-American and Asian populations are significantly lower in CAFO-dense regions while median household income and elderly populations exhibit no statically significant relationship.

A previous study used a longitudinal analysis to show that greater percentages of Hispanic, low-education, and low-income populations live near CAFOs in eastern North Carolina when compared to random points throughout the same region (Horton, 2012). It is possible that higher Hispanic populations near CAFOs are explained by preferential employment of recent immigrants in CAFOs due to the taxing physical and mental conditions (Acury and Marín, 2009; Imhoff, 2010). This would indicate that not only are Hispanics disproportionately exposed to reduced quality of life due to proximity to CAFO facilities, but that they are also disproportionately exposed to the physical and environmental dangers of working in such facilities. The relationship between CAFO siting and proximity to children has been addressed and demonstrated in several previous studies (Donham, 2000; Sigurdarson and Kline, 2006). Concern for the relationship between CAFO siting and proximity to children arises from the high vulnerability of children to toxic emissions and airborne illnesses from concentrated livestock facilities (Committee on Environmental Health, 1993; Barrett, 2006; Mirabelli et al., 2006).

Our study found no relationships between CAFO density and income or the proportion of African-American populations – a finding that is contested by similar analyses which show that low-income and African-American populations tend to be unequally exposed to CAFOs (Edwards and Ladd, 2010). It is possible that CAFOs are less clustered in low-income areas of Ohio and that African Americans are located primarily in urban areas that were not included in our analysis, but it is also likely that the scale of the analysis influenced the results of every relationship studied in this paper. Scale plays an important role in environmental justice studies as relationships between toxic facilities and socioeconomic population groups may change or become more or less significant when moving from the census tract to the county or zip-code level (Sheppard et al., 1999). A limitation of this study, therefore, is that it can only describe relationships at the census tract level, and future research should include analysis of relationships at both finer (census block or block group) and coarser resolutions (county or zip-code).

Conclusions

Ohio is one of the largest egg-producing states in the US, and is experiencing a trend of intensification in livestock production. As a result, CAFOs are becoming more prominent on Ohio horizons, resulting in contamination of surface water, toxic airborne emission, and odor and aesthetic issues. Certainly, CAFOs do not only negatively impact the health and quality of life of surrounding residents. CAFOs in the US strongly impact the local and regional economy, putting small, family farms out of business and driving away development in other economic sectors. At the global scale, meat production is responsible for up to 24 percent of the world's greenhouse gas emissions and the livestock sector uses approximately 8 percent of the world's entropic water resources (Steinfeld et al., 2006), issues that have largely remained unaddressed in US discussions of climate change and agriculture. Furthermore, the long-term confinement of thousands of animals in small spaces, where they are rarely able to turn around, see sunlight, or have physical contact with their offspring, has long been considered an inhumane and unethical practice (Imhoff, 2010). All of these impacts have long-lasting effects on the physical and emotional well-being of communities, nations, and our global society, and places like Iowa and North Carolina have sacrificed the well-being of their states in favor of CAFOs, likely with irreversible consequences. These arguments must be considered in future siting and construction of CAFOs not only in the US but in developing countries that are pushed toward intensification by international organizations and foreign investment.

References

Arcury, T. A. and Marín, A. J. (2009) 'Latino/Hispanic farmworkers and farm work in the eastern United States: the context for health, safety, and justice', in *Latino Farmworkers in the Eastern United States*, Springer, New York

Barrett, J. R. (2006) 'Hogging the air: CAFO emissions reach into schools', *Environmental Health Perspectives*, vol 114, no 4, p. A241

Bogue, D. (1985) *Population in the United States: Historical Trends and Future Projections*, Free Press, New York

Committee on Environmental Health (1993) 'Ambient air pollution: Respiratory hazards to children', *Pediatrics*, vol 91, no 6, pp. 1,210–1,213

Donham, K. J. (2000) 'The concentration of swine production: Effects on swine health, productivity, human health, and the environment', *Veterinary Clinics Of North America Food Animal Practice*, vol 16, no 3, pp. 559–598

Donham, K. J., Wing, S., Osterberg, D., Flora, J. L., Hodne, C., Thu, K. M. and Thorne, P. S. (2007) 'Community health and socioeconomic issues surrounding concentrated animal feeding operations', *Environmental Health Perspectives*, vol 115, no 2, p. 317

Edwards, B. and Ladd, A. (2010) 'Environmental justice, swine production and farm loss in North Carolina', *Sociological Spectrum: Mid-South Sociological Association*, vol 20, no 3, pp. 263–290

EPA (2012) *America's Children and the Environment*, 3rd edition, EPA, Washington, DC

ESRI (2011) 'The American Community Survey', *Esri Data Brochures and White Papers*, www.esri.com/data/esri_data/literature, accessed 13 November 2013

Horton, J. (2012) 'The siting of hog CAFOs in eastern North Carolina: A case of environmental injustice?', PhD thesis, University of Michigan at Ann Arbor

Imhoff, D. (2010) *The CAFO Reader: The Tragedy of Industrial Animal Factories*, Watershed Media, Healdsburg, California

Kumar, C. M. (2002) 'GIS methods for screening potential environmental justice areas in New England', MA thesis, City Planning, Massachusetts Institute of Technology, Cambridge

Liu, F. (2001) *Environmental Justice Analysis: Theories, Methods and Practice*, CRC Press LLC, Boca Raton, FL

Maantay, J., Chakraborty, J. and Brender, J. (2010) 'Proximity to environmental hazards: Environmental justice and adverse health outcomes', prepared for the US Environmental Protection Agency

Merchant, J., Naleway, A., Svendsen, E., Kelly, K., Burmeister, L., Stromquist, A., Taylor, C., Thorne, P., Reynolds, S., Sanderson, W., and Chrischilles, E. (2005) 'Asthma and farm exposures in a cohort of rural Iowa children,' *Environmental Health Perspectives*, vol 113, no 3, pp. 350–356

Mirabelli, M.C., Wing, S., Marshall, S.W., Wilcosky, T.C. (2006) 'Race, poverty, and potential exposure of middle-school students to air emissions from confined swine feeding operations', *Environmental Health Perspectives*, vol 114, no 4, pp. 591–596

Osterberg, D. and Wallinga, D. (2004) 'Addressing externalities from swine production to reduce public health and environmental impacts', *American Journal of Public Health*, vol 94, no 10, pp. 1,703–1,708

Pew Commission (2008) *Putting Meat on the Table: Industrial Farm Animal Production in America*, Johns Hopkins Bloomberg School of Public Health, Baltimore, MD

Sheppard, E., Leitner, H., McMaster, R. and Tian, H. (1999) 'GIS-based measures of environmental equity: exploring their sensitivity and significance.' *Journal of Exposure Analysis and Environmental Epidemiology*, vol 9, no 1, pp. 18–28

Sigurdarson, S. T. and J. N. Kline (2006) 'School proximity to concentrated animal feeding operations and prevalence of asthma in students', *CHEST Journal*, vol 129, no 6, pp. 1,486–1,491

Steinfeld, H., Gerber, P., Wassenaar, T., Castel, V., Rosales, M. and De Haan, C. (2006) *Livestock's Long Shadow: Environmental Issues and Options*, FAO, Rome

Thorne, P. (2007) 'Environmental health impacts of concentrated animal feeding operations: Anticipating hazards – searching for solutions', *Environmental Health Perspectives*, vol 115, no 2, p. 296

USDA NASS (2008) 'Livestock Slaughter', USDA, Washington, DC

Welch, B. L. (1947) 'The generalization of student's problem when several different population variances are involved', *Biometrika*, vol 34, pp. 28–35

Wilson, S. M., Howell, F., Wing, S. and Sobsey, M. (2002) 'Environmental injustice and the Mississippi hog industry', *Environmental Health Perspectives*, vol 110, no 2, p. 195

Wing, S., Cole, D. and Grant, G. (2000) 'Environmental injustice in North Carolina's hog industry', *Environmental Health Perspectives*, vol 108, no 3, p. 225

9

NEOLIBERAL GOVERNANCE AND ENVIRONMENTAL RISK

'Normal accidents' in North Carolina's hog industry

Elisabeth A. Stoddard

Introduction

In the last twenty years, North Carolina's hog industry has faced a series of disasters, from massive spills of hog waste during coastal storms to, most recently, outbreaks of infectious disease. These incidents have been described by the industry, as well as the state, as unpredictable accidents or 'acts of God' (Hayes, 1999; Barnes, 2001; Stevens, 2013). However, I argue that these events are examples of 'normal' or expected accidents (Prudham, 2004; Perrow, 2011). These so-called accidents are produced by the intentional tolerance of risk built into the state's neoliberal governance reforms.

In this chapter, I examine hog waste spills following three hurricanes in North Carolina as 'normal' accidents. I also briefly discuss the recent outbreak of porcine epidemic diarrhea virus, an ongoing 'normal' accident whose full repercussions are not yet known. The idea of a 'normal' accident was developed by sociologist Charles Perrow in the 1980s. Perrow argues that accidents are built into today's complex industrial systems, making these accidents 'normal' or expected (Perrow, 2011). I adopt Prudham's (2004) use of the concept of 'normal accidents', which he applies to neoliberal governance. Prudham argues that neoliberalism makes risk inevitable by 'building *organized irresponsibility* into regulatory systems' (Prudham, 2004, p.345). I argue that neoliberalism in North Carolina makes disasters inevitable by building an intentional tolerance of risk into the regulation of the swine industry.

While neoliberal governance has some common characteristics (e.g. deregulation), its impact on particular species, ecosystems and communities can differ significantly (McCarthy and Prudham, 2004; Bakker, 2009; Heynen et al., 2007). North Carolina's ten million hogs and their waste (held in open air waste lagoons) are concentrated on the state's flood plains among low-income, minority communities (Nicole, 2013). I draw from the literature on the political ecologies of risk to make four arguments about neoliberal governance and 'normal' accidents in the state's hog industry. First, the neoliberal governance of the hog industry is the 'root cause' (Wisner et al., 2004) of these environmental disasters. Second, the state's neoliberal policies have targeted historically marginalized communities, producing unequal risk and environmental injustice (Stith and Warrick, 1995; Morgan, 1998; Wing et al., 2002; Nicole, 2013). Third, I demonstrate that the state's intentional tolerance of risk has created a situation in which public and private vulnerability to disasters is highly differentiated. Hog corporations are allowed to create risks that inevitably lead to disasters, which the public then pay for with their environmental resources and tax dollars (Kilborn, 1999; Hayes, 1999).

Finally, I argue that North Carolina communities may be facing increasing risk to 'normal' accidents. North Carolina's coast is experiencing rising sea levels, and may face an increase in the frequency and intensity of hurricanes and other severe weather in a changing climate (Riggs and Ames, 2003; Paerl et al., 2006; Sallenger Jr et al., 2012). This may increase the susceptibility of hog waste lagoons on the coastal plain to flooding, posing threats to public and environmental health (Wing et al., 2002). In addition, in an ever-growing global economy, the US hog industry is expanding its international relationships (Huffstutter and Plume, 2012; Breuer, 2013; Rovira, 2013). This may increase the vulnerability of North Carolina's industrial swine production network to the global spread of infectious disease (Knobler et al., 2006; Rovira, 2013). In the event of a disease outbreak, the disposal of swine carcasses can pose serious threats to air and water quality (Ellis, 2001; Kastner et al., 2004; Miller, 2012). These increasing threats are occurring as North Carolina's government rolls out a second wave of neoliberal reforms (Kaufman, 2011; Dukes, 2013; Adams, 2013; Blythe, 2013).

In the rest of this chapter, first, I review the literature on the political ecologies of risk that analyze the ways in which neoliberal governance create environmental threats and 'normal accidents'. Second, I examine the first wave of neoliberal governance reforms to the state's hog industry. I argue that neoliberal tax breaks and deregulation put ten million hogs and their waste on the flood plain, creating the context for a series of normal accidents. Third, I analyze the 'normal' accidents of hurricanes Bertha, Fran and Floyd. I discuss the ways in which the neoliberal governance of the hog industry created a highly differentiated experience of vulnerability between the industry and the public, especially resident minority communities. Fourth, I describe the community resistance to neoliberal governance and the hog industry, as well as the roll-out of a second wave of neoliberal reforms. Last, I briefly analyze the ongoing 'normal' accident of porcine epidemic diarrhea virus. I argue that the fast spread of infectious viruses is built into the hog industry through a neoliberal strategy of flexible accumulation. While these implications of the outbreak are not yet fully known, the rising numbers of swine carcasses for disposal create potential threats to human and environmental health. Finally, I conclude that North Carolina's communities may face increasing risks, as sea levels rise on the coast and as the state rolls out a second wave of neoliberal governance reforms. This 'double exposure' (Leichenko and O'Brien, 2008) of

North Carolina communities to neoliberal economic policies and to environmental change may increase the risk for 'normal' accidents.

Neoliberal governance and the production of environmental risk

Neoliberalism has been described as a political 'project to restore, renew, and expand the conditions for capital accumulation, and ... to restore power to economic elites' (Heynen et al., 2007, p.4 citing Harvey, 2005). Neoliberalism is a broad term and a wide-ranging phenomenon, but with varied and diverse experiences on the ground (McCarthy and Prudham, 2004; Heynen et al., 2007). However, there is a set of discourses, ideologies and practices that is central to neoliberal governance strategies (Heynen et al., 2007; McCarthy and Prudham, 2004; Harvey, 2005). For the purposes of this chapter, this includes:

1 the deregulation and restructuring of state and federal monitoring and enforcement rules;
2 deep cuts to social and environmental programs and personnel, reducing the government's capacity to monitor and enforce rules;
3 a shift from a legally required regulatory framework to a voluntary one; and
4 a shift to a flexible accumulation strategy, where production systems have to respond quickly to the whims of the market (McCarthy and Prudham, 2004; Heynen et al., 2007; Bonanno and Constance, 2008).

McCarthy and Prudham (2004) and others argue that neoliberalism is an inherently environmental project (Heynen et al., 2007; Bakker, 2009; Peet et al., 2011). Neoliberalism is understood to be both the result and driver of a restructuring of social relationships with nature (e.g. enclosure). The neoliberalization of nature has allowed the environment to be 'freed-up' for the market, where it is managed as a commodity (McCarthy and Prudham, 2004). Neoliberalism has not only created a shift in how the environment is governed, it has also become a source of new environmental risks and 'normal' accidents (Wisner, 2003; Prudham, 2004; Collins and Jimenez, 2012).

Political ecologists and others have analyzed a number of ways in which neoliberal governance shapes environmental risk. I have condensed this analysis into three broad themes for the purposes of this chapter:

1 neoliberal governance can be the underlying cause of disasters;
2 neoliberal governance processes expose marginalized communities to environmental disasters; and
3 neoliberal governance creates highly differentiated experiences of vulnerability to environmental risks. These categories and practices are not mutually exclusive; instead they shape and inform one another.

In the first of these themes, a number of political ecologists have shown that neoliberalism can be, what Wisner et al. (2004) call, the 'root' or underlying cause of environmental disasters (Pelling, 2003; Wisner, 2003; Prudham, 2004; Collins, 2008; Brett and Oviatt, 2013; Bolin, 2007; Wisner et al., 2004). In these cases, environmental disasters are, in large part, *produced* by neoliberal governance policies. For example, Prudham (2004) argues that neoliberal governance strategies in Ontario's provincial government undermined agriculture and water quality regulation. The deregulation and restructuring of the province's water quality infrastructure created the conditions for E. coli bacteria to enter the public's drinking water in May of 2000, killing seven people and sickening over 2,000 others.

Second, other scholars have demonstrated the ways in which neoliberal governance can disadvantage certain communities, forcing socially and economically marginalized people into unsafe areas where they are exposed to environmental threats (Wisner, 2001; Peet and Watts, 2004; Robbins, 2004; Wisner et al., 2004; Bolin, 2007; Peet et al., 2011). For example, Wisner et al. (2004) examine policies in the Philippines that reduce the livelihood securities of rural Filipinos, forcing people into the coastal city of Manila to work as informal recyclers in the city's solid waste dump. In 2001, heavy rains from a monsoon flooded the city and dislodged compacted garbage, killing 700 workers and their families living in fragile shacks nearby.

Third, political ecologists have also examined how neoliberal policies can make vulnerability to environmental disasters highly differentiated. In these cases, environmental monitoring and enforcement is deregulated or restructured so that profits are prioritized and costs are socialized, often onto communities with the least political power (Wisner, 2003; Peet and Watts, 2004; Wisner et al., 2004; Bolin, 2007; Collins, 2008; Collins and Jimenez, 2012). Collins and Jimenez (2012) explain, 'neoliberal institutional arrangements have increasingly enabled them [wealthy corporations] to transfer risks to less powerful people and to expropriate awards' (p 56). They reference Collins (2008) who argues that Arizona's neoliberal policies (e.g. deregulation, insurance, and disaster-relief subsidies) have facilitated the ability of the wealthy to locate in fire-prone areas, while the costs are socialized as increased fire risks at the expense of public resources and finances.

In the remainder of this chapter, I argue that the neoliberal governance of North Carolina's hog industry is the root cause of a series of environmental disasters on the flood plain, creating the conditions for these 'normal' accidents. I examine the ways in which marginalized communities have been targeted by the hog industry, which has concentrated itself in low-income, minority communities, making them differentially vulnerable to industry disasters (Wing et al., 1996; Wing et al., 2002; Charleston, 2004; Donham et al., 2007; Nicole, 2013). In addition, I demonstrate how deregulation and emergency disaster-relief subsidies have enabled the hog industry to operate and rebuild in an areas with high environmental risks, while the costs are socialized as pollution at the expense of public health, resources and finances (Hayes, 1999; Kilborn, 1999; Ellis, 2001; Noble, 2010; Ford, 2011).

The neoliberal governance of North Carolina's hog industry: The first wave

North Carolina, like many communities, saw the first wave of neoliberal governance reforms in the 1970s (Harvey, 2005; Heath Jr. and Hess III, 2007; Heynen et al., 2007). The institutionalization of neoliberalism came in response to a political environment of strong environmental regulations and a crisis in the state's tobacco industry (Charleston, 2004; Heath Jr. and Hess III, 2007; Heynen et al., 2007). In the 1970s, tobacco was the state's number one agricultural commodity (Charleston, 2004). However, with the development of mechanical harvesters, tobacco was no longer labor dependent. As a result, low-income tobacco farmers could not compete and began seeking other farm jobs and opportunities (Charleston, 2004).

While in the throes of the tobacco crisis, there was also a state backlash against federal environmental regulations that were seen as impeding economic development, like the Clean Water Act of 1970 (Heath Jr. and Hess III, 2007). In response, a series of statutes were enacted by the state's General Assembly between 1974 and 1978. Known as the Hardison Amendments, the statutes prevented the state government from adopting air and water quality regulations that were stricter than the federal requirements. These amendments prevented the state expansion of environmental regulations for the next two decades (Heath Jr. and Hess III, 2007).

The growing neoliberal agenda in North Carolina facilitated the ability of the hog industry to move into the state, and specifically onto the state's coastal flood plain (Charleston, 2004). Socially and economically marginalized communities on the flood plain, who lacked political clout and employment opportunities, became a target for swine development policies and plans (Wing et al., 1996; Edwards and Ladd, 2000; Charleston, 2004). In the first wave of neoliberal reforms, Senator Wendell Murphy and his colleagues helped to pass a series of legislation that opened the door for the industrial penetration and domination of hogs on the state's coastal flood plain – creating the context for a series of 'normal' accidents (Stith and Warrick, 1995; Morgan, 1998; Charleston, 2004).

In 1985, two senate bills treated the hog industry to a gas tax reduction and exempted the industry from sales taxes on materials and equipment used to build hog houses. These exemptions resulted in a loss in public revenue of over $900,000 – the equivalent of over two million dollars today (Stith and Warrick, 1995). In 1987, three more bills were passed, exempting hog farms owned by corporations from feed inspection fees, from taxes on building materials and equipment, and from property taxes on feed mills used for hog farms (Stith and Warrick, 1995). In 1991, a bill restructured the definition of a 'farm' to include confined animal feeding operations or CAFOs for zoning purposes (Stith and Warrick, 1995). CAFOs, with thousands of densely stocked pigs – whose manure is collected in multi-acre, open-air waste lagoons – replaced small-scale outdoor hog farms in North Carolina at record rates in the 1990s (Edwards and Ladd, 2000; Gullick et al., 2007; Gillespie and Flanders, 2010). Adding CAFOs to the definition of farm prevented counties from using their zoning authority to restrict the citing of industrial-scale hog farms near residences, schools and other areas (Stith and Warrick, 1995; Morgan, 1998).

A second bill in 1991 weakened the environmental penalties for farms that discharged hog manure into streams. A third bill allowed the North Carolina Pork Producers Association to collect money through a hog levy and use the money to lobby the state legislature and fight lawsuits against the industry (Stith and Warrick, 1995). In addition, a 1991 amendment prevented the state from adopting waste effluent standards for animal feeding operations, if they were not already required by federal law (Stith and Warrick, 1995; Morgan, 1998). Finally, in 1993, House Bill 33 prevented researchers who were studying the impact that hog farms have on water quality from accessing agriculture department records with information on farm sites and sizes (Stith and Warrick, 1995).

The result of these neoliberal governance reforms enabled the hog industry to grow exponentially in an environmentally risky area, prone to floods and coastal storms, with limited oversight. In a span of six years, from 1989–1995, there was an 85 percent increase in the number of hogs produced in eastern North Carolina, moving the state from the fifteenth to the second largest hog producer in the country (Wing et al., 1996). By 1992, there were two million hogs concentrated on the flood plain, producing twice the amount of manure as the state's human population (ibid.). Four years later, the number of hogs more than quadrupled to over nine million, with the hogs producing over nine million tons of waste each year – creating the context for the disasters of hurricanes Bertha, Fran and Floyd (Walker et al., 2000; Leung, 2003).

The 'normal' accidents of hurricanes Bertha, Fran and Floyd

Bertha

On July 12, 1996, Hurricane Bertha hit North Carolina's coastal plains (Barnes, 2001). After hours of heavy winds and rain, the lagoon of a 2,400-head hog farm burst, spilling 1.8 million gallons of raw feces and urine into Swift Creek and the Neuse River (Kirby, 2010). An industry representative claimed that they 'had done nothing wrong, and blamed the accident on an unpredictable act of nature' (ibid., p.172). However, an inspection a few months earlier found that a number of lagoons on the flood plain could not withstand heavy rains, let alone a hurricane (ibid.). A few days later, dead and dying fish and crabs were found in the Neuse River Basin's streams, having died from low levels of oxygen in the river. The storm swept excess nutrients into the river (much of it hog waste), which created algal blooms that sucked available oxygen from the river (Kirby, 2010).

Human communities also faced threats from water contamination. Prudham (2004) explains that the impacts of neoliberal reforms are highly specific to the particular biophysical environment. The sandy soils and shallow water table on the coastal plain make the communities in this area especially vulnerable to groundwater pollution (Warrick and Stith, 1995b). Nitrates and bacteria from hog waste (and other contaminants) can move quickly through the sandy soil into ground water supplies below (Warrick and Stith, 1995b; Wing et al., 2002). In addition, the flat land of the coastal plain makes storing water in reservoirs impossible (Warrick and Stith, 1995b). As a result, more than half the population in this area is dependent upon well water, increasing their chance of exposure to harmful bacterial and other substances from flooded hog waste (Warrick and Stith, 1995b; Wing et al., 2002). An editorial in Raleigh's *News and Observer* contended that this was not an 'act of nature'; it was a 'normal' or expected accident. 'Nature did not plunk down 2,400 hogs on [this farmer's] land, just as nature did not create the hundreds of waste lagoons across the coastal plain' (*News and Observer* Editorial 1996, cited in Kirby 2010, p.173). It is the state's neoliberal governance of the hog industry that was the root cause of this disaster, not 'nature'. Tax exemptions, limited zoning authority, weakened environmental oversight and penalties, and the targeting of low-income communities are what 'plunked down' over nine million hogs and nine million tons of hog waste on the state's coastal plain, causing these 'normal' accidents (Wing et al., 2002; Leung, 2003; Kirby, 2010).

Fran

Two months later, Hurricane Fran hit North Carolina. Thousands of hogs drowned, trapped in confinement on the flood plain (Barnes, 2001). As the rains continued, twenty-two lagoons were inundated by rising flood waters (Leavenworth and Richissin, 1996; Wing et al., 2002). The lagoons overflowed, spilling into nearby rivers and streams. Farmers pumped out tons of hog waste onto their fields, desperately trying to avoid an overflow. However, with the fields saturated with water, most of the waste ran off into surrounding wetlands (Kirby, 2010).

Another round of fish kills ensued. The state's environmental officials argued that the fish kills were not caused by hog manure, but were due to natural materials in swamps being flushed into the rivers during the storm. Again, some scoffed at the idea that this 'accident' was caused by nature. Reporters from the *News and Observer* examined the breach of the lagoon at one flooded farm: 'The Ham farm was built in the Neuse River's floodway, an area so vulnerable to flooding that federal guidelines caution against the development of any kind' (Leavenworth and Richissin 1996, in Kirby 2010, p.175). However, lax zoning laws and political decisions in the state's neoliberal political establishment led to the permitting of Ham farm directly in the floodway (Kirby, 2010).

Floyd

Three years later, in 1999, Hurricane Floyd ripped through North Carolina's coast. Thirty thousand pigs drowned, confined to cages and pens (Barnes, 2001; Kirby, 2010). To prevent water contamination, farmers were ordered to not apply hog waste to saturated fields. However, environmental enforcement was not made a priority, so farmers (trying to avoid a lagoon breach) pumped out thousands of gallons of hog waste anyway (Kirby, 2010). Once again, deadly fish kills followed, and local communities faced numerous threats to their water supplies – from hog waste to decomposing hog carcasses (Ellis, 2001; Wing et al., 2002; Kirby, 2010).

When the storm quieted, state officials were faced with the task of disposing of 30,000 hog carcasses. The Secretary of Agriculture explained, 'Water contamination caused by decomposing livestock carcasses poses one of the most immediate threats to public health, and we will do all we can to help communities and farmers eliminate this hazard as quickly as possible' (Ellis, 2001). With the shallow water table, sandy soils, and high concentrations of hogs on the flood plain, rendering and burning the animals were deemed the safest options (ibid.).

However, rendering facilities were damaged during the storm, and burning the waterlogged hogs became unfeasible (Ellis, 2001; Kirby, 2010). As a result, 80 percent of the hogs were buried by farmers, who were paid by the pound to bury their pigs on their land (Ellis, 2001; Kirby, 2010). This created serious problems, as farmers buried animals in areas saturated with standing water. Dead hogs lose about six liters of body fluid in the first week after death (Ellis, 2001). With thousands of carcasses buried in saturated water, carcass runoff threatened well water and local streams (ibid.).

Bob Epting, a member of the state's environmental management commission and critic of the hog industry, requested a map of where animals were buried (Shiffer, 2000). However, he was told that environmental officials lacked the capacity to monitor the construction and placement of the burial sites. As a result, no one knew the exact location of the tens of thousands of buried pigs (ibid.). 'I wouldn't sit here and tell you none of them were buried in places they shouldn't have been', said a state official, who helped to run the animal disposal program after Floyd (ibid.).

Differential public-private vulnerability and environmental injustice

The neoliberal governance of the hog industry was not only the root cause of this series of 'normal' accidents, it also created a highly differentiated experience of vulnerability between the industry and the public. Seventy-five percent of the massive carcass disposal effort was paid for by the USDA's Emergency Watershed Program at a cost of over five million dollars (Ellis, 2001). These kinds of subsidies pay for the industry's 'normal' accidents through public funds. This public safety net for private corporations enables the hog industry to continue its risky practices at the expense of taxpayer money and the health of resident low-income, minority communities.

Pender County, a low-income, minority community on the flood plain, was inundated with contaminated floodwaters after Hurricane Floyd (ExchangeProject, 2008). The county is the fifth largest hog producer in the state (PCHD, 2010), and is in the region with the highest concentration of pigs per square feet (ACDS, 2007). Pender County, one of many low-income, minority communities targeted by the industry for development, was disproportionately impacted by the 'normal' accidents of Hurricane Floyd (Wing et al., 2002; ExchangeProject, 2008). They also faced greater barriers to accessing disaster relief funds than wealthier counterparts did, including the hog industry (ExchangeProject, 2008).

In the days after Floyd, many Pender County residents were sent to the emergency room with illnesses as a result of exposure to standing contaminated water (ibid.). Two of the major water contaminants were hog waste and dead livestock (ibid.). One resident, interviewed for the Southern Oral History Project in 1999, explained:

> I think that the major problem with the devastation was not really the water but the actual contaminants that were in the water. Used to be when they had floods … the water would recede and people could go and pick their crops and no problems. But now everything is so contaminated. The contamination is still here. Wells are still contaminated … There's been a lot of illness in the community, a lot of sickness, a lot of sores that won't heal, a lot of upper respiratory problems.
>
> (ExchangeProject, 2008)

Deregulation and emergency disaster-relief subsidies enabled the hog industry to operate and rebuild in areas with high environmental risks, while the environmental and health consequences for local communities remained largely unaddressed.

Following Floyd, the North Carolina Pork Council requested a year's exemption from the Clean Water Act and one million dollars in aid to rebuild their operations on the flood plain (Hayes, 1999; Kilborn, 1999). A spokesperson for the Council defended the request saying:

> It's no different from anybody else who has gotten flooded out … You know, we wanted our producers to be able to recover and have the opportunity to recover and rebuild just like everybody else in the state who has experienced this horrible catastrophe.
>
> (Hayes, 1999)

Donn Webb, of the Alliance for a Responsible Swine Industry, expressed his outrage at the efforts of the industry and state to prioritize the profits of the industry and socialize the costs of their 'normal' accidents.

> 'These people knew this could happen', Webb says, pointing to yet another lagoon brimming with hog waste. 'We told them they shouldn't ever build [hog CAFOs and waste lagoons] in the wetlands and flood plains. We knew it. They knew it. But it was cheap land. It was a cheap way to do anything, without any regard for the safety of the people that were already living in the wetlands … Don't make the hardworking taxpayer of the United States pay for the mistakes that the corporate hog people have made,' Webb says. 'They brought this on themselves. They should pay for it. Not us.'
>
> (Hayes, 1999)

Community resistance and the second wave of neoliberal governance reforms

The hurricanes of the 1990s made visible what minority communities on the flood plain were subject to on a daily basis (Wisner et al., 2004). Air and water pollution from North Carolina's swine farms cause respiratory and gastrointestinal problems for workers, local residents, and children attending school within a three-mile radius of an industrial hog farm (Wing and Wolf, 2000; Bullers, 2005; Mirabelli et al., 2006a, 2006b). Swine workers are exposed to drug-resistant strains of bacteria, which they can carry home to their families and neighbors (Rinsky et al., 2013). Neighbors of hog farms also suffer from a reduced quality of life. Exposed to chronic odors and unable to open their windows or play outdoors, many people suffer from stress, high blood pressure, anxiety and depression (Bullers, 2005; Wing et al., 2013).

Community resistance

However, the chronic pollution and objections to the state's prioritizing of corporate priorities over community welfare gave birth to a formidable collective of hog industry opponents (Wing et al., 1996; Rocheleau, 2007; Wing et al., 2008; Kirby, 2010). The Concerned Citizens of Tillery, the Alliance for a Responsible Swine Industry, the Rural Empowerment Association for Community Help, the Neuse Riverkeepers, the Waterkeeper Alliance, the North Carolina Environmental Justice Network and others organized to fight for needed regulation in the industry. Against a powerful opponent, they have had a number of successes.

In 1995, resistance efforts created the context for the Swine Farm Siting Act, which requires new hog farms to be 1,500 feet from a residence and 2,500 feet from a school (SSRI, 2007). In the same year, community organizations put pressure on the state to conduct an in-depth inspection of over 3,500 hog farms, in what was called The Blue Ribbon Commission on Agricultural Waste (Kirby, 2010). The commission found egregious violations, which led to legally requiring industrial hog farms to have permits to operate, to have 50-foot buffers between their farms and bodies of water, and to submit to annual inspections (Valentine and Carl, 1996; Kirby, 2010).

Community organizers were integral to the passing of the 1997 Clean Water Responsibility Act, which began a ten-year moratorium on the building on new hog farms and waste lagoons in North Carolina (SSRI, 2007; Kirby, 2010). In 2000, organizers served as committee members and informal advisors in a seven-year project they initiated through a legal settlement, known as 'The Smithfield Agreement' (Kirby, 2010). The goal of the agreement was to develop environmentally superior waste treatment technologies (known as ESTs) that would be legally required to replace waste lagoons, if deemed economically feasible (EDF, 2000; Williams, 2009; Kirby, 2010). ESTs were required to eliminate the discharge of swine waste into ground and surface waters, reduce air pollution and odor, and reduce the release of pathogens from the farms and lagoons into the environment (Williams, 2009).

In 2006, community organizations, represented by a lawyer named Nicollete Hahn, finalized a settlement with Murphy-Brown LLC, a subsidiary of Smithfield Foods and one of the world's largest producers of hogs (Niman, 2009; Kirby, 2010). In the settlement, Murphy-Brown agreed to install weather alert technology on their farms to prevent the spraying of hog waste in heavy winds and rain. They agreed to pay independent researchers to evaluate leaking lagoons and to improve pollution-control measures. Finally, they agreed to get Clean Water Act permits for all of their 275 hog farms in the state (Niman, 2009; Kirby, 2010). These were significant stopgap measures to reduce industry pollution until an alternative to hog waste lagoons was found (Kirby, 2010).

The second wave of neoliberal governance reforms

In 2007, five technologies or ESTs developed through the Smithfield Agreement were proved successful in eliminating the discharge of hog waste and reducing air pollution, odors and pathogens (Williams, 2009; Kirby, 2010). However, none of the ESTs were deemed economically feasible. The industry argued that any technology that increased their costs by more than nine cents per pound of pig was economically unfeasible (Williams, 2009; Kirby, 2010). Research showed that the five technologies would increase costs by 11–40 cents per pound, depending on the technology (Williams, 2009). These additional cents per pound would be passed onto the consumer. The industry argued that with more than an additional nine cents per pound, it would not be able to compete in the global pork market (Kirby, 2010).

Community organizations, outraged and disheartened by the outcome, pushed for a bill that would:

1   ban the building of lagoons on new and existing hog farms,
2   ban the building of new hog barns or expanding existing ones without adopting an EST technology, and
3   provide a grant for each producer who installed one of the five technologies developed through the Smithfield Agreement (ibid.).

In April of 2007, the bill unanimously passed in the Senate and was expected to pass in the House.

However, later that spring, Governor Easley pulled the bill from the House and worked with the industry to push through a different bill. The new bill still banned the building of new lagoons or hog houses without ESTs, but it offered a grant for a different, less environmentally protective technology that would increase the profits of the hog industry and ensure the longevity of hog waste lagoons on the flood plain (ibid.). The bill would provide money for a pilot program to capture methane from lagoons, which would be used to sell electricity at a subsidized price that would be passed onto consumers (Sturgis, 2007; Kirby, 2010). In true neo-liberal fashion, this legislation rolled back the more restrictive regulations in the original bill and turned the industry's hog waste into a commodity that was to be subsidized by the state's citizens.

This legislative maneuver was the beginning of a second wave of neoliberal governance reforms in North Carolina. In 2009, North Carolina's senate unanimously passed a bill to halt swine CAFO regulatory rules being developed by the Environmental Management Commission (Sturgis, 2009). At the time, the law required hog CAFOs to be inspected twice each year, with visual checks only – no environmental sampling. The proposed rule, now halted, would have increased water quality monitoring around hog CAFOs to three times each year, with environmental sampling at three different sites around the farm (ibid.). Further, in 2011, the passage of Senate Bill 501 undermined the 2007 moratorium by allowing hog farmers to replace or expand existing barns without upgrading their waste system to an EST (Ford, 2011).

To add insult to regulatory injury, in 2011, the state reduced the number of required inspections for CAFOs to once each year. In classic neoliberal form, it also shifted (partially) from a water quality monitoring framework that is legally required to a voluntary one (Stillwell, 2011; Heynen et al., 2007). Annual inspections by the Division of Water and Soil Conservation were no longer required, though two inspectors were made available for producers interested in participating in voluntary inspections (Stillwell, 2011). The Division of Water Quality (DWQ) would perform one visual inspection of water quality on swine CAFOs once each year, without any environmental testing (ibid.). In October 2013, at a North Carolina Environmental Justice Summit meeting, community members expressed concern about older lagoons that are expected to begin to break down and leak once they are about 20 years old (Kirby, 2010). Christine Lawson, supervisor of the Division of Water Resources' Animal Feeding Operations, responded to the question of a community member who asked if the annual inspections could detect a crack or break in the lagoon's lining. Lawson explained 'if there is a crack or a hole in the lagoon's lining, there is no way – with our visual inspections – to tell if there is actually a crack or if waste is leaking into the ground water' (Lawson, 2013).

In 2011, North Carolina's legislature also brought back the 1970s Hardison Amendments in the form of the Regulatory Reform Act of 2011. Like the Hardison Amendments, the Regulatory Reform Act prohibits the state from implementing environmental regulations that are stronger than federal standards (Stillwell, 2011). Cuts to the state's environmental regulatory bodies continued in 2012 and 2013. North Carolina's Department of Environment and Natural Resources (NCDENR) was reorganized, eliminating 70 positions and cutting its budget by over four million dollars (Dukes, 2013; Smith, 2013). Despite the cuts to the environmental agency's funding and personnel, in September of 2013, NCDENR turned down two grants from the federal government, worth over $580,000 for water quality monitoring (Binker, 2013).

In July of 2013, North Carolina community members, still suffering from swine CAFO odors and water pollution, filed 588 nuisance complaints against Smithfield Foods, the largest pork producer in the world (now owned by China's Shuanghui International Holdings Ltd) (Neff, 2013). In the same year, the state's Senate and House of Representatives pushed through a bill that would require complainants who lose in court to pay the legal fees of the farmers that defend the lawsuit (Neff, 2013). The bill is awaiting the governor's signature.

This second wave of neoliberal regulatory reforms comes at the same time as researchers are finding that rising sea levels are threatening North Carolina's coast, which may increase flooding on the state's coastal plains (Phillips, 2012; Sallenger Jr et al., 2012). This may increase the susceptibility of hog waste lagoons on the coastal plain to flooding, posing increasing threats to public and environmental health (Wing et al., 2002). Ironically, this research comes in the same year (2012) that North Carolina's legislature passed a bill preventing state agencies from basing laws on predictions of increase rates in sea-level rise (Phillips, 2012). Facing both rising sea levels and a second wave of neoliberal reforms, North Carolina's coastal communities may find themselves 'doubly exposed' to threats from neoliberal economic and environmental changes, increasing their risks to 'normal' accidents (Prudham, 2004; Leichenko and O'Brien, 2008).

The ongoing 'normal' accident of porcine epidemic diarrhea virus

In April of 2013, two cases of porcine epidemic diarrhea virus (PEDv) were found in North Carolina (Lange, 2014). PEDv is a highly contagious virus that causes severe diarrhea, vomiting, and dehydration in pigs, with a 100 percent mortality rate in young piglets (Slenning, 2013). By January of 2014, there were almost 1,800 confirmed cases of PEDv in North Carolina (Allen, 2014), and the virus had spread to over 20 states (De Groot, 2014) – killing up to four million pigs (Johnston, 2014). The outbreak of PEDv has been described as an accident, with the virus sneaking across the US border and 'marching' its way through the nation's hog industry (Stevens, 2013).

I argue, however, that the spread of PEDv is another case of a 'normal' accident of the swine CAFO industry in North Carolina and the broader United States. Conditions for the fast spread of infectious viruses are built into the system through just-in-time production, a neoliberal strategy of flexible accumulation (Boyd and Watts, 1997; Bonanno and Constance, 2008; Kotz and McDonough, 2010; Vansickle, 2012). Just-in-time production avoids overproduction by producing hogs 'just in time' for the next phase of production (e.g. nursery, weaning, growing) (Whiting et al., 2011). In just-in-time production, North Carolina's hogs are moved across the state, and to the Midwest, every few months for each phase of production (Paarlberg et al., 2009; Miller, 2011; Vansickle, 2012). As a result, 625,000 hogs move daily across the state and country (Vansickle, 2012; Campbell and Chen, 2014).

With over a half a million of hogs on US roads each day, just-in-time production also creates miles of exposure routes for the spread of disease (Slenning and Tickel, 2010; Vansickle, 2012; Campbell and Chen, 2014). Veterinarian James Roth explains, 'One of the reasons that we are so vulnerable to [infectious disease] is because we … depend on just-in-time movement to be efficient' (Vansickle, 2012).

The three firms that run North Carolina's swine industry obtain their inputs (e.g. feed, labor) from across the globe, extending their giant arms across the earth to access the cheapest inputs (Warrick and Stith, 1995a; Huffstutter and Plume, 2012; Stevens, 2013). It is believed that PEDv entered the United States through a feed additive from China (Stevens, 2013; Lange, 2014). Once the virus entered the country, just-in-time production facilitated its movement across the state and country. PEDv can remain infective in manure for 2–4 weeks (Young, 2014). Research found PEDv infective hog manure on transport trucks and tires and on the shoes and clothing of the truckers that move the 625,000 hogs across the country each day (Santiago, 2013; Campbell and Chen, 2014; SDSU, 2014). A study in Iowa tested the floors of 50 convenience stores frequented by swine transport truckers; all 50 tested positive for the virus (SDSU, 2014). It is just-in-time production that enabled PEDv to 'march' its way across the country, creating the 'normal' accident that is killing millions of pigs.

North Carolina's industry is geographically concentrated, with high animal stocking densities, to take advantage of cheap rent, to increase scale efficiency, and to facilitate just-in-time production (Furuseth, 1997; PCIFAP, 2008). This concentration of farms and animals also facilitates the spread of infectious disease. Snelson (2001) explains, 'The US [has] trended towards larger livestock production units … Diseases may well move more quickly, and be more difficult to control and eradicate, in these large farms where facilities are overstocked and production expectations are maximized' (Snelson, 2001). Concentrating thousands of hogs and their manure in one place has created the potential for large reservoirs of PEDv and large populations of susceptible pigs (Helm, 2006; UMN, 2013).

The pork production network is configured around neoliberal approaches to capital accumulation. First, low rent, lax regulations, and economies of scale have led to the concentration of millions of hogs and their manure. Second, just-in-time production moves hundreds of thousands of these pigs across the country each day. These practices have created miles of exposure routes for the PEDv virus, large reservoirs of PEDv virus held in swine waste lagoons, and large, concentrated populations of susceptible pigs. These neoliberal practices of concentration and circulation are root causes of the PEDv outbreak. Neoliberal accumulation strategies have created a pork production network that is extremely sensitive to the spread of infectious disease, creating the 'normal accident' of PEDv outbreak.

PEDv is not a zoonotic disease that can be transmitted to humans (Slenning, 2013). However, its high mortality rate (Paulson, 2013) presents challenges and threats associated with carcass disposal, especially on North Carolina's flood plain. This 'normal' accident is ongoing, and its full repercussions for the pigs, the industry, local communities, and the environment are not yet known (Strom, 2014). However, what we do know is that all carcass disposal methods, especially for large populations of animals, can pose threats to human and environmental health (Kastner et al., 2004; Harper et al., 2008) – with potentially serious impacts for environmental justice communities in the flood plain.

In infectious disease outbreaks, on-site above-ground composting or burial are preferred to avoid the spread of disease (Kastner et al., 2004; Harper et al., 2008; USDA and APHIS, 2012). However, the industry's location on the flood plain, with a high water table and sandy soils, makes this method a serious threat for water contamination (Ellis, 2001). Also, with the hog industry situated in 'hurricane alley' (Barnes, 2001), composting is not ideal because coastal storms could push partially composted remains into waterways, threatening water sources (Miller, undated). Carcass incineration can also pose environmental and public health risks thorough air and ash pollution (Kastner et al., 2004; Harper et al., 2008). Carcass disposal through rendering is environmentally superior, but not ideal because of the potential to spread the virus during transport to rendering, and due to the limited number of rendering facilities available (Kastner et al., 2004; Harper et al., 2008). The socio-ecological landscape targeted by neoliberal policies to enable the production and concentration of ten million hogs on the flood plain is the same landscape that makes the safe clean-up of this, so-called, 'normal' accident nearly impossible.

Conclusion

This paper uses the concept of a 'normal' accident to examine a series of disasters in North Carolina's hog industry. These disasters were not and are not 'acts of God'. They are the result of two decades of neoliberal governance reforms that prioritize the profits of the industry, while socializing the costs as environmental and public health risks. Tax exemptions, limited zoning authority, weakened environmental oversight and penalties, and the targeting of low-income communities put ten million hogs and 9.5 million tons of hog waste on the state's flood plain. The institutionalization of neoliberalism in the political-ecological fabric of the hog industry is the root cause of the disasters of hurricanes Bertha, Fran and Floyd. The neoliberal configuration of the pork production network – simultaneously concentrating pigs and place and moving them across the landscape – is what enabled PEDv to hitchhike across the state and country.

Neoliberal government representation not only enables the hog industry through tax breaks and deregulation, but also through subsidized insurance and disaster relief. This creates a highly differentiated experience of vulnerability between the industry and the public. The public safety net for private corporations allows the hog industry to continue its risky practices. This draws money away from already dwindling public resources, which could be utilized for environmental protection and restoration for the benefit of public, economic and environmental health. In addition, by providing disaster relief for the hog industry without requiring pollution controls, the government further marginalizes the environmental justice communities on the flood plain, for whom 'normal' accidents of air and water pollution are a daily occurrence.

North Carolina is currently experiencing a second wave of neoliberal governance reforms. This second wave comes as sea levels rise on the state's coast and the industry expands its global economic reach. This double exposure of North Carolina communities to neoliberal economic policies and to environmental change may increase the risk for 'normal' accidents. It remains to be seen whether the pressures and counter-actions of North Carolina's environmental advocates and justice organizations will eventually be successful in making the hog industry's disasters less 'normal'.

Acknowledgements

This research was supported by The Society for Women Geographers and The Robert and Patricia Switzer Foundation.

References

ACDS 2007. Agricultural Trends Profile for Duplin County, NC. Columbia, MD: Agriculture and Community Development Services, LLC.

Adams, A. 2013. *Soul-crushing takeover of NC DENR brings resignation* [Online]. Raleigh, NC: News and Observer. Available: www.newsobserver.com/2013/12/15/3457917/ soul-crushing-takeover-of-nc-denr.html [Accessed February 10 2014].

Allen, W. 2014. *Pig Virus May Lead to Higher Cost for Barbeque* [Online]. Gastonia, NC: Gaston Gazette. Available: www.gastongazette.com/spotlight/pig-virus-may-lead-to-higher-cost-for-barbecue-1.264967?page=0 [Accessed February 20 2014].

Bakker, K. 2009. Neoliberal nature, ecological fixes, and the pitfalls of comparative research. *Environment and Planning A*, 41, 1781–1787.

Barnes, J. 2001. *North Carolina's hurricane history*, University of North Carolina Press.

Binker, M. 2013. *DENR Turns Down Grant for Water Monitoring in Gas Drilling Areas* [Online]. Raleigh, NC: Capital Broadcasting Company. Available: www.wral.com/ denr-turns-down-grant-to-help-with-water-monitoring-in-fracking-areas/12917090/ [Accessed February 18 2014].

Blythe, A. 2013. *NC 'Moral Monday' demonstrations bring 49 arrests* [Online]. Raleigh, NC: News and Observer. Available: www.newsobserver.com/2013/05/13/2890544/ nc-moral-monday-demonstrations.html [Accessed February 10 2014].

Bolin, R. 2007. Race, Class, Ethnicity, and Disaster Vulnerability. *In:* Rodriguez, H., Quarantelli, E. L. and Dynes, R. (eds), *Handbook of Disaster Research.* New York: Springer Science and Business Media LLC.

Bonanno, A. and Constance, D. 2008. *Stories of Globalization: Transnational Corporations, Resistance, and the State*, Park, PA, The Pennsylvania State University Press.

Boyd, W. and Watts, M. 1997. Agro-Industrial Just-In-Time. *In:* Goodman, D. and Watts, M. (eds), *Globalising Food: Agrarian Questions and Global Restructuring.* New York: Routledge.

Brett, J. and Oviatt, K. 2013. The Intrinsic Link of Vulnerability to Sustainable Development. *In:* Thomas, D. S. K., Phillips, B. D., Lovekamp, W. E. and Fothergill, A. (eds), *Social Vulnerability to Disasters.* 2nd ed. Boca Raton, FL: Taylor and Francis Group, LLC.

Breuer, A. 2013. Expanding the US Pork Industry Through FTAs. *Choices: The Magazine of Food, Farm, and Resource Issues*. Washington, DC: Agricultural and Applied Economics Association (AAEA).

Bullers, S. 2005. Environmental stressors, perceived control, and health: the case of residents near large-scale hog farms in eastern North Carolina. *Human Ecology*, 33, 1–16.

Campbell, E. and Chen, L. 2014. *Virus Killing 5 Million Pigs Spurs Hog-Price Rally: Commodities* [Online]. New York: Bloomberg News. Available: www.bloomberg.com/news/2014-02-06/virus-killing-5-million-pigs-spurs-hog-price-rally-commodities.html [Accessed February 20 2014].

Charleston, D. 2004. Feeding the Hog Industry in North Carolina: Agri-Industrial Restructuring in Hog Farming and Its Implications for the US Periphery. *Sociation Today*, 2.

Collins, T. W. 2008. The political ecology of hazard vulnerability: marginalization, facilitation and the production of differential risk to urban wildfires in Arizona's White Mountains. *Journal of Political Ecology*, 15, 21–43.

Collins, T. W. and Jimenez, A. M. 2012. The Neoliberal Production of Vulnerability and Unequal Risk. *In:* Dooling, S. and Simon, G. (eds), *Cities, Nature, and Development: The Politics and Production of Urban Vulnerabilities*. Burlington, VT: Ashgate Publishing Company.

De Groot, A. 2014. *The Big Bad PEDv that's Blowing the Pig Farm Down …* [Online]. Providence, RI: EpiVax, Inc. Available: www.epivax.com/blog/the-big-bad-pedv-thats-blowing-the-pig-farm-down/ [Accessed February 20 2014].

Donham, K. J., Wing, S., Osterberg, D., Flora, J. L., Hodne, C., Thu, K. M. and Thorne, P. S. 2007. Community health and socioeconomic issues surrounding concentrated animal feeding operations. *Environmental Health Perspectives*, 115, 317–320.

Dukes, T. 2013. *Job cuts coming for water regulators as DENR trims costs* [Online]. Raleigh, NC: WRAL. Available: www.wral.com/job-cuts-coming-for-water-regulators-as-denr-trims-costs/12880102/ [Accessed February 10 2014].

EDF. 2000. *Environmentalists Applaud Action Requiring Smithfield Foods To Eliminate NC Hog Lagoons* [Online]. New York: Environmental Defense Fund. Available: www.edf.org/news/environmentalists-applaud-action-requiring-smithfield-foods-eliminate-nc-hog-lagoons [Accessed February 17 2014].

Edwards, B. and Ladd, A. E. 2000. Environmental Justice, Swine Production, and Farm Loss in North Carolina. *Sociological Spectrum*, 20, 263–290.

Ellis, D. B. 2001. *Carcass Disposal Issues in Recent Disasters, Accepted Methods, and Suggested Plan to Mitigate Future Events*. Master of Public Administration, Southwest Texas State University.

ExchangeProject 2008. Maple Hill, NC (Pender County). *In:* EDUCATION, D. O. H. B. A. H. (ed.), *Real People-Real Stories*. Chapel Hill, NC: The University of North Carolina at Chapel Hill.

Ford, S. 2011. *Living with Those Lovely Lagoon* [Online]. Raleigh, NC: News and Observer. Available: www.newsobserver.com/2011/05/01/1164638/living-with-those-lovely-lagoons.html [Accessed February 13 2014].

Furuseth, O. J. 1997. Restructuring of Hog Farming in North Carolina: Explosion and Implosion. *The Professional Geographer*, 49, 391–403.

Gillespie, J. R. and Flanders, F. B. 2010. *Modern Livestock and Poultry Production*, Clifton Park, NY, Cengage Learning Inc.

Gullick, R. W., Brown, R. A. and Cornwell, D. A. 2007. Source Water Protection for Concentrated Animal Feeding Operations. Newport News, VA: American Water Works Association Research Foundation and US Environmental Protection Agency.

Harper, A. F., Derouchey, J. M., Glanville, T. D., Meeker, D. L. and Straw, B. E. 2008. Swine Carcass Disposal Options for Routine and Catastrophic Mortality. Ames, IA: Council for Agricultural Science and Technology (CAST).

Harvey, D. 2005. *A brief history of neoliberalism*, New York, Oxford University Press.

Hayes, E. 1999. Hog Industry Produces 37 BILLION Gallons Toxic Waste In N. Carolina. *ABCNews.com*, November 5, 1999.

Heath Jr, M. S. and Hess III, A. L. 2007. The Evolution of Modern North Carolina Environmental and Conservation Policy Legislation. *Campbell Law Review*, 29, 535–761.

Helm, J. 2006. Biosecurity: Protecting Animal Agriculture Swine Production. *In:* Anonymous (ed.), *Swine Training Manual*. Clemson, South Carolina: Clemson University Cooperative Extension.

Heynen, N., McCarthy, J., Prudham, S. and Robbins, P. 2007. Introduction: False Promises. *In:* Heynen, N., McCarthy, J., Prudham, S. and Robbins, P. (eds), *Neoliberal Environments: False Promises and Unnatural Consequences*. New York: Routledge.

Huffstutter, P. J. and Plume, K. 2012. *Exclusive: North Carolina firms ink deals to import 826,733 tons of corn* [Online]. London: Reuters. Available: www.reuters.com/article/2012/09/26/us-usa-corn-imports-idUSBRE88P1KH20120926 [Accessed February 11 2014].

Johnston, T. 2014. *PEDv cases spike in the U.S., cause concern in global pork market* [Online]. Chicago: Meatingplace. Available: www.meatingplace.com/Industry/News/Details/47832?loginSuccess [Accessed February 20 2014].

Kastner, C., Erickson, L., Kastner, J., Nutsch, A. and Phebus, R. 2004. Carcass Disposal: A Comprehensive Review. *In:* GROUP, N. A. B. C. C. C. D. W. (ed.). Manhattan, Kansas: National Agricultural Biosecurity Center, Kansas State University.

Kaufman, L. 2011. *G.O.P. Push in States to Deregulate Environment* [Online]. New York: New York Times. Available: www.nytimes.com/2011/04/16/science/earth/16enviro.html?_r=2&hp& [Accessed February 10 2014].

Kilborn, P., T. 1999. Hurricane Reveals Flaws in Farm Law as Animal Waste Threatens N. Carolina Water. *The New York Times*, October 17, 1999.

Kirby, D. 2010. *Animal Factory*, New York, St. Martin's Press.

Knobler, S., Mahmoud, A., Lemon, S. and Pray, L. E. 2006. The Impact of Globalization on Infectious Disease Emergence and Control: Exploring the Consequences and Opportunities: Workshop Summary. Washington, DC: National Academies Press.

Kotz, D. M. and McDonough, T. 2010. Global Neoliberalism and the Contemporary Structure of Accumulation. *In:* McDonough, T. and Reich, M. (eds), *Contemporary Capitalism and its Crises: Social Structure of Accumulation Theory for the Twenty-First Century*. New York: Cambridge University Press.

Lange, K. 2014. *Pork producers on the lookout for deadly PED Virus* [Online]. Fargo, NC: WDAY News. Available: www.wday.com/event/article/id/93580/ [Accessed February 20 2014].

Lawson, C. October 18, 2013 2013. *RE: The 2013 North Carolina Environmental Justice Summit.*

Leavenworth, S. and Richissin, T. 1996. Waste Lagoons that Withstood Fran Overflowing Now Due to Rain. *News and Observer*, September 12, 1996.

Leichenko, R. M. and O'Brien, K. 2008. *Environmental Change and Globalization: Double Exposures*, New York, Oxford University Press.

Leung, R. 2003. *Pork Power: Are Hog Farmers Creating a Waste Hazard?* [Online]. New York: CBS News. Available: www.cbsnews.com/news/pork-power/ [Accessed February 17 2014].

McCarthy, J. and Prudham, S. 2004. Neoliberal nature and the nature of neoliberalism. *Geoforum*, 35, 275–283.

Miller, D. 2011. North Carolina Pork Industry Reboots. *National Hog Farmer*. New York: Penton.

Miller, L. (undated) Agricultural Disposal MaTCh Tool: Matrix, Decision Tree, Checklist. *FADPreP*. Riverdale, MD: The United States Department of Agriculture and The Animal and Plant Health Inspection Service.

Miller, L. 2012. Global Lessons from FMD Outbreaks: Implications for the US. *Wide Area Recovery and Resiliency Program*. Denver, CO.

Mirabelli, M. C., Wing, S., Marshall, S. W. and Wilcosky, T. C. 2006a. Asthma symptoms among adolescents who attend public schools that are located near confined swine feeding operations. *Pediatrics*, 118, e66–e75.

Mirabelli, M. C., Wing, S., MarshalL, S. W. and Wilcosky, T. C. 2006b. Race, poverty, and potential exposure of middle-school students to air emissions from confined swine feeding operations. *Environmental Health Perspectives*, 114, 591.

Morgan, R. 1998. Legal and Political Injustices of Industrial Swine Production in North Carolina. *In:* Thu, K. M. and Durrenberger, E. P. (eds), *Pigs, Profits, and Rural Communities*. Albany, NY: State University of New York Press.

Neff, J. 2013. Hundreds file complaints over hog-farm waste. *News and Observer*.

Nicole, W. 2013. CAFOs and Environmental Justice: The Case of North Carolina. *Environmental Health Perspectives*, 121, 182–189.

Niman, N. H. 2009. *Righteous Porkchop: Finding a Life and Good Food Beyond Factory Farms*, New York, HarperCollins.

Noble, M. 2010. Paying the Polluters: Animal Factories Feast on Tax Payer Subsidies. *In:* Imhoff, D. (ed.), *CAFO: The Tragedy of Industrial Animal Factories*. San Rafael, CA: Earth Aware.

Paarlberg, P. L., Seitzinger, A. H., Lee, J. G. and Matthews, K. H. J. 2009. Supply Reductions, Export Restrictions, and Expectations for Jog Returns in a Potential Classical Swine Fever Outbreak in the United States. *Journal of Swine Health and Production*, 17, 155–162.

Paerl, H. W., Valdes, L. M., Joyner, A. R., Pieierls, B. L., Piehler, M. F., Riggs, S. R., Christian, R. R., Eby, L. A., Crowder, L. B., Raums, J. S., Clesceri, E. J., Buzzelli, C. P. and Luettich JR., R. 2006. Ecological Response to Hurricane Events in the Pamlico Sound System, North Carolina, and Implications for Assessment and Management in a Regime of Increased Frequency. *Estuaries and Coasts*, 29, 1033–1045.

Paulson, S. K. 2013. *Porcine Epidemic Diarrhea Virus Migrates To U.S., Threatens Pork Prices* [Online]. New York: Huffington Post. Available: www.huffingtonpost. com/2013/07/10/porcine-epidemic-diarrhea-virus-pork-prices_n_3575321.html [Accessed February 20 2014].

PCHD 2010. 2010 Pender Community Health Assessment. Burgaw, NC: Pender County Health Department.

PCIFAP 2008. Putting Meat on the Table: Industrial Farm Animal Production in America. Washington, DC: Pew Charitable Trusts.

Peet, R. and Watts, M. 2004. Liberating Political Ecology. *In:* Peet, R. and Watts, M. (eds), *Liberation Ecologies*. 2nd ed. New York: Routledge.

Peet, R., Robbins, P. and Watts, M. 2011. Global Nature. *In:* Peet, R., Robbins, P. and Watts, M. (eds), *Global Political Ecology*. New York: Routledge.

Pelling, M. 2003. *Natural disaster and development in a globalizing world*, New York, Routledge.

Perrow, C. 2011. *Normal accidents: Living with high risk technologies*, Princeton University Press.

Phillips, L. 2012. *US Northeast coast is hotspot for rising sea levels: Report comes after North Carolina senate proposes bill to ban predictions of increase in rates of sea-level rise*. [Online]. Nature: International Weekly Journal of Science. Available: www.nature.com/news/

us-northeast-coast-is-hotspot-for-rising-sea-levels-1.10880   [Accessed   February   18 2014].

Prudham, S. 2004. Poisoning the well: neoliberalism and the contamination of municipal water in Walkerton, Ontario. *Geoforum*, 35, 343–359.

Riggs, S. R. and Ames, D. V. 2003. *Drowning the North Carolina Coast: Sea Level Rise and Estuarine Dynamics*, Raleigh, NC, North Carolina Sea Grant

Rinsky, J. L., Nadimpalli, M., Wing, S., Hall, D., Baron, D., Price, L. B., Larsen, J., Stegger, M., Stewart, J. and Heaney, C. D. 2013. Livestock-Associated Methicillin and Multidrug Resistant Staphylococcus aureus Is Present among Industrial, Not Antibiotic-Free Livestock Operation Workers in North Carolina. *PloS one*, 8, e67641.

Robbins, P. 2004. *Political Ecology: A Critical Introduction*, Malden, MA, Blackwell Publishing.

Rocheleau, D. E. 2007. Neoliberal environments, technologies of governance and governance of technologies. *In:* Heynen, N., McCarthy, J., Prudham, S. and Robbins, P. (eds), *Neoliberal Environments: False Promises and Unnatural Consequences*. New York: Routledge.

Rovira, A. 2013. *Addressing the Growing Epidemic of PEDV* [Online]. National Hog Farmer. Available: http://nationalhogfarmer.com/health/addressing-growing-epidemic-pedv [Accessed February 10, 2014 2014].

Sallenger Jr, A. H., Doran, K. S. and Howd, P. A. 2012. Hotspot of accelerated sea-level rise on the Atlantic coast of North America. *Nature Climate Change*, 2, 884–888.

Santiago, V. 2013. *U.S. Trucks Test Positive for PED Virus* [Online]. Ames, IA: Farms. com. Available: www.farms.com/ag-industry-news/u-s-trucks-test-positive-for-ped-virus-018.aspx [Accessed February 20 2014].

SDSU. 2014. *Three Million Pigs Possibly Lost Due to PEDV* [Online]. Minneapolis, MN: South Dakota State University and National Hog Farmer. Available: http://nationalhogfarmer. com/health/three-million-pigs-possibly-lost-due-pedv [Accessed February 20 2014].

Shiffer, J. 2000. A Hog Issue that Just Won't Die. *The News and Observer*, September 19, 2000, p.A3.

Slenning, B. D. 2013. *Epidemiology Expert on Spread of Porcine Epidemic Diarrhea Virus* [Online]. Raleigh, NC: NC State College of Veterinary Medicine. Available: www. cvm.ncsu.edu/news/2013-07-29-Epidemiology-Expert-on-Spread-of-PEDV.html [Accessed February 20 2014].

Slenning, B. D. and Tickel, J. L. 2010. Foreign Animal Diseases and Food System Security: Decision Making for Appropriate Responses. *In:* Voeller, J. G. (ed.), *Wiley Handbook of Science and Technology for Homeland Security*. New York: John Wiley & Sons, Inc.

Smith, R. W. May 20, 2013 2013. The Senate Budget and the Environment: Money. *SmithEnvironment Blog: Environmental Law and Policy from a North Carolina Point of View* [Online]. Available from: www.smithenvironment.com/the-senate-budget-and-the-environment-money/ [Accessed February 18, 2014 2014].

Snelson, H. 2001. Foot and Mouth Disease in the UK - My Experience. *North Carolina Healthy Hogs Seminar*. Greenville, NC: North Carolina Swine Veterinary Group.

SSRI. 2007. *North Carolina in the Global Economy: Overview* [Online]. Durham, NC: Social Science Research Institute, Duke University. Available: www.soc.duke.edu/NC_GlobalEconomy/hog/overview.shtml [Accessed February 16 2014].

Stevens, J. 2013. *ISU vet: PEDV now spread to 20 states* [Online]. Fort Dodge, IA: Farm News. Available: www.farm-news.com/page/content.detail/id/519676/ISU-vet--PEDV-now-spread-to-20-states.html?nav=5005 [Accessed February 13 2014].

Stillwell, L. 2011. New Laws Affect Hog Farms. Raleigh, NC: Sampson County Livestock Agent Swine and Waste Management.

Stith, P. and Warrick, J. 1995. *Murphy's Law: for Murphy, Good Government Means Good Business* [Online]. Raleigh: The News and Observer. Available: www.pulitzer.org/archives/5897 [Accessed February 14 2014].

Strom, S. 2014. Farmers Gain Weapon Against Devastating Pig Virus. *The New York Times*, October 9.

Sturgis, S. 2007. *N.C. Enviros Rally Against Not-So-Clean Energy Bill* [Online]. Durham NC: The Institute for Southern Studies. Available: www.southernstudies.org/2007/07/nc-enviros-rally-against-not-so-clean-energy-bill.html [Accessed February 18 2014].

Sturgis, S. 2009. *Boss Hog's attempted regulatory coup in North Carolina* [Online]. Durham, NC: Institute for Southern Studies. Available: www.southernstudies.org/2009/08/boss-hogs-attempted-regulatory-coup-in-north-carolina.html [Accessed February 18 2014].

UMN. 2013. *Tracking PEDV in North Carolina* [Online]. Minneapolis, MN: University of Minnesota and National Hog Farmer. Available: http://nationalhogfarmer.com/health/tracking-pedv-north-carolina [Accessed February 20 2014].

USDA and APHIS 2012. Foot-and-Mouth Disease (FMD) Response Plan: The Red Book. *Foreign Animal Disease Preparedness and Response Plan.* Washington DC: United States Department of Agriculture and The Animal and Plant Health Inspection Service.

Valentine, T. and Carl, E. A. 1996. The Blue Ribbon Study Commission on Agricultural Waste. *In:* ASSEMBLY, T. N. C. G. (ed.), *Part IV of chapter 542 of the 1995 Session Laws.* Raleigh, NC: The North Carolina General Assembly.

Vansickle, J. 2012. Protecting Our Borders: Education is Paramount to Preserving National Food Security and Public Health. *National Hog Farmer.* Minneapolis: Penton.

Walker, J., Nelson, D. and Aneja, V. P. 2000. Trends in ammonium concentration in precipitation and atmospheric ammonia emissions at a coastal plain site in North Carolina, USA. *Environmental science & technology*, 34, **3527**–3534.

Warrick, J. and Stith, P. 1995a. *Money Talks: The Smell of Money* [Online]. Raleigh, NC: The News and Observer. Available: www.pulitzer.org/archives/5899 [Accessed February 19 2014].

Warrick, J. and Stith, P. 1995b. *New Studies Show that Lagoons are Leaking: Groundwater, rivers affected by waste* [Online]. Raleigh: News and Observer. Available: www.pulitzer.org/archives/5893 [Accessed February 17 2014].

Whiting, T. L., Steele, G. G., Wamnes, S. and Green, C. 2011. Evaluation of methods of rapid mass killing of segregated early weaned piglets. *The Canadian Veterinary Journal*, 52, 753–758.

Williams, C. M. 2009. Development of Environmentally Superior Technologies in the US and Policy. *Bioresource Technology*, 100, 5512–5518.

Wing, S. and Wolf, S. 2000. Intensive livestock operations, health, and quality of life among eastern North Carolina residents. *Environmental Health Perspectives*, 108, 233.

Wing, S., Freedman, S. and Band, L. 2002. The Potential Impact of Flooding on Confined Animal Feeding Operations in Eastern North Carolina. *Environmental Health Perspectives*, 110, 387–391.

Wing, S., Grant, G., Green, M. and Stewart, C. 1996. Community based collaboration for environmental justice: south-east Halifax environmental reawakening. *Environment and Urbanization*, 8, 129–140.

Wing, S., Horton, R. A., Muhammad, N., Grant, G. R., Tajik, M. and Thu, K. 2008. Integrating epidemiology, education, and organizing for environmental justice: community health effects of industrial hog operations. *American journal of public health*, 98, 1390–1397.

Wing, S., Horton, R. A. and Rose, K. M. 2013. Air pollution from industrial swine operations and blood pressure of neighboring residents. *Environ Health Perspect*, 121, 92–96.

Wisner, B. 2001. Risk and the Neoliberal State: Why Post-Mitch Lessons Didn't Reduce El Salvador's Earthquake Losses. *Disasters,* 25, 251–268.

Wisner, B. 2003. Changes in Capitalism and Global Shifts in the Distribution of Hazard and Vulnerability. *In:* Pelling, M. (ed.), *Natural Disaster and Development in a Globalizing World.* New York: Routledge.

Wisner, B., Blaikie, P., Cannon, T. and Davis, I. 2004. *At Risk: Natural Hazards, People's Vulnerability, and Disasters,* London, Routledge.

Young, L. 2014. *Porcine epidemic diarrhea virus continues to spread* [Online]. Rochester, MN: Agri News. Available: www.agrinews.com/porcine/epidemic/diarrhea/virus/continues/to/spread/story-5921.html [Accessed February 20 2014].

PART III

Biopolitics, knowledge and the materialism of meat

10

BREED CONTRA BEEF

The making of Piedmontese cattle

Annalisa Colombino and Paolo Giaccaria

Introduction

In the spring of 2014, one of the authors (Paolo) was visiting the Green Market on Union Square, NYC, one of the most renowned farmers' markets in the United States, performing a direct connection between producers and consumers of food, allegedly alternative to the mass retail channel (Tiemann, 2008), but also promoting what Sharon Zukin terms, from a critical standpoint, 'the consumption of authenticity' (2008). Exactly in the middle of the square, a farmer from Pennsylvania displayed a sign to attract customers claiming 'Piedmontese Only'. Less than half a mile away, on Madison Square, at Eataly – the sumptuous sanctuary of 'high-quality' Italian food – the sophisticated New York consumer could already purchase a taste of Piedmontese beef at the butcher's counter and at the Manzo restaurant (literally 'beef' in Italian) since the opening of the food mall, on 30 August 2010.

The Piedmontese was officially recognized as a cattle breed in the 1850s. In 1996 it became the first presidium established by Slow Food in Bra, Piedmont.[1] Its beef is now well renowned among gastronomists and listed in Michelin-starred restaurants (NAPA, 2010, p.6) and it is Eataly's official beef in Italy and the US. But, what is, exactly, the link connecting these moments and places and which establishes a relationship between an apparently endangered cattle breed in the motherland of Slow Food and the sophisticated consumption practices of the world elites in New York City? La Granda, in its twofold role as a sociocultural and economic actor, provides the most obvious nexus, which articulates the connection between the past and present of the Piedmontese breed and the refined New York City cosmopolitan consumer.

La Granda is the name of the Slow Food presidium of the Piedmontese breed founded by veterinarian Sergio Capaldo in 1996 to summon a small number of breeders and preserve the rearing of this apparently endangered cattle breed. La

Granda Trasformazione is the meat-processing company, owned by Capaldo and Eataly's founder Oscar Farinetti, established in 2004 to supply the Italian branches of the food mall with premium Piedmontese beef directly from the Slow Food presidium (Colombino and Giaccaria, 2013a).[2] La Granda, rather obviously, does not directly supply the beef for Eataly New York. The beef sold at the butcher counter and used to cook at Manzo's is more simply called 'Piedmontese' and is supplied by North American companies. The breed has in fact been reared in the US since 1979.[3] However, La Granda and its founder play a key role in maintaining the consortium's original quality conventions (Boltanski and Thevenot, 2006) – fixed and codified by the *disciplinare di produzione* (specifications of production), the document that establishes how exactly the cattle must be farmed, including strict rules on fodder and hygiene – by organizing workshops and training for Eataly's butchers. Importantly, as we claim in this chapter, La Granda is only the final outcome of a contested process, originated in the second half of the nineteenth century, which has radically modified the political ecology of the Piedmontese breed.

In this chapter, we 'follow' (Cook et al., 2006) the Piedmontese starting with a peculiar event that took place in 1886 in Guarene d'Alba, a small locality in the province of Cuneo (in Piedmont, Northern Italy) and ending on the butcher's counter at Eataly, in contemporary New York City. In discussing some of the spatio-temporal trajectories of the Piedmontese, we bring to light the process that undergirds the transformation of a specific morphological feature – known today as the 'double muscle factor', and appearing randomly in some animals of this bovine population in the second half of the nineteenth century – from a (monstrous) anomaly to be eliminated into a key trait to be preserved. Consistently with a political ecology/actor-network theory approach (Bennett, 2010; Latour, 1999), we show how the current status of the Piedmontese, as a cattle breed that produces what is marketed as premium beef, is not a reflection of the animal's genetic characteristics (see Holloway et al., 2011; Morris and Holloway, 2013). Rather, it is a matter of 'natureculture' (Haraway 2008; see also Latimer and Miele, 2013), that is the result of the complicated negotiations among veterinarians, livestock technicians, farmers and butchers, which have taken place from the second half of the nineteenth century to the present day.

This chapter is structured into three parts. First, we follow the development of the making of the Piedmontese breed from 1886 until the late 1950s. We bring into light how an intense and heated debate between experts and breeders focused on the 'nature' of the breed. Second, we move on to discuss how this contested negotiation between academics and practitioners eventually 'fixed' the purpose and 'nature' of the Piedmontese as a breed for meat, through the inclusion in this bovine population of animals previously constructed as 'anomalies', and the exclusion of other animals beforehand considered as 'normal'. The last part of this chapter deals with the shifting status of the Piedmontese breed from an apparently endangered local animal species in the mid-1990s into a food specialty for the cosmopolitan consumer in contemporary New York.

Breeding the monster? Negotiating survival and extinction: 1886–1956

What is scientifically known today as the 'double-muscled Piedmontese cattle' is the result of the breed's specialization in meat production obtained through selection started towards the end of the nineteenth century and accelerated since 1960 with the institution of Anaborapi, the National Association of the Piedmontese breeders. Towards the end of the nineteenth century the Piedmontese bovine population was rather heterogeneous. In an 1872 book, Domenico Vallada, professor of veterinary science, described five different varieties of bovines that can be associated to the contemporary Piedmontese (Coalvi, 2008). As we discuss in this chapter, the selection of the breed has contributed to the vanishing of these five varieties to privilege those animals that presented the *groppa doppia* (literally, 'double back', called 'double muscling' or 'double muscle factor' in English; see Arthur, 1995), which was the morphological trait randomly emerging in some Piedmontese animals at the end of the nineteenth century, and which today makes the Piedmontese an animal specialized in meat production (see Figure 10.1). The *groppa doppia* is a characteristic of several breeds worldwide (most notably the Belgian Blue cattle breed) first documented by George Culley, a livestock observationist in 1807 (Kambadur et al., 1997).[4] In the case of the Piedmontese, the double-muscle factor was officially recorded in 1886 in Guarene d'Alba (Raimondi, 1956, p.6). In practice, the *groppa doppia* refers to a morphological mutation in the conformation of the animals presenting this trait and results in more muscular masses particularly in the hindquarter of the bovines.[5]

As we show in this chapter, the history of the Piedmontese breed from the beginning of the twentieth century until 1960 is the tale of a struggle between different actors (breeders, veterinarians, livestock technicians, bureaucrats) who can be seen as the spokespersons for conflicting biological, morphological and racial taxonomies. What was at stake particularly during this period was the definition of the official standard of the Piedmontese breed, which, in turn, concerned a definition of what was normal and what was abnormal, of the rule and the exception. Ultimately at stake was the relationship between the maximization of the production of the bovine breed's labour, milk and meat, and the reproduction of animal capital (Shukin, 2009), which had to be preserved and increased. More specifically, the negotiations about the status and destiny of the Piedmontese breed occurred through two different channels: the official discourse, in which veterinarians and livestock technicians kept claiming that the *groppa doppia* represented an anomaly and, ultimately, a threat for the breed itself;[6] and the semi-official discourse,[7] in which farmers and technicians collaborated as they were convinced that the *groppa doppia* animals could be improved and specialized in meat production (see Figure 10.2).

As far as the official narration is concerned, the Italian scientific debate engaged in an intense dialogue with the European academic literature, sifting the different propositions about the aetiology of this mutation. Already in the 1920s, Vittorino

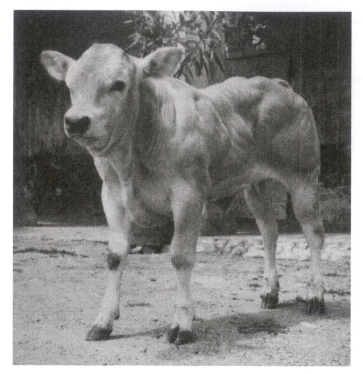

FIGURE 10.1 A groppa doppia calf.

Courtesy of Anaborapi, Carrù, Italy

FIGURE 10.2 The selection of the breed .

Courtesy of Anaborapi, Carrù, Italy

Vezzani, director of the Istituto Zootecnico e Caseario per il Piemonte (Piedmont's Zootechnics and Dairy Sciences Institute), discarded the hypothesis of a teratological nature ('un fatto di ordine teratologico') of the *groppa doppia*, in favour of an explanation related to the mechanisms of Mendelian inheritance (Vezzani, 1927, p.13). Yet, some echoes of the teratological hypothesis survived when academics described the *groppa doppia* animals' problems: imperfections in the calves such as enlarged tongues and ambulation problems, rickets, small genitals, infertility and frigidity, calving and parturition difficulties – were among the main identified issues affecting the life and reproduction of these peculiar bovines (see Mascheroni, 1931, pp.77–78).

The official, state-regulated, selection of the Piedmontese breed started in the 1930s. State veterinarians and livestock technicians excluded the animals with the *groppa doppia* from the breed improvement's programme because of the abovementioned problems they could transmit to their progeny. In 1932, Turin's Ispettorato Compartimentale Agrario (Municipal Agricultural Inspectorate) started a 'rational and methodical selection of the breed' (Bonadonna, 1959, p.671). The best cows and bulls were selected among 'normal Piedmontese cattle' (Raimondi, 1956 and 1958) and registered on the Herd Book. The opening of the Herd Book established a functional control over cows and bulls. The Ispettorati Provinciali dell'Agricoltura (Provincial Agricultural Inspectorate) of Alessandria, Asti, Cuneo and Turin were responsible for the selection. In 1935 the Ministry of Agriculture and Forests established the first standard of the breed, which aimed at making of the Piedmontese a bovine population comprising animals specialized primarily in work and then in milk and meat production (Esmenard and Dassat, 1948, p.3; MIAF 1935). The *groppa doppia* animals were still considered abnormal and therefore excluded from the selection units and ignored by the breed improvement practices established in the 1935 standard. It must be noted that, however, due to lack of funds, in the following years, the number of controlled and selected animals was very limited (Bonadonna, 1959, p.671). The lack of controls contributed to the spread of the double-muscled cattle.

In fact, the animals with the *groppa doppia* turned out to be an excellent source of income for farmers who, throughout the entire twentieth century, took on the risk of rearing cattle banned from the official reproduction of the Piedmontese livestock (see Raimondi, 1962). Why were these 'anomalous animals' economically more advantageous than the normal Piedmontese cattle? It was observed that the animals with the *groppa doppia* had a different conformation from the normal Piedmontese: more muscles, especially in the hindquarters; poor accumulation of fat; smaller skeleton and internal organs and thinner skin, when compared to the normal Piedmontese. These factors determined a higher dressing percentage after slaughtering; namely, a larger amount of beef that butchers could sell. Furthermore, it was noticed that the beef of the *groppa doppia* animals was tenderer than the meat extracted from the carcasses of the normal Piedmontese.[8]

These characteristics were also well known across the whole value chain, from production to consumption. The butchers in Piedmont's urban areas were eager to pay more money for purchasing the carcass of an animal with the *groppa doppia* (Vezzani, 1927; Raimondi, 1956). They could in fact earn more from these animals for three main reasons. First, they could extract more meat. Second, consumers preferred the meat of the *groppa doppia* animals, as it was tenderer and its colour paler than that of the normal Piedmontese. Third, because the *groppa doppia* animals' beef was always tender and pale (ibid.), butchers could cheat consumers and sell it as if it were *sanato* (i.e. the specialty beef obtained from calves nourished with milk) and sell forequarters cuts as if they were hindquarters (these latter providing the most expensive cuts). In Vezzani's words (1927, p.17), 'as a matter of fact, butchers in Turin slaughter [and sell] only double-muscled cattle'.[9]

Therefore, particularly after the First World War, farmers who wanted to increase the economic value of their livestock started to use the double-muscled Piedmontese for reproduction and specialize this breed in the production of beef (Raimondi, 1956; Vezzani, 1927). This is the moment in which the *groppa doppia* was transformed from an erratic genetic mutation into a conscious, yet roughly managed, trait for the selection of the breed. The semi-official selection of the Piedmontese cattle breed took place thanks to the collaboration of those experts who, despite the official harsh critiques, recognized that the abnormal cattle could represent, especially in times of economic crisis, the main resource for the survival of farmers. In particular, some livestock technicians and veterinarians, who supported the selection and improvement of the cattle with the *groppa doppia*, established in Alba, on 12 March 1927, an association of the breeders of the Piedmontese with the local *cattedra ambulante di agricoltura* (Vezzani, 1927, p.19).

Since end of the nineteenth century, the *comizi agrari*, the *cattedre ambulanti di agricoltura* (institutions created in 1866 in Italy to support agriculture and disseminate techniques and innovations in agriculture among farmers) and the *esibizioni zootecniche* (agricultural fairs) played a crucial role in the selection of the Piedmontese breed, by encouraging farmers to use stud-farms for the reproduction of their livestock (cf. Dassat, 1949, p.12). As the animals with the double-muscle factor were more profitable for farmers, they tended to privilege mating their dams with bulls presenting this trait (Raimondi, 1956; Vezzani, 1927). This practice contributed to the homogenization of the breed towards a population that increasingly tended to present the *groppa doppia* feature (Raimondi, 1956, 1958, 1962), despite official statements discouraging their reproduction (Raimondi, 1958). Until the establishment of Anaborapi in 1960, farmers have therefore been the main decision-makers and bearers of risk in the process of breed selection, improvement and specialization aimed at increasing meat production.[10] The role of academic veterinarians, livestock technicians and practitioners has been nevertheless fundamental. On the one hand, academic discourses somehow mirrored the 'official *versus* semi-official' divide. Even those academics that praised the exclusion of the bulls with *groppa doppia* from the programmes of *reproduction*, such as Raimondo Raimondi, recognized the *production* value that these animals secured to the breeders and their households. On the other hand, some academic and professional veterinarians, such as Francesco Maletto and Attilio Bosticco, and many other anonymous local practitioners, became what we might term 'vet-activists', engaged in solving the problems inherent to the reproduction of the *groppa doppia* specimens. It is impossible to formulate a consistent hypothesis about these experts' multifaceted attitude. Perhaps some of them felt trapped in between the loyalty to formal academic understanding of the *groppa doppia* and the acknowledgment of its role in securing an income for family farms living in some of the poorest areas of northern Italy. It is also likely that personal academic rivalries played a role in establishing divides and alliances. One of our interviewees, a retired professor of veterinary science now in his late seventies, claimed that cattle with the *groppa doppia* were understood as 'monsters' during fascism, thus suggesting that the ambience of the 1930s might have played a role in maintaining and fostering the teratological imagination about double-muscled bovines.[11]

Normalizing the breed: 1956–1976

The years from 1956 to 1960 marked for the Piedmontese breed a fundamental turn in the process of negotiation between the rule and exception, between the production and reproduction of 'animal capital' (Shukin, 2009). We can make sense of this shift by following a key actor in the debate, Raimondo Raimondi, deputy-director of Piedmont's Institute for Zootechnics and Dairy Sciences. In the 1940s Raimondi was a key figure moving in between the semi-official and the official discourse on the Piedmontese by publishing several academic papers and by participating at meetings with the farmers of the Piedmontese. On the one hand, he recognized the economic value of the *production* of double-muscled calves and their social utility in sustaining farmers' household economy. On the other hand, Raimondi maintained that the *groppa doppia* was a deviation from the codified and desirable standards of the Piedmontese breed and that double-muscled bulls had to be excluded from reproduction programmes.

His 1956 article represents the turning point in the process of the breed's normalization and therefore deserves proper attention. Raimondi was then aware that the 'battle' against the *groppa doppia* was a lost one. What had started as a random mutation appearing in the second half of nineteenth century had now spread across the Piedmontese bovine population: the animals with the *groppa doppia* largely outnumbered the 'normal Piedmontese cattle' (Raimondi, 1956, p.8). Raimondi recognized that the collaboration between breeders and vet-activists contributed to solving most of the 'teratological issues' associated with the *groppa doppia* (ibid., pp.6, 12). He admitted that the socio-economical and technological change taking place in Italy after the Second World War made obsolete the breed's triple specialization of the 1935 standard, and that both milk and meat production had to be improved through selection in the reproduction process (ibid., pp.12–13). He recognized that the most likely and profitable choice would have been further fostering the usage of double-muscled dams in combination with selected bulls with *groppa doppia* (ibid., pp.14–16). He even envisaged the possibility of experimenting with the reproduction of some animals by using double-muscled bulls at the Zootechnics Institute where he was working in Turin (ibid., p.12).

Yet, Raimondi supported a different solution. First, he highlighted the existence of what he termed 'una situazione paradossale', a paradoxical situation:

> the production of double muscled Piedmontese calves is exclusively a matter of butchery.[12] Today more than a few agree that without the providential birth of these calves, it is likely that the Piedmontese breed could not be economically sustainable. As a consequence, the following paradoxical situation emerged: the 'double muscling' phenomenon represents an undeniable economic resource for our breeders; yet, at the same time, it is also considered as a possible means for the close out of the breed.
>
> (Raimondi, 1956, p.9, emphasis in the original)

In writing about the 'close out of the breed' (*liquidazione della razza*, in the original Italian text), he was referring to the normal Piedmontese, as it had been codified in the 1935 standard. The teratological prejudice was somehow still at work, as the double-muscled cattle were considered (not without contradictions)[13] infertile and, when generating life, only capable of delivering faulty animals destined to die (cf. Mascheroni, 1931).

Raimondi, a few pages later, envisioned an alternative policy for the Piedmontese breed, identifying what he called the 'bovino Piemontese migliorato' (literally, 'improved Piedmontese bovine'), an evolution of the normal animal. His policy advice is somehow surprising, as it evokes the Slow Food presidia credo (i.e. the safeguarding of small traditional agricultural productions from industrial agriculture and homologation) 30 years earlier the birth of the movement:

> We think that ... it would be urgent and of the greatest importance to define within each province ... the zones to be preserved and allocated predominantly to reproduction, and in which, therefore, the provincial commissions for the approval of bulls should, in general, allow only the use of subjects of the normal type.
>
> (Raimondi, 1956, p.19, emphasis in the original)

It must be noted that Raimondo Raimondi was an experienced academic who acted as a spokesperson for the Ministry of Agriculture and Forest's position when presenting to the farmers the second standard for the Piedmontese breed approved in 1958 (Raimondi, 1958). The new ministerial directive (MIAF, 1958) established that the improvement of the breed had to target first the increase of milk and, secondly, beef production, thus discarding the work criterion included in the 1935 standard (see also Anaborapi, 2005, 2008; Bonadonna, 1959, pp.687–688). Raimondi's support of the second standard was perhaps his final attempt to protect the normal Piedmontese livestock from the spread of the double-muscle factor, literally the last bulwark against the *groppa doppia*. Therefore, the authorities represented by official experts such as Raimondi encouraged farmers to collaborate and avoid using for reproduction double-muscled bulls and dams. As Sartore and Chiappone note, 'until 1960, bulls which were characterized by muscular hypertrophy were officially *banned* from reproduction' (1982, p.461; our emphasis). In commenting on the 1958 standard, Raimondi launched his final call for the enrolment of farmers against the *groppa doppia* deviation:

> the work for the breed's reconstruction cannot longer wait, at stake is the downfall of the breed itself … *Yet, only with farmers' collaboration will the implementation* [of the new breed's standard] *be possible. Piedmontese breeders must and cannot back out of the responsibility of saving this breed; a breed on which their farms' income depends. Therefore it is indispensable that, even with some sacrifices, namely, giving up some beef calves, everybody gives their own contribution.*
>
> (Raimondi, 1958, p.13, emphasis in the original)

Unfortunately for Raimondo Raimondi, times were not ready for conservation projects and preservationist feelings, which were underlying his plan to establish conservation zones for the normal Piedmontese. Italy, in the late 1950s, had just entered its amazing economic growth, known as the 'boom years', and the policy-making concern was oriented towards production, rather than reproduction.

Only two years later, in 1960, in Turin, a handful of breeders of Piedmontese cattle, led by Francesco Maletto, professor of veterinary sciences at the University of Turin, founded Anaborapi, the National Association of the Piedmontese Cattle Breeders. The establishment of this association – soon to be recognized by the Ministry of Agriculture and Forests as *the* (official) *Institution* for the Piedmontese breed – was the formal attempt of a takeover in the 'world of the Piedmontese', imposing the groppa doppia as the key feature to be targeted by the – soon to be approved – new standard for the Piedmontese breed. Anaborapi became the 'spokesperson' at the Ministry of Agriculture for the Piedmontese breeders interested in increasing meat production (cf. Bosticco, 2010). It became also responsible for managing the Herd Book and implementing the genetic selection and improvement of the livestock (ibid.). The fact is that Anaborapi completely ignored Raimondi's call for the 'reconstruction of the [normal] breed', as it implemented reproductive programmes involving bulls and dams with the *groppa doppia* trait. As a consequence of Anaborapi's activities, in 1966 the Ministry again modified the breed standard: selection had to increase both milk and meat production. However, and importantly, the new standard established that increasing the production of meat, rather than the production of milk, was the most important aim to achieve through selection. The 1966 standard, therefore, represented the first official step towards the transformation of the Piedmontese into a beef breed (Coalvi, 2008, p.55).

In the meanwhile, Anaborapi's technicians and veterinarians continued their efforts to enhance the double-muscled variant of the Piedmontese. In particular, reproductive traits were selected through progeny tests targeted to establish the genetic value of the bulls through the examination of their offspring. Nowadays the whole process lasts a few months. Yet, during Anaborapi's early steps, it took ten years to successfully accomplish the first progeny test and to set the correct procedures and protocols.[14] The first cycle of the progeny tests with double-muscled bovines was in fact completed in 1970 and this success paved the road to the approval of the new, the last and current, fourth breed standard.

The 1976 standard established that, while milk production had not been neglected by selection, the Piedmontese was primarily a breed for meat production.[15] De facto, after a long negotiation and struggle about what the Piedmontese breed had to be, the fourth standard fixed a renewed notion of normality, defining that the *groppa doppia* was the rule and not the exception, subsequently bridging the divide between production and reproduction.[16] As we have shown, this struggle had been playing out for more than 70 years on different tables, entailing and assembling heterogeneous cultural, scientific, economic, ideological elements into long series of technological, scientific, normative canons. Since 1976, the fourth standard guides contemporary Anaborapi's practices of genetic selection and improvement. Anaborapi's technicians, today, basically operate to create an animal with no, or as little as possible, 'imperfections' (i.e. enlarged tongues and ambulation problems in calves, and parturition difficulties in dams), and able of producing large amounts of beef (thanks to the inclusion of the *groppa doppia* as valuable and 'normal' trait of the Piedmontese in the 1976 standard of the breed).[17]

Saving the breed (again)? 1976–2014

The Piedmontese breed's path to success was apparently paved and smooth. A few years after the approval of the fourth standard, Anaborapi wrote a new chapter in the history of the Piedmontese, by dispatching one bull (named Brindisi) and four dams (called Banana, Biba, Bisca and Binda) to Saskatchewan, Canada, in the autumn of 1979. The following year, five more bulls (Captain, Champ, Corallo, Camino and Domingo) were shipped to Canada. Subsequently, in the early 1980s three bulls (Istinto, Imbuto and Iose) and two cows (India and Gazza) were exported again from Italy to the United States.[18] These animals supplied the original genetic base for the Piedmontese breed in North America. Today, there are livestock of Piedmontese in several countries: China, Argentina, New Zealand, Australia, Great Britain, Ireland, Denmark, Germany, the Netherlands, Mexico and Switzerland (see Bosticco, 2009, 2010). It must be noted that the Piedmontese breed attracts international attention as it can be used for crossbreeding and improving 'meat yield, meat tenderness and feed efficiency' (Arthur, 1995, p.1507). Farmers and companies in the meat industry are interested into the Piedmontese because they can produce tender and lean beef with 'more quality cuts than other breeds' (Natural Farms).[19] Furthermore, it 'offers great potential to lean beef marketing programs' (ibid.). The Piedmontese fills, especially in the USA, a niche market where it is advertised as premium and 'healthy' beef as this latter has very little fat and it is tender (Certified Piedmontese®).[20] With an increase of the demand for leaner meat, interest for the Piedmontese has grown in different parts of the world (Arthur, 1995, p.1494).

The Piedmontese's current fortune is directly linked to the genealogy we highlighted in this chapter. The success of the *groppa doppia* beef among the Pennsylvania breeders and the sophisticated NYC consumers purchasing Piedmontese beef at Eataly also relies on the same factors that seduced producers and consumers in Piedmont since the early twentieth century: high dressing percentage and tender, lean and tasteful meat. However, we still cannot put a (happy) end to the (success) story of the Piedmontese by stopping at the establishment of Anaborapi and the 1976 breed standard. What is still missing, and must be clarified, are the reasons why in the 1990s a debate arose in the emerging Slow Food movement about the need of a presidium to protect specifically the Piedmontese breed.

Slow Food's very notion of presidium is grounded in the fact that there is an agri-food production threatened by extinction unless urgent action is undertaken. This was not the case for the Piedmontese cattle breed. Since its foundation in 1980, Coalvi, the consortium for the valorization of the Piedmontese breed,[21] has been promoting the consumption of Piedmontese beef, coordinating the work of more than 1,400 breeders, about 85 slaughterhouses and nearly 200 butchers.

It cannot be forgotten that exogenous factors do play a role in the fortunes of a commodity. In the case of the Piedmontese, exogenous threats came in the early 1980s from the diffusion of large-scale retail, reducing the profitability of a breed like the Piedmontese that, despite its high dressing percentage, needs more time for fattening. As a consequence, many breeders redeveloped their business, replacing the Piedmontese with French cattle breeds, such as the Limousin and Charolais, which could be fattened using mass feeding techniques and, eventually, bootleg hormone injections. Also the EU's Common Agricultural Policy played a role. Its large-scale development plan, enforcing a spatial division of labour among European countries, acted as an incentive to shift from meat to milk production in Italy, further reducing the diffusion of the Piedmontese in favour of Holstein Friesians cattle. These changes in both the market conditions and public policies brought about a breakneck decline in the number of Piedmontese heads of cattle (Cumino, 2012; Ponzio, 2012; Quaglino and Albera, 2012; interviews). While after the Second World War there were about 700,000 Piedmontese cows and bulls (Dassat, 1949, pp.10–11; see also Raimondi, 1962, p.1), the number fell to less than 200,000 in 2004 before inverting the trend and reaching the 260,000–265,000 units in the current period (Anaborapi, 2013, p.6).

These external shocks somehow proved that Raimondo Raimondi's concerns were well grounded: the drive towards the selection and improvement of the *groppa doppia* saved the Piedmontese breed but, at the same time, exposed it at a risk. As mentioned above, since 1960 Anaborapi drove the selection of the breed towards meat production and, with the approval of the 1976 standard, the improvement of milk productivity was nearly abandoned. As Raimondi noticed in 1962, when it comes to milk, the productivity of the double-muscled Piedmontese is about 20 percent lower compared to normal cattle (1962, p.42). The issue was even more complex and brings us to the very heart of the genealogy that is central to our narration. On the one hand, the selection and improvement that Anaborapi carried out since 1960 transformed the Piedmontese into a truly 'meat machine'. As Vezzani figuratively reported, 'in these [double muscled] calves, the butchers say "the leg is in each part [of the animal] and each part is leg"'. Others significantly argue that these calves have the leg also in the head' (1927, p.11). On the other hand, Coalvi (the consortium that promotes the commercialization of the Piedmontese beef) implemented an inclusive policy towards the Piedmontese breeders, setting loose production standards and regulations.

Coalvi's commercial discourse was (and still is) clear: the Piedmontese's characteristics (low fat, tenderness, delicate taste, pale colour, texture) are embedded in the genetic uniqueness of the breed, are 'natural' and hence there are not significant beef quality variations between breeders. The combination of two discourses – Anaborapi's technical and Coalvi's commercial discourse – produced in the 1990s what we called the 'philogenetic narrative', connoting the Piedmontese's beef quality as genetically determined, as an objective matter of fact (Colombino and Giaccaria, 2013b). The paradoxical consequence is that small-scale breeders and vet-activists transformed the *groppa doppia* from an anomaly into the standard, and saved the Piedmontese breed by encouraging farmers to keep rearing it, but at the same time waived farmers' agency and handed it to Anaborapi and Coalvi, which became the official spokespersons, the gatekeepers respectively of the Piedmontese genetic assets and of the commercial valorization of the breed. In fact, the 'phylogenetic discourse' that sustains Anaborapi and Coalvi's idea of beef quality (epitomized by a Coalvi manager's statement 'the breed makes the quality') relies almost exclusively on the genetic substrate of the breed. The practical consequence of this 'truth' articulated by the phylogenetic discourse is that *anyone* can rear the Piedmontese and obtain high quality beef (Scaglia, 2012, interview). In Anaborapi's and Coalvi's discourses and practices even the fattening depends on the animal itself, as its genetic character dictates the proper feeding (see Colombino and Giaccaria, 2013b, pp.147–149). The typical Coalvi breeder receives the proper semen from Anaborapi, feeds the cattle with the right, standardized, diet, and, finally sells it to the butchers associated with Coalvi.

This is the context that partially explains Slow Food's decision to enforce a presidium for the Piedmontese cattle, despite the fact the livestock was not numerically endangered.[22] What was in danger of extinction, according to the Slow Food discourse, were the traditional skills and knowledges of the breeder. Once again, in the mid-1990s, a non-academic vet-activist, Sergio Capaldo played a pivotal role in gathering a handful of young breeders around a Slow Food presidium, willing to experiment old practices of feeding and fattening their cattle.

At the beginning, the La Granda presidium gathered seven breeders and 78 head of cattle. Capaldo's intuition was to refresh the sources of the success of the *groppa doppia* across the twentieth century; namely the profitability of animal capital and the quality of the beef. Double-muscled animals used to be about 30 percent more profitable for breeders than the normal Piedmontese (Raimondi, 1962, pp.54–56).

Yet, the diffusion of large-scale retail impacted on small breeders' profits, and even Coalvi's retail network was no longer to guarantee to farmers the previous returns (Giordano, 2012, interview; Quaglino and Albera, 2012, interview). As a consequence, Capaldo concentrated his efforts in repositioning the presidium's beef at the top end of the market. This required harsh bargaining with retailers, caterers and butchers, in order to secure to his associates an average surplus of 25 per cent more than the price paid on the market (Capaldo, 2012, interview). In turn, this strategy – which is encapsulated in *La Granda*'s specification of production (which relies on the use of 'natural' and possibly local fodder and 'traditional' rearing techniques), turned out to be successful in enhancing – according to food critics, gourmets and gastronomists – the quality of the presidium's beef. In order to do so, Capaldo basically empowered the breeders' agency by returning to them the know-how and the competences of 'properly' feeding and fattening their cattle (see Giordano, 2012, interview). The original group grew slowly from seven to 65 farmers by sharing 'good practices' and social capital, which contributed to enabling them to produce the premium beef that has captured food connoisseurs, chefs and, later, important economic actors in the world of food culture and gastronomy such as Eataly's founder Oscar Farinetti (Sartorio, 2008). Again, external factors played a key role: the mad cow disease in the late 1990s and early 2000s, the new popular concern with health and obesity and the birth of the food mall Eataly in 2007 contributed to creating the conditions for the international success of La Granda and, more precisely, of the Piedmontese cattle breed. Of course, also Anaborapi's dissemination action, 'mobilizing bulls and cows' and commercializing semen for artificial insemination across the world, contributed to making the Piedmontese breed's international success possible. Yet, the work of a vet-activist and of a few dozens of breeders was essential to transform a local beef into an international commodity, sold in New York City, the heart of cosmopolitan food consumption.

The presence of the Piedmontese beef in a stall at New York's Green Market cannot simply be explained with a direct causal relationship between Slow Food's success and influence in affecting foodies' sophisticated consumption practices and the strategic location of Eataly – which materializes gastronomes' fantasies for 'high quality' food and specialties – in New York City. Neither can it be explained as a reflection of the animal's and beef's intrinsic qualities, nor it can be justified by telling a story of the Piedmontese that constructs it as an endangered breed, which, as in the case of many Slow Food presidia, immediately turns into a food specialty. The commercial success of the Piedmontese in the niche market targeted to international food connoisseurs and cosmopolitan urban elites can be better explained when considering this breed complicated and centennial genealogy. A series of struggles, negotiations, tensions, imaginaries have been pivoting on the characters of the breed in order to set its standard and define the balance between production and reproduction of its animal capital. All these elements are still interacting in a dialogical tension, in the interplay of a plurality of stakeholders: there is not such thing as an end in the interaction of heterogeneous actors.

Notes

1 Slow Food presidia are an evolution of a project started in the 1990s, originally called *Arca del Gusto* (literally 'arc of taste'), which were officially presented in 2000 at the *Salone del Gusto*, the 'glocal' food fair that Slow Food organizes every autumn in Turin, Italy.

2 In this chapter, unless otherwise specified, by La Granda we refer indistinctly to the presidium and the meat processing company.

3 More specifically, Eataly's Piedmontese beef is supplied by Pat La Frieda, a New York-based luxury meat retailer and by farms working for Great Plain Beef (see www.eataly.com/nyc-butcher-counter/ and www.greatplainsbeef.com, accessed 7 October 2014).

4 This trait is termed in different national contexts after the morphology of the cattle, which visually recalls horses' backs' silhouettes, as in the French *veau à cul de poulain* and the Italian *vitello a groppa di cavallo*, or refers to the hypertrophic muscles of the hind leg, as in the German's *Doppellender* and the different Italian denominations *vitello della groppa doppia* or *vitello della coscia*.

5 Today we know that the double muscling is the result of a spontaneous mutation of the myostatin gene (Wheeler et al. 2001). This mutation has caused a malfunctioning of the myostatin, a protein responsible for controlling muscular growth and which causes the growth of muscular masses (hypertrophy, the increase of the volume of muscular fibres), and an increase of the numbers of muscular fibres (hyperplasia). This mutation is considered at the origin of the two main factors that determine the higher economic value of the animal: the higher dressing percentage (i.e. more meat after slaughtering) compared to other beef cattle breeds, and the tenderness of the meat (see Albera, 2006; Fiems, 2012). As we show in this chapter, these are two factors that farmers, butchers, veterinarians, and livestock technicians knew well since the beginning of the twentieth century (see e.g. Mascheroni, 1931, pp.68–78).

6 Until the late 1950s, the main argument against the use of *groppa doppia* animals for reproduction concerned the supposed infertility of the cows and the incapacity of delivering healthy calves (Raimondi, 1958).

7 We write 'semi-official' and not 'unofficial' because some exemplars of the cattle with the *groppa doppia* were exhibited and received prizes at important national events such as the *Mostra Zootecnica* (livestock exhibition) at Milan's Fair (Vezzani, 1927, p.19).

8 Today we know that the tenderness is also the result of the genetic mutation of the myostatin, which causes muscular hyperplasia; that is, more muscular fibres, which are poor of connective tissue (collagen), which translates into tender beef (see Arthur, 1995; De Stefanis, 2012).

9 Translations from sources in Italian are our own.

10 Possible risks in using the double-muscled bulls for reproduction could include the death of the dam for parturition difficulties and the birth of calves with severe health problems.

11 The fact that some German and French academic veterinarians (e.g. Putsch and Dechambre cited in Vezzani, 1927) strongly supported the teratological hypothesis, might be a factor to be taken into account (see ibid., p.13). However, more archival work on technical and historical documents is needed to offer a sound answer to this question, and to cross-check and integrate the arguments formalized in the academic articles and position papers we have been able to collect so far.

12 By 'matter of butchery', Raimondi meant that the Piedmontese animals presenting the *groppa doppia* trait were and had to be used only for the production of beef and not for the reproduction of the herd.

13 If the *groppa doppia* characters implied infertility, impotence and rickets, how is it that 50 years of tentative reproductive programmes, semi-officially managed by breeders and vet-activists, made the double-muscled specimens the majority of Piedmontese cattle?

14 Today from each bull brought to Anaborapi's Genetic Station semen doses are collected and then used on dams registered on the Herd Book. After delivery, calves are examined

to determine the genetic potential of the bulls. After this evaluation, before being qualified for artificial insemination, the bulls are tested for their sexual functionality. This stage implies the training of the bulls in the 'artificial service' (*monta artificiale*) and the examination of the quality of the semen. If the bull has a good libido, its semen is tested (for appearance, volume, concentration, motility of the spermatozoa). If the bull has a good semen production then it qualifies for being an AI bull and, after a sanitary inspection, it is then moved to the Centro Tori (Artificial Insemination Station) where the semen is produced, controlled, stored and then sold nationally and internationally.

15 According to the 1976 standard, the improvement of the Piedmontese must target: precocity (the early achievement of the age for slaughtering); growth rate; feed conversion index; dressing percentage; the characteristics of the carcass; beef quality; fertility; and longevity (see www.anaborapi.it/index.php?option=com_content&view =article&id=44:statuto&catid=5:piemontese-presenta&Itemid=7, accessed 7 October 2014).

16 Our account of the Piedmontese cattle breed finds a theoretical echo in Biermann and Mansfield's (2014) recent paper about the biopolitical nature of conservation biology. More specifically, our findings support their claim that 'decisions [made by conservation biology on which life forms should live and which should be allowed to die] rely on distinctions between normalcy and aberrance, between biological advantages and threats ... The division between what must be maximized, or made to live, and what must be diminished, or allowed to die, is based not on inherent value of an organism but rather on its supposed relation to the population' (Biermann and Mansfield, 2014, p. 261).

17 In order to create the 'perfect animal' through selection, today Anaborapi employs genetic markers and Estimated Breeding Values (see Holloway et al., 2011). It must be noted that the affirmation of genetics markers and Estimated Breeding Values in livestock rearing is truly *biopolitics*, which deeply penetrates into the reproduction of animal capital. This is because 'such practices involve not just the insertion of animal bodies into farming assemblages involving technologies, human beings, land, architectural spaces, and so on for the purposes of changing and "maximizing" those bodies, but also the selection of individuals and populations as the bearers of particular traits to suit the particular ends of capitalist enterprise. What we have here, in other words, is not just the operation of a new "norm" but one whose benchmarks presuppose the production and sale of animal food products *as a commodity for profit*' (Wolfe 2014, pp.35–36, original emphasis).

18 It is worthwhile to notice that the denomination of the bulls and cows follow the genealogical naming typical of pets' pedigree.

19 See www.naturalfarms.com/e-p-s-p-ranch/the-piedmontese-story/, accessed 7 October 2014.

20 'The healthier beef option', www.piedmontese.com/about_healthier-option.aspx, accessed 7 October 2014.

21 It is important to notice that Coalvi's original name was 'Consorzio di valorizzazione della Piemontese sottorazza Albese' (consortium for the valorization of the Alba's Piemontese sub-breed). The reference to the Albese sub-breed is probably the last mirroring of the harsh debate that brought the *groppa doppia* specimens, whose selection started originally in Alba's area, to become the ideal-type of the Piedmontese breed.

22 According to a Slow Food manager we interviewed, in the mid-1990s there were about 300.000 head of Piedmontese cattle.

References

Albera, A. (2006) 'Selection for beef traits and calving performance in Piemontese cattle', PhD thesis, Wageningen University, Department of Animal Sciences, Wageningen, Netherlands

Anaborapi (2005), 'L'evoluzione della Piemontese dalle origini ai giorni nostri', in Regione Piemonte (ed.), *Patrimonio zootecnico del Piemonte. La Razza Bovina Piemontese*, Regione Piemonte, Torino, Italy, pp. 9–18

Anaborapi (2008) *La Razza Piemontese*, Anaborapi, Carrù, Italy

Anaborapi (2013) *Relazione tecnica e statistica*, Anaborapi, Carrù, Italy

Arthur, P. F. (1995) 'Double muscling in cattle: A review', *Australian Journal of Agricultural Research*, vol 46, no 8, pp. 1493–1515

Bennett, J. (2010) *Vibrant Matter: A Political Ecology of Things*, Duke University Press, Durham and London

Biermann, C. and Mansfield, K. (2014) 'Biodiversity, purity, and death: Conservation biology as biopolitics', *Environment and Planning D*, vol 32, pp. 257–273

Boltanski, L. and Thevenot, L. (2006) *On Justification: Economies of Worth*, Princeton University Press, Princeton, NJ

Bonadonna, T. (1959), 'Razza Piemontese', in Bonadonna, T. (ed.), *Le razze bovine*, Progresso Zootecnico, Milan, pp. 666–689

Bosticco, A. (2009) 'L'introduzione della razza bovina Piemontese in Cina: contributo al miglioramento quanti-qualitativo della produzione di carne', *Large Animal Review*, vol 15, pp. 117–122

Bosticco, A. (2010) 'Storia della Razza Piemontese dal 1941 al 1960', in *La Razza Piemontese*, no 7, pp. 6–7

Capaldo, S. (2012) Founder of the Piedmontese Breed Slow Food Presidium and La Granda Trasformazione Srl, interviewed on 17 February

Coalvi (2008) *Oro Rosso*, Coalvi, Carrù, Italy

Colombino, A. and Giaccaria, P. (2013a), 'Alternative Food Networks tra locale globale: il caso del pesidio della razza bovina piemontese', *Rivista Geografica Italiana*, no 122, pp. 225–240

Colombino, A. and Giaccaria, P. (2013b) 'Il sistema agrogastronomico piemontese: tra qualità e radicamento: il caso della carne di razza Piemontese' in P. Giaccaria, F. S. Rota and C. Salone (eds), *Praticare la territorialità. Riflessioni sulle politiche per la green economy, l'agroindustria e la cultura in Piemonte*, Carocci, Roma, pp. 135–154

Cook, I. et al. (2006) 'Geographies of Food: Following', *Progress in Human Geography*, vol 30, no 5, pp. 655–666

Cumino, P. (2012) Piedmont Regional Government, Agriculture Section, interviewed on 20 April

Dassat, P. (1949) 'Aspetti dell'allevamento bovino in Piemonte' in *Cronache economiche*, no 62, pp. 9–12

De Stefanis, Gianluigi (2012) Professor of Agrarian Sciences, University of Turin, interviewed on 21 March

Esmenard, G. and Dassat, P. (1948) *Partecipazione piemontese alle mostre internazionali zootecniche di Milano (annesse al I° congresso internazionale di fisiopatologia della riproduzione animale e di fecondazione artificiale)*, Tipografia Mario Ponzio, Pavia

Fiems, L. O. (2012) 'Double Muscling in Cattle: Genes, Husbandry, Carcasses and Meat', *Animals*, no 2, pp. 472–506

Giordano, S. (2012) President of La Granda Consortium and farmer, interviewed on 6 March

Haraway, D. (2008) *When Species Meet*, University of Minnesota Press, Minneapolis

Holloway, L., Morris, C., Gilna, B. and Gibbs, D. (2011) 'Choosing and rejecting cattle and sheep: Changing discourses and practices of (de)selection in pedigree livestock breeding', *Agriculture and Human Values*, no 28, pp. 533–547

Kambadur, R., Sharma, M., Smith, T. P. L. and Bass, J. (1997) 'Mutations in *myostatin* (*GDF8*) in double-muscled Belgian Blue and Piedmontese cattle', *Genome Research*, no 7, pp. 910–915

Latimer, J. and Miele, M. (2013) 'Naturecultures? Science, affect and the non-human', *Theory Culture and Society*, no 30, pp. 5–31

Latour, B. (1999) 'On recalling ANT', *Sociological Review*, vol 47, no 1, pp. 15–25

Mascheroni, E. (1931) *I bovini da carne*, G. B. Paravia C, Torino, Italy

MIAF (Ministero dell'Agricoltura e delle Foreste) (1935) 'Standard della Razza Bovina Piemontese', Decreto Ministeriale, Rome, 21 March

MIAF (1958) 'Standard della Razza Bovina Piemontese', Decreto Ministeriale, Rome, 23 July

Morris, C. and Holloway, L. (2013) 'Genetics and livestock breeding in the UK: Co-constructing technologies and heterogeneous biosocial collectivities', *Journal of Rural Studies*, vol 33, pp.150–160

NAPA (2010) 'Piedmontese beef is the star at celebrity chefs dinner in LA', *Your Piedmontese Voice*, vol 6, no 1, p. 6

Ponzio, Raffaella, (2012) Slow Food manager in charge of Italian presidia, interviewed on 17 February

Quaglino, Andrea and Albera, Andrea (2012), Anaborapi director and researcher expert in genetic selection, interviewed on 3 March

Raimondi, R. (1956) 'La razza bovina piemontese e le sue attuali possibilità di miglioramento', *Zootecnica*, no 11, pp. 3–19

Raimondi, R. (1958) 'Aspetti tecnici ed economici della produzione carnea bovina piemontese', paper presented at the first regional convention of the provincial breeders association, Torino, 30 March

Raimondi, R. (1962) *La razza bovina piemontese*, Paravia, Milano

Sartore, G. and Chiappone, E. (1982) 'Herd structure of pedigree Piedmont cattle', in J. W. B. King and F. M. Bnissier (eds), *Muscle Hypertrophy of Genetic Origin and Its Use to Improve Beef Production*, Martinus Nijhoff Publishers, The Hague, pp. 460–470

Sartorio, A. (2008) *Il mercante di utopie*, Sperling & Kupfer, Milan

Scaglia, Graziano (2012), owner of meat processing company and farmer associated with Coalvi, interviewed on 12 April

Shukin, N. (2009) *Animal Capital: Rendering Life in Biopolitical Times*, Minnesota University Press, Minneapolis and London

Tiemann, T. K. (2008) 'Grower-only farmers markets: Public spaces and third places', *Journal of Popular Culture*, vol 41, no 3, pp. 467–487

Vallada, D. (1872) *Abbozzo di Taurologia*, Unione Tipografico-Editrice Torinese, Torino

Vezzani, V. (1927) 'La Formazione della sottorazza albese in seno alla razza bovina piemontese', in *Rivista di Zootecnica*, vol 4, no 6–7, pp. 3–19

Wheeler, T. L., Shackelford, S. D., Casas, E., Cundiff, L. V. and Koohmaraie, M. (2001) 'The effects of Piedmontese inheritance and myostatin genotype on the palatability of longissimus thoracis, gluteus medius, semimenbranosus, and biceps femoris', *American Society of Animal Science*, vol. 79, no 12, pp. 3,069–3,074

Wolfe, C. (2014) *Before the Law: Humans and Other Animals*, University of Chicago Press, Chicago

Zukin, S. (2008) 'Consuming authenticity: From outposts of difference to means of exclusion', *Cultural Studies*, vol 22, no 5, pp. 724–748

11

BIOPOWER AND AN ECOLOGY OF GENES

Seeing livestock as meat via genetics

Lewis Holloway

Introduction

In this chapter I focus on some of the implications of what has been represented as a radical change in livestock breeding for thinking about meat in relation to living farm animals: the use of genetic techniques in selecting breeding animals. The chapter draws on Foucault's theorization of biopower to describe some of the key dimensions of this shift, articulating this concept with an argument that breeders' engagement with these techniques is part of a changing political ecology of livestock farming at the inter-related scales of the gene, the body, the herd or flock, the farm and the meat production system. Drawing on research funded by the UK's Economic and Social Research Council ('Genetics, genomics and genetic modification in livestock agriculture: emerging knowledge practices in making and managing farm livestock', RES-062-23-0642; see Holloway and Morris, 2008, 2012, 2014; Morris and Holloway, 2009, 2014), I begin by outlining the background to a significant shift in how meat-producing nonhuman animals (focusing here on sheep and beef cattle) are bred in UK agriculture, as there has been an emphasis placed on the deployment of genetic techniques alongside or instead of 'traditional' visual assessment of animals. This represents a change from assessing animals' 'quality' based on proximate 'looking' and touching (along with knowledge of pedigree and health records) to a more virtual mode of assessment based on differing kinds of genetic data theoretically available when the animal is corporeally remote. The chapter then briefly outlines Foucault's conception of biopower and shows how and why this theory is valuable in exploring changing techniques of livestock breeding, before looking at how biopower can inform a political ecological understanding of farmed animals and livestock breeding vis-à-vis meat. I then turn to primary and secondary empirical evidence from UK-based research with a wide range of actors in UK beef and sheep farming to explore some key issues of the geneticization of meat-producing animals, focusing on a reorientation of how animals are represented, from fleshy bodies towards assemblages of genes and data, with implications for the ontological status of 'meat' as far as breeders and other actors are concerned. The chapter ends with some comments on the practical and ethical implications of this reorientation for livestock breeding and the political ecologies of livestock farming and meat systems.

Geneticizing livestock breeding

The use of genetic techniques for breeding livestock has become increasingly prevalent in agricultural systems in the UK and elsewhere, something referred to by some as the 'geneticization' of livestock breeding (Gannett, 1999) and regarded as part of a wider geneticization of knowledges of life (Haraway, 1997; Keller 1992, 2000; Rose, 2001). For some, the reorientation of breeding towards genetics has been seen as revolutionary (Archibald and Haley, 2003, Bishop and Woolliams, 2004; Bulfield, 2000; see also Holloway, 2005, Holloway and Morris, 2008), and while this may be hyperbolic it is clear that a powerful discourse of geneticization has emerged. Farmers are thus persistently encouraged to move away from what are represented as outdated traditions of breeding 'by eye', and to adopt selection techniques which depend in different ways on a sense of the genetic composition of farmed animals. As a result, breeders' tacit, practical and perhaps aesthetic knowledges of livestock (Holloway and Morris, 2014), gained in many cases from very long-term experience of livestock breeding and close relationships with animals, have become downplayed in sometimes dismissive terms by those who would promote what are often represented as more progressive, scientifically informed selection techniques which purport to be able to see 'under the skin' of an animal and to quantify its genetic value, enabling supposedly objective calculations to be made about which animal to mate with which in the pursuit of livestock productivity.

Relevant techniques include 'estimated breeding values' (EBVs) and genetic markers (see Holloway, 2005; Holloway and Morris, 2007, 2008; Morris and Holloway, 2009; Holloway et al., 2009). EBVs are based on the principles of classical genetics and produce what is referred to as an animal's 'genetic value' (Bulfield, 2000). They are statistical calculations, based on records from individual animals and their relatives, of the probability that an animal will pass on specific heritable qualities to their offspring. EBVs for different specific traits (e.g. growth rate) can be combined to create more general indices, such as the 'beef value', to aid breeders with their selection decisions. Genetic markers are at a more experiment stage as far as most UK breeders are concerned although they have been more widely adopted elsewhere, for example in the US and Australia. Markers, identified from animals' blood or hair samples, are actual genetic material associated with a heritable quality such as meat tenderness. Commercially available tests can be purchased for use with a breeder's own animals, allowing them to select for particular genetic traits, and breeders can also purchase (usually male) animals specifically bred to 'contain' particular genes.

The aim of using both techniques is to progressively enhance the genetic 'quality' of livestock populations, and they are heavily promoted by government and commercial agencies, agricultural scientists and the farming press as 'the way forward' for livestock farming and meat production (Holloway and Morris, 2008). They are viewed, for example, as a key part of farming's response to recent concerns about future food security (Technology Strategy Board, 2013). And yet the use of genetic techniques such as EBVs and markers is not uncontested (something evident in the persistence of efforts made to persuade breeders to adopt them). While there are many enthusiastic users, many breeders, in the UK at least, have been resistant to 'adopting' genetic techniques, or have been sceptical of their value even while using them, on a number of grounds (see Holloway and Morris, 2012). These include a perceived difference between animals' 'quality' as measured by eye and by genetic techniques, a continued preference to rely on visual assessment, knowledge of pedigree and long experience to determine what a 'good animal' actually is, and the strength (again particularly in the UK) of the practice of breeding 'for the show ring', which makes particular aesthetic demands on animals and breeders which may, many argue, conflict with the commercial demands of efficient meat production. Regardless, in terms of the discourses and practices of livestock breeding, geneticization is having a powerful transformative effect. The next section outlines a way of conceptualizing these transformations, drawing on the idea of biopower, summarizing how this theorization of human power-knowledge relations can be used in the context of nonhuman animals (for more detail see Holloway et al., 2009; Holloway and Morris, 2012) and suggesting how in the case of breeding livestock this can be articulated with a political ecological perspective.

Livestock breeding, biopower and a changing political ecology of meat farming

There is an extensive literature which describes and works with Foucault's conceptions of biopolitics and biopower, deploying his ideas in a diverse range of disciplinary and empirical fields. Here only a very brief outline can be provided. In essence, Foucault's descriptions of biopower (Foucault, 1990, 2003, 2007) relate a turn to the *fostering of life* as the focus of power-knowledge relations from the late eighteenth century in Western Europe. Biopower implies a focus on the enhancing, or optimization, of life. This was, Foucault argues, associated with the establishment of new forms of scientific and demographic knowledge-practices concerning humans as living entities and as populations. As such, for Foucault, biopower consists of a duality: an anatamopolitics centred around the capacities and subjectification of individuals, and a biopolitics focused around the metrics of populations (e.g. birth and death rates, productivity). Rose (2007, p.53) suggests that biopower emerged from struggles to understand and intervene in the specific problems of constituting and managing populations and 'the vital processes of their subjects … a multitude of attempts to manage their life, to turn their individual and collective lives into information and knowledge, and to intervene on them'. For Foucault, then, biopower is centered

> on the body as a machine: its disciplining, the optimisation of its capabilities, the extortion of its forces, the parallel increase of its usefulness and docility, and its integration into systems of efficient and economic controls.
>
> (Foucault, 1990, p.139)

This process, for Foucault, was an essential part of a shift towards industrial capitalism, which 'would not have been possible without the controlled insertion of bodies into the machinery of production and the adjustment of the phenomena of population to economic processes' (ibid., p.141).

A useful heuristic framework for understanding particular incidences of biopower in operation is provided by Rabinow and Rose (2006). They argue that biopower comprises first, the establishment of truths concerning life by those regarded as holding appropriate authority to determine truth; second, specific and systematic interventions in the 'life' of individuals and populations; and third, modes of subjectification in which individuals actually come to work upon themselves as living beings, becoming projects of self-improvement dependent on aligning their consciousness and behaviour with truth discourses and strategies concerning the improvement of their life. Of particular relevance for this chapter is that Rabinow and Rose (see also Gibbon and Novas, 2008) identify the 'truths' about life told by genetic science as one key source for intervention in contemporary life.

Fostering life through interventions in the life processes which constitute populations demands the production of data on individuals and collectives, and means that ideas of normalization become important, along with techniques for measuring and representing distributions around norms. The norm becomes something which circulates between and ties together anatamopolitics and biopolitics (see Nealon, 2008). Systems of measurement assess the individual and relate them to population level standards. Following that, it becomes important to develop techniques for interventions which can shift population-level norms in desirable directions. Deleuze for example, in his book on Foucault, writes that biopower implies 'administering and controlling life in a particular multiplicity, provided the multiplicity is large (a population) and the space spread out or open' (1988, p.61). This sense of a spread out or open field is echoed in Nealon's (2008) argument that relations of biopower extend beyond institutional settings and saturate the spaces of everyday life and entire populations.

Now, Foucault's theorization of biopower was oriented towards his accounts of historical changes in power–knowledge relations with regard to human individuals and populations. Several writers have, however, engaged with biopower in their explorations of the nonhuman world in its relations with humans (see for example Haraway,1997; Holloway et al., 2009; Rutherford, 2011; Shukin, 2009; Twine, 2010; Wolfe, 2013). For these authors, nonhuman life, including nonhuman animals, can be conceptualized as co-enrolled, with people, into relations of biopower. They argue that the focus of biopower on the fostering or enhancement of life makes its power–knowledge relations something which permeates nonhuman as well as the human species. Going a little further, it can be argued that it is in particular human–nonhuman animal relations such as those associated with agriculture, that biopower can be seen in operation in heterogeneous associations, co-fostering human and nonhuman life towards enhanced levels of efficiency and productivity. Rabinow and Rose's (2006) threefold heuristic for biopower – emphasizing truths, interventions and subjectification – can describe such agricultural relations. 'Truths' produced about farming and about livestock (for example, that farming should be 'efficient' or 'productivist', or that livestock are best understood through genetic as opposed to phenotypic assessments) are clearly in play, and interventions (breeding, feeding and killing animals, and deploying veterinary science) follow. Both clearly affect the humans *and* animals involved. Subjectification is a little more difficult as it is problematic to regard nonhuman animals as able to be subjectified so that they act in accordance with truths concerning (for example) genetics or productive farming. However if we understand livestock farming as a heterogeneous assemblage of humans and nonhumans, then the subjectification of the human components of the assemblage, so that they farm and breed animals in accordance with genetic truths for example, is a process which has material effects on the assemblage overall, and on its nonhuman animal components specifically.

It can thus be argued that biopower is an effective conceptualization of contemporary livestock farming. The practice involves the controlled production of animal bodies suited for insertion into particular farming and food system assemblages, and it involves interventions which adjust animal bodies (for example, their bodily compositions of meat, fat and bone), behaviours (for example by manipulating light levels and stocking densities), and the processes (such as birth and death rates) which direct their population-level characteristics towards the particular economic ends of the meat industry. Genetic knowledge-practices are increasingly playing a role here: genetic 'truths' about animal bodies influence selection and mating decisions, affecting future population (herd or flock) characteristics. Geneticization, along with other metrics, also leads to envisaging animal populations in terms of distributions around norms of (for example) growth rate or muscle depth. Individuals can be compared according to their EBVs, for instance, or measured against a breed average or norm. Such comparisons are likely to influence decisions about which animals will be used for further breeding and which will be culled from the breeding population. They thus have real effects on both individuals and (future) populations together, rendering some animals more expendable and killable (Haraway, 2008; Holloway et al., 2011) while enhancing the value of others for their future contribution to breeding populations and, ultimately, the meat industry.

Articulating biopower with concepts drawn from political ecology provides a further useful dimension to the analysis of geneticization in meat production systems. Like biopower, political ecology, in its focus on the ineluctable interconnectedness of politics and ecology (Harvey, 1996; Robbins, 2012) in practices such as agriculture, is concerned with issues of life and death, and with the politics of establishing 'truths' about things which influence future practice. Farming is an inherently ecological set of practices, as it is fundamentally entangled with (both affected by and affecting) the flows and circulations of various things which constitute and are constituted by agro-ecological networks (e.g. nutrients, water, genes, and living entities including crop plants and livestock). But farming is also a highly politicized set of practices, as the political ecology of farming is supported and steered by political-economic interests and by associated, powerful discursive formations such as those associated with productivism, 'food security' or 'sustainable intensification'. In the UK context, for instance, the role of the European Union's (EU) Common Agricultural Policy (CAP) in structuring agro-ecological relationships is highly evident, even if very complex, while at the more local scale within the UK, politicized structures affecting the governance and regulation of on-farm agro-ecologies again serve to emphasize the value of a political ecological perspective on farm practice. To give an example related to meat production, in England, the English Beef and Lamb Executive (EBLEX), part of the Agriculture and Horticulture Development Board (AHDB, a non-departmental public body which operates independently of, but is sponsored by, the Department for Agriculture, Food and Rural Affairs, Defra) collects a statutory levy payment on all beef cattle and sheep entering the food system, using that to fund research into 'improving' agricultural production and promoting the meat to consumers. EBLEX is thus a powerful political-ecological actor able to create knowledge and truth about beef and sheep meat production, and to influence the direction of the meat sector in England in its farming practices and in the fostering of particular sorts of biopolitical intervention in the lives of farmed animals: it has, for example, been a vociferous advocate of the use of genetic techniques in beef and sheep breeding. As well as illustrating the conceptual linkage here between political ecology and biopower, this helps to emphasize a key point. The political ecology of farming does not just concern the 'non-domesticated' elements of farming ecologies, including the non-living elements (nutrients, soil, water etc.) and the 'wild' species (plants, microorganisms and invertebrate and vertebrate macro-organisms associated with and affected *by* farming), but crucially also enrols the 'farmed' elements too. In particular, for this chapter, the lives and deaths of farmed animals are political ecological in the sense that political-economic institutions and discursive frameworks profoundly affect the animals as individuals and populations, through the fostering of particular biopolitical interventions in their lives, breeding and bodies. The promotion and deployment of genetic techniques is a good illustration of this, and in the rest of the chapter I look at how such techniques become bound into, are promoted by, and affect the political ecologies of beef cattle and sheep farming in the UK through their reconfiguring of animal bodies and their meatiness as a product of genetics and genetic calculability.

Genetic techniques and reconfiguring the meat of animal bodies

In this section I draw on two parts of the data collected during the research project identified above. These parts represent two scales at which the geneticization of meat production is articulated: the scale of the *national breed society* and a larger scale representing the wider *commercial meat sector* in the UK. How both have become reorganized to take genetic techniques into account is of interest, but more conceptually, both are linked as part of an emerging political ecology of meat, involving a governance regime dependent on genetic knowledge to make the sector more efficient and productive at these different scales. Meat production thus depends on the interplay of these scales as part of an ecological regime of biopower. At both scales, the concept of population is crucial, whether this refers to a farm's herd or flock, or to the national herd/flock of cattle or sheep. At the same time, genetics become individualized as associated with specific animals, and thus how individuals stand, genetically, in relation to breed populations is also critical to making sense of their status within emergent meat political ecologies.

Genetics and meat on the farm: breed society perspectives

Here, I outline beef cattle and sheep breed society perspectives on the implications of geneticization for breeding practices, specifically focusing on how concepts related to the *meat* of their animals' bodies are re-articulated and made newly available for intervention within the localized ecologies of farms and herd/flock populations. Breed societies are institutions which take responsibility for the 'improvement' and promotion of particular pedigree livestock breeds, and are thus crucial in determining the extent to which, and how, the breed and its breeders engage with genetic techniques. Most of those involved in running breed societies are also breeders themselves. In the UK, breed societies tend to have charitable status. The larger societies associated with the numerically more important breeds employ professional staff, while smaller societies associated with numerically less important, minority or rare breeds, tend to be run by volunteers. Different breed societies, and different breeders, have widely differing perspectives on genetic techniques (see for example Holloway et al., 2009; Holloway and Morris, 2012). In this subsection I draw on in-depth interviews conducted in 2008 with four representatives of some of the numerically and commercially most significant breeds (three beef cattle and one sheep) in the UK, selecting these as it is these numerically important breeds which tend to be most deeply involved with the development and use of genetic techniques. They thus are most useful in exploring the implications of these techniques for the changing practices and political ecologies of meat production. Interviews were conducted in confidence, I thus refer to BS1, BS2, BS3 (cattle breed societies) and BS4 (sheep breed society). Alongside material from these interviews, I also refer to a recent article in the UK trade journal *Farmers Weekly* which discusses farmers' deployment of genetic techniques in their farming practices in relation to a sense of the 'meat' their animals can represent.

At the simplest level, the EBV technique allows breeders to quantify certain carcass and meat-related characteristics, and to relate these to the genetic value. EBVs depend on the systematic and reliable collection of data from living animals. Some are actual measurements, such as weight and muscle-depth records; others are proxy measurements (for example a cow's 'milkiness' might be recorded on the basis of the growth rate of her calf). These might more properly be referred to as 'capta' (see Kitchin and Dodge, 2011), implying a set of actual measurements recorded from the wider set of available measurements which in theory *could* be taken. The selection of particular capta illustrates a logic of measurement in which certain characteristics are deemed useful within a context of breed 'improvement' and the need to respond to certain market demands. In livestock breeding, sets of capta related to carcass production are clearly important, alongside other sets relating to so-called 'maternal' characteristics such as ease of birth and milk production.

Focusing on meat production, for example, one interviewee said that,

> We input all the information and put in things like birth weight, and 200, 400 and 600 day weights. We scan the animals, live scan. We are scanning for eye-muscle area, fat depth, marbling. So we record all the data here and put it into the computer system and we are also linked to Australia … and it gets analysed, then it is fed back down the line here.
>
> (BS1)

Another said that,

> EBVs come from background data from sire and dam, so the more information you've got, the correct accuracy of the figures, and also they're measuring different weights at so many days, 200, 300, 400, 500 day weight and that's all ploughed into the system and crunched up. The muscle score is measured, the muscle depth, the fat depth, you know, elements like that all go into giving you a figure for an animal … So you are selecting on figures.
>
> (BS3)

Recording might also begin to focus on meat *quality* as well as quantity, for example, as suggested here:

> … you are scanning for your eye muscle areas which is your ribeye steak and you are scanning for your marbling. Which obviously gives you tenderness quality, eating quality for the marbling through the beef, you are measuring that on a live animal, and obviously, these traits are heritable, so you're going to get that in the next generation.
>
> (BS1)

Once performed, EBV measurements thus enter into wider realms of calculation, in which they can be combined and manipulated to create new indices (such as an overall beef value, for example), which are designed to help farmers make sense of the complexity of the 'raw' capta. The manipulability of capta enhances the sense in which the 'genetics' of an animal, rendered as an EBV, comes to represent a particular truth about the life of farmed animals: this life is something which can be measured and itself manipulated on the basis of genetic knowledge-practices. And going beyond the individual animal, EBVs become important in the understanding of breed populations too. Comparisons of animals' 'genetic value' can be made for the different characteristics captured by EBVs, or by comparing the indices derived from combinations of specific capta. Breed norms or averages can be established for each EBV, with individuals then compared against that norm. These processes then allow, stimulate, or even make imperative, particular breeding practices or interventions, as breeders deploy EBVs in deciding which animals to keep for breeding (and, of course, which to rear for meat and cull from the future population of the breed), and in deciding which animals to mate in order to produce and 'improve' (in the sense of them having 'better' EBVs as well as 'better' bodies) future generations.

To illustrate, another representative discussed their practice as follows:

> What we can do then is to take EBVs plus economic factors and create an index, right … and each of the societies can decide how we are going to calculate them. Now the calf has a yield index, basically it is telling you the level of profitability that you are likely to get out of a calf [sired by] that bull.
>
> (BS2)

Such practices allow the digital envisaging of existing and future, as yet unbred, animals, as part of a set of interventions which guide the future of the breed population in particular directions. In the series of comments below, for instance, the interviewee (BS2) is looking at EBVs on a computer screen. The numbers conjure up fleshy animals for him, and he begins to show how his envisioning of these animals, and the performance of calculations using EBVs, informs intervention practices which foster the 'improvement' of future generations of the breed population.

> [This bull is] top of the breed for growth, carcass traits, that's retail beef yield is quite good … The eye muscle area happens to be down a bit, but it's just above breed average, but he is top of the breed for everything else … [looking at another bull] he is quite a well muscled beast, tremendous length and I mean basically it will drive our genetics forward so we don't lose these traits.
>
> … with that cow its eye muscle area is awful right, so I need to pull up a bull with good eye muscle area and so I go into here and I want something at least above average on eye muscle area, which is 1.1. So, I put in here eye muscle

area 1.1, submit that, so a minimum of 1.1 on eye muscle area and … that will pull up 37 animals … I can then go to the semen catalogue and pick any of those bulls and if I use one of those bulls on that [cow] it will improve that data … I can go a stage further and I can go to 'mating predictor' and I can put in the identity of the sire … and the dam's identity … and it will tell me the EBVs of the subsequent calf, and [the programme] reckons it will be no more than 5 per cent out either way.

We see here in this detailed commentary, recorded while the interviewee was pulling up information on different animals on a computer screen and talking through a decision-making process, how he uses EBV capta to try and 'correct' what have been identified by genetic techniques as defects in specific animals, something referred to in interview as 'plugging the gaps' in a population by mating animals according to a forecast of their offspring's genetic 'qualities'.

Two further points can be made. First, the use of EBVs and other genetic techniques depends on the establishment of a 'truth' of geneticization, in the sense that Rabinow and Rose (2006) argue is key to the operation of biopower. This truth has to be made visible to breeders to become accepted: they have to trust and believe in the truths concerning their animals revealed by genetic techniques. A recent *Farmers Weekly* article thus included a comment from a sheep breeder that, using genomic marker techniques,

> This animal, 08147, came back as being in the top 5% for fat yield and top 10% for meat traits, which was just exceptional. The phrase 'trust and verify' sums up what genomics is all about. You trust some of the traits, but genomics allows you to verify, giving you the confidence to use ram lambs and speed up the genetic gain.
>
> (Alderton, 2014, p.34)

Secondly, going beyond the individual breeder and into the political ecology of the meat system more widely, genetic techniques become entangled with systemic processes of ensuring productivity, and meat quality and traceability, within a supply chain. I discuss this further from the industry perspective in the next subsection, but here outline breeders' takes on the importance of this point.

The following comment, for example, points to how the use of EBVs is manipulable to suit different rearing systems: the political economic structure and demands of the meat sector is here given particular inflections by on-farm ecologies.

> … you need to have a carcass and as quick as possible to get to that carcass on your system. So that's why we give the different weight indices, if it's a one-year [rearing] system, or if you are going to finish off calves in 18 months … if you're in cereal growing, or a good grass area, you want them away at 14 to 16 months, then you want something with a large 400 day weight, big carcass.
>
> (BS1)

Alongside responding to local ecological differences, breeding practices also have to co-respond to market demands for particular types and qualities of fleshy body:

> We've been using EBVs and indices … and we've managed to get the fat levels down [but] we've been listening to what our customers have said and a number of them have said they've actually had a job to try and get the lambs to finish, to handle right, there is just not enough fat on them … you need a bit of fat cover, but if you are going to handle a lamb, you can feel the fleshing, especially over the spine, you just need that bit of fat to get them to handle right.
>
> (BS4)

As this interviewee suggests, EBVs can cause problems as their use in steering populations in particular directions (e.g. to reduce fat cover) can conflict with other ways of knowing animal bodies – in this case the manual handling of bodies to assess their quality in other ways. This is sometimes seen as a problem with EBVs more widely: a focus on 'improving' numbers only can lead to what might be later seen as the misdirecting of population-level traits which then need correction, as the following comment suggests.

> A number of people [have] just gone for high final index score EBV and the way it was tilted [i.e. calculated], on weight gain, muscle depth when we do the ultrasound scanning and, as it was then, basically, the leaner the better, and they were getting very high scores and these lambs were being used [for breeding] across the group and it was having a detrimental effect really on what our customers were wanting, so we just had to tilt it back a bit to correct it.
>
> (BS4)

In terms of deploying genetic techniques within a meat system political ecology where trust in quality increasingly needs to be secured, a future is imagined which closely ties calculations of animals' genetics to meat processors', retailers' and consumers' demands for guaranteed quality and consistency. One interviewee thus imagined a future of:

> the whole traceability of the animal, this animal is destined eventually for beef and when we've taken a hair sample, this animal, complete traceability through, will turn up on your plate … and it's guaranteed to be 10 out of 10 for tenderness and 8 out of 10 for marbling, 7 out of 10 for taste and it's guaranteed, because that is a tremendous marketing advantage for whatever breed of animal you've got. Obviously you've got to work with the processors, from the supermarkets, from the consumers, but we want to move from this relatively small pedigree top of the pyramid right through to the 600,000 [breed name]-sired calves which are destined for meat production.

You know, if we can get all the information on all of those calves, that would give us tremendous power.

(BS3)

Along with the other points made, this final comment sums up the particular nature of a geneticized political ecology of meat production. In essence, specific, genetically inflected interventions are being made in ecologies at different scales (for example the localized ecologies and domestic biodiversities of breed populations on farms, farm-scale ecologies which entangle cattle or sheep populations with other components of agro-ecological systems, and national or even international domestic livestock agro-ecologies). At the same time, farm-scale interventions (in essence, which animal to breed with which) are co-produced with political economic/bio-economic institutions (e.g. processors, retailers, breed societies, genetics companies, government agencies) which act as authorities establishing biopowerful genetic truths about life which demand interventions aimed at constituting particular sorts of animal life.

Geneticization and the commercial meat sector

Following the above discussion of farmers' and breeders' perspectives, here I turn to briefly examine a wider political ecology of genetic intervention in farm and national-scale bovine and ovine populations by looking at the perspectives and activities of some of the commercial and associated institutions involved in fostering and steering the use of genetic techniques in livestock breeding. I outline material from two sources: the first, an EBLEX publication distributed in Spring 2014; the second an interview conducted with a meat processing company representative in 2008.

EBLEX's (2014) *Beef Breeding Bulletin Extra* focuses on encouraging more breeders to use EBVs, including showing them how to access the capta and how to base decision-making on them. In doing so, EBLEX contributes to a metrics of livestock breeding in which knowing and practising genetics is a crucial part of an ecology of farm management which aims to make meat production more efficient at different scales (the individual body, the farm-level herd/flock and the national-level livestock population). Meat production depends on the interplay of these scales – and on the metrical knowing of each as part of an ecological regime of biopower. EBLEX's need to continue promoting EBVs to what is represented as a reluctant or 'backward' population of beef and sheep farmers is itself interesting, in that the claims to truth and authority made by proponents of genetic techniques are by no means fully accepted, although they are enthusiastically embraced by many. EBLEX thus exemplifies one dimension of the *politics* of this meat political ecology. As mentioned above, the agency is linked to government, and has political authority to sanction its funding by compulsory levy. More widely, it embodies the political economics of agricultural and food system productivism. These features affect its interventions in cattle and sheep breeding, that is, in the ecologies of farm life. This *Bulletin* is interesting in the way it exemplifies relations of biopower functioning through this meat political ecology. Three brief points are worth making.

First, there is a focus on how EBVs can foster animal life in enhancing qualities which align with a productivist agenda. And second, in doing this, the *Bulletin* continues a process of cementing and legitimizing the authority of science to determine genetic truths about life. In particular, this is achieved by reference to ten case studies of trials conducted at research institutes, agricultural colleges and companies, all of which provide evidence for the benefits of using genetic techniques in breeding beef cattle. These benefits are determined in various ways, including the greater financial value of animals sired by bulls with high 'genetic merit', their greater weight, speed in reaching slaughter, higher 'killing out percentage' (i.e. useable proportion of the carcass), and superior carcass conformation. Summarizing this survey of trials, EBLEX's breeding specialist comments that:

> The evidence is overwhelming. High EBV bulls can significantly increase herd profitability. This BRP Breeding Bulletin explains why this is so and which traits to look for when selecting a bull. It also shows how EBVs should be interpreted to optimize their impact.
>
> (EBLEX, 2014, p.1)

Third, the *Bulletin* attempts to 'nudge' reluctant breeders towards using EBVs themselves; that is, it tries to intervene in their subjectivity as breeders, and in their breeding practices. It provides basic guidance on how to find and interpret EBV data, illustrating the different sorts of graphic illustrations of EBVs which are used. There's also a quiz, in which readers are prompted to 'have a go!' at selecting which bull to use for particular breeding goals, purely on the basis of EBV data. This 'game' tries to demystify the use of EBVs and make them accessible to all breeders. At the same time, however, it is quite reductive, presenting breeding decisions as simple and one-dimensional, and, in suggesting that a breeder can just use the numbers to make a decision, can effect a disempowering of the breeder through an exporting of decision-making authority to the organization which calculates and presents EBVs.

The second example of a wider political ecology of genetic intervention is of a meat processing company which has formed a meat network based around contractual relations between itself and farmers who are paid to rear carefully bred calves in carefully specified ways (see Holloway et al., 2014 for more detail). Through such intensive, genetically informed, integration, animals are bred and reared to be of consistent and appropriate quality for the company's downstream customers in the meat supply chain. A company representative mapped out the biopowerful interventions made here in the life of livestock animals and in on-farm ecologies and practices:

> What we're trying to do is a total system in that, all to do with meat quality basically. So we've got a bull that we know is genetically superior …

> producing us calves that grow quickly. We've got a rearing system which …
> it's a very prescribed system, all right, different from other organisations …
> We actually contract the rearer to rear our calves, pay them a fee, we put in
> all the medicines, all of the feed, all of the milk powder. So we dictate to that
> rearer … we dictate protocol, health protocols, feed protocol as well.

In this example, genetic knowledge–practices are presented as part of a wider integrated set of interventions which mesh together in the pursuit of efficiency and quality. But for the interviewee, genetic truth is the basis of the rest of the system. As he said, 'genetics is the initial foundation step all right. If you get the genetics right, and you get the right bull with the right potential, then it leads on to more efficiencies down the chain'. On the basis of this 'truth', the company has worked in partnership with a major UK cattle-breeding company which supplies semen from high quality bulls for artificial insemination, to select one particular Aberdeen Angus bull with the desired genetic characteristics. Semen is supplied to breeders in the network, who use it to breed the calves which will be reared under the precise terms of the contract described above. For the company, involvement in genetic intervention was planned to increasingly intensify through experimenting with genetic markers as well as EBVs:

> This bull here, we'll do a total gene marker on him, as much as we can, then
> get our bull, the progeny of that bull on farms, through the system, and we
> could monitor all the way through … even to the meat end [i.e. retailer and
> consumer] of the operation, it's going to come out with some validated evidence, you know.

What is described here mirrors the comments made by the representative of BS3 above, suggesting a further integration of breeding and rearing with the rest of the meat supply chain, using a process of traceability to monitor meat quality and to collect more capta which would be fed back into further rounds of political economic intervention in the life and ecologies of livestock farming. Genetic truths about breeding would be more deeply embedded, leading to further interventions in life, in on-farm practices, and in the subjectification of those who breed and rear animals under contract to the company.

Both examples referred to in this subsection point to an ongoing redistribution of power and knowledge in meat political ecological networks. This takes on particular inflections in relation to the emergence of genetic knowledge-practices, where off-farm political and economic actors are involved in the calculation and representation of genetic information. The articulation of biopower through this political ecology of agricultural life focuses attention on how genetic interventions affect human subjectivity and animal life together. Breeders thus become expected to align their practices with (what become established as) genetic truths, with consequences for the lives and bodies of the animals they farm.

Conclusions

This chapter has outlined some of the implications of geneticization of livestock breeding for the lives of animals and breeders caught up in meat production systems. It has framed the geneticization of livestock breeding in terms of a mode of biopower that is articulated through changing meat system political ecologies, which are played out at a range of different, interconnected scales: genes, bodies, farm- and national-scale breed populations, and meat systems consisting of farms, other economic actors (e.g. processors and retailers) and political and quasi-political institutions. This political ecological network is increasingly centred around discourses of genetic truth, and the interventions which result affect breeders' subjectivities and knowledge-practices, and animals' bodies and lives (and deaths). Breeders become subject to a process of 'nudging' towards using genetic techniques, and may acquire new identities as a result – for example as 'progressive' or 'backward'. Animals may become more valued or prized, or conversely more killable, by being associated with particular genetic qualities.

Ecologically, what can be referred to in terms of domestic animal biodiversity is affected by geneticization. How animals are viewed in relation to others of their breed is changed (e.g. by quantitative comparisons of their 'genetic merit', and by the ability to assess individuals in relation to breed norms), with potentially significant effects on the genetic composition of breeds and of species, particularly when combined with other technologies such as artificial insemination and embryo transfer which enable a single, genetically highly valued animal to be parent to very large numbers of offspring. In terms of biopower, what is being intervened in and changed are the metrics of the population, its collective life channelled towards particular political-economic ends (e.g. productivism, or food security).

Finally then, geneticization can be said to allow a further intensification of biopowerful interventions in the political ecologies of livestock breeding systems which, for many, are ethically problematic. How millions of animals are bred, reared and slaughtered is already a cause for concern for many. Geneticization is potentially associated not only with a genetic reductivism in respect of animals (so that they risk being seen only as the product of their genes) but with further ethical issues associated with genetic interventions in the life of individuals and populations, and with the effects of that on farming ecologies which are necessarily *political* ecologies since they are affected by an agricultural political economy focused on an agenda of continued industrialized livestock farming and increasing farm output and efficiency. A narrowing of biodiversity, for example, may reduce farm system resilience, while a focus on breeding for a narrow range of valued genetic characteristics (e.g. size, growth rates and muscle depth) might mean neglecting other characteristics(such as disease resistance) important to animals' welfare and, again, to the resilience of farming systems. Many breeders and others are alive to these issues and are cautious as a result about the deployment of genetic techniques as the sole determinant of breeding decisions.

Countering genetic truths there are thus alternative perspectives on livestock breeding, and a process of negotiation between different ways of selecting which animals to breed with which, which takes place on individual farms as well as within the wider political ecology of the meat system. Geneticization is currently proving to be a powerful truth, however, and understanding some of its consequences, particularly in the context of recent drives for the 'sustainable intensification' of agriculture, remains important.

References

Alderton, S. (2014) 'Genomics can write success in your flock's DNA', *Farmers Weekly* 17 January, pp. 30–34

Archibald, A. and Haley, C. (2003) 'What can the genetics revolution offer the meat industry?', *Outlook on Agriculture*, vol 32, pp. 219–226

Bishop, S. and Woolliams, J. (2004) 'Genetic approaches and technologies for improving the sustainability of livestock production', *Journal of the Science of Food and Agriculture*, vol 84, pp. 911–919

Bulfield, G. (2000) 'Farm animal biotechnology', *Trends in Biotechnology*, vol 8, pp. 10–13

Deleuze, G. (1988) *Foucault*, Continuum, London

EBLEX (2014) *Beef Breeding Bulletin Extra*, Spring, AHDB, Warwickshire

Foucault, M. (1990) *The History of Sexuality Volume 1: An Introduction*, Penguin, Harmondsworth

Foucault, M. (2003) *Society Must Be Defended*, Penguin, London

Foucault, M. (2007) *Security, Territory, Population: Lectures at the College de France 1977–1978*, Palgrave Macmillan, Basingstoke

Gannett, L. (1999) 'What's in a cause? The pragmatic dimensions of genetic explanations', *Biology and Philosophy*, vol 14, pp. 349–374

Gibbon, S. and Novas, C. (2008) 'Introduction: Biosocialities, genetics and the social sciences', in S. Gibbon and C. Novas (eds), *Biosocialities, Genetics and the Social Sciences*, Routledge, London

Haraway, D. (1997) *Modest_witness@second_millennium.femaleman_meets_oncomouse: Feminism and Technoscience*, Routledge, London

Haraway, D. (2008) *When Species Meet*, University of Minnesota Press, Minneapolis and London

Harvey, D. (1996) *Justice, Nature and the Geography of Difference*, Blackwell, Oxford

Holloway, L. (2005) 'Aesthetics, genetics and evaluating animal bodies: Locating and displacing cattle on show and in figures', *Environment and Planning D: Society and Space*, vol 23, pp. 883–902

Holloway, L. and Morris, C. (2007) 'Exploring biopower in the regulation of farm animal bodies: Genetic policy interventions in UK livestock', *Genomics, Society and Policy*, vol 3, pp. 82–98

Holloway, L. and Morris, C. (2008) 'Boosted bodies: Genetic techniques, domestic livestock bodies and complex representations of life', *Geoforum*, vol 39, pp. 1709–1720

Holloway, L. and Morris, C. (2012) 'Contesting genetic knowledge-practices in livestock breeding: Biopower, biosocial collectivities and heterogeneous resistances', *Environment and Planning D: Society and Space*, vol 30, pp. 60–77

Holloway, L. and Morris, C. (2014) 'Viewing animal bodies: Truths, practical aesthetics and ethical considerability in UK livestock breeding', *Social and Cultural Geography*, vol 15, pp. 1–22

Holloway, L., Morris, C., Gilna, B. and Gibbs, D. (2009) 'Biopower, genetics and livestock breeding: (Re)constituting animal populations and heterogeneous biosocial collectivities', *Transactions, Institute of British Geographers*, vol 34, pp. 394–407

Holloway, L., Morris, C., Gilna, B., Gibbs, D. (2011) 'Choosing and rejecting cattle and sheep: Changing discourses and practices of (de)selection in pedigree livestock breeding', *Agriculture and Human Values*, vol 28, pp. 533–547

Holloway, L., Morris, C., Gibbs, D. and Gilna, B. (2014) 'Making meat collectivities: Entanglements of geneticisation, integration and contestation in livestock breeding', in M. Goodman and C Sage (eds), *Food Transgressions: Making sense of contemporary food politics*, Ashgate, London

Keller, E. (1992) *Secrets of Life, Secrets of Death: Essays in Language, Gender and Science*, Routledge, London

Keller, E. (2000) *The Century of the Gene*, Harvard University Press, Cambridge, MA

Kitchin, R. and Dodge, M. (2011) *Code/Space. Software and Everyday Life*, MIT Press, Cambridge, MA

Morris, C. and Holloway, L. (2009) 'Genetic technologies and the transformation of the geographies of UK livestock agriculture: A research agenda', *Progress in Human Geography*, vol 33, pp. 313–333

Morris, C. and Holloway, L. (2014) 'Genetics and livestock breeding in the UK: Co-constructing technologies and heterogeneous biosocial collectivities', *Journal of Rural Studies*, vol 33, pp. 150–160

Nealon, J. (2008) *Foucault Beyond Foucault: Power and Its Intensifications Since 1984*, Stanford University Press, Stanford, CA

Rabinow, P. and Rose, N. (2006) 'Biopower today', *Biosocieties*, vol 1, pp. 195–217

Robbins, P. (2012) *Political Ecology: A Critical Introduction*, Wiley-Blackwell, Oxford

Rose, N. (2001) 'The politics of life itself', *Theory, Culture and Society*, vol 18, pp. 1–30

Rose, N. (2007) *The Politics of Life Itself: Biomedicine, Power and Subjectivity in the Twenty-first Century*, Princeton University Press, Princeton, NJ

Rutherford, S. (2011) *Governing the Wild: Ecotours of Power*, University of Minnesota Press, Minneapolis

Shukin, N. (2009) *Animal Capital: Rendering Life in Biopolitical Times*, University of Minnesota Press, Minneapolis

Technology Strategy Board (2013) *Feeding the Future: Innovation Requirements for Primary Food Production in the UK to 2030*, Technology Strategy Board, Swindon

Twine, R. (2010) *Animals as Biotechnology: Ethics, Sustainability and Critical Animal Studies*, Earthscan, London

Wolfe, C. (2013) *Before the Law: Humans and Other Animals in a Biopolitical Frame*, University of Chicago Press, Chicago

12

COWS, CLIMATE AND THE MEDIA

Keith C. L. Lee, Joshua P. Newell, Jennifer R. Wolch and Pascale Joassart-Marcelli

Introduction

With the shift toward large-scale concentrated animal feeding operations (CAFOs), media coverage of livestock production has focused on issues ranging from livestock-borne diseases to worker's rights to greenhouse gas (GHG) emissions. The latter is particularly important given growing evidence for anthropogenic climate change and its connection to livestock production (Steinfeld et al., 2006). Continued public uncertainty about anthropogenic climate change, however, threatens the adoption and enforcement of appropriate mitigation and adaptation policies (Leiserowitz, 2006; Boykoff, 2007). As media representations of climate science have in part fueled climate skepticism, analysis of how the media portrays different climate-related issues is required if scientists and policymakers are to improve their engagement and communication with the public. Doing so will help secure broader-based public support for climate policy. Yet despite livestock production's sizeable contribution to GHG emissions, academic literature lacks systematic media content analysis of how the media cover the livestock–climate change connection. This chapter addresses this gap by comparing media coverage of livestock production's contribution to climate change with broader coverage of other livestock-related issues. This is followed by a deeper analysis of how the media has represented the livestock–climate change connection.

The food system's contribution to climate change is often framed in terms of food miles. However, the global transportation sector emits less than livestock production, which contributes up to 18 percent of world GHG emissions and accounts for nearly 80 percent of all agriculture-related emissions (Steinfeld et al., 2006). Deforestation associated with grazing and feed production (e.g. corn and soy) underpins livestock's climate change impact (Gill, Smith, and Wilkinson, 2010). Additionally, livestock's digestive systems and manure produce GHGs such as nitrous oxide and methane (Steinfeld et al., 2006). CAFOs also have large heating, cooling, lighting, ventilation and waste disposal energy demands, which also increase GHG emissions (Lappé and McKibben, 2010).

Cattle (including beef cattle and dairy cows sent to slaughter) are the largest livestock-based source of GHG emissions. These emissions vary considerably according to type of animal, method of production and the geography of where the animals are raised and slaughtered. The livestock industry faces growing pressure to mitigate these emissions and has responded with an array of preventative and 'end of pipe' approaches that further intensify the livestock production process (Clemens and Ahlgrimm, 2001), while allowing them to continue to expand operations and sell more meat. In concert with the livestock production industry, bioengineering and pharmaceutical firms have developed measures such as increasing animal productivity through improved genetics, greater use of growth hormones, antibiotics, steroids, disease control, controlled grazing and altering animal feeds. 'End of pipe' measures include better manure management and use of manure or litter for biogas production. The industry warns that 'productivity-enhancing technologies' are necessary for limiting deforestation and GHG emissions from beef production (Capper and Hayes, 2012).

Livestock production's impacts are not limited to climate change, but include additional environmental, public health, socio-economic and animal welfare costs. Other environmental impacts associated with intensive beef production include water pollution and water use, biodiversity and aquatic system threats, air pollution and land degradation (Gerbens-Leenes, Nonhebel, and Ivens, 2002; Mallin and Cahoon, 2003; Koneswaran and Nierenberg, 2008; Emel and Neo, 2011). Livestock production consumes nearly three-quarters of all agricultural land globally, as well as 8 percent of total water use (Steinfeld et al., 2006, xxii).

Livestock production and consumption each have their respective public health impacts. CAFOs are responsible for public and worker health issues associated with increasingly antibiotic-resistant bacteria and the spread of infectious diseases, including influenza (Gilchrist et al., 2007). Increased meat consumption has been linked with health maladies including obesity, cancer, heart disease and diabetes (Chao et al., 2005; Micha, Wallace, and Mozaffarian, 2010; Michaelowa and Dransfeld, 2008).

Industrial beef production is representative of the wave of corporate consolidation in the broader meat industry. Four corporations (Tyson Foods, JBS, Cargill and National Beef) produce approximately 80 percent of the beef products sold in the US. Concerned scholars write of the industry's close interconnections with government subsidies, financialization, industry group advertising, (e.g. 'Beef, it's what's for dinner') and pharmaceutical companies (Bonanno et al., 1994; Morgan, Marsden, and Murdoch, 2006). Specific socio-economic concerns include family versus corporate ownership of farms, living wages and livelihoods for farmers and farm workers, sourcing food 'locally', and supply chain transparency. In theoretical parlance, differences between beef production systems parallel those of ecological modernization and agro-ecology (Marsden and Sonnino, 2005): that is, sustainability through intensification and efficiency as opposed to sustainability through reimagined (and reconstituted) urban and rural food provisioning networks that attempt to undo social and economic inequalities.

Last but not least, CAFOs create significant animal welfare issues. Concerns over animal welfare relate to cases of slaughterhouse animals so injured or sick that they cannot stand up unassisted (so-called 'downer' animals) and conditions that deprive animals of social interaction, limit time outdoors, restrict normal behaviors and result in a range of serious health and behavioral problems (Mader, 2003; West, 2003).

Media coverage of these issues contributes to public awareness and can support or impede structural changes such as developing more sustainable food systems and policies that address the wide range of impacts of livestock production. Despite widespread media coverage of livestock-related issues and growing scientific evidence linking meat production and climate change, systematic content analysis of this relationship in media coverage has been surprisingly minimal.

This chapter extends previous research that combines actor-network theory (ANT) with framing theory to develop the basis for 'story-networks' – networks of actants and artifacts that shape how a media report or 'story' is framed (Lee et al., 2014). We do this by coding livestock-related articles from a major US newspaper, the *Los Angeles Times*, over the 1999 through 2010 period to understand how various actants and artifacts shaped different story-networks. Specifically, we address the following questions:

1 What livestock-related themes did the *Los Angeles Times* cover from 1999–2010?
2 How did coverage of these themes change over this period?
3 Which actors (human or nonhuman) contributed towards news coverage of livestock-climate change related issues and how did they do so?
4 How were these stories framed?

The chapter illustrates how distinctive story-networks emerge, framing the livestock–climate change linkage as either an issue to be addressed through technological innovation, individual lifestyle choices, or policy action. In these story-networks, varying configurations of actants and artifacts were involved, including the cattle themselves. We conclude the chapter by reflecting on our theoretical approach and directions for future research.

Climate change, livestock and the media: frameworks for understanding

This section reviews media analysis studies and introduces framing theory and ANT. These theoretical frameworks provide the foundation for the 'story-network' concept, which we use to describe how different configurations of actors and artifacts create narratives for media stories. This framing solidifies these narratives in different stories through repeated messaging over time. News stories and their characteristics are thus influenced not only by the media but also by the actors and artifacts involved in generating the news. Broadly, this reflects the socially constructed nature of knowledge. This refers to how scientific knowledge of environmental issues such as climate change is not insulated from politics – the political ecology of knowledge. The practice of science, often taken for granted as objective, instead involves a web of social relations which not only generates its own politics, but is open to influence from the politics it often seeks to inform (Demeritt, 2001). As a result, the nature of knowledge is molded by the power relationships within and among the groups involved in its production and the users of knowledge. While our focus is on the media and not on formal scientific knowledge, the political nature of knowledge production readily applies and informs our exposition of the following theoretical frameworks.

Media analysis and framing theory

Media analyses focus on how mass media shapes public perceptions and attitudes. Their findings illuminate how media's ability to shape public perception depends on how it chooses its primary sources and frames its stories (Bennett, 1996; Goodman and Goodman, 2005). Several studies have examined climate change media coverage and found it reflects and influences short-term public concern about the issue (Carvalho and Burgess, 2005; Sampei and Aoyagi-Usui, 2009; Trumbo, 1996). Media analyses have also found that the media sometimes convey inaccurate information, possibly to balance two sides of a story. Antilla (2005) concluded the media would sometimes cite climate skeptics to appear journalistically balanced, often giving undue weight to sensational, less scientific approaches and exaggerating the extent to which issues were debated (Bennett, 1996; Goodman and Goodman, 2005).

Media analyses have also sought to explain temporal changes in the coverage of issues like climate change. Downs theorized changes in coverage by arguing that public attention to an issue consists of: (1) 'the pre-problem stage;' (2) 'alarmed discovery and euphoric enthusiasm;' (3) 'realizing the cost of significant progress;' (4) 'gradual decline of intense public interest;' and (5) 'the post-problem stage,' where public interest in the problem is low, but higher than at the beginning (Downs, 1972, pp. 39–40). Though frequently cited, scholars have criticized Downs's model for failing to account for the media's agency in determining news coverage. Boykoff and Boykoff (2007) argue that professional norms in journalism, including personalization, dramatization, novelty and balance (often confused for objectivity) also shape media coverage. Though actual news content undoubtedly plays a role, these norms lead to the emergence of particular narratives and frames that influence public perceptions of the issues being covered.

Other studies not only examine potential cyclicality in media coverage, but also illustrate how narratives and discourses employed by the media change over time. Subsequent work (Trumbo, 1996; McComas and Shanahan, 1999; Carvalho and

Burgess, 2005) suggested that climate change coverage follows a cyclical pattern, similar to Downs's theory, that is augmented by the media's construction of different narratives over time: during the early stages of the cycle, the media most frequently covered articles grounded in science that highlight the need for political reform. These articles frequently linked major scientific findings to climate change-related events, such as massive US-wide heat waves. Scientists were most often quoted during this upswing of attention. Next, politicians and industry became more involved actors in media reports of climate change, often lending moral judgments and providing solutions (Trumbo, 1996; Carvalho and Burgess, 2005). Articles then began to depict controversy among scientists over climate change, which is suggestive of media attempts to maintain journalistic balance and create drama (McComas and Shanahan, 1999). At the end of the cycle, the media started to frame the issue in terms of the large investment costs and behavioral change burdens required to mitigate climate change, leading to a gradual decline in attention (Trumbo, 1996; McComas and Shanahan, 1999; Carvalho and Burgess, 2005).

To our knowledge, only Neff et al. (2009) have examined media coverage of livestock–climate change linkages over time. They analyzed stories in 16 major US newspapers from 2005 to 2008 and concluded that although coverage of food–climate change connections increased over time, it did not reflect the scale of the food system's effects on climate change. This coverage focused on food in general rather than specific food system components. The study found that articles initially allocated responsibility to individuals but over time shifted towards business and government, suggesting a growing salience of food system–climate change impacts for political leaders, experts and advocacy groups. The study did not attempt to identify how different stakeholders might have influenced the newspaper coverage.

Research shows how framing shapes public perceptions and attitudes. Framing theory helps us understand how information is presented and which aspects are included or omitted. Iyengar (1994) divided frames into episodic and thematic framing. Stories framed episodically examine one 'episode,' rather than the larger processes at work. For example, prior studies demonstrate that episodic media coverage of health problems (e.g. obesity) often blames individuals' eating behavior rather than structural or genetic reasons (Saguy and Almeling, 2008; Borra and Bouchoux, 2009). In contrast, thematically framed stories provide contextual information about an issue, such as the policies that have made fats and sugars more affordable and readily available. Thematic stories tend to build broad-based public concerns (Iyengar, 1994; Wallack et al., 1999) or create pressure for institutional reform (Wallack et al., 1999; Dorfman, Wallack, and Woodruff, 2005), thereby attributing responsibility to government or society. Although few news stories are purely episodic or thematic, one type is usually predominant in each story (Iyengar, 1994).

Framing also refers to the narratives news stories employ and reflects how public understandings of different issues are cognitive and cultural (Goffman, 1974). Understanding this aspect of framing helps us understand how the media shape opinion (Entman, 1993; Scheufele, 1999). Gamson et al. (1992) suggest that media framing is influenced by social actors with stakes in different social realities presented by the media. Trumbo (1996) suggests that framing is dictated by the ability of different parties to communicate messages and the media's discretion in choosing which sources to use. We later employ ANT to make these interactions more nuanced and explicit.

Different frames involve different themes, sources and actors. Here, we use 'theme' to refer to the general subject area the media chooses to align its stories with. For example, articles about CAFOs could highlight themes such as animal rights issues, workers' rights, or health and nutrition, depending on the angle and sources employed. A manufacturer can be generous for providing a low-priced item or, conversely, be irresponsible for cutting costs on pollution abatement. Frames shape our understanding of who is responsible; they direct the public to pressure certain responsible parties (Wallack et al., 1999). By studying livestock-related stories, we can understand how news is framed and, accordingly, who is made responsible.

Actor–network theory

ANT was developed in the 1980s by Bruno Latour, Michel Callon and John Law (Law, 1998; Callon and Latour, 1981; Latour, 1993) and views the world as comprising multiple actor-networks that are heterogeneous, complex and dynamic (Castree, 2002). This perspective breaks down traditional dualistic boundaries (e.g. nature/culture, structure/agency) that shape how most knowledge is constructed. Actor-networks include assemblages of human and nonhuman actants, which can include everything from people and plants to institutions and scientific research. Networks are made 'real' not necessarily by actants' intrinsic properties but by actants' positions relative to each other. Actor-networks' success depends on the ability to enroll other actants through translation: an actor's ability to exert authority over another in speech or action (Callon and Latour, 1981).

ANT's potential to transcend nature-society dualism partly explains its allure. It helps resist such dualisms by providing a relational vocabulary, providing neutral ground between natural and social sciences (Ivakhiv, 2002). Nature is understood as neither 'natural' nor 'social' but as a hybrid. ANT is therefore 'co-constructionist', seeking to identify how relations and entities come into being together (Murdoch, 1997). ANT also challenges how we think about actants with respect to power. We generally conceive power based on what we perceive to be intrinsic resources and liabilities of these actants. ANT turns this conception on its head by ascribing power not to the actants themselves but to the links that bind actants and entities together (Murdoch, 2000).

ANT can augment framing theory by identifying actants, who they influence and what artifacts they use to enroll other actants in their story-networks. In this chapter, actants include humans, animals and objects that have agency in shaping story-networks by contributing to or having a stake in the events or circumstances covered by the media. We distinguish between these three using the terms 'actors', 'animal actants', and 'artifacts', respectively.

ANT differs from traditional communication models (Shannon and Weaver, 1949; Berlo, 1960) that consider the process to be linear and one in which the media reframes existing information for the public. Couldry (2008) highlights that ANT can blur dualistic boundaries between media institutions and broader society and show how media power is spatially dispersed in actor-networks. However, ANT's treatment of power, especially between actants, has been critiqued as insufficient (Castree, 2002; Fine, 2005). In particular, 'social' rather than 'natural' actants have been demonstrated to have more 'power' (Castree, 2002) – through a surplus of money, for example (Massey, 1993; Hudson, 2001 quoted in Fine, 2005).

This critique is important when considering media discourses as outcomes of contestation among different actants (Gamson et al., 1992). Better understanding these outcomes requires a version of ANT that interrogates power more subtly and explicitly. In addition to actants' individual characteristics, their positions within networks, network structure and the type and terms of their connections are important in determining the kinds of power exerted and the outcomes of actant interaction (Rocheleau, 2011; Rocheleau and Roth, 2007). Similarly, Hobson (2007) suggests that animal agency is shaped by their placement in different networks, i.e. their relationships with other actants.

In our analysis of livestock–climate change articles, we draw upon these elaborations on ANT and framing theory to conceptualize news stories as 'story-networks' – webs of actants and artifacts with different degrees of power to influence stories' framing and their communicated messages. The media is an actant that others have to pass through and, thus, is intrinsically endowed with power. However, the story-network's actants are also vital; they shape the story's framing, its different themes and the sources that inform it, thus shaping the meaning of events for the broader public. Our research seeks to understand what kinds of messages are reaching the public about livestock and climate change. To this end, we combine ANT and framing theory to identify and examine key actants associated with different frames and themes. The relationships between actants explain the story-network; we focus on the ways in which different actants exert power and how this influences the framing of the story.

Methodological approach

Our methodological model assumes story-networks comprise multiple actants and the media. Different degrees and types of power held by each actant shape these networks and interact with the media to shape news articles. We identify the key actants in media coverage of livestock issues and assess how frequently they are cited or referenced, using them as gateways into the actor-networks underlying different news stories. We draw conclusions about how actants' relationships to each other and the media affect their representation. Finally, we assess whether and how these effects interact with the media to impact how articles frame livestock–climate change issues.

Specifically, we examined newspaper articles in the *Los Angeles Times*. This newspaper was selected for three reasons. First, the *Times* is a major national media outlet, with a searchable online archive. Second, California is the nation's leading agricultural state, making its media sensitive to issues affecting that sector. Third, focusing on a single media source helped to some extent hold constant differences in editorial philosophy and strategy. We used electronic search engines to identify articles, determined their annual frequency and quantified different coded actants. To keep the amount of data manageable, we systematically searched for livestock-focused, full-text news articles and editorials of any length (except for letters to the editor) published between January 1, 1999 and December 31, 2010, excluding articles that only tangentially referred to livestock. We selected these years as they span a period when scientific awareness of livestock–climate change linkages was growing steadily.

We identified six themes from reading the articles:

1   climate change;
2   animal welfare;
3   workers' rights and safety;
4   human health and nutrition (including food safety);
5   environmental impacts (excluding climate change); and
6   business and technology.

We tabulated the total number of articles in each theme for each of the study period's 12 years to identify trends and changes in issue coverage over time. As our aim was to explore how the media portrayed livestock–climate change connections, we focused most on articles in the climate change theme.

To understand what voices livestock-related articles exposed the public to and which voices influenced the livestock–climate change discourse, we quantified three types of actants quoted or mentioned in the *Los Angeles Times*. We termed human actants as 'actors', defining actors as human individuals or organizations that had a stake in, or would be affected by, the event that led to the article. All human actors also received another code based on their affiliation. These included 'state', 'private sector', 'academic', 'industry association' (i.e. associations representing the livestock industry's interests) or 'public interest' (including non-governmental organizations and other members of civil society).

We also counted animals, both when the media portrayed them as having agency and when they were mentioned in general. Lastly, we included key nonhuman actants (for example, a new piece of legislation, or a journal article); these were termed 'artifacts'. We coded and counted actants once, even if they were mentioned multiple times in an article. Following Iyengar (1994), we also coded each article as episodic or thematic. To identify how the media represented livestock–climate change linkages, we identified the actants that referenced these linkages. We coded those that acknowledged the linkages as a problem as 'positive', those that acknowledged only some of the linkages or did not necessarily view climate change as a problem as 'neutral', and those that expressed skepticism over livestock's climate change impacts as 'negative'. All coding was done using Atlas.ti software (Scientific Software Development, 2012).

We divide our findings into four areas: changes in the frequency of livestock-related articles over time, the number and types of actants we identified in climate change articles, how these articles were framed and different actants' attitudes to climate change–livestock linkages.

Media themes over time

Our analysis of coverage by general theme reveals that livestock-related articles in the *Los Angeles Times* from 1999–2010 (Figure 12.1) most commonly focused on human health (175), followed by animal welfare (105), environmental impacts (41), business and technology (36), workers' rights and safety (30) and climate change (19). The annual article total increased from 14 in 1999 to 72 in 2010, suggesting an overall increase in media interest in livestock-related issues. Workers' rights and safety and climate change were the only themes to end the period without an overall increase in article frequency.

Articles on environmental impacts primarily focused on water pollution and waste from livestock production, although in 2009 and 2010 there was notable growth in articles covering sustainable agriculture trends (e.g. urban backyard chicken farming). Animal welfare articles covered animal rights activism (notably People for the Ethical Treatment of Animals) and associated legislation, with peaks in 2003 and 2008. Health articles were the most temporally consistent, generally discussing nutrition (including diets and certain foods' nutritional impact),

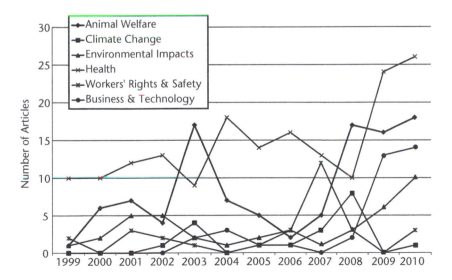

FIGURE 12.1 Annual number of articles by theme.

food-borne illnesses and food product recalls. Workers' rights and safety articles were consistently low-frequency except for a peak in 2007; they featured changes in labor and immigration policy and their impact on immigrant farm workers and employers. Business and technology articles covered government deliberation over genetically modified food standards and the impacts on American livestock businesses of mad cow disease and Japanese bans on American beef. Although consistently low at first, coverage took off in 2009 and 2010, focusing on rapidly rising costs of meat and the recession-induced competitive tactics of large meat retailers, such as fast food restaurants.

Climate change articles were least common ($n = 19$, 5 percent) and appeared irregularly over the study period. Although 2003 saw some coverage, coverage only increased and peaked in 2007 and 2008 with articles covering climate change mitigation policy, diet change and methane capture technology. However, they nearly disappeared in 2009 and 2010. Meanwhile, the annual total of livestock-related articles increased from 14 in 1999 to 72 in 2010, suggesting that climate change lagged other livestock-related themes in attracting media coverage. Otherwise, health articles were most frequent (43 percent), followed by animal welfare (26 percent), environmental impacts (10 percent), business and technology (9 percent) and workers' rights and safety (7 percent).

The cause of increases in article frequencies was clear where multiple news articles mentioned specific events. For example, Proposition 2 in California mandated larger chicken cages, the subject of a large number of the articles in 2008. Another example is 2007, when 10 of 12 articles discussed the Bush administration's efforts to tighten federal policies governing the hire of illegal immigrants. Otherwise, it was difficult to explain trends in article frequencies without further research or being speculative, especially when articles covered issues possibly triggered by factors not mentioned in the articles. For example, the 2008 climate change articles only once mentioned Al Gores's Academy Award-winning climate change documentary, *An Inconvenient Truth*, and never specifically mentioned the release of the UN FAO report, *Livestock's Long Shadow*, but both can plausibly be linked to the rise in climate change stories that year.

Actants and artifacts

Among human actants, climate change articles most commonly featured state actors, which comprised 18 percent of all actants. This reflected the prominence of policy- and legislation-related news stories in this theme. Next most frequent were public interest actors, such as environmental NGOs (nongovernmental organizations) and livestock industry associations (11 percent each). Private sector actors, mainly food services and energy companies, comprised 10 percent. Academics represented 8 percent of all actants and were cited in connection with their research on livestock's climate change impacts and mitigation. Animals comprised 28 percent of all actants and were almost evenly split among those animals mentioned generally and those to which the media assigned agency. Artifacts in the climate change theme made up the remainder (15 percent) and included studies and reports, tech-nologies such as biogas energy and grass-based feeding strategies, new policies and a documentary.

Framing analysis

The climate change articles can be roughly divided into three categories; each solidifies a different facet of the livestock-climate change nexus for the public. The first category of articles ($n = 6$) emphasized technological innovations for climate change mitigation (e.g. bioengineering of feed and cattle and manure biodigestion). The second category ($n = 4$) highlighted carbon footprint-reducing individual lifestyle changes, such as eating less beef and buying locally. The third category ($n = 9$) focused on climate change regulations and legislation. Table 12.1 shows how the actants identified (and their subtypes) were distributed among these three categories.

Episodic stories comprised 32 percent of the climate change articles. The low percentage contrasts with Iyengar's (1994) finding that typical news stories are epi-sodic. Half of the technology and lifestyle articles were episodic; these highlighted specific actors' development of mitigation technologies, or individuals' actions or responses concerning lifestyle changes. The sole episodic policy article cov-ered Tom Vilsack's appointment as Secretary of Agriculture, focusing on his track record and expected agricultural policy. Artifacts commonly featured in episodic articles included technology (processes, equipment) and items individuals easily relate to, such as diets.

Thematic technology and lifestyle articles provided more background than episodic articles on technological innovation or behavioral change and involved more academic, state and public interest actors. Thematic policy articles discussed legislative issues and mainly referenced state actors. They often featured academ-ics in connection with their research and NGO representatives who advocated or expressed support for certain reforms, often referring to their own research. Common artifacts in thematic stories included academic studies and reports, new technologies and techniques for farming that might be incorporated into legislation.

Attitudes of actants to the climate change–livestock linkage

Many articles made statements or quoted actors acknowledging the linkage between livestock and climate change as problematic (54 percent; coded as positive). Most were academics that discussed emissions data, GHG-reduction approaches and livestock's contribution to climate change. Just one private sector actor supported the linkage: Bon Appétit Management Co., a self-described sustainable food ser-vices company (Weiss, 2008).

State actors often referenced livestock-climate change connections; these were about half positive and half neutral. Different sectors and levels of the government

TABLE 12.1 Proportional distribution of actants in climate change theme by type and story-network.

Actant types		No. of actants by story-network			Total	% of total	% of actants by story-network		
		Technology	Lifestyle	Policy		Actants	Technology	Lifestyle	Policy
State		7	3	9	19	18	37	16	47
Livestock industry association		2	1	8	11	11	18	9	73
Academic		5	3	–	8	8	63	38	–
Animal	General animal	9	3	2	14	13	64	21	14
	Animal actor	4	9	2	15	14	27	60	13
Private sector	Energy utility	2	1	–	3	3	67	33	–
	Beef/dairy company	2	–	–	2	2	100	–	–
	Energy technology/services	1	1	–	2	2	50	50	–
	Food services company	–	2	–	2	2	–	100	–
	Car company	1	–	–	1	1	100	–	–
Public interest	Environmental NGO	1	–	5	6	6	17	–	83
	Social justice NGO	1	–	1	2	2	50	–	50
	Business development NGO	1	–	–	1	1	100	–	–
	Consumer advocacy group	–	–	1	1	1	–	–	100
	Public policy think tank	–	–	1	1	1	–	–	100

Actant types	No. of actants by story-network				% of total	% of actants by story-network		
	Technology	Lifestyle	Policy	Total	Actants	Technology	Lifestyle	Policy
Artifact Study/report	1	3	2	6	6	17	50	33
CC mitigation technology	3	–	–	3	3	100	–	–
Policy	–	–	3	3	3	–	–	100
Consumer practice	–	2	–	2	2	–	100	–
Beef production technology	–	1	–	1	1	–	100	–
Film	–	1	–	1	1	–	100	–
Total	40	30	34	104	100			

tended to disagree whether the connection warranted action. For example, then California Attorney General Jerry Brown threatened to sue the Environmental Protection Agency (EPA) for not regulating GHG emissions from farm equipment, aircraft and ships (Sahagun, 2008).

Our study supports Trumbo's (1996) analysis of a decade of climate change coverage in five major US newspapers, which suggests that the private sector would downplay or disregard the connection's significance, as most private sector actors acknowledged the linkage by emphasizing opportunities involving end-of-pipe mitigation strategies such as manure-based energy generation. However, they did not address indirect sources of emissions (e.g. deforestation), which require systemic changes (e.g. curtailing livestock production), or necessarily acknowledge livestock production as a problematic cause of climate change. These actors were therefore identified as neutral (27 percent).

Trumbo (1996) suggests that governmental support of climate change policies follows a cycle where support for such policies wanes as the costs become clearer. Our findings suggest this varies by level of government. For example, several articles highlighted California's leadership in implementing state-led climate initiatives despite the costs. In contrast, other contemporaneous articles discussed politicians' use of economic arguments to oppose federally proposed climate change policies. The following header is an apt example: 'Of greenhouse gases and greenbacks, Senate debate on a proposal to impose pollution regulations is likely to center on the financial stakes' (Simon, 2008).

Actors coded as having negative attitudes (19 percent) were generally livestock industry members and either publicly questioned livestock's climate change impacts (Shogren, 2003) or lobbied against climate change legislation. For example, the industry responded to an EPA report on livestock's climate and air pollution impacts by immediately criticizing the costs of possible pollution fees (Associated Press, 2008). This illustrates how industry might disregard climate change and instead focus on and distort the costs of proposed reforms. Government's tendency to back down when faced with such opposition (Trumbo, 1996) presents obstacles to structural reforms. This places greater responsibility for climate change mitigation on individuals and NGOs.

Discussion

Given livestock production's major contribution to climate change (Koneswaran and Nierenberg, 2008; Steinfeld et al., 2006), the scarcity of climate change-themed articles in relation to the other themes we identified is disturbing. It is unclear whether this is due to (1) a perception that such stories do not sell newspapers, (2) a paucity of newsworthy material related to this theme, or (3) climate change advocates being ineffective at building relationships with the media. Our study provides some evidence for the last possibility. Only half of the actants (primarily academics) in the theme acknowledged the climate change–livestock linkage, although media attempts at journalistic balance may have been responsible. Also supporting (3) is that academics were not only the minority in the climate change theme, but also in the animal welfare, workers' rights and safety and environmental impacts themes.

Why news coverage of climate change–livestock issues after 2008 suddenly declined remains unclear. The 2009 'Climategate' controversy[1] may have affected the legitimacy of climate change science in the American public's eyes, at least in the short term. Another possibility is that the Great Recession drew attention toward economic issues. Nevertheless, our findings suggest that academics and other climate change advocates could build closer relationships with media, using strategies such as press releases or collaborating to produce educational material with mainstream appeal.

We divided the climate change articles into three categories: technology, lifestyle and policy. Each category can be considered a group of story-networks that share similar configurations of actants and reflect a specific narrative about climate change. Different configurations of actants in relation to each other (and to the media) provide each group of story-networks their common characteristics, enabling their identification as a distinct category within the livestock–climate change nexus. These categories are stabilized through repetition and reproduction, in the process shaping public understandings of what should be done about livestock and climate change.

Story-networks in the technology category, for example, included private sector actants (e.g. energy utilities, beef producers and food service companies) in addition to several artifacts (e.g. the technologies they developed and the studies they relied upon). These artifacts reveal the enrollment of other actants (e.g. scientists), who were not prominent in the story but nonetheless instrumental in developing the technology. Additionally, by mitigating bovine climate change impacts, private sector actors exerted a 'taming' effect[2] on cattle, their manure, microbes and other actants involved in the release of greenhouse gases. Stuart (2011) described how such actants occasionally destabilize (i.e. threaten the legitimacy of) the industrial food system with disease outbreaks; these actants' contribution to climate change constitutes a similar, but less direct destabilization that nonetheless requires 'taming'. Media's focus on mitigation technologies, however, draws attention away from actants responsible for organizing individual animals into CAFOs and multiplying their individual emissions, consumers demanding cheap beef, government subsidies for cattle feed production and actants driving indirect impacts such as land-use change. These actants are in fact the root causes of livestock-linked climate change, but escape responsibility in the media, as we shall see next.

By shifting blame to bovine digestive systems and by deploying GHG mitigation technology, this story-network configuration helps preserve a hegemonic industrial livestock production system. Certain articles played up animals' agency in causing climate change by focusing on their inherent biological properties, i.e. their digestive systems and direct emissions from manure. Human actants' roles (e.g. demand for meat, deforestation, CAFOs) received far less attention. In contrast, media in health-related story-networks rarely blamed the biological characteristics of animals for causing heart disease and other meat-related health conditions. Articles that represented animals as actants placed responsibility for GHG emissions on livestock and discussed production-oriented technological fixes rather than food system level reform. Other scholars have also observed such responsibility shifting in the industrial food system (Stuart, 2011; Gouveia and Juska, 2002).

Lifestyle-focused stories provided another example of a network configuration that yields a different interpretation of what should be done. Though the media continued to mention animals' agency, climate change mitigation became a matter of individual consumer choice: either eat less meat or switch to 'greener' alternatives such as grass-fed beef. These story-networks suggested that consumers exert economic power over private sector actants. For instance, Bon Appetit's promotion of a low-carbon diet was a response to increased consumer concern about the climate. Consumer awareness can be linked to actants like the United Nations Intergovernmental Panel on Climate Change, which urged consumers to reduce meat consumption and suggested governments start campaigns to reduce national meat consumption (Los Angeles Times, 2008).

However, the absence of such national campaigns, reflected by this category's minimal number of state actors, suggests continued government subsidies for meat production. The beef lobby's strength (Los Angeles Times, 2007) reflects the continuation of economic power forged by private sector–state relations. These actant connections lead to the reaffirmation of faith in markets, thereby obscuring needed system-level food production reforms. There is a tendency for climate change mitigation to be framed as a matter of individual choice, when in fact structural change through democratic participation and political leadership is equally, if not more important (Maniates, 2002).

Story-networks in the policy category involved two-way connections between state and livestock industry actors. Pro-mitigation state-level actions pressure industry by enrolling academic studies on climate change and promoting end-of-pipe reduction policies. Industry actants respond through lobbyists by threatening to block such policies unless they are watered down. These oppositional efforts center the debate on the economic costs of reform, thereby enrolling consumers accustomed to low beef prices and those employees dependent on the livestock industry. As a result, policy and legislation articles focused primarily on the economic costs and benefits of climate change mitigation, detracting from the needed industrial food system reforms. As noted already, this is consistent with Trumbo's (1996) analysis concerning waning government support for climate change mitigation over time. There is also some evidence to support McComas and Shanahan's (1999) finding that media narratives towards the end of climate change media coverage cycles emphasize the costs of mitigation amidst increasing politicization of the issue. This is reflected in how six of the eight policy-oriented articles were written in 2008.

The media shape story-networks through the act of investigation and by marshaling actants in the service of a story. Story-networks are shaped by the journalist's interests, the actants whose interests are at stake and the demands of the general audience. Despite the prominence of the three categories discussed above, some articles briefly problematized the entrenched industrial livestock production system. For example, one article stated:

> Cows lived in harmony with the atmosphere for thousands of years. Then humans developed a taste for the animals and their dairy products and nature's equilibrium was disturbed. Simple barnyard creatures were transformed into agents of climate change, not by their own doing, but because people dramatically multiplied their numbers so they would produce more milk, cheese and meat.
>
> (Polakovic, 2003)

Nonetheless, the article reverted to discussing promising technologies for reducing individual animals' emissions, rather than discussing industry structure. The article's title, *Getting the Cows to Cool It*, aptly reflects this shift of responsibility.

The configuration of actants in a story-network shapes how responsibility is allocated (Gouveia and Juska, 2002) and predisposes a story to episodic or thematic framing. Technology and lifestyle-oriented stories are easier to frame episodically; the opposite is true for policy articles. However, by influencing the media's perception of how best to sell a story, the public can strongly influence the story's ultimate framing. Although media may portray certain actants as responsible for change, change is also attributable to other actants in the story-network. Illustrative of this is how consumer concern over climate change prompted Bon Appetit's apparent game-changing promotion of a low-carbon diet (Weiss, 2008).

Besides animal welfare, climate change articles had a higher proportion of episodic articles than other themes. Episodic stories primarily covered technology and lifestyle change, thereby framing climate change mitigation as a matter of individual choice and action. Emphasizing organic or local food purchasing as a lever for change (Pollan, 2010) is an example of this. Due to the schism in the American public's opinion towards climate change (Leiserowitz, 2006), presenting livestock–climate change issues in terms of individual choice and action rather than employing a normative, policy-oriented approach is arguably the least controversial option. In general, our findings reflect Neff et al.'s (2009) discussion of contrasts in media between framing climate change mitigation as individual choice versus institutional responsibility. Episodic articles may be easier to relate to and, in theory, be better for raising awareness of livestock–climate change interactions. However, this may not be the most appropriate strategy. Portraying climate change mitigation as a matter of individual choice is problematic, as already discussed, since this may undermine the importance of structural change. Therefore, the media should frame climate change–livestock linkages at both individual and system levels.

About half the time, animals were portrayed as actants with agency in the climate change theme versus more general references where the media did not explicitly assign them agency. However, even when the media did not treat animals as actants, human actors occasionally spoke on their behalf, providing animals with a proxy voice. ANT enables us to recognize this as an example of nonhuman actants exerting their influence through their respective actant networks. This is clearest in the campaigns of animal rights activists, but a livestock industry association member provides a more subtle example: 'It's a natural process that a ruminant animal goes through ... There's not much you can do about it. If you want to control methane emissions in the world, controlling it from cows has to be pretty low on the totem pole' (Polakovic, 2003). This statement illustrates how man's dependency on their domesticated relationship with cows allows the latter to enroll human actors in their defense against disproportionate blame for climate change. It is ironic however, that the very same relationship is also responsible for multiplying the once limited agency of individual animals in causing climate change.

This example reveals the complexity of actant relations in story-networks and catalyzes a deeper examination and untangling of nonhuman actants' roles in the making of news, as well as the contrasting effects different actants may have on reader perceptions and behavior. Ultimately, this may shift public perceptions and behavior of the livestock–climate change connection. A possible effect might be to unite the interests of animal rights and welfare activists and climate change advocates. ANT, by emphasizing both nonhuman and human actants, can be used to introduce even greater nuance to our understandings of the media. Used in conjunction with framing theory, ANT provides a foundation for the story-network approach. This permitted us to highlight how it is not just the media, but also the interaction of various actants in power-infused relationships that help attribute responsibility to different actors in society.

Conclusion

More research investigating relationships between the media and livestock–climate change-related actants is necessary. Additional research could expand the geographic range of this study, which focused on one newspaper. Although a national media outlet, the *Los Angeles Times* concentrates much of its coverage on Southern California. It is also a relatively liberal newspaper in terms of editorial policy. Future studies could focus on additional newspapers and locations to understand how coverage of the issue varies by geography and political alignment. Online news articles, readers' comments and their integration with social media provide rich future data sources for understanding how media portrayals of livestock and climate change affect public perceptions and attitudes.

It would also be beneficial to investigate relationships between the media and different actants to explain how these relationships have developed over time and how media framing influences public opinion and behavior. ANT allowed us to identify and quantify the key actants involved in news generation. As each actant is a network unto itself, the relative influence of each actant can be assessed by tracing the components of actants' individual networks. Ethnographic and institutional work would expand our understanding of how networks of actants evolve and shape the media.

By combining ANT with framing theory, we provide the theoretical framework and language of story-networks to understand and describe media content, to identify key actants and their linkages within the articles and to reveal how journalists obtain their information and from whom. When combined with framing theory, ANT allowed us to link key actants with each article's framing and content, shedding light on why certain frames or biases may exist. Although we attempted to bring both living and non-living actants into the analysis, we focused primarily on human actants. Further research should therefore delve deeper into the role of nonhuman actants, especially animals.

Notes

1 This involved an email hacking at the University of East Anglia's Climatic Research Unit, leading to allegations that scientists had manipulated climate change data to suppress critics. Subsequent investigations found no evidence of fraud or misconduct.
2 Gouveia and Juska (2002, p.375) employ 'taming' as a metaphor that describes an actor's exertion of power over another that captures 'the coercive nature of disciplining technologies deployed ... to manufacture consent among humans and non-humans.'

References

Antilla, L. (2005) 'Climate of scepticism: US newspaper coverage of the science of climate change', *Global Environmental Change*, vol 15, no 4, pp. 338–352

Associated Press (2008) 'Livestock farmers raise stink over EPA report', *Los Angeles Times*, 6 December, http://articles.latimes.com/2008/dec/06/business/fi-cowtax6, accessed 31 March 2014

Bennett, W. L. (1996) *News: The politics of illusion* (3rd ed), Longman, White Plains, NY

Berlo, D. K. (1960) *The Process of Communication: An Introduction to Theory and Practice*, Rinehart and Winston, New York, NY

Bonanno, A., Busch, L., Friedland, W. H., Gouveia, L. and Mingione, E. (1994) *From Columbus to ConAgra: The Globalization of Agriculture and Food*, University Press of Kansas, Lawrence, KS

Borra, S. T. and Bouchoux, A. (2009) 'Effects of science and the media on consumer perceptions about dietary sugars', *Journal of Nutrition*, vol 139, no 6, pp. 1214S–1218S

Boykoff, M. T. (2007) 'From convergence to contention: United States mass media representations of anthropogenic climate change science', *Transactions of the Institute of British Geographers*, vol 32, no 4, pp. 477–489

Boykoff, M. T. and Boykoff, J. M. (2007) 'Climate change and journalistic norms: A case-study of US mass-media coverage', *Geoforum*, vol 38, no 6, pp. 1,190–1,204

Callon, M. and Latour, B. (1981), 'Unscrewing the big leviathan: How actors macro-structure reality and how sociologists help them to do so', in K. Knorr-Cetina and A. V. Cicourel (eds), *Advances in Social Theory and Methodology: Toward an Integration of Micro- and Macro-Sociologies*, pp. 277–303, Routledge & Kegan Paul, Boston, MA

Capper, J. L. and Hayes, D. J. (2012) 'The environmental and economic impact of removing growth-enhancing technologies from U.S. beef production', *Journal of Animal Science*, vol 90, no 10, pp. 3,527–3,537

Carvalho, A. and Burgess, J. (2005) 'Cultural circuits of climate change in U.K. broadsheet newspapers, 1985–2003', *Risk Analysis*, vol 25, no 6, pp. 1,457–1,469

Castree, N. (2002) 'False antitheses? Marxism, nature and actor-networks', *Antipode*, vol 34, no 1, pp. 111–146

Chao, A., Thun, M. J., Connell, C. J., McCullough, M. L., Jacobs, E. J., Flanders, W. D., Rodriguez, C., Sinha, R., Calle, E. E., (2005) 'Meat consumption and risk of colorectal cancer', *Journal of the American Medical Association*, vol 293, no 2, pp. 172 –182

Clemens, J. and Ahlgrimm, H.-J. (2001) 'Greenhouse gases from animal husbandry: Mitigation options', *Nutrient Cycling in Agroecosystems*, vol 60, no 1–3, pp. 287–300

Couldry, N. (2008) 'Actor network theory and media: Do they connect and on what terms?' in A. Hepp, F. Krotz, S. Moores, and C. Winter (eds), *Connectivity, Networks and Flows: Conceptualizing Contemporary Communication*, pp. 93–111, Hampton, Cresskill, NJ

Demeritt, D. (2001) 'The construction of global warming and the politics of science', *Annals of the Association of American Geographers*, vol 91, no 2, pp. 307–337

Dorfman, L. E., Wallack, L. and Woodruff, K. (2005) 'More than a message: Framing public health advocacy to change corporate practices', *Health Education & Behavior*, vol 32, no 3, pp. 320–336

Downs, A. (1972) 'Up and down with ecology: The issue attention cycle', *Public Interest*, vol 28, no 1, pp. 38–50

Emel, J. and Neo, H. (2011) 'Killing for profit: Global livestock industries and their socio-ecological implications', in R. Peet, P. Robbins, and M. Watts (eds), *Global Political Ecology*, pp. 67–83, Routledge, New York, NY

Entman, R. M. (1993) 'Framing: Toward clarification of a fractured paradigm', *Journal of Communication*, vol 43, no 4, pp. 51–58

Fine, B. (2005) 'From actor-network theory to political economy', *Capitalism Nature Socialism*, vol 16, no 4, pp. 91–108

Gamson, W. A., Croteau, D., Hoynes, W. and Sasson, T. (1992) 'Media images and the social construction of reality', *Annual Review of Sociology*, vol 18, pp. 373–393

Gerbens-Leenes, P. W., Nonhebel, S. and Ivens, W. P. M. F. (2002) 'A method to determine land requirements relating to food consumption patterns', *Agriculture, Ecosystems & Environment*, vol 90, no 1, pp. 47–58

Gilchrist, M. J., Greko, C., Wallinga, D. B., Beran, G. W., Riley, D. G. and Thorne, P. S. (2007) 'The potential role of concentrated animal feeding operations in infectious disease epidemics and antibiotic resistance', *Environmental Health Perspectives*, vol 115, no 2, pp. 313–316

Gill, M., Smith, P. and Wilkinson, J. M. (2010) 'Mitigating climate change: The role of domestic livestock', *Animal*, vol 4, no 3, pp.323–333

Goffman, E. (1974) *Frame Analysis: An Essay on the Organization of Experience*, Harper & Row, New York, NY

Goodman, A. and Goodman, D. (2005) *The Exception to the Rulers: Exposing Oily Politicians, War Profiteers, and the Media That Love Them*, Hyperion, New York, NY

Gouveia, L. and Juska, A. (2002) 'Taming nature, taming workers: Constructing the separation between meat consumption and meat production in the US', *Sociologia Ruralis*, vol 42, no 4, pp. 370–390

Hobson, K. (2007) 'Political animals? On animals as subjects in an enlarged political geography', *Political Geography*, vol 26, no 3, pp. 250–267; doi:10.1016/j.polgeo.2006.10.010

Ivakhiv, A. (2002) Toward a Multicultural Ecology. *Organization & Environment*, vol 15, no 4, pp. 389–409; doi:10.1177/1086026602238169

Iyengar, S. (1994) *Is Anyone Responsible?: How Television Frames Political Issues*, Chicago: University Of Chicago Press.

Koneswaran, G. and Nierenberg, D. (2008) 'Global farm animal production and global warming: Impacting and mitigating climate change', *Environmental Health Perspectives*, vol 116, no 5, pp. 578–582

Lappé, A. and McKibben, B. (2010) *Diet for a Hot Planet: The Climate Crisis at the End of Your Fork and What You Can Do About It*, Bloomsbury USA, New York, NY

Latour, B. (1993) *We Have Never Been Modern*, Harvard University Press, Cambridge, MA

Law, J. (1998) 'After ANT: Complexity, naming and topology', *Sociological Review*, vol 47, no. S1, pp. 1–14

Lee, K. C. L., Newell, J. P., Wolch, J., Schneider, N., and Joassart-Marcelli, P. (2014) '"Story-Networks" of Livestock and Climate Change: Actors, Their Artifacts, and the Shaping of Urban Print Media', *Society & Natural Resources*, vol 27, no. 9, pp 948–963

Leiserowitz, A. (2006) 'Climate change risk perception and policy preferences: The role of affect, imagery, and values', *Climatic Change*, vol 77, no 1–2, pp. 45–72

Los Angeles Times (2007) 'Pollution on the hoof', *Los Angeles Times*, 15 October, http://articles.latimes.com/2007/oct/15/opinion/ed-methane15, accessed 31 March 2014

Los Angeles Times (2008) 'What's not for dinner', *Los Angeles Times*, 9 September, http://articles.latimes.com/2008/sep/09/opinion/ed-meatless9, accessed 31 March 2014

Mader, T. L. (2003) 'Environmental stress in confined beef cattle', *Journal of Animal Science*, vol 81, no 14, pp. E110–E119

Mallin, M. A. and Cahoon, L. B. (2003) 'Industrialized animal production: A major source of nutrient and microbial pollution to aquatic ecosystems', *Population and Environment*, vol 24, no 5, pp. 369–385.

Maniates, M. (2002) 'Individualization: Plant a tree, buy a bike, save the world?', in T. Princen, M. Maniates and K. Conca (eds), *Confronting Consumption*, pp. 43–66, MIT Press, Cambridge, MA

Marsden, T. and Sonnino, R. (2005) 'Rural devopment and agri-food governance in Europe: Tracing the development of alternatives', in V. Higgins and G. Lawrence (eds), *Agricultural Governance: Globalization and the New Politics of Regulation*, pp. 50–70 Routledge, New York, NY

Massey, D. (1993) 'Power-geometry and a progressive sense of place' in J. Bird, B. Curtis, T. Putnam, and L. Tickner (eds), *Mapping the Futures: Local Cultures, Global Change*, pp. 59–70, Routledge, London

McComas, K. and Shanahan, J. (1999) 'Telling stories about global climate change', *Communication Research*, vol 26, no 1, pp. 30–57

Micha, R., Wallace, S. K. and Mozaffarian, D. (2010) 'Red and processed meat consumption and risk of incident coronary heart disease, stroke, and diabetes mellitus', *Circulation*, vol 121, no 21, pp. 2271–2283

Michaelowa, A. and Dransfeld, B. (2008) 'Greenhouse gas benefits of fighting obesity', *Ecological Economics*, vol 66, no 2–3, pp. 298–308

Morgan, K., Marsden, T. and Murdoch, J. (2006) *Worlds of Food: Place, Power, and Provenance in the Food Chain*, Oxford University Press, New York, NY

Murdoch, J. (1997) 'Inhuman/nonhuman/human: Actor-network theory and the prospects for a nondualistic and symmetrical perspective on nature and society', *Environment and Planning D*, vol 15, pp. 731–756

Murdoch, J. (2000') Networks: A new paradigm of rural development?', *Journal of Rural Studies*, vol 16, no 4, pp. 407–419

Neff, R. A., Chan, I. L. and Smith, K. C. (2009) 'Yesterday's dinner, tomorrow's weather, today's news? US newspaper coverage of food system contributions to climate change', *Public Health Nutrition*, vol 12, no 7, pp. 1,006–1,014

Polakovic, G. (2003) 'Getting the cows to cool it', *Los Angeles Times*, 7 June, http://articles.latimes.com/2003/jun/07/local/me-cowgas7, accessed 31 March 2014

Pollan, M. (2010). 'The food movement, rising.' *The New York Review of Books*, 10 June, http://www.nybooks.com/articles/archives/2010/jun/10/food-movement-rising, accessed 23 January 2015

Rocheleau, D. (2011) 'Rooted networks, webs of relation, and the power of situated science: Bringing the models back down to earth in Zambrana', in M. J. Goldman, P. Nadasdy, and M. D. Turner (eds), *Knowing Nature: Conversations at the Intersection of Political Ecology and Science Studies*, pp. 209–226, University of Chicago Press, London

Rocheleau, D. and Roth, R. (2007) 'Rooted networks, relational webs and powers of connection: Rethinking human and political ecologies', *Geoforum*, vol 38, no 3, pp. 433–437

Saguy, A. C. and Almeling, R. (2008) 'Fat in the fire? Science, the news media, and the "obesity epidemic"', *Sociological Forum*, vol 23, no 1, pp. 53–83

Sahagun, L. (2008) 'State may sue EPA over pollution', *Los Angeles Times*, 1 August, http://articles.latimes.com/2008/aug/01/local/me-briefs1.S1, accessed 31 March 2014

Sampei, Y. and Aoyagi-Usui, M. (2009) 'Mass-media coverage, its influence on public awareness of climate-change issues, and implications for Japan's national campaign to reduce greenhouse gas emissions', *Global Environmental Change*, vol 19, no 2, pp. 203–212

Scheufele, D. A. (1999) 'Framing as a theory of media effects', *Journal of Communication*, vol 49, no 1, pp. 103–122

Scientific Software Development (2012) ATLAS.ti (Version 6.2), Scientific Software Development, Berlin

Shannon, C. E. and Weaver, W. (1949) *The Mathematical Theory of Communication*, University of Illinois Press, Urbana, IL

Shogren, E. (2003) 'EPA Plans Farm Pollution Amnesty', *Los Angeles Times*, 25 September, http://articles.latimes.com/2003/sep/25/nation/na-pollute25, accessed 31 March 2014

Simon, R. (2008) 'Of greenhouse gases and greenbacks', *Los Angeles Times*, 2 June, http://articles.latimes.com/2008/jun/02/nation/na-climate2, accessed 31 March 2014

Steinfeld, H., Gerber, P., Wassenaar, T. D., Castel, V. and de Haan, C. (2006) *Livestock's Long Shadow: Environmental Issues and Options*, United Nations Food and Agriculture Organization, Rome

Stuart, D. (2011) '"Nature" is not guilty: Foodborne illness and the industrial bagged salad', *Sociologia Ruralis*, vol 51, no 2, pp. 158–174

Trumbo, C. (1996) 'Constructing climate change: Claims and frames in US news coverage of an environmental issue', *Public Understanding of Science*, vol 5, no 3, pp. 269–283

Wallack, L., Woodruff, K., Dorfman, L. E. and Diaz, I. (1999) *News for a Change: An Advocate's Guide to Working with the Media* (1st ed), Sage, Thousand Oaks, CA

Weiss, K. R. (2008) 'With low-carbon diets, consumers step to the plate', *Los Angeles Times*, 22 April, http://articles.latimes.com/2008/apr/22/local/me-lowcarbon22, accessed 31 March 2014

West, J. W. (2003) 'Effects of heat-stress on production in dairy cattle', *Journal of Dairy Science*, vol 86, no 6, pp. 2,131–2,144

13

THE POLITICAL SCIENCE OF FARM ANIMAL WELFARE IN THE US AND EU

Connie Johnston

Introduction

The welfare of farmed animals has become an important topic of public concern, regulation, and research funding in the United States and Europe, with industry and policymakers looking for scientific guidance on modifying existing industrial farming infrastructure and practices. The concept of welfare has proved slippery, however, with multiple ethical perspectives on the issue, multiple physiological and psychological dimensions for the animals, and varying opinions among scientists on how to measure it. This complexity has given rise to polarization on these issues and often geographically uneven regulation.

This chapter analyzes findings from research on government-supported farm animal welfare science programs in the US and the European Union. Governments in both locations are responding to public concerns and as a result have significantly funded research on animal welfare. The governmental research vehicles also hold in tension the animals' status as both economic units and individual living creatures that can subjectively experience good or poor welfare.

Industrial agriculture has placed large numbers of animals together, requiring intensive management, with some of the same types of risks (e.g. disease outbreaks or violent confrontations) paralleling those of human populations. Population-level management and animal husbandry practices are subject to regulation, but are only one aspect of agricultural animals' lives that places them in the domain of the state. As evidenced by advocacy on their behalf, farm animals are also becoming more than simply material objects to be managed – they are also being conceptualized at a societal level as *subjects* that can experience good or poor welfare. I assert that the animals are acquiring a type of political subjectivity in the US and Europe and, as part of this process, their own individual subjectivities are often both invoked and investigated. Scientific knowledge of the animals' physiologies and psychologies allows them to be governed as productive units in a population, but also understood as at least semi-subjective individuals that deserve protection. It is important to examine the resources brought to bear in this situation, as scientific knowledge plays a role in addressing both human concerns for the animals and governance of their populations in the agricultural industry (Irwin, 2008; Thorpe, 2008). Scientific knowledge of the animals as both natural objects and welfare-experiencing subjects is inherently political and politicized, as it is used by citizens, animal advocates, legislators, and industry to codify their (frequently conflicting) positions. Inasmuch as farm animals are important actors in multiple ecological networks, the political ecologies of animal welfare and animal subjectivity provide an umbrella for this analysis, which draws primarily upon tools from science and technology studies.

In what follows, I first review pertinent scholarship, including Agamben's theorizing of bare versus social life and, foundational for him, Foucault's concept of biopower. I then give an overview of the US and European trajectories of farm animal welfare regulation in order to demonstrate the longstanding role of the state in governing the treatment of these animals, this role increasing beginning in the twentieth century. Second, I describe in more detail the empirical cases – three government-supported farm animal welfare science research vehicles – that illustrate the development, relative to US and European societies and the state, of these animals as welfare-possessing subjects. The next section introduces the perspectives of the scientists who are responsible for the material practice and realization of this research. Finally, I analyze this empirical data in terms of the animals as political subjects.

The nonhuman as political

A number of scholars have recently engaged with political theory and the nonhuman. For example, Braun and Whatmore (2010) argue for including the nonhuman material world, in its sentient and non-sentient forms, in political theory, along with the role of science and technology. Similarly, Bennett (2010) asserts that it is not only humans that act together politically, and Stengers (2010) calls for 'decenter[ing] political theory from the abstract concept of "humans"' (p13). More specifically oriented to sentient nonhumans, Donaldson and Kymlicka (2011) argue for a new political theory direction in animal rights scholarship.

Several geography scholars have also theorized animals in particular as enrolled in human political processes. For example, Emel and Wolch (1998) engage in this analysis as they delineate the myriad locations and contexts of animals in human social life, illustrating, first, the embeddedness and reach of animals into human society, both in intended and problematic ways and, second, as moving conceptually into a group of beings worthy of protection, brought about by political activism. In 'Urban wild things' (2005), Hinchliffe et al. use a study of water vole populations, habitat, and behavior in a UK urban environment as a case study for an expanded notion of 'ecologized' politics, a recognition that human life and sociopolitical processes are not separate from the nonhuman world. The authors also argue for the potential of more direct engagement by humans with the nonhuman world to substantively alter existing policymaking paradigms.

Hobson explicitly engages with animals as political subjects in her 2007 article on bears used for bile 'farming' in Asia and the efforts by a non-governmental organization to gain protections for them. Hobson contrasts what was thought to be known about the bears in the wild – that they are solitary – with what came to be learned about the ones who were rehabilitated in captivity – that they could live and interact positively in larger social groups. Echoing Emel and Wolch's points, she claims that, more broadly, the animals are involved in formal political structures in that they play an important role in national/international economies. Hobson further claims that nonhumans are also involved in less formal political processes, both in their abilities to adapt and in the ways in which they affect individual humans, leading them to act on the animals' behalf.

Biology in political theory

Bare versus subjective life

Giorgio Agamben, engaging with Foucault's scholarship on the modern state in *Homo Sacer* (1998), puts forth a theory of the relationship between sovereign power and biological life. Central to Agamben's argument is the distinction between *zoē* (bare life) and *bios* (social life), although he argues that the distinction is blurred within the modern democratic state. According to Agamben, Foucault's thesis that modern politics is distinguished by the inclusion of biological life into political life does not go far enough. Agamben asserts that the actual *foundation* of the modern state's form is the incorporation of human biological life into the political realm, saying that, corresponding with the birth of modern democracy, 'man [sic] as a living being presents himself [sic] no longer as an *object* but as the *subject* of political power' (Agamben, 1998, p9). The additional aspect that Foucault does not include, according to Agamben, is the ability to create exceptions, which is the province of the state and the seat of its power. Through this ability, states are able to both bring bare life into the political domain, while at the same time maintaining bare life as excluded (and able to be killed).

Biopower and populations

Foucault famously developed the concept of 'biopower', which he defined as 'the set of mechanisms through which the basic biological features of the human species became the object of a political strategy' (2007, p1). In other words, in developing political tools and strategies, governing institutions have increasingly utilized scientific knowledge about the biological qualities of (in Foucault's case) humans. Part and parcel of this line of theorizing is Foucault's analysis of populations. He says, 'The population is pertinent as the objective, and individuals, the series of individuals, are no longer pertinent as the objective, but simply as the instrument, relay, or condition for obtaining something at the level of the population' (Foucault, 2007, p42). Here Foucault is indicating that governing entities moved from concerning themselves with managing individuals to managing populations, to which generalized biological knowledge could be applied. These twin developments – the use of biological knowledge and the shift in focus from the individual to the population – have allowed modern states 'a whole field of new realities in the sense that they are the pertinent elements for mechanisms of power' (ibid., p75). In addition to states' options, Jasanoff (2005) has asserted that the increasing body of bio-scientific knowledge has expanded *citizens*' options as well, as they have 'a new arena on which to demand and contest the exercise of state power' (p36).

In his review of Foucault's contribution to state theory, Marinetto (2007) explicates Foucault's ideas on the concurrent disciplining and production of the subject, stating that '[t]he subjective side of power is contingent upon freedom of choice and autonomy of the individual. Hence, social order and regulation are not achieved simply through discipline' (p37). With respect to Foucault's theory of governmentality, the autonomy of individuals – and their perceived choices related to self-regulation – disciplines without the threat of force and also allows a particular type of subject to come into being.

Informed by Foucault's theories of governmentality, Miele et al. (2005) explore farm animal welfare as part of agricultural governance in Europe. The authors define governmentality as 'the collective ways of thinking that underpin particular governmental strategies' (p3), arguing that the European public has an ambivalent view of farm animals, seeing them as both creatures to be protected but also as exploitable. Miele et al. conclude that the complex of governmental and non-governmental actors involved in farm animal welfare issues is forming a type of governmentality. Despite discussing regard for the animals' subjectivity in many aspects of European society, the authors do not discuss the animals as *themselves* objects of governance or as enrolled in political processes. However, in describing the significant role that animal science plays in animal activism and policy, their analysis echoes Jasanoff's point that not only the state, but also citizens, have increased options related to the use of state power. Further, their assertion of societal ambivalence toward farmed animals can be construed as a manifestation of the 'blurred distinction' between *zoe* and *bios* put forth by Agamben.

Holloway (2007) engages in a Foucauldian analysis of 'bovine subjectivity' through a study of automated milking system (AMS) use in the UK. Holloway states that management of the farms that use AMS rely on cows' learning of the systems and, he suggests, their internalization of this milking regime. Foucault's biopower is applicable at both the level of the individual and the population as cows are able to use the system in an individualized way, and AMS technology creates efficiencies at the herd level. Echoing Marinetto, using AMS not only gives the cows a 'choice' of when to be milked, and thereby at least gestures toward some level of subjectivity, but also requires a particular type of bovine subject – one that is willing/able to use AMS.

Farm animal welfare trajectories

United States

The first known acknowledgement of farm animals' welfare needs appears in the Massachusetts Colony's *Body of Liberties* from 1641 and dealt with the driving of livestock from one place to another (Whitmore, 1890). No further regulations appear in the US until the 1800s, these occurring in a few, primarily northeastern states and, again, focused mainly on livestock and on the prevention of cruelty (Favre and Tsang, 1993). State-based legislation continues in the US today.

Currently, there are only two pieces of federal regulation that deal directly with farm animal welfare: the Twenty-eight Hour Law and the Humane Methods of Slaughter Act, both of which exclude poultry. The Twenty-Eight Hour Law, first passed in 1873, covers the transportation of animals across state lines and requires that they must be unloaded after no more than 28 hours and given the opportunity to eat, drink, and rest (Chu, 2010). The 1958 Humane Methods of Slaughter Act stipulates that livestock in all federally inspected facilities be rendered insensible to pain before entering the slaughter process, or that they be slaughtered in accordance with religious ritual (Becker, 2008).

Building on the momentum of growing public knowledge and sentiment about the cramped 'battery' cages in which most egg-laying hens are kept, in 2011 the Humane Society of the United States and the United Egg Producers (the egg industry's main trade association) together drafted a bill that would double the cage space and provide other welfare enhancements for hens in US egg production. The bill, introduced into Congress in 2012, was referred to committee, where it remains as of the time of this writing (US Congress, 2012, 2013).

Most farm animal welfare law in the US is state-based, however. The most commonly regulated issues concern confinement (primarily crates that house veal calves and gestating sows). As of this writing nine states (Florida, Ohio, Maine, Oregon, Arizona, Rhode Island, California, Colorado and Michigan), with effective dates ranging from 2008 to 2025, have banned sow gestation crates and eight (Ohio, Maine, Colorado, Michigan, Arizona, Rhode Island, California and Kentucky) have banned veal crates. California and Michigan have both enacted restrictions on battery cages, with California passing a law that by 2015 all whole eggs sold in the state must be produced (regardless of location) in accordance with its state welfare standards. Several other states have bills pending, as of this writing, to ban or restrict confinement practices. The most comprehensive attention given to the matter of farm animal welfare has arguably been by the state of Ohio, which in 2009 passed a constitutional amendment requiring the establishment of care standards and set up the Ohio Livestock Care Standards Board (AWI, 2014; EL, 2012; HSUS, 2012a, 2012b, 2012c, 2014; ODA, undated; Rumley, undated).

From a non-regulatory position, recent public concern, animal advocacy group pressure, and damaging undercover videos have prompted a number of corporations to change their practices. Sow gestation crates and laying hen battery cages have garnered the most attention, with the likes of McDonald's, Burger King, Costco, Safeway and General Mills committing to transition away from using suppliers that employ severe confinement systems. Additionally, the US Veal Producers Association agreed in 2007 to phase out veal crates by 2017 (Eckholm, 2010).

European Union

The UK has been at the forefront of European farm animal welfare legislation, and its policies are often standard setting. Therefore a good starting point for the EU trajectory is Britain's 1822 'Martin's Act' (Radford, 2011a), which made it an offense to 'wantonly and cruelly beat, abuse, or ill-treat members of the various livestock species driven to markets' (Martin, 1822). This Act was followed by the 1911 'Protection of Animals Act', which was intended to cover 'any domestic or captive animal' (UK, 1911). British concern for animal welfare began to have significant influence on the continent in the mid-twentieth century, due to both the creation of the European Union and the British focus on the plight of industrially farmed animals.

A seminal event was the publishing of Ruth Harrison's *Animal Machines* (1964), which detailed many of the intensive (and by Harrison's account inhumane) husbandry practices that had by that time already become routine in Britain's industrialized farms. Harrison's book is widely credited with the establishment of the Brambell Committee, which investigated these practices and subsequently published the *Brambell Report* (Brambell Committee, 1965). This investigation and report in many ways laid the foundations for more Europe-wide legislative recognition of farmed species' physiological and behavioral needs, for example with the Council of Europe's 1976 European Convention for the Protection of Animals Kept for Farming Purposes (Radford, 2011a). Although the conventions of the Council are not directly enforceable, this document signifies the beginnings of broader efforts within European society to establish standards of care for farm animals (Radford, 2011b). In 1979, the British government established the Farm Animal Welfare Council which expanded and refined five basic living conditions stipulated in the *Brambell Report* and created 'The Five Freedoms' (freedom *from* hunger and thirst; discomfort; pain, injury or disease; distress and freedom *to* express normal behavior) (FAWC, 2009). These freedoms have become the basis for many of the farm animal welfare standards applied outside of Britain, especially across Europe (Radford, 2011b) and by the World Organisation for Animal Health (OIE, 2013).

Another important driver of consideration of animal welfare at the EU level was the entrance of Denmark (1973) and Sweden (1995) as member states, as these countries had their own histories of animal welfare legislation (Radford, 2011b). From the early 1990s through the 2000s, EU organizing/governing documents have included animal welfare and accorded it increasing importance. A good example is the 1997 Treaty of Amsterdam which not only raised the level of codification of animal welfare but also officially recognized animals as *sentient beings*.

TABLE 13.1 EU-wide directives.

Species and welfare objective	Year effective
Pigs	
Sow stalls/tethering prohibition	2013 (stalls)/2006 (tethering)
Sow hunger minimization	2003
Fully slatted floors in sow housing prohibition	2003 (existing farms)/2013 (new farms)
Enrichment provision requirement	2003 (fattening pigs)/2013 (sows)
Routine tail docking prohibition	2003
Routine teeth clipping/grinding prohibition	2003
Minimal requirements for castration[1]	2003
Early weaning	2003
Calves	
Veal crate prohibition	2006
Calf tethering prohibition	1998
Solid food/iron provision requirement	1998
Laying hens	
Barren battery cage prohibition	2012
Alternative housing systems minimum requirements	2007
Mandatory product labelling of farming method	2004
Beak trimming	2002
Forced moulting[2]	1999
Broiler chickens	
Maximum stocking densities[3]	2010
Required management practices[4]	2010
Product labelling standards[5]	2010

[1] The 2011 European Declaration on Alternatives to Surgical Castration in Pigs proposed that all surgical castration be performed with anasthesia and/or prolonged analgesia (effective 2012) and that castration be abandoned by 2018.

[2] While not prohibiting forced moulting per se, Council Directive 98/58/EC requires that animals be adequately fed at appropriate intervals. Forced moulting is achieved by depriving hens of food for long periods of time.

[3] A maximum stocking density of 33 kg/m² is stipulated, but higher densities (up to 42 kg/m²) are allowed if Member States meet certain criteria.

[4] These include personnel training, chickens' access to dry litter, and twice daily inspections.

[5] The farming method is not required to be disclosed on a label. However, if producers voluntarily label, they must adhere to certain labelling standards.

Sources: Stevenson (2012); EC (2007, 2008b)

Although the practical effect of such inclusions is diminished by the fact that none of these codifications represent binding laws and that qualifications are made for cultural and religious particularities within member states, they can be considered a broad recognition of some level of (European) societal obligation to treat animals in accordance with their physiological and psychological needs (Radford, 2011b, EC, 1992, 1997, 2008a).

Beyond these more general gestures toward concern for animal welfare, the EU has enacted numerous farm animal protection *laws*, the first in 1974 requiring that livestock and poultry be rendered unconscious prior to being slaughtered. This directive has been replaced, as of 2009, by the Slaughter Regulation, which covers not only consciousness at the time of slaughter but, additionally, operations related to the slaughter process and slaughterhouse management (Stevenson, 2012). In 1998 the EU enacted the General Farm Animals Directive, Article 3 of which says, 'Member States shall make provision to ensure that the owners or keepers take all reasonable steps to ensure the welfare of animals under their care and to ensure that those animals are not caused any unnecessary pain, suffering or injury' (EC, 1998, p3). While this is a very broad statement open to much interpretation, a number of more specific provisions are provided in the document's Annex. As of late 2011, there were also EU-wide directives related specifically to pigs, calves, laying hens, and broiler chickens (summarized in Table 13.1) and the EU Transport Regulation (Stevenson, 2012; EC, 2007, 2008b). Finally, member states have enacted animal protection legislation that exceeds EU standards (see Table 13.2).

TABLE 13.2 EU member state legislation.

Country	Practice									
	D	PS	GC	ST	VC	VT	BC	FC	BT	C
UK	X	X	X	X	X	X	2012		2011	
Sweden	X	X	X	X	X	X	X		X	
Netherlands	X	X	2008	X	2007	X	2012			
Denmark	X	X	2013	X	2007	X	2012			
Germany	X	X	2013	X	2007	X	2009	2012		
Finland	X	X	2006	X	2007	X	X		X	
Other EU	X	X	2013	X	2007	X	2012			
Switzerland	X			X	X	X	X	X		2009
Norway	X	X	X	X	X	X	2012		X	X

Notes: D: density and housing limits; PS: humane poultry slaughter (except in religious slaughter); GC: gestation crates, ST: sow tethers, VC: veal crates, VT: veal tethers; BC: battery cages; FC: furnished cages; BT: beak trimming; C: castration without anesthesia.

Blank box indicates no legislation; X indicates legislation already in place; dates shown are when the legislation is to be in place.

Source: Matheny and Leahy, 2007

US/EU overarching similarities in industrial agriculture

As evidenced by the range of welfare issues that US and EU legislation have tried to address, animal agriculture in both locations shares, or at least has shared, many similar features. This statement should not be taken to mean that there are not distinct differences between the US and the EU (or, for that matter, within them). However, the historical beginnings and prevalence of industrial animal agriculture are similar in both locations, and many of the practices that raise welfare concerns have existed and/or do exist in both as well.

Second World War technologies aided the development of industrial farming practices. For example, antibiotics created to fight the spread of infectious diseases among soldiers were utilized post-war to minimize the spread of disease between large numbers of animals housed in close confinement. In a complementary way, animal nutrition science in the mid-twentieth century showed how to control animals' food to both provide basic nutrition and promote growth. This manufactured food could be utilized on a large scale and, like antibiotics, allowed for larger numbers of individuals to be raised together because the need for extensive grazing/foraging land was eliminated. Additionally, genetic science allowed for more precise breeding practices that selected for traits maximizing the animals' bodily productivity.

As a result of these innovations, human contact with and knowledge of *individual* animals diminished, and practices such as breeding became much more technical endeavors. These changes, aimed at production efficiencies, also led to welfare issues – some physiological, some behavioral. For example, on the physiological side, the housing of egg-laying hens in 'battery cages' (small, stacked wire cages that house multiple birds) led to the very basic welfare concern that the hens cannot move at all in a normal fashion, including extending their wings. In terms of behavior, many problems arose because of the mixing of large numbers of individual animals in close, and often barren, quarters. An example of undesirable behavior is tail-biting in pigs, which occurs in environments in which the pigs have a lack of physical separation as well as a dearth of material objects with which to interact. This behavior has led to the practice of (unanesthetized) tail-docking of piglets.

These overarching similarities in farming practices contrast with the differing welfare and legislative trajectories reviewed in the preceding section, but both have laid the foundations for the government-sponsored research vehicles discussed in the next section.

Government-supported research

The US research vehicles

The US research vehicles used as case studies are the Livestock Behavior Research Unit (LBRU) in West Lafayette, IN, and the multi-state North Central Regional Association's 'Applied Animal Behavior and Welfare' program (AABW). Both of these vehicles gained significance for US farm animal welfare research in the early 2000s (FAIR, 2002, introduction; USDA, 2002).

The LBRU received funding from the US Congress in the early 1990s and was conceptualized as a research center partnering the US Department of Agriculture's Agricultural Research Service and Purdue University. Currently, the LBRU's mission statement encompasses both welfare and productivity issues. In fiscal year 2010, the LBRU received $1.4 million in total funding, approximately $1 million of this amount from the federal agricultural appropriations bill (LBRU, 2007, 2010; Dr D. Lay, 2011, pers. comm.).

The AABW project grew from, in the 1980s, a small group of scientists interested in the behavioral aspects of animal welfare, to a major consortium of farm animal scientists (primarily at large land-grant universities) researching topics deemed of high priority at the national and/or regional level (Dr J. Swanson, 2010, pers. comm.; SAES, 2006). Unlike the LBRU, the AABW's projects are not necessarily funded *directly* by the federal government. There are, however, federal funds routed to the individual universities through federal appropriations bills (Dr J. E. Minton, 2011, pers. comm.). Similar to the LBRU's mission, the justification for AABW cites animal welfare, but relates it to productivity. The rising importance of welfare to consumers is acknowledged, as is the effect of more restrictive welfare criteria being put in place internationally (NCRA, 2010).

The EU research program

The European research program used as a case is the Welfare Quality® project (WQ), which lasted five years (2004–2009). The WQ project was 'designed to provide practical science-based tools and strategies to assess and improve the welfare of farm animals on a European scale' (STOA, 2009, p4). The total project cost was €17 million, with €14.6 million contributed by the European Commission. One of the WQ project's main objectives was to balance the science with social and economic demands, and therefore the research included input from both animal and social science fields. WQ had 40 European partners (from 13 countries) and four from Latin America. The partners were universities and public and private research institutes (Welfare Quality, undated).

Scientists' views

As part of this research, I interviewed 25 animal scientists involved with the research entities described above (see Figure 13.1). For the WQ project I also interviewed three social scientists. (No social scientists have been involved with the LBRU or AABW.)

Defining welfare

A primary interview question was how the scientists defined farm animal welfare. A range of answers was given, but all at least gestured at the complexity of the concept. Almost without fail but often utilizing varying terms, the interviewees indicated that welfare is both physiological and psychological, although for both

FIGURE 13.1 Author before a Welfare Quality on-farm assessment at a commercial pig farm in Spain.

Source: Connie Johnston

the US and EU scientists, the aspect that was clearly stated by most of the respondents was related to the animals' physical condition and/or health.

Apart from the overarching similarity in a broad definition of welfare, one significant yet nuanced difference between the US and European scientists' responses is worth discussion. A number of the European, but few US, respondents referenced an animal's ability to 'cope with its environment', a definition from the noted UK animal welfare scientist Donald Broom (1986). And the same numbers of EU interviewees referenced the 'Five Freedoms' (discussed above), which are much more common in European farm animal welfare discourse. These differences, based on two long-standing definitions, between the US and EU respondents suggest a more localized uptake of knowledge in a person's concept formation, despite the 'movement' of scientific research, results, and knowledge between practitioners in different locations. Additionally, the longer history of thinking about and researching animal welfare in Europe (and particularly in the UK) may have provided foundational definitions that many of those scientists called forth during the interview.

Despite this difference, the US's shorter history of focus on welfare in animal science, and the differences in the respective research vehicles, there was more similarity than dissimilarity in the individual scientist's responses. Given that the AABW program and the WQ project (although not the LBRU) reference public concern/opinion as justifications for their research, it is perhaps most surprising that only two researchers overall discussed welfare as a *human-defined* concept.

Pressing concerns

The potential omission of human society is taken up, however, when the scientists were asked their views on the most pressing current farm animal welfare concerns. (The interviewees were not, however, asked to give just *one* concern or to *rank* multiple concerns.) For the US in particular, most respondents referenced society, although in a variety of contexts ranging from societal demands for animal products to US versus European funding for scientific research. Interestingly, three US scientists (one, however, originally from Europe) almost exclusively discussed societal aspects as being the most pressing current animal welfare concern. One said that 'the biggest problem in the farm animal welfare discussion is the polarization that exists' (2012, interview), while another said, 'I think the most pressing issue for people is … is what we're doing sort of morally acceptable from the standpoint of are we hurting the animals to get what we want out of them?' (2012, interview). The third referenced several different things – for example, international trade barriers and the public's lack of good information about livestock production (2012, interview). Two European respondents discussed society, with one referencing a disconnect between public perceptions of major animal welfare issues and the aspects that concern scientists (2011, interview), and the other expressing a view of progress: 'And now … that everybody can have access to meat, now is the question … can we do a step forward and adapt these intensive conditions to the welfare of the animals?' (2011, interview).

Aside from these responses, the issue that predominated for the scientist-interviewees was animals' environments, with a majority of EU and almost all the US scientists referencing concerns in this domain. (Environment was not necessarily given as *the* most important issue, however, but was discussed by most of the interviewees.)

Management was also a stated concern, although more so for the US scientists. Half of the respondents overall tied management (or husbandry) concerns to issues of scale, with all but one European and one US scientist saying that larger numbers of animals create potential management problems. Expressing this view, one European researcher states that the problems relate to 'the very limited time [caretakers] can really spend in observing, in managing and those things – making contact with animals will become an increasing problem' (2011, interview).

Farmed animals as political subjects

The scientists' interview responses reviewed above illustrate both Emel and Wolch's delineation of the ubiquity of nonhuman animals in human society and

Hinchliffe et al.'s assertion of the inextricability of animal life from our sociopolitical processes. There were several comments that incorporated a social dimension, with this dimension being most prominent with regard to the interviewees' views on pressing welfare issues. The responses indicate that many animal scientists do not view farm animal welfare as simply an issue for scientific investigation, but one that is shaped by the wider society. (In fact, a central premise of the WQ project was a joint science-society addressing of these issues.) And while many of these respondents did not invoke the political domain per se, in present-day US and European society, the political is inherent in these societies' actions relative to farm animal welfare, evidenced by the government sponsorship of these research entities. With regard to scientists' concepts of welfare, overall those from the US and EU differed in a foundational component of their definition, with more of those from the EU drawing on definitions of European provenance. Although this difference does not necessarily demonstrate farm animals as political subjects, it does point toward the influence of sociopolitical milieus in the articulation of a concept. For farm animals in the US and Europe, the way they are conceptualized may in fact be linked to long-standing definitions related to their welfare. A related point arises from the two responses that aligned the definition of welfare with societal values, again gesturing toward the embeddedness of these animals in the surrounding culture.

The bears in Hobson's case are in many ways very similar to the animals raised for consumption in the US and Europe. Cattle, chickens, and pigs on industrial farms have gained much popular attention in recent decades as people have been affected by their plight and have mobilized politically on their behalf. Additionally, knowledge has been gained about these animals' emotional lives and cognitive capacities (e.g. see Coulon et al., 2009; Della Chiesa et al., 2006), showing them, like the Asian bears (and the water voles), to be more complex beings than previously thought. More broadly, as demonstrated in the preceding sections on the welfare trajectories and the review of the LBRU, AABW, and WQ research vehicles, farm animals' lives and well-being have been on regulatory agendas well before, but especially since, the twentieth century, and have garnered sufficient attention to be included in governmental budgets. In fact, this inclusion of farm animal welfare research in state budgets suggests that animal welfare is increasingly considered an aspect of societal welfare in its own right, as this research would likely *not* be expected to benefit humans through increased agricultural output (Barnes, 2001).

Considering farmed animals as subjects in terms of their enrollment in political processes, I would like to further suggest that social and scientific processes in the US and EU are also producing them as political subjects in conceptual terms, of moving them across the border of *zoe* to *bios*. I contend that we can apply Agamben's theoretical approach in that in the US and Europe farmed animals currently occupy a blurred, liminal space between bare and social life: they are living organisms that are explicitly produced to be killed for their biological properties, but US and European societies are increasingly working at defining moral and legal obligations to them, utilizing science as a means to legitimate (or delegitimate) claims for those obligations. States and their publics, through combinations of legislative, judicial, and activist processes, are placing these beings who begin and end their lives in industrial systems as simply biological matter, into the political domain as a type of subject. In the last several decades, the US and European publics have increasingly become aware of industrial farming practices, and the welfare of farmed animals has become an object of concern, activism, legislation, and scientific research. In terms of scientific research in particular, not only is knowledge of the animals' biologies used for managing their (often large) populations, but more is also becoming known about the animals' psychological lives, causing many in the field of animal science to regard them as (at least minimally) subjective beings. As one scientist said, referring to pigs:

> from my point of view I have no, no doubt that they are highly intelligent … and we rely on their intelligence for, you know, managing a lot of systems. If you think about [electronic sow feeding] systems, you know, you couldn't do that with an animal that didn't have the ability to think, make decisions, and learn.
>
> (2012, interview)

This response echoes those of the majority of the other interviewees when asked about animal subjectivity. Yet these animals are still in a perpetual state of exception as they are constituted as 'able to be killed'. It is their (potential) subjectivity, however, that gives, or should give, humans pause. This was expressed by a number of interviewees, though perhaps most assertively in the following response:

> there are the people who are genuinely concerned [about farm animals' subjective welfare] … [I]f you study animals' emotional states, if you look at their capacity for learning and so on it just raises and further heightens concerns that people have about eating food animals in general. So for the food animal industries … there are people who are legitimately concerned about what may be made of this sort of research … and thus they would be understandably sort of hesitant to put money into that kind of thing, which is unfortunate because of course if you talk to John Q. Public on the street these are the questions that person has about food animals.
>
> (2012, interview)

As this scientist indicates, concerns expressed by the public at large (see also Rauch and Sharp's 2005 survey) suggest that they care about farm animals' subjective capacities, for example to experience fear and to have preferences. In addition to these animal scientists' opinions, recognition of farmed animals as having at least some level of subjectivity is interspersed in regulatory language (e.g. the EU's recognition of animals as sentient) and the justifications of the research vehicles examined in this chapter. Returning to Agamben's theories with regard to *zoē* and *bios*, US and European societies are not only utilizing knowledge of farmed animals as biological beings for productivity and governance, but are also recognizing them as more than just 'bare life', as human citizens engage in formal and informal political processes to shape policy and attitudes toward them.

I further suggest that, as with Agamben's, Foucault's analysis can be productively applied to the case of farm animals as well. As discussed earlier, Western animal science research expanded dramatically in the mid-twentieth century. That animal agricultural industries and related science fields have charged themselves with obtaining biological knowledge of farm animals in the most comprehensive sense and at the most minute levels cannot be disputed. Often, the goal of this knowledge is to wring maximum productivity out of the individual animal body. In recent decades this field of scientific research has added to this productivity orientation a welfare component, with welfare research adding a new dimension to biopower. A survey of recent study topics of the LBRU, AABW, and WQ project evidence the range of knowledge sought, with these vehicles' research including: pain (from beak trimming in hens, lameness in pigs, and castration in calves); heart-rate variability, stress, and well-being in pigs; osteoporosis in chickens; diet and ulcers in sows; dairy cow leg stress; and breeding strategies to reduce pig aggression. These topics indicate the broad spectrum of biopower that encompasses both productivity and welfare. In addition to physiological requirements, as knowledge of farmed animals' emotional, social, and behavioral needs is also gained, new tools are available for management and, importantly, for addressing societal concerns about welfare. As noted previously, these nonhuman populations are subject to some of the same issues as those of humans in terms of minimizing disease and damage, and with respect to managing health and well-being at the population level. Antibiotics developed during the Second World War became a means of minimizing disease risks for both human and animal populations. The Foucault quotation above is applicable here, in that biological knowledge of disease and its transmission between animals (human and non) supported the 'shift in focus from the individual to the population' and resulted in modern states having new 'realities' that could be deployed in the service of industry.

We can see that scientific knowledge of farmed animals' physiologies and psychologies is supported by the state through funding of research programs that retain production objectives, but now incorporate welfare as well. Additionally, Foucault's theory of the individual-population relationship is relevant here, as this knowledge of animals' capacities is deployed and individual animal subjects often participate in the efficient functioning of the overall industrial farm population. The bare lives of the animals can be seen to be merged with their subjective selves in production and this is especially apparent in the quotation above that describes pigs as learning, disciplined subjects. This merging further blurs the distinction between their existence as productive units with their existence as political subjects.

Conclusion

In this chapter I have suggested that present-day industrially farmed animals in the US and EU are moving into a conceptual realm of political subjectivity. This subjectivity is evidenced in part by the history of, and increasing, state regulation of their treatment. Inherent in this regulation, significant government support is being provided for scientific research not only directed at boosting productivity by managing the animals as living matter, but also as living beings that can experience good or poor welfare, increasingly shown to be subjective. I have further suggested that this situation fits within Agamben's theorizing of bare versus social life, in that these animals are literally brought into existence as bare, material life to be killed. However, as both the public and animal science engage with their individual subjectivity, their sociopolitical subjectivity, at least on a conceptual level, is developing as well. As with the focus on the population in governing human lives in societies, to manage animals in industrial-scale agriculture there is also a focus on the population level, and I have contended that Foucault's concept of biopower can be productively applied to animal populations. Within the processes of producing scientific knowledge about these animals, their physiologies and psychologies, individual subjects also begin to emerge.

References

Agamben, G. (1998) *Homo Sacer: Sovereign Power and Bare Life*, Stanford University Press, Palo Alto, CA

AWI (2014) 'Farm Animal Anti-Confinement Legislation', www.awionline.org/content/farm-animal-anti-confinement-legislation, accessed 19 May 2014

Barnes, A. P. (2001) 'Towards a framework for justifying public agricultural R & D: The example of UK agricultural research policy', *Research Policy*, vol 30, pp. 663–672

Becker, G. S. (2008) 'USDA Meat Inspection and the Humane Methods of Slaughter Act', *CRS Report for Congress*, 26 February

Bennett, J. (2010) 'Thing-Power' in B. Braun and S. J. Whatmore (eds), *Political Matter: Technoscience, Democracy, and Public Life*, University of Minnesota Press, Minneapolis, pp. 35–62

Brambell Committee (1965) *Report of the Technical Committee to Enquire into the Welfare of Animals kept under Intensive Livestock Husbandry Systems (The Brambell Report)*, HMSO: London

Braun, B. and Whatmore, S. J. (2010) 'The Stuff of Politics: An Introduction', in B. Braun and S. J. Whatmore, (eds), *Political Matter: Technoscience, Democracy, and Public Life*, University of Minnesota Press, Minneapolis, pp. ix – xl

Broom, D. M. (1986) 'Indicators of poor welfare', *British Veterinary Journal*, vol 142, pp. 524–526

Chu, V. S. (2010) *Brief Summaries of Federal Animal Protection Statutes*, Congressional Research Service, Washington, DC

Coulon, M., Deputte, B. L, Heyman, Y. and Baudoin, C. (2009) 'Individual Recognition in Domestic Cattle (*Bos taurus*): Evidence from 2D-images of heads from different breeds', *Plos One*, vol 4, no 2, pp. 1–8

Della Chiesa, A., Speranza, M., Tommasi, L. and Vallortigara, G. (2006) 'Spatial cognition based on geometry and landmarks in the domestic chick (*Gallus gallus*)', *Behavioural Brain Research*, vol 175, pp. 119–127

Donaldson, S. and Kymlicka, W. (2011) *Zoopolis: A Political Theory of Animal Rights*, Oxford University Press, Oxford

EC (1992) 'Treaty on European Union', *Official Journal C 191*, www.eurlex.europa.eu/en/treaties/dat/11992M/htm/11992M.html#0103000044, accessed 15 November 2012

EC (1997) 'Treaty of Amsterdam Amending the Treaty on European Union, the Treaties Establishing the European Communities and Related Acts', *Official Journal C 340,* www.eurlex.europa.eu/en/treaties/dat/11997D/htm/11997D.html#0110010013, accessed 15 November 2012

EC (1998) *Council Directive 98/58/EC*, Brussels

EC (2007) *Council Directive 2007/43/EC*, Brussels

EC (2008a) 'Consolidated version of the treaty on the functioning of the European Union', *Official Journal of the European Union*, vol 115, no 47

EC (2008b) *Council Directive 2008/120/EC*, Brussels

Eckholm, E. (2010) 'Farmers lean to truce on animals' close quarters', *The New York Times*, 11 August, www.nytimes.com/2010/08/12/us/12farm.html, accessed 12 August 2010

EL (2012) 'Kraft's Oscar Mayer Pledges to Ban Pig Gestation Crates', www.environmentalleader.com/2012/07/09/krafts-oscar-mayer-pledges-to-ban-pig-gestation-crates/, accessed 15 November 2012

Emel, J. and Wolch, J. (1998) 'Witnessing the animal moment', in: J. Wolch and J. Emel (eds), *Animal Geographies: Place, Politics, and Identity in the Nature-Culture Borderlands*, Verso, London, pp. 1–24

FAIR (2002) *Animal Products for the Next Millennium: An Agenda for Research and Education*, Federation of Animal Science Societies, Savoy, IL

Favre, D. and Tsang, V. (1993) 'The development of the anti-cruelty laws during the 1800s', *Detroit College of Law Review*, vol 1993, no 1, pp. 1–35

FAWC (2009) 'Five freedoms', www.fawc.org.uk/freedoms.htm, accessed 15 August 2012

Foucault, M. (2007) *Security, Territory, Population*, G. Burchell, trans., Picador, New York.

Harrison, R. (1964) *Animal Machines: The New Factory Farming Industry*, Vincent Stuart Publishers, Ltd., London

Hinchliffe, S., Kearnes, M., Degen, M. and Whatmore, S. (2005) 'Urban wild things: A cosmopolitical experiment', *Environment and Planning D: Society and Space*, vol 23, pp. 643–658

Hobson, K. (2007) 'Political animals? On animals as subjects in an enlarged political geography', *Political Geography*, vol 26, pp. 250–267

Holloway, L. (2007) 'Subjecting cows to robots: Farming technologies and the making of animal subjects', *Environment and Planning D: Society and Space*, vol 25, pp. 1,041–1,060

HSUS (2012a) 'An HSUS report: Welfare issues with tail docking of cows in the dairy industry', www.humanesociety.org/assets/pdfs/farm/HSUS-Report-on-Tail-Docking-of-Dairy-Cows.pdf, accessed 15 November 2012

HSUS (2012b) 'Barren, cramped cages: Life for America's egg-laying hens', www.humanesociety.org/issues/confinement_farm/facts/battery_cages.html, accessed 15 November 2012

HSUS (2012c) 'Rhode Island enacts legislation to prohibit extreme confinement crates for pigs and calves and the routine docking of cows' tails', www.humanesociety.org/news/press_releases/2012/06/rhode_island_gestation_crates_ban_062112.html, accessed 15 November 2012

HSUS (2014) 'Kentucky becomes eighth state to ban cruel veal crates', www.humanesociety. org/news/news_briefs/2014/03/KY_veal_crate_ban_031014.html, accessed 19 May 2014

Irwin, A. (2008) 'STS perspectives on scientific governance', in E. J. Hackett, O. Amsterdamska, M. E. Lynch and J. Wajcman (eds), *The Handbook of Science and Technology Studies* (3rd edition), The MIT Press, Cambridge, MA, pp. 583–608

Jasanoff, S. (2005) *Designs on Nature: Science and Democracy in Europe and the United States*, Princeton University Press, Princeton, NJ

LBRU (2007) 'A history of the LBRU', *LBRU Update*, Spring

LBRU (2010) 'Laboratory Plan', September

Marinetto, M. (2007) *Social Theory, the State and Modern Society: The State in Contemporary Social Thought*, Open University Press, Berkshire, UK

Martin, R. (1822) 'Act to Prevent the Cruel and Improper Treatment of Cattle', *Statutes of the United Kingdom of Great Britain and Ireland*, www.animalrightshistory.org/animal-rightslaw/ romantic-legislation/1822-uk act ill-treatment-cattle.htm, accessed 15 November 2012

Matheny, G. and Leahy, C. (2007) 'Farm animal welfare, legislation and trade', *Law and Contemporary Problems*, vol 70, pp. 325–358

Miele, M., Murdoch, J. and Roe, E. (2005) 'Animals and ambivalence: Governing farm animal welfare in the European food sector', in V. Higgins and G. Lawrence (eds), *Agricultural Governance: Globalization and the New Politics of Regulation*, Routledge, Oxford, UK, pp. 169–185

NCRA (2010) 'NC1029: Applied Animal Behavior and Welfare (NCR131), Statement of Issues and Justification', www.nimss.umd.edu/homepages/outline.cfm?trackID=13156, accessed 3 January 2011

ODA (Undated) 'Ohio livestock care standards', www.agri.ohio.gov/LivestockCareStandards, accessed 15 November 2012

OIE (2013) 'OIE's achievements in animal welfare', www.oie.int/animal-welfare/animal-welfare-key-themes/, accessed 15 March 2014

Radford, M. (2011a) 'Welfare legislation', *Course on Animal Welfare Science, Ethics and Law*, Cambridge, UK, 9–20 September

Radford, M. (2011b), 'The impact of European Union law', *Course on Animal Welfare Science, Ethics and Law*, Cambridge, UK, 9–20 September

Rauch, A. and Sharp, J. S. (2005) *Ohioans Attitudes About Animal Welfare: A Topical Report from the 2004 Ohio Survey of Food, Agricultural and Environmental Issues*, The Ohio State University, Columbus, OH

Rumley, E. R. (Undated) 'States' Farm Animal Welfare Statutes', The National Agricultural Law Center, www.nationalaglawcenter.org/assets/farmanimal/index.html, accessed 15 November 2012

SAES (2006) *Guidelines for Multistate Research Activities*, USDA, Washington, DC

Stengers, I. (2010) 'Including nonhumans in political theory: Opening Pandora's box?', In B. Braun and S. J. Whatmore (eds), *Political Matter: Technoscience, Democracy, and Public Life*, University of Minnesota Press, Minneapolis, pp. 3–34

Stevenson, P. (2012) *European Union Legislation on the Welfare of Farm Animals*, Compassion in World Farming, London

STOA (2009) 'Animal-based welfare monitoring: Final report', M. Bokma-Bakker and G. Munnichs (eds), Rathenau Institute, The Hague

Thorpe, C. (2008) 'Political theory in science and technology studies', in E. J. Hackett, O. Amsterdamska, M. E. Lynch and J. Wajcman (eds), *The Handbook of Science and Technology Studies* (3rd edition), The MIT Press, Cambridge, MA, pp. 63–82

UK (1911) 'Protection of Animals Act', www.legislation.gov.uk/ukpga/Geo5/12/27, accessed 15 November 2012

US Congress (2012) H.R. 3798 (112th): *Egg Products Inspection Act Amendments of 2012*, www.govtrack.us/congress/bills/112/hr3798, accessed 15 November 2012

US Congress (2013) H.R. 1731: *Egg Products Inspection Act Amendments of 2013*, www.govtrack.us/congress/bills/113/hr1731, accessed 19 May 2014

USDA (2002) *USDA Stakeholder Workshop for Animal Agriculture*, www.ars.usda.gov/docs.htm?docid=1083&page=1 accessed 3 January 2011

Welfare Quality (Undated) 'Welfare Quality®: Science and society improving animal welfare in the food quality chain', www.welfarequality.net/everyone/26536/5/0/22, accessed 1August 2010

Whitmore, W. H. (1890) *A Bibliographical Sketch of the Laws of the Massachusetts Colony from 1630–1686*, Rockwell and Churchill, City Printers, Boston

14

BATTLING THE HEAD AND THE HEART

Constructing knowledgeable narratives of vegetarianism in anti-meat advocacy

Harvey Neo

Introduction

Livestock production and consumption straddle the realms of environmentalism (Emel and Neo, 2010; Lee and Newell, this volume) and cultural imperatives (Giaccaria and Colombino, this volume) and are highly political and politicized. For the former, livestock production has been increasingly implicated in climate change politics and policies since the United Nations Food and Agriculture Organization published its landmark thesis on the negative environmental impacts of meat production in 2007 (FAO, 2007; see also Mäkiniemi and Vainio, 2013). Such environmental impacts run the gamut from the release of greenhouse gases, to water body pollution to land contamination from livestock wastes to zoonotic diseases that are born out of shoddy production practices. These impacts have been invariably measured and analysed by science and in many cases scientific research offers potential solutions to mitigate them. Meat consumption (or its non-consumption) is also a marker of culture (Kalof et al., 1999; Shukin, 2009) and religion (Donner, 2008; Nath, 2010; Miller, 2011). For example, followers of Jainism are all vegetarians, with a significant proportion of them being vegans (who not only avoid meat but all animal by-products as well). A significant proportion of Hindus in India are vegetarians as well. Above all, the production and consumption of meat is besieged with all forms of politics. These include explicit confrontations over animal and human labour welfare issues, the clearing of forests for cattle ranching and the demise of smallholder producers as well as a more general ethical-political debate over the very consumption of meat itself.

The focus of this chapter is to evaluate the efforts of anti-meat advocates to convince more people to practise vegetarianism. The central argument is that the protean nature of meat production *and* consumption challenges anti-meat advocates to construct persuasive narratives of the vegetarianism message. While such narratives are largely 'knowledge' driven (speaking to the level headedness of consumers), there exists considerable scope to infuse normative exhortations in them (appealing to the 'hearts' of consumers). In short, the anti-meat narratives are strategic elaborations of knowledge about livestock production and consumption that fuse politics, ecology and ethics. Drawing on primary research done in Singapore, this chapter shows the ambiguity and challenges faced by anti-meat advocates in their quest to construct narratives that balance science and emotional appeal to not consume meat. In so doing, it will hopefully illuminate ways to best reduce consumers' intake of meat and, more ambitiously, to completely stop their consumption of meat.

Following this introduction, I will briefly describe the state of global vegetarianism activism. Following that, I will delineate both the 'science-based' rationale for vegetarianism and the normative-based arguments for vegetarianism. In so doing, I argue that the political ecology of meat actually does not allow for such a neat dichotomy between facts and 'feelings'. I exemplify this latter argument through the notion of a 'knowledgeable narrative' of vegetarianism. Such a narrative aims to infuse consumers with knowledges about vegetarianism in a comprehensive manner, and is a narrative that vegetarian advocates strive to achieve.

Vegetarianism advocacy

In a recent study, researchers analysed 29 countries, representing 54 percent of the world's population, and extrapolated that there are 75 million vegetarians by choice in the world and 1.45 billion vegetarians by necessity (Leahy et al., 2010). The latter are defined as consumers who are too poor to afford meat but would likely consume meat once their income level rises. This suggests that with the rising global economic growth, there will be a significant increase in meat consumption in the near future. Among many other global projections, the United Nations Food and Agriculture Organization, for example, has predicted that meat consumption in East Asia will rise to 650 kilocalories per person per year in 2050 (the corresponding figures in 1970 and 2000 are 100 and 400 respectively). Nonetheless, this ever-increasing appetite for meat is accompanied by persistent advocacy to increase the number of vegetarians (by choice).

The roots of organized vegetarianism advocacy can be traced to 1908 when the International Vegetarian Union was formed. Indeed, the first known quasi-vegetarian society in the Western world – The British and Foreign Society for the Promotion of Humanity and Abstinence from Animal Food (the precursor for United Kingdom's Vegetarian Society) – was formed even earlier in 1843. Then, the two main reasons for establishing vegetarian societies and promoting vegetarianism were to encourage healthy living and to promote a more humane relationship with animals. The former is rooted largely in a scientific discourse that appeals to the rationality of consumers to eat what is best, while the latter appeals to the morality of consumers to eat what is ethical. Today, the International Vegetarian Union lists hundreds of affiliate vegetarianism societies worldwide and organizes an annual World Vegetarian Congress.

Vegetarianism advocacy is somewhat unique as compared with other socio-environmental movements in that its members are expected to make visible, material changes to their lifestyles (to a meat-free diet). Individual vegetarians and vegans also negotiate a very personal politics at a day-to-day level as when they are in social gatherings where food is served. In their frequent interactions with families, friends and colleagues on their dietary choices and in explaining to them their reasons for adopting a meat-free lifestyle, vegetarians and vegans are essentially politicizing vegetarianism in subtle ways. Put another way, they are exemplifying the fact that 'the personal is political' and that being vegetarian is arguably a form of embodied social action that impacts on the immediate social sphere of vegetarians. Indeed, research has shown that people generally change their diets through personal social interaction with already committed vegetarians (Maurer, 2002).

The proliferation of vegetarian societies around the world attests to the fact that activism and education on meat intake reduction and avoidance is ever-present. The specific politics of vegetarianism activism are however played out variously in different places and at different scales, drawing upon multiple rationales. Large-scale events that are held to promote vegetarianism for health reasons are generally collegial and non-confrontational. For example, 'Meatout', a result of grassroots social activism, is held in the first day of spring in the United States to educate communities, friends and families to reduce meat consumption. First organized in 1985, the nationwide event aims also to persuade people that a vegetarian diet is more wholesome. In that sense, it is not overt in promulgating the vegetarianism message.

There have also been city-level efforts to promote vegetarianism through the symbolic declaration of a Meatout day (or 'veggie day') each week. The earliest city to adopt this was the Belgian city of Ghent where each Thursday is designated as a 'veggie day'. Other cities that have adopted a meat-free day each week include Cape Town in South Africa, Bremen in Germany and São Paulo in Brazil. While such a gesture is impossible to be legally enforced, it is to the credit of vegetarianism activists to have successfully launched such high-profile sociopolitical campaigns, amidst scepticism from various quarters (for example, the restaurant industry). Indeed, there are signs that such 'Meatout' initiatives are increasingly replicated in universities and private companies. The Meatless Monday movement, which originated in the USA in 2003, has been growing from strength to strength, targeting various sites to institute a meatless day. For example, through their advocacy efforts, more than 150 colleges in the USA have implemented a meat-free day in their cafeterias (www.meatlessmonday.com/meatless-monday-campus/).

An increasingly important realm for vegetarianism activism is the meat commodity chain where livestock producers have marketed meat consumption as a viable and enviable dietary choice. A good example would be the pork producers in the United States who have for years advertised pork as the 'other white meat'. Similarly, the attempts by these producers to sell leaner cuts of meat are aimed at people who are wont to reduce meat consumption for health reasons. Such attempts however are unlikely to sway people who object to meat consumption for environmental and ethical grounds. For example, the United Nations Food and Agriculture Organization has argued that the livestock sector releases 18 percent of greenhouse gas emissions (measured in CO_2 equivalent) and this finding has provided good fodder to revalorize vegetarianism advocates' environment-based objections to meat consumption. Animal advocacy groups like PETA (People for the Ethical Treatment of Animals) have continually exposed the cruelty prevalent in the meat production process through undercover documentation. For advocates, such social-political exposés highlight the fact that animal cruelty is collateral to the modern production of cheap meat; it compels ordinary consumers to think of their culpability in the meat commodity chain.

Anti-meat narratives

While advocacy efforts are variable, as are the specific spaces and scales they are targeting, the justifications for adopting a vegetarian diet have not fundamentally changed in essence. The reasons for not eating meat have always drawn on three broad albeit interlinked concerns of health, animal welfare and environmental well-being (all of which have been alluded to above). Each of these reasons are in turn the product of scientific (sometimes, pseudo-scientific) rationale and ethical exhortations. This mix of objective facts with normative views in relation to a no-meat diet needs to be unpacked so that that contradictions and challenges of vegetarianism advocacy can be understood better.

For example, while there is broad consensus that consuming too much meat is bad for one's health (Leitzmann, 2003; Walker et al., 2005), it is much more debatable whether eliminating meat completely from one's diet (as opposed to merely reducing meat intake) is the best health option for people. Indeed, the Academy of Nutrition and Dietetics (2012), formerly known as the American Dietetic Association, recommends that our diet should be made up of 50 percent fruits and vegetables, 25 percent of lean meat, poultry or fish and 25 percent of grains, with suitable amounts of fat-free or low-fat milk, yogurt or cheese. Yet, it is not uncommon to find vegetarian activists promoting a meat-free diet as the healthiest one (Compassion in World Farming Trust, 2004). To be sure, the notion of an 'ideal' diet, be it from the Academy of Nutrition and Dietetics' perspective or vegetarianism groups' standpoint, is highly contestable. As Nestle (2002) argues, any normalized or idealized form of diet is neither benign (i.e. free from values) nor entirely objective (i.e. completely 'scientific'). Rather, it is an outcome of complex sociopolitics of regulators, food conglomerates, consumers and non-governmental organizations. In other words, the idea of a meat-free diet as *the* healthiest diet is arguably discursively constructed even as it is rooted partly in science.

In addition, this narrative that draws on health issues is essentially an extension of a broader existential question: are humans 'naturally' omnivores or herbivores? Put another way, what activists are arguing is not just that a vegetarian diet is healthier, but that it is also more natural. This is one important way in which advocates framed their narrative such that it intersects in interesting ways the questions of scientific truth, morality and naturalness. Loren Cordain (2010), an evolutionary nutritionist at Colorado State University, argues that the 'best' diet is one that mirrors that of hunters and gatherers. It is a diet which is the most 'natural' and free from the artifice that resulted from cooking and modern agriculture. However, it is also a diet where individuals derive more than half of their required daily calories intake from meat.

The concern for animal welfare manifests itself in two different beliefs. The first animal welfare concern relates to the way in which meat is produced in modern livestock systems. These systems, variously known as factory farms and concentrated animal feeding operations (CAFOs), are often criticized for severely compromising the physical and mental welfare of animals (Ilea, 2009). The overall drive towards hyper-intensification of meat production is said to have commodified animals into mere inanimate objects in an intricate network of contract farming (MacLachlan, 2005; Neo, 2010). Others have pointed how such systems of production have exploited human labour as much as animals (Watts, 1994; Neo and Emel, forthcoming). Predicating a switch to vegetarianism on account of the cruelty of modern animal farming means that vegetarian activists are logically and morally compelled to acquiesce to the consumption of animals which are raised in a more humane and natural manner than CAFOs. For example, there has been a persistent niche in organic livestock farming that purportedly subjects animals to the lowest level of suffering (Alrøe et al., 2001; Ilbery and Maye, 2005; Neo and Chen, 2009). Furthermore, for most meat eaters, while it may be clear to them that subjecting animals to extreme and unnecessary cruelty is unnatural and wrong, there remains still a persistent cognitive dissonance that prevents them from effecting any real change to their purchasing or dietary habits (Smart, 2004). In part, this is due to the spatial disconnect between the spaces of consumption and production, where the raising and slaughtering of animals are well hidden.

The second justification relating to animal welfare takes the more absolute position that it is morally objectionable to kill and consume animals. Consuming meat is fundamentally wrong and unnatural (and this intersects somewhat to the appeal to health discussed earlier). Clearly, there is some conflation of that which is morally objectionable and that which is unnatural. In any case, this position means that how well and comfortable meat animals are raised is not relevant because they are still ultimately killed for human consumption (Pluhar, 2010). Such a view towards animals can be in the first instance deeply influenced by religious beliefs (Miller, 2011); hence it is not so much a moral concern for animals per se that drives such vegetarianism, than a direct religious imperative. For example, vegetarianism in India is rooted in the Hindu concept of *ahimsā* ('non-violence'). It is also an important ideological conduit that unites the vegetarian movement and the animal rights movement (Maurer, 2002, p62). Vegetarians who believe that it is morally wrong to rear animals for human consumption are generally the most consistent and committed ones (ibid.); nonetheless studies have shown that the vast majority of people who initially attempted a vegetarian diet did so for health reasons (Morris and Kirwan, 2006; Fox and Ward, 2007).

Finally, vegetarianism activists have also used the rhetoric of environmentalism for advocacy. This is a fairly recent strategic framing although the environmental impacts of meat production are not unknown. As recently as 2002, Maurer (2002, p62) observed that 'the vegetarian movement overlaps less with the environmental movement than with the animal rights and health food movements'. To be sure, as mentioned earlier, the landmark publication of *Livestock's Long Shadow* in 2006 by the United Nations Food and Agriculture Organization catalysed international attention to the links between environmental degradation and meat production (see also Jarosz, 2009). The rationale for aligning the vegetarian cause with the environmentalist cause is thus understandable as the latter is an established moral-ethical concern recognized by most people. However, compared to the health and animal welfare justifications, appealing to the environment to persuade people to turn vegetarian is not straightforward, in terms of framing and eventual results. Not least, it will be plagued with the same kinds of problems confronting the success of the environmental movement, and as will be discussed later, some activists also have reservations about the seeming devaluation of animals in such a strategic framing.

While for heuristic reasons, I have briefly discussed the three justifications for vegetarianism separately; in reality, all vegetarian activism touch upon all three in various permutations and to different extent. Indeed, vegetarians are often moti-vated by different justifications at different phases of their lives (Fox and Ward, 2007). Regardless on the exact framings of vegetarianism and the individual beliefs of activists; as a collective movement, the most important goal for activists is to persuade consumers that meat consumption is both unnatural and immoral. Put simply, it is to frame vegetarianism as a form of ethical food consumption. In the next section, I will briefly introduce the research context before developing the substantive argument.

Singapore and the Vegetarian Society (Singapore)

Singapore, with a total land area of 718 square km, is a tiny island state south of Peninsula Malaysia. It gained self-rule from the British colonial rulers in 1959. With no natural resources and a small population, doubts about its viability prompted the ruling elites to push Singapore into a merger with the Malaysian Federation in 1963. Two years later, Singapore was unceremoniously booted out of the Federation when it became apparent that the political ideology (and ambi-tion) of Singapore's People's Action Party (PAP) clashed with those of the central authorities in Kuala Lumpur (Turnbull, 1989). Among other clashes, the mul-ticultural governing style of the PAP was seen as increasingly at odds with the central government's 'Malay-centric' disposition. Singapore remains a multiracial and multicultural country with a majority population of Chinese (74.2 percent of the resident population of 5.3 million), and substantial Malay (13.2 percent) and Indian minorities (9.2 percent).

Reflecting the multicultural population, the cuisine in Singapore is similarly varied. Extrapolating on 2003 data, Leahy et al. (2010) estimated that 0.21 per cent of all households in Singapore are vegetarian or vegan. Given that there are about 1.17 million households in Singapore (Singapore Statistics, 2013), there are thus almost 2,457 vegetarian households in Singapore. With an average household size of 3.47 persons, a crude estimate of the number of vegetarians in Singapore is about 8,500. This is likely to be an underestimation given that many vegetarians live in mixed dietary habit households. In any case, the number of occasional vegetarians in Singapore is significant. Many Buddhists, Taoists and Catholics abstain from meat on particular religiously symbolic days of the month.

Formalized vegetarian advocacy began fairly recently with the leading advocacy group, the Vegetarian Society (Singapore), or VSS, formed less than 20 years ago in 1999. The VSS juggles many different vegetarianism-related projects simultaneously (for example, compiling a directory of vegetarian eateries in Singapore). However, their activities are driven by their goal of ultimately seeing more vegetarians in Singapore. The VSS is a registered charity (with tax exemptions benefit) and a member of the International Vegetarian Union. In its mission statement, the VSS states that:

> We strive to build a more humane and harmonious world for everyone on the planet as well as for our fellow creatures. Environmental degradation, global warming, the high incidence of cancer, heart and other diseases have resulted in much untold physical, emotional and financial hardship. Much of this is unnecessary and PREVENTABLE if only we knew and made the right choices. VSS' efforts are directed at the prudence of PREVENTION through awareness, and we believe that education is the key.
>
> (VSS, 2014, emphasis in original)

In this short mission statement, it is already apparent that the VSS underpins its advocacy with the three rationales of vegetarianism elaborated above. In the next section, I will explicate the advocacy efforts of the VSS through interviews with key members of the organization and analyses of their outreach efforts, focusing on their challenges in framing the most appropriate and effective advocacy message. To be sure, the VSS also has to be cognizant of the broader socio-politics of Singapore, particular the wariness of the dominant political party of any other sources of social power that might weaken their grip on Singapore politics. This means that the VSS need to navigate potential pitfalls in the way that they advance their agenda.

Constructing knowledge and narratives on vegetarianism

It is this concern over wider social politics that VSS activists feel that few positive results will be achieved by highlighting the environmental impacts of meat consumption. As a senior member of the society elaborates:

> I think Singaporeans in general are not that environmentally aware. Sure you might argue that the younger generations have better environmental

consciousness but I don't see how anything concrete and material will come out of saying things like 'Save the world, don't eat meat!' It is already an uphill task asking Singaporeans to recycle as it is! So I think we need a different approach. You do not want the vegetarianism message to be collateral of another bigger message – environmentalism.

Unpacking this apprehension, one can see that this VSS member treats environmentalism as a normative issue that does not necessarily resonate with the wider population. The message of environmentalism is also seen as too broad and vague to begin with and framing vegetarianism advocacy in the context of environmentalism might result in advocates needing to narrate two different arguments.

In contrast with this, many advocates interviewed felt that linking vegetarianism with health appeals to the 'head' (or logic) of consumers and hence stands a better chance of being internalized. Dave, an active member of the VSS with years of advocacy explains why the VSS has relied more on the health justification to persuade people to become vegetarians:

> We need to be smart about what we do and how we do it. Is it wise to align with the environmental groups, like the Nature Society [of Singapore]? I am not too sure. The thing is the government has a dim view of such groups … I am sure you know of some bad blood between the Nature Society and the government in the past. So we say that if you want what is best for you, in terms of your health and mental well-being, you should consider becoming vegetarian. In fact, we have been trying to work out something with the Ministry of Health.

It may not seem explicit but what Dave is trying to do is to articulate a notion of ethics that believes that in order to be ethical, one needs to start with taking responsibility with one's body. Consumers are thus not drawn to look at the moral well-being of distant others, but inwards to themselves and how a non-meat diet (as a type of moral objective) is ethical in and of itself. In other words, distant others and an out-there unethical global economy is not immediately relevant to the (would-be) moral subject. Anti-meat advocacy that is premised upon health consideration essentially seeks to transform non-vegetarians' understandings of what it means to be ethical to oneself. While this idea is not uncommon, it is controversial in some respects and can be seen in discourses on obese people and smokers: how the former 'owe' it to themselves to lose weight (see Guthman, 2011) and quit smoking (Chapple et al., 2004) so that they can become 'better' people. However, to such rationalizations, there too exist limitations, as Gregory, another VSS member explains: 'This is a dilemma because as a nutritionist, I cannot say that a diet without meat is necessarily better than a diet with very little meat. I think if you want to sustain a long-term vegetarian diet, it has to be more than for health reasons.'

Indeed, Gregory's argument takes us back to the point of the 'ideal' healthy diet explicated earlier. While valorizing health in their advocacy seems like a logical thing to do, it remains to be seen if omitting meat completely from one's diet is truly best for everybody. As it stands now, the scientific jury is still out on this. In that sense, appealing to facts about health and a meat-free diet might not go far enough to persuade people to *stop* eating meat; although it might cause more people to consume *less* meat.

It seems then that constructing narratives of vegetarianism that draw on the science of dietary practices or the normative appeal to environmentalism (which in turn is underpinned by the science of environmental degradation) are both problematic in the eyes of some advocates. A young Singaporean vegetarian in her late twenties elaborated, when queried about the challenges she faced in changing her diet:

> It is not easy … For me, I know that some sacrifices … are bound to occur. Maybe I am still young and only have been a vegetarian for less than five years but I think it is hard to be committed to vegetarianism. You must really believe that you *need* to stop consuming meat.

What then are some of the other beliefs that drive vegetarians and in turn frame their advocacy narratives? We return to the point about the 'naturalness' of a meat-free diet, briefly mentioned above. This evokes both the notions of nature/ environment as well as health/body. In this narrative, becoming vegetarian is not only good for the environment and for our health, it is also argued to be the 'natural' thing to do.

Mary, a member of VSS speaks for many in the group when she opines:

> I don't think the kind of meat we eat now can be considered natural. It is completely unnatural for us to eat meat now with all the toxins and hormones and what-nots floating in the production system. Our bodies are just polluted by all these poisons! Maybe if we go back to using our bare hands to kill animals, then it can still be considered natural. Otherwise, now the meat we are eating is making people more aggressive, more impatient because of all the unnatural chemicals in them. It is true. Believe you me.

Here, something that is unnatural is at the same time deemed as socially immoral and unethical. This is not an uncommon position given geography's longstanding effort to disrupt the nature-social dichotomy (Castree and Braun, 2001). Suffice to say, outside of the vegetarian social sphere, not many will agree that consuming meat is unnatural – as evinced by the ever-increasing meat production and the normalization of meat as part of a balanced diet. It is telling that quite a number of vegetarians have similarly expressed the unnaturalness of meat consumption even if official/public discourse used in their public campaign often sidesteps this belief. Interestingly, meat analogues have also been ironically criticized by some vegetarians as highly unnatural too.

The plight of (food) animals figures least in the advocacy efforts of the activists. Yet, it is an issue that provokes the most discussion and insights in my interviews with them. The following are some responses to the questions: 'How do you feel about animals in the livestock industry? How can we use animal welfare and animal rights to validate the vegetarianism cause?'

> Sometimes, we need to think for a moment. What kinds of lives do animals live? Do we want that kind of life? The global meat industry is most perverse. One good strategy is to get all those undercover videos [of factory farming] out to more and more people.

> There is no way that what we are doing is sustainable. We cannot continue to demand for more meat, cheaper meat and not expect animals to suffer more and more. The difficult part is to let people see that all this is unsustainable.

> I feel strongly about taking another living thing. Animals are sentient beings. It is as wrong to kill a human being or a dog or a cat as it is a pig, a chicken or whatever. Killing something so that you live is not right. And we can live without killing … I often ask myself, why do so few others share my view? I think it is hard to push the animal's right [to live] message to people. Singaporeans won't buy it unless they've already bought it … you know what I mean?

> How do we connect the facts of the modern meat industry with some kind of emotional connection and concern? It is not as easy as it seems because there is always a kind of mental disconnection. We need to speak to both the 'head' and the 'heart' of people.

Sentiments as expressed by the last interviewee have prompted the VSS to collaborate with a local animal rights group in Singapore, ACRES (Animal Concerns Research and Education Society) to launch a high profile public campaign in the public train system in 2014. Juxtaposing cute images of pets (e.g. puppies and kittens) and livestock (e.g. cows and pigs), the campaign asks plainly: 'Why love one and eat the other?' While somewhat subtle, the campaign aims to balance the emotive, normative message of love and the factual brutality of factory farming at the same time.

In highlighting the immorality of factory farming, advocates might have to entertain the idea that it may be acceptable to consume organically raised animals which likely had the highest welfare accorded to them. Yet, many advocates argue that such 'organic' meat is not ethical because killing for animal meat – regardless of the process used to produce them – is morally wrong. To substitute conventional meat with organic meat does not negate the fact that a morally wrong death has occurred.

The latter point is a constant refrain by many activists. For example, Mark explains at length:

> It is fine to have organic vegetables or fruits because the point is to save the environment, reduce pollution and all that. But I think it is laughable to talk

about organic meat. Sure, organically raised animals might have better lives compared to their 'normal' counterparts in many aspects; but they share the most critical similarity. Death! How can eating organic meat be more ethical? I think it is a scam.

Non-activist vegetarians have also appealed to animal rights in their decision to adopt a meat-free diet. A Singapore resident in his forties speaks of how he abruptly stopped consuming meat when he was about 14 years old:

> I know it sounds unbelievable. I literally woke up one day, realizing that it is completely wrong to kill animals. It was like a sudden enlightenment and I stopped eating meat from that day onwards. It was admittedly hard in the initial days but I have never tasted meat since then.

As mentioned earlier, notwithstanding their strong personal views about the critical importance of animals in influencing their decision to become vegetarians, all the activists acknowledged that to sell the vegetarianism message through the animal rights approach might not be fruitful. Instead, they have continually emphasized the health and environmental benefits of not consuming meat. This remains a somewhat perplexing contradiction.

Conclusion: towards a knowledgeable narrative of vegetarianism

While many advocates reflected that their turn to vegetarianism is undergirded by a moral concern of animal rights and welfare – in other words, an emotional appeal to their hearts – they nonetheless believe that most people would not have the same level of moral fortitude as they have. Hence, it is better to construct narratives for vegetarianism that are based on 'facts', and which would directly benefit the consumers.

In part, this strategy is based on their reading of the 'Singaporean psyche' where civic consciousness and idealism struggle against pragmatism and brutal calculations of cost/benefits (Neo, 2007). It is against this larger backdrop that advocates in the VSS (and likely other non-governmental organizations) constantly struggle to come up with meaningful narratives that will inform the public about doing the right thing.

I suggest that narratives aimed at social change need to be 'knowledgeable'. To construct a knowledgeable narrative is not to just draw on facts, logic and science; not least, oftentimes, such facts are contested and unresolved. More importantly, knowledge is more than a combination of fact-based cognition, but includes moral, ethically rooted aesthetics about the world we live in. This position points to a problematic dichotomy on narratives which tries to link knowledge, choice and ethical consumption. As Barnett et al. (2011, p13) have argued, the knowledge gap model, in focusing on 'the consumer' and the pursuit of 'facts', 'might not throw much explanatory light on the set of processes involved in the growth of the variety of alternative economic practices subsumed under ethical consumption', obfuscating the 'role of campaign organizations as prime movers in the politicization of consumption'. Put another way, the autonomy of consumer choice is tied to larger institutional processes beyond that of an individual and her or his knowledge.

Furthermore, knowledge gaps alone cannot explain why, even when equipped with the relevant knowledge, most consumers persist to consume less than ethically. An instinctive response is that consumers do not care enough about their moral responsibilities owed to others, both far (Eden et al., 2008) and near (Renting et al., 2003). Hence, they *knowingly* choose not to do what they know to be ethical. This is often described as the moral-cognitive dissonance model of ethical consumption. At a conceptual level, while both the 'information gap narrative' and the 'moral-cognitive dissonance model' of ethical food consumption research are useful advocacy frameworks, they present a somewhat static and dichotomized understanding of ethical consumption (in this case vegetarianism). Barnett et al. (2011, p32; see also Eden et al., 2008) argue that the limitation of this narrative is that it

> dissembles the extent to which ethical consumption practices do not simply aim to facilitate the practical realization of already existing but somehow frustrated ethical commitments, but are part of broader projects which aim to transform self-understanding of wants, needs, desires and satisfactions.

This suggests that advocacy efforts must consistently collapse any distinctions between 'facts' and values and indeed, emphasize the transformative potential of vegetarianism in reordering their moral bearings. For if, by their own admission, most of them become vegetarians due to their empathetic awareness towards animal suffering, why should they assume other people to behave differently?

References

Academy of Nutrition and Dietetics (2012) 'Dietary guidelines and MyPlate' www.eatright. org/resources/food/nutrition/dietary-guidelines-and-myplate

Alrøe, H. F., Vaarst, M. and Kristensen, E. S. (2001) 'Does organic farming face distinctive livestock welfare issues? A conceptual analysis', *Journal of Agricultural and Environmental Ethics*, vol 14, no 3, pp. 275–299

Barnett, C., Cloke, P., Clarke, N. and Malpass, A. (2011) *Globalizing Responsibility: The Political Rationalities of Ethical Consumption*, Wiley-Blackwell, London

Castree, N. and Braun, B. (2001) (eds), *Social Nature: Theory, Practice and Politics*, Blackwell Publishers, London

Chapple, A., Ziebland, S. and McPherson, A. (2004) 'Stigma, shame and blame experienced by patients with lung cancer: qualitative study', *British Medical Journal*, vol 328, pp. 1,470–1,474

Compassion in World Farming Trust (2004) *The Global Benefits of Eating Less Meat*, CIWF Trust Report, Petersfield

Cordain, L. (2010) *The Paleo Diet*, Wiley and Sons, Hoboken, NJ

Donner, H. (2008) 'New vegetarianism: Food, gender and neoliberal regimes in Bengali middle-class families', *South Asia: Journal of South Asian Studies*, vol 31, no 1, pp. 143–169

Eden, S., Bear, C. and Walker, G. (2008) 'Mucky carrots and other proxies: Problematising the knowledge-fix for sustainable and ethical consumption', *Geoforum*, vol 39, pp. 1,044–1,057

Emel, J. and Neo, H. (2010) 'Killing for profit: Global livestock industries and their socio-ecological implications', in R. Peet, P. Robbins, and M. Watts (eds), *Global Political Ecology*, Routledge, London

FAO (2007) *Livestock's Long Shadow*, FAO, Rome

Fox, N. and Ward, K. (2007) 'Health, ethics and environment: A qualitative study of vegetarian motivations', *Appetite*, vol 50, no 2–3, pp. 422–429

Guthman, J. (2011) *Weighing In: Obesity, Food Justice, and the Limits of Capitalism*, University of California Press, Berkeley, CA

Ilbery, B. and Maye, D. (2005) 'Alternative (shorter) food supply chains and specialist livestock products in the Scottish-English borders', *Environment and Planning A*, vol 37, pp. 823–844

Ilea, R. C. (2009) 'Intensive Livestock Farming: Global Trends, Increased Environmental Concerns, and Ethical Solutions', *Journal of Agriculture and Environmental Ethics*, vol 22, pp. 153–167

Jarosz, L. (2009) 'Energy, climate change, meat and markets: mapping the coordinates of the current world food crisis', *Geography Compass*, vol 3, no 6, pp. 2065–2083

Kalof, L., Dietz, T., Stern, P. and Guagnano, G. (1999) 'Social Psychological and Structural Influences on Vegetarian Beliefs', *Rural Sociology*, vol 64, no 3, pp. 500–511

Leahy, E., Lyons, S. and Tol, R. (2010) 'An estimate of the number of vegetarians in the world', Economic and Social Research Institute, Dublin, Ireland, Working Paper No. 340

Leitzmann, C. (2003) 'Nutrition ecology: The contribution of vegetarian diet', *American Journal of Clinical Nutrition*, vol 78, no 3, pp. 6,575–6,595

MacLachlan, I. (2005) 'Feedlot growth in Southern Alberta: A neo-Fordist interpretation', in A. Gilg, R. Yarwood and S. Essex (eds), *Rural Change and Sustainability: Agriculture, the Environment and Communities*, CABI Publishing, London

Mäkiniemi, J. and Vainio, A. (2013) 'Moral intensity and climate-friendly food choices', *Appetite*, vol 65, pp. 54–61

Maurer, D. (2002) *Vegetarianism: Movement or Moment?*, Temple University Press, Philadelphia

Miller, I. (2011) 'Evangelicalism and the early vegetarian movement in Britain c. 1847–1860', *Journal of Religious History*, vol 35, no 2, pp. 199–210

Morris, C. and Kirwan, J. (2006) 'Vegetarians: Uninvited, uncomfortable or special guests at the table of the alternative' food economy?' *Sociologia Ruralis*, vol 46, no 3, pp. 192–213

Nath, J. (2010) '"God is a vegetarian": The food, health and bio-spirituality of Hare Krishna, Buddhist and Seventh-Day Adventist devotees', *Health Sociology Review*, vol 19, no 3, pp. 356–368

Neo, H. (2007) 'Challenging the developmental state: nature conservation in Singapore', *Asia Pacific Viewpoint*, vol 48, no 2, pp. 186–199

Neo, H. (2010) 'Geographies of subcontracting', *Geography Compass*, vol 4, no 8, pp. 1,013–1,024

Neo, H. and Chen, L.-H., (2009) 'Household income diversification and the production of local meat: The prospect of small scale pig farming in Southern Yunnan, China', *Area*, vol 41, no 3, pp. 300–309

Neo, H. and Emel, J. (forthcoming) *Geographies of Meat*, Ashgate, London

Nestle, M. (2002) *Food Politics: How the Food Industry Influences Nutrition and Health*, University of California Press, Berkeley, CA

Nordgren, A. (2012) 'Ethical issues in mitigation of climate change: The option of reduced meat production and consumption', *Journal of Agriculture and Environmental Ethics*, vol 25, pp. 563–584

Pluhar, E. B. (2010) 'Meat and morality: Alternatives to factory farming', *Journal of Agriculture and Environment Ethics*, vol 23, pp. 455–468

Renting, H., Marsden, T. and Banks, J. (2003) 'Understanding alternative food networks: Exploring the role of short food supply chains in rural development', *Environment and Planning A*, vol 35, pp. 393–411

Shukin, N. (2009) *Animal Capital: Rendering Life in Biopolitical Times*, University of Minnesota Press, Minneapolis

Singapore Statistics (2013) 'Population and population structure', www.singstat.gov.sg/statistics/browse-by-theme/population-and-population-structure

Smart, A. (2004) 'Adrift in the mainstream: challenges facing the UK vegetarian movement', *British Food Journal*, vol 106, no 2, pp. 79–92

Turnbull, C. M. (1989) *A History of Singapore*, Oxford University Press, Singapore

VSS (2014) 'About Us', www.vegetarian-society.org/AboutUs

Walker, P., P. Rhubart-Berg, S. McKenzie, K. Kelling, and R.S. Lawrence (2005) 'Public health implications of meat production and consumption'. *Public Health Nutrition*, vol 8, pp. 348–356

Watts, M. J. (1994) 'Life under Contract: Contract Farming, Agrarian Restructuring, and Flexible Accumulation', in P. D. Little and M. J. Watts (eds), *Living Under Contract: Contract Farming and Agrarian Transformation in Sub-Saharan Africa*, University of Wisconsin Press, Madison

PART IV

The governance of meat production systems

15

PRODUCING HALAL MEAT

The case of Halal slaughter practices in Wales, UK

Mara Miele and Karolina Rucinska

Introduction

Provision and consumption of halal and kosher meat are essential aspects of Muslim and Jewish religious lives, respectively. *Halal*, meaning 'lawful', or 'permissible' when used in the context of food, implies that the meat is produced according to Islamic rules. These vary from specifying the types of animals to the method of killing (Anil et al., 2009; Anil, 2012). *Kosher*, which means 'fit', 'ritually permitted', 'clean' or 'in accordance with the rules', refers to meat produced from animals killed by the Jewish method of slaughter, called *shechita*, an essential step in the production of kosher meat, but not the only one (Zivotofsky et al., 2009, Bergeaud-Blackler et al., 2013).

To non-Muslim and non-Jewish people, these two concepts are often associated only with the act of killing animals without stunning prior to the throat cut. However, as the above definitions show, halal and kosher encompass many aspects of food production: both Judaism and Islam do not permit an animal to be dead at the time of the kill and Judaism does not allow the kill of any injured animals, therefore they do not accept current methods of stunning (Zivotofsky et al., 2009). In Islam, on the other hand, certain stunning methods are accepted as long as they do not lead to the death of the animal and they meet other religious requirements – for example the provision of healthy animals, reciting the Tasmiyah (Anil et al., 2009). Therefore, production of meat according to Islamic rules does not necessarily involve a non-stun kill although this issue remains controversial among many Muslim scholars and halal certifiers (Lever and Miele, 2012).

Here we present the results of research carried out in 2012 that aimed to map halal slaughter practices in Wales and the changes that a growing demand for halal food might have caused (Lever and Miele, 2012) as well as the challenges of complying with the recent changes to EC Regulation 1099/2009 concerned with the protection of animals at the time of killing (Miele et al., 2013).

The EU regulation on the protection of animals at the time of killing (EC Regulation 1099/2009) maintains the possibility of the derogation from stunning in the case of religious slaughter for the production of kosher and halal meat, and in most European countries the derogation is adopted for both shechita and halal slaughter. However, this new EU Regulation, which came into force on 1 January 2013, introduces new arrangements for slaughter licences and more attention is given to the welfare of animals (e.g. refinement of stunning methods, animal handling methods, post-cut care, etc.). The new regulation includes the following definitions:

> *slaughterhouse*: any establishment used for slaughtering terrestrial animals which falls within the scope of Regulation (EC) No. 853/2004; *stunning*: any intentionally induced process which causes loss of consciousness and sensibility without pain, including any process resulting in instantaneous death; *slaughtering*: the killing of animals intended for human consumption; *competent authority*: the central authority of a Member State competent to ensure compliance with the requirements of this Regulation or any other authority to which that central authority has delegated that competence.

Regarding this delegation of authority, the religious authority in the EU Member States, on whose behalf slaughter is carried out, shall be competent for the application and monitoring of the special provisions, which apply to slaughter according to certain religious requirements. As regards said provisions, the religious authority shall operate under the responsibility of the official EU member state veterinarian, as defined in the Regulation 1099/2009 (Velarde et al., 2014). Stunning before slaughter is therefore a statutory requirement in Europe and is done to induce unconsciousness in animals, so that slaughter causes no anxiety, pain, suffering or distress. The stunning of farm animals prior to slaughtering can be performed using different methods: mechanical, electrical and gas methods (ibid.). In the majority of the countries of the European Union, religious slaughter is exempt from stunning. But in recent time a number of countries have banned religious slaughter without stunning for animal welfare reasons, see for example Norway, Iceland, Switzerland, Sweden and Poland, even though this last country lifted the ban for 'domestic consumption' of halal meat. In February 2014 Denmark joined them, with agriculture minister Dan Jørgensen saying: 'Animal rights come before religion' (Avasthy, 2014), causing a heated debate since for the previous ten years religious slaughter without stunning was not practised in Denmark and this new rule was interpreted as a sign of antisemitism and islamophobia by the religious minorities in Denmark. In the UK,[1] Ireland, the Netherlands, Germany, Italy and France – the countries with large halal markets – the two methods, with stunning and without stunning, are practised.[2] The coexistence of non-stunned and stunned halal slaughter raises issues of a different nature in the political arena, since it opens up a discussion, on the one hand, about religious freedom and the right to practise one's religion for Muslims and, on the other hand, about non-Muslim consumers' right to information.[3] This latter problem has gained increasing attention with the growth of the halal market because parts of the carcasses of the animals killed with religious slaughter practices (both with and without stunning) are currently sold unlabelled in the conventional market to consumers who are not informed about the method of slaughter of the animals that originated the meat they buy. Recently, a BBC report claimed that 'more than 25 per cent of meat sold in our shops comes from animals not stunned before slaughter' (Lowther, 2012). These concerns were echoed in the House of Commons by an MP who asserted that 'state schools, hospitals, pubs, sports arenas, cafes, markets and hotels [are] serving halal meat to customers without their knowledge' (ibid.). These views signal a number of concerns resulting from the rapid development of a two-tier halal market in the UK. Nevertheless, a lack of transparent and up-to-date data on the number of animals slaughtered for religious reasons does not allow a clear understanding of the relevance of this problem, for it provides no indication of the scale of animals killed without stunning. In this chapter we reviewed the available data on religious slaughter in the UK with a focus on Welsh abattoirs, and supplemented these data with face-to-face interviews with the key informants from the competent authorities, managers of slaughterhouses in Wales practising halal slaughter, as well as the presidents of the main certifying bodies operating in Wales.

This chapter consists of the following parts. First, we provide an overview of current trends in the market for halal meat and other animal products in the UK. Second, we present the results of the interviews with the key informants from the competent authorities and the managers of the slaughterhouses in Wales practising halal slaughter, and we discuss current trends in the halal meat market in Wales. We conclude with some reflections about the complexity of the emerging geographies of religious and conventional animal slaughter.

Slaughterhouses performing halal slaughter in the UK and in Wales

In 2002 Mintel published a report in which it estimated that in the UK ten abattoirs were licensed to carry out religious slaughter in order to supply halal meat, most of which was poultry (Mintel, 2002). Today the picture is very different; there is a higher number of abattoirs carrying out religious slaughter and the majority of animals are stunned before the cut of the throat.

The Food Standard Agency (FSA) survey carried out across Wales, England and Scotland in September 2011 shows that the majority of animals destined for the halal trade in both red and white meat sectors are stunned (FSA, 2012b) (see Table 15.1 and Box 15.1).

TABLE 15.1 UK slaughterhouse survey.

Survey conducted during September 2011	Total UK		Halal					Shechita			
	Number killed (thousands)	Abattoirs	Number killed (thousands)	% total	Stunned		No. abattoirs	Number killed (thousands)	% total	Stunned after cut	No. abattoirs
					before cut	after cut					
Cattle	44	194	1.7	4%	84%	1%	16	1.3	3%	10%	4
Poultry	16,102	73	4766	30%	88%	0%	29	71.2	<1%	0%	5
Sheep/Goats	308	202	154.8	50%	81%	1%	39	1.9	<1%	0%	4

Source: FSA (2012b, pp.5–6)

Box 15.1 Percentage of animals slaughtered without stunning

- 1,727 (4 per cent) of the UK total (43,772) cattle were slaughtered at 16 establishments: 84 per cent of these were stunned before slaughter, and less than 1 per cent stunned after bleeding;
- 154,795 (50 per cent) of the UK total (307,512) sheep and goats were slaughtered at 39 establishments: 81 per cent of these were stunned before slaughter and less than 1 per cent stunned after bleeding;
- 4,766,237 (30 per cent) of the UK total (16,101,844) poultry were slaughtered at 29 establishments: 88 per cent of these were stunned before slaughter (FSA, 2012b).

According to the FSA (interview), at the time of their survey (September 2011) there were two abattoirs located in Wales that practised religious slaughter without stunning. In our study (carried out between April and October 2012), all the interviewed abattoirs practising halal slaughter declared that they practised stunning before slaughtering. It is possible that those abattoirs that do not practise stunning before slaughter have declined participation in this study or have changed their practices since.

The FSA data (2012a) show that out of 100 authorised meat plants operating in Wales under Regulation (EC) No. 853/2004 laying down specific hygiene rules on the hygiene of foodstuffs (see FSA, 2012a) 28 plants were abattoirs during the time of the study, two businesses terminated their operations, one of them was a halal abattoir (BBC, 2012) and the other was a conventional small business. A map illustrating the geographical spread of the 28 plants is shown in Figure 15.1. While we invited all the existing slaughterhouses to participate to the study, only 11 accepted to take part and the manager was interviewed (see Table 15.2).

TABLE 15.2 Abattoirs in Wales.

	Number of plants	
	Contacted:	22
	of which:	
Interviewed	11	
Declined	4	
Agreed but did not reply	7	
Not reachable		4
	Total	26

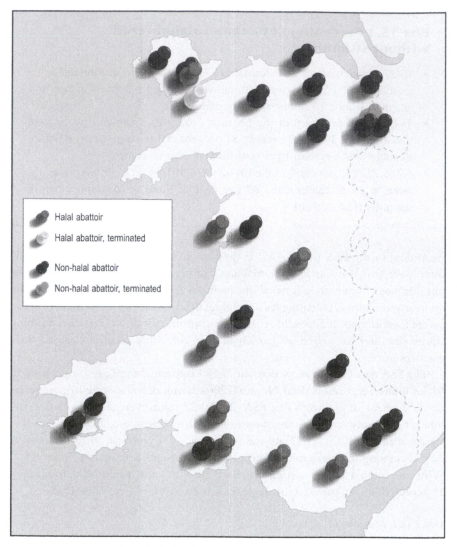

FIGURE 15.1 Map of abattoirs in Wales.

It has emerged that out of the 11 abattoirs that participated in the study only seven performed halal slaughter with stunning (for a detailed study sample, see Table 15.3). None of the plants carried out shechita slaughter for production of kosher meat.

Interviews with slaughterhouse managers

The interviews with the slaughterhouse managers addressed the challenges posed by the enforcement, from 1 January 2013, of EC Regulation 1099/2009 (on the protection of animals at the time of killing) that is imposing higher animal

TABLE 15.3 Study sample.

		Abattoir Number										
		1	2	3	4	5	6	7	8	9	10	11
Method of communication	Phone interviews								Y	Y		
	In-depth interviews	Y	Y	Y	Y	Y	Y					
	Online survey										Y	
	Postal survey							Y				Y
Species	Ovine	Y	Y	Y	Y							
	Bovine and Ovine					Y					Y	
	Ovine, Bovine, Porcine						Y	Y	Y	Y		Y
	Poultry											
Halal slaughter		Y	Y	Y	Y	Y	Y	Y	N	N	N	N
Certified by	Halal Authority Board			Y								
	Halal Food Authority	Y	Y	Y								
	EHDA					Y						
Member of	Freedom Foods	Y			Y							
	Red Tractor	Y				Y					Y	
	BRC	Y	Y			Y					Y	
	Soil Association	Y	Y								Y	
	ABM	Y	Y			Y					Y	
	Welsh Organic Scheme											
	Welsh Meat Promotions									Y		
	Welsh Lamb									Y		

Note: *At the time of the study poultry was slaughtered at four abattoirs; three of them were reached but none of them agreed to provide any information about Halal slaughter. However, interviews with one abattoir manager and HAB director indicated that Halal slaughter could have been carried out at two premises belonging to a large group.

welfare standards, and explored the ways in which the abattoirs practising halal slaughter in Wales were planning to implement the new requirements. Second, they aimed to collect up-to-date information on personnel and practices and the number of animals killed for the halal market in order to obtain an understanding of the development of the halal meat sector in Wales. Furthermore, they aimed to assess the likelihood and potential extent of conventional abattoirs entering the halal market.

The majority of abattoirs have been operating for decades, although ownership changes may have occurred over the years. Of the abattoirs interviewed five were, at the time of the study, private firms, one of which was owned by a person from New Zealand. One abattoir was recently acquired by VION, a large food group based in the Netherlands and operating in Germany, the Netherlands and the UK.

Three abattoirs were small family businesses with small throughput (up to 1,500 lambs per week) whereas the others were large businesses, part of a group of abattoirs and cutting plants, with high throughput (up to 300,000 lambs per week).

The small abattoirs employed between 7 and 40 people compared to the large abattoirs with 100 to over 600 members of staff (or 3,500 in the case of one group). In all the abattoirs staff turnover was low due to the current economic climate and lack of alternative jobs in the surrounding rural areas. In previous years large plants have had problems with retaining staff in the cutting and retail sections of their operations as a result of the prevalence of 'low skill' and 'low pay' jobs. The seasonality of work (e.g. due to the life cycle in ovine species) caused problems with retaining staff at times. However, none of the abattoirs ever experienced high staff turnover for skilled, better paid jobs, such as for the slaughtermen. The employees in the large slaughterhouses perform specific tasks – for example, in lairage, slaughter, cutting and boning – and they would not take on other tasks unless previously trained and licensed. In small abattoirs, however, slaughterhouse staff would be responsible for and required to perform a number of tasks. In most cases the workers are employed by the company, although, due to a seasonality of work (spring lambs and Eid Qurbani festival), there are many seasonal/contract workers who come back each year.

In terms of nationality, the majority of the workforce is Welsh, from neighbouring localities, or British, followed by Polish. In the large plants, Hungarians, Czechs and Slovaks are also employed. Small slaughterhouses employ between 1 and 2 Muslim slaughtermen, whereas larger ones employ between 2 to 4 people for this task. The majority of Muslim slaughtermen were of British nationality, but there was also one Pakistani, one Turk, one Bosnian and one Moroccan.

The age of the workforce varies between 18-year-olds and people in their sixties. It has emerged that many local men or women joined these companies in their teens and stayed for many years, even until their retirement age. Women represented a very small proportion of the workforce with none employed at the slaughtering end of production. Some are employed in cutting and packaging, but the majority held administrative roles.

Lambs and sheep were the only animals slaughtered according to the halal standard in the seven abattoirs that participated in the study; some of the slaughterhouses also slaughtered cattle and pigs for the conventional market.

TABLE 15.4 Number of abattoirs per animal species slaughtered.

Type of species	Number of plants
Lamb and sheep (halal)	7
Cattle (non-halal)	5
Pigs* (non-halal)	3
Horse** (non-halal)	1

Notes: * Pigs are not Halal according to Islam, they are one of animal species considered *haram*.
** Licensed only but no horse has been killed.

Source: interviews.

Lambs at three large abattoirs were sourced from many localities throughout the UK, although most would be Welsh lambs, especially in the period from July to December. The exact numbers of Welsh lambs could not be estimated as animals often are delivered to collection points from many areas of the UK. Small abattoirs source only lambs from Wales within a close proximity (4–10 miles) of the abattoir.

Slaughter numbers of lambs and sheep in general are higher than those of other animal species. Table 15.5 shows the numbers of animals killed per week and per year at the establishments interviewed.

Practices of halal slaughter in Wales

All abattoir managers stated that they (and their companies) considered the halal market only because they can stun the animals before the throat cut. All companies had a clear view on stunning being the only acceptable and approved method to kill an animal. The use of the non-penetrative captive bolt as a stunning method for cattle has not been approved by the current halal certifying bodies, including the HFA which accepts the stunning of sheep and poultry; therefore none of the abattoirs in Wales supply halal beef. All the abattoir managers declared that they would not undertake slaughter without stunning to produce meat for a religious market, for animal welfare concerns.

For the halal slaughter both large and small abattoirs stun before the throat cut (*dhabiha*), which is done in accordance with the following halal requirements:

> The animal must be healthy and alive before slaughter; a Muslim slaughtermen must carry out the cut; it is required the reciting of Tasmiyah; the blood of the animal must flow out of the body before death and in sufficient quantities.
> (Velarde et al., 2014)

An example from an interview with Interviewee 1:

> We stun using Jarvis head-to-back stunning equipment but the head to back is head only. The back part is disconnected, we then cut the throat via the halal slash cut, and all the slaughtermen who carry out the sticking operation are HFA approved … So we basically stun everything head only so it can recover, and which meets all the big customers' requirements. We also use a Muslim slaughterman so that they can say the prayer, etc. We have been HFA approved for about three to four years now.

In four out of seven cases, all lambs[4] were slaughtered this way and were sold (whole carcasses) as either halal meat for the halal market – domestic and export – or as non-halal meat to conventional – domestic only – markets. Small abattoirs

TABLE 15.5 Number of animals slaughtered at interviewed abattoirs.

Abattoir No.	Animal species	Per week	Per Year
1.	Lamb	30,000	
	Cattle	50,000	
2.	Lamb		1,000,000
	Cattle		20,000
3.	Lamb	10,000*	600,000**
4.	Lamb	1,500	
	Cattle	50	
	Pigs	10	
5.	Lamb	50–200***	
	Cattle	300****	
6.	Lamb	~100	
	Pigs	~100	
	Cattle	15–40	
7.	Lamb	300–400	
	Cattle	10	
	Goats	0	
	Pigs	15–30	

Notes: * used to be 1.5 million; ** used to be 35,000 per week before foot-and-mouth disease; *** a figure for halal from last year, with a capacity for 600 lambs a week; **** with a capacity for 120 cattle a day.

Source: interviews.

would perform a halal kill only on those lambs destined for the halal market. In all cases, there was no distinction in price for the carcasses destined to different markets and all managers described the current market situation as difficult:

Interviewer: What are these changes [in the market]? Better quality, diversified demand?

Interviewee 3: Better quality, but less demand.

Interviewer: Less demand?

Interviewee 3: Because of the pricing.

Interviewer: Less of demand in Europe for the export market? Or for the domestic market?

Interviewee 3: It is all over.

Interviewer: And is it recent?

Interviewee 3: I reckon the last two, three years. In the last three years it has been going down.

Interviewer: But you said that you have been working for 24 years, so was it going up before then?

Interviewee 3: It was skyrocketing until 2001 and we had foot and mouth disease, and since FMD it has been going down. Pre–FMD we were doing 35,000 a week – after FMD the highest we have got to is 25,000. So this would be 10,000 lambs less a week. We used to do one and a half million [lambs per year] – we plan to do 600,000 this year.

The halal market constituted a significant proportion of the sales; however, because the same method of slaughter was used for all lambs, the abattoir managers were unable to give the exact numbers. Their estimates for the halal market varied from 10 per cent to 65 per cent of the volume, where the vast majority of halal carcasses would go to the export markets, mainly to France:

Interviewer: What do you think about the development of the halal market? After all, according to what you have said, only 10 per cent is labelled halal. Is it an expanding market? Will it grow in your opinion?

Interviewee 2: I think that it will grow. The biggest issue that we have at the moment is oversupply, in the UK. As far as lamb goes there is an oversupply. As far as beef goes there is an undersupply – there is a shortage of cattle in the UK. We have an overcapacity for lamb and an undercapacity for beef. The export market for lambs is very difficult at the moment. As an industry we have lost a lot of money on lambs' skins as the Chinese do not want them anymore, the fashion of sheepskin boots seems to have gone – that was holding the price up a lot – like all fashions it does not last forever. There is an overstock of lambs' skins waiting to be processed in the Far East, which has forced the price back as much as £5 a head. So that has cost us and the farmers a considerable amount of money, not only that with the Euro uncertainty at the moment, that has pushed that up 6 cents in the last 12 months, that has had a massive effect as well. So our profit margin has been eaten away at both ends, on the raw material and the selling price. Because of that there are a lot of Spanish and Portuguese lambs in the French market at the moment, considerably cheaper than we can produce them for. So we are struggling to get our lambs into the French market at the moment.

The remaining two small abattoirs no longer supply the halal market on a regular basis because they experienced difficult business relationships with some of the customers (delay in payments). Clearly, small businesses, given the current low margins, cannot afford 'slaughtering animals and wasting carcasses' (interviewee 4) when the customers are not regular in their payments.

Halal meat market in the UK

The halal meat market is rapidly expanding because large retailing companies started to offer halal meat, as did fast-food restaurants and takeaway outlets. The big fast-food chains are now competing with the halal-only rivals such as Chicken Cottage and Perfect Fried Chicken, as a recent report from the Guardian has indicated, nowadays 'more than 100 KFC outlets around the country are currently running an open-ended trial with finger-lickin' halal. Pizza Express uses halal approved chicken, as do about one-fifth of Nando's 270-odd restaurants in Britain' (Henley, 2013). These new supply-chain actors require a formal certification that guarantees the halal quality of the meat that they sell. So in recent times a number of certifying bodies emerged in the UK that proposed various rules for halal slaughter, sometimes with considerable differences. It could also be said that, even if there is a growing number of halal-labelled foods in non-ethnic shops and restaurant, there are not many other types of information for Muslims about the ways in which they can identify halal meat derived from animals produced and consumed on a mass scale. In the case of halal meat, there are currently two ways of practising halal slaughter: 'It is this situation that has sparked strong competition between certifying bodies promoting different notions of "*authentic* halal"' (Lever and Miele, 2012, p. 2).[5] The abovementioned requirements for halal meat production can vary depending on the accepted method of slaughter defined by certifying bodies. At the time of the interviews the three large abattoirs in Wales were certified by the Halal Food Authority and the Halal Authority Board, which both allow stunning in sheep and poultry. While all three large abattoirs practise halal slaughter on all animals (lambs), they only sell a small portion of the carcasses as certified halal, as indicated in this interview excerpt:

Interviewee 2: As I said, export – some export customers require halal, particularly in France at certain times of the year. The UK supermarkets do not require halal, but it is there if they require it. With the UK trade, based on UK wholesalers, butchers and shops, only a small percentage – 30 per cent of our total kill – requires halal and they would be our ethnic customers, would specifically ask for halal.

Interviewer: But do you do all halal slaughter? All the lambs?

Interviewee 2: Everything is eligible for halal, head-only stun and cut to the throat.

Interviewer: Do you know roughly what percentage goes to the halal market, certified as halal?

Interviewee 2: As certified halal? Probably less than 10 per cent.

In the past, one abattoir was certified by the 'European Halal Development', which used to approve stunning. However, after a name change to European Halal Development Agency (EHDA),[6] this certifier began to support non-stun halal practices and the abattoir changed certifier, now they are certified by the newly constituted (March 2012) Halal Authority Board (HAB), which allows stunning.

The two small abattoirs do not have a certification by an accredited certifying body, they rely on a letter from the local imam, attesting that the slaughterman was a Muslim and that the procedures were acceptable for producing halal foods. The abattoir managers have stated that their knowledge of halal religious requirements is limited:

Interviewee 2: From our point of view, they will audit to ensure that we have a licensed Muslim slaughterman, and that we operate within the four (is it four?) pillars of the Koran (I am not 100 per cent on it) and that all those requirements are filled. I am more interested in animal welfare and hygiene standards.

It has been asserted by all the managers that it was important that the slaughterman was trusted by the local Muslim community and known in the local mosque. This view was true especially in the case of the small abattoirs that did not have a formal certification. The issue of trust has been raised in all cases, although large abattoirs saw the certification, whose cost ranges from £50,000 to over £100,000 per year (with considerable variation depending on number of animals certified) as tangible proof of genuine halal slaughter and as a means of enabling them to sell their products worldwide:

Interviewee 1: It was a big requirement for the French market, a lot of our export lambs go to France, and a lot of French customers want the halal stamp. Also they want some form of accreditation to say that your slaughter method meets their requirements.

On the other hand, for the two small abattoirs that did not hold a formal halal certificate, the personal knowledge and trust of their customers was sufficient to sell their products:

Interviewee 4:   We have never been required to provide a certificate. The customer only needs to know that the throats have been slit by a Muslim slaughterman. It has always been this way. Various certifying bodies approached us and asked us £1000 fee for a certificate, which we didn't want to pay. What for? If our customers never asked for it, because they trust us, then what is it for?

Interviewee 6:   We were always led to believe that such and such a person was prominent in this mosque, so everything was OK. I think that the person doing the cutting had a certain standing, but there was never any independent verification.

All abattoirs supply meat all year round although due to the life cycle of the ovine species there is a peak in production usually between July and December for British lambs. This is when lambs are at their best and abattoirs work at full capacity. During the early season, lambs are sold as spring lambs in the supermarkets. Seasonality is especially important for the organic market and so it also follows this pattern.

Interviewee 3:   Between now (June) and December, December, January, February sees a decline, April–May is the worst time and then we start climbing back up again in June.

Interviewee 2:   The lamb processing cycle is very short when you compare it to pigs and cattle. Pigs have large litters and they can breed all year round, they are indoors so there is a constant supply. Cattle are a long time maturing animal, they can be three years old before they are brought into slaughter, so there is that constant feed of cattle. Lambs are all born at certain times of the year depending on what part of the country they are from and it sweeps up, as the weather gets better. They also mature very quickly as well, so a 12-month-old lamb is a totally different eating quality animal to a 5-month-old lamb, so there is a very short window in which to process.

One abattoir imports New Zealand lambs from Christmas to July to meet a demand for a domestic and export market although the number of slaughtered animals would be three times lower than in the British season. In addition, seasonality of production in these abattoirs follows a demand for lambs around Ramadan (a month in which Muslims fast during the day) and a festival named Eid Qurbani/ Eid al Adha ('Festival of Sacrifice', also referred to as Eid, which takes place approximately two months and ten days after the month of Ramadan). The Islamic calendar is lunar, therefore Ramadan followed by Eid Qurbani migrates through the seasons. In 2012 the month of Ramadan started on 20 July and Eid Qurbani took place on 26 October. During Ramadan, Muslims fast during the day and eat after the sunset (*Iftar*).

There might be some preferences toward the types of meat being consumed, for example one abattoir supplies the French market with:

Interviewee 1: Male lambs with testicles intact.[7] France in particular would be looking for a lot of lambs around Ramadan. They would buy a lot of male lambs with testicles intact – we would leave the testicles on the carcass and sell the whole carcass. There would be a big flush for two, three days before then, any festival it really ramps up.

Eid Qurbani/Eid al Adha is an important festival during which Muslims commemorate the willingness of Abraham to sacrifice his son Isaac as an act of obedience to God, before God intervened to provide him with a sheep to sacrifice instead. Depending on the region of the world, cattle, goats, camels and sheep can be slaughtered in large numbers. In the UK, Eblex reports that the vast majority of Muslim consumers purchase and eat more meat during this time (2010, p. 14).

The Eid festival boosts the number of sheep slaughtered in the Welsh abattoirs visited, even in those that no longer supply the halal market on a regular basis. In those cases, often, a few individual customers order lambs. Export sales of large abattoirs go up around this time. The abattoir managers could not estimate the exact numbers.

The majority of slaughterhouses in Wales practising halal slaughter supply domestic and export markets, with only two exceptions. Out of seven companies, five supply both markets where a large percentage of operations would be directed for export.

The other two companies, currently, do not sell to the export market, although one of them has plans to move into the New Zealand market, considering that it is owned by a person from New Zealand.

In general, large abattoirs have a capacity to supply all major British retailers, wholesalers and butchers, whereas small abattoirs mainly supply wholesalers, few butcher shops and some of their own shops. In terms of halal supply, it has to be noted that because certain slaughterhouses use the same method of slaughter for all animals, some abattoir managers could not point out exactly how much of their operations would supply the halal market. Keeping the seasonality of production (Eid) in mind, the patterns of supply vary, as one manager put it: 'Some times of the year it can be that up to 80 per cent of our kill will be required [to be halal]'.

Some abattoirs have supplied to the domestic halal market since the beginning of their operations. In many cases abattoirs have been carrying out halal slaughter (with stun) since the 1980s to meet a demand from local Muslim communities. In one case the owner was Muslim, although in all other cases abattoirs were run by Welsh individuals or families who reoriented their operations toward an 'ethnic' market. Moving to the halal market was not problematic for larger abattoirs as they had a capacity to meet the demand and, in turn, secure a sound business relationship with customers both in the UK and abroad (large retailers). In the case of smaller abattoirs this is a problematic area and there are some barriers to entry to these markets.

In the UK, especially in England, where the Muslim population is larger than in Wales, the halal market and its suppliers are well established and prominent. As the slaughterhouse managers explained, entering a saturated market is a risk, which might yield little return. Apart from one abattoir, which has been supplying Birmingham, Manchester and Sheffield for decades, others have directed their operation towards the export market.

In terms of volume the exact numbers are unknown; however, one manager has declared that 10 per cent of the 30 per cent of lambs sold to small butchers and wholesalers is sold as halal.

From the interviews it emerged that the volume of halal meat sold in Wales is very low. One small abattoir sells 60 lambs a week to halal butchers in South Wales. Table 15.6 provides information about the geographical spread of customers.

The sheep export market continues to grow despite the economic crisis in the Eurozone (Eblex, 2012, p. 5). Eblex further informs that shipments to France were up 4 per cent on the year, and continued to account for over 60 per cent of all exports (2012, p. 5). The growth of the German market was also significant, an 11 per cent increase on the figure from the previous year, as shown in the same report. Also the Irish and Belgian markets show an expansion. Interestingly, also exports outside Europe – to Vietnam and Hong Kong – increased significantly. The relevance of the French market for halal meat was already pointed out in several studies (see for example Zivotofsky et al., 2009, p. 35) given that France has the largest percentage of Muslims among EU countries and Islam is France's second religion (10 per cent) behind Catholicism (85 per cent). Data from 2008 show that 4.2 million lambs and 634,000 ewes were slaughtered that year in the country. After the British, the French are second in Europe for the consumption of lamb and mutton (ibid.). And this is confirmed by the interviews with the managers of slaughterhouses in Wales. Therefore it is not surprising that four out of seven interviewed abattoirs in Wales export halal lambs mainly to France. Out

TABLE 15.6 Domestic halal market supply.

	Type of customer	Destination
Large abattoirs	Wholesalers, butcher shops, individuals	M4 corridor, Birmingham, Sheffield, Manchester, and across the UK
Small abattoirs	Butcher shops, individuals	Swansea, Cardiff

Source: interviews.

of these, three abattoirs were large and only one family business exports solely to France. In terms of volume, the halal export market in Welsh abattoirs varied from 10,000 to 30,000 lambs per week. The French market would take up a majority of the export, in one case up to 70 per cent. For the small abattoir, the French Halal market constituted 65 per cent of all operations.

Conclusions

'The future is bright', according to the President of the HFA. But is it? And, for whom?

A report by Pew Centre Research (2011) argued that the global Muslim population is now 1.8 billion and rising fast, and it predicted that Muslims will account for 30 per cent of the world's population by 2025. About 50 per cent of Muslims are under 25 years old and as many are becoming more affluent they engage with new technologies and are interested in brands and fashion, which make them a very interesting segment of the global market.

A report from the market research firm Dinar Standard found that the global halal food and lifestyle market, worth $1.62 trillion in 2012, is set to grow to $2.47 trillion by 2018 (Power, 2014). Lever et al. have argued that the global halal food market is worth around $547 billion and the European market around $77 billion a year (Lever et al., 2010, p. 1). Europe has seen a rise in the demand for halal food due to a growing number of Muslim immigrants and increased consumption of meat characteristic of vertical mobility among second and third generations of Muslims (Bergeaud-Blackler, 2007; Bonne and Verbeke, 2007; Lever and Miele, 2012).

According to Henley (2013), traditionally, halal has been a difficult market for major supermarkets in the UK, partly because of its scattered nature and partly because there is no single halal cuisine. In the UK, consumers looking for halal products might come from Pakistan, Turkey, the Middle East, North Africa, Bangladesh or India. But all the main supermarkets, including Sainsbury's, Tesco and Morrisons, now sell ranges of halal products at selected stores. Boots sells halal baby food. The World Halal Forum estimates sales of all types of halal food combined totalled £2.6bn in Britain in 2011. And Britain's Muslim population is growing: in the 2001 census, 3 per cent of the population of England and Wales – 1.5 million people – said they were Muslims. In the 2011 census, the corresponding figures were nearly 5 per cent, or 2.7 million people. The Pew Foundation has estimated Britain's Muslim community will continue to expand, to 8.2 per cent of the population, or around 5.6 million people, by 2030. Moreover, a survey by Eblex, the organisation for the British beef and sheep industry, found that 90 per cent of Muslims eat halal meat, and Muslims eat proportionately more fresh meat than the rest of the population, accounting for up to 15 per cent of UK meat sales. In response to this trend there has been a significant growth in the offer of goods and services aimed at Muslims. However, Britain has been slow to tap into this new consumer trend, and other countries are addressing Muslim desires and new purchasing power in the market:

> Malaysia has become the leader in halal certification and in promoting the global halal industry. Each year Kuala Lumpur hosts World Halal Week, bringing together a remarkable array of Islamic scholars, scientists, producers of halal products and services and big multinational companies. Malaysia is also home to the first international university to teach Islamic finance.
>
> (BBC Radio 4, 26 August 2012)

Current trends in the halal meat market in the UK

In the UK the halal market is of significant size and growing. Mintel's Halal Food UK report (2002) showed that in 2001 halal meat had an 11 per cent share of all meat sales in the UK, despite the fact that Muslims accounted for only 3 per cent of the population. The same report estimated the size of the fresh halal meat market, frozen and convenience food at £460 million, and with the addition of halal takeaway and restaurant food it reached a market value of around £700 million in 2001 (Mintel, 2002). The same report also suggested that the halal market would expand significantly in the coming years. This report identified several causes for this trend: a diverse background and profile of the consumers (Muslim and non-Muslims going to ethnic restaurants), the fragmented supply, the lack of a common halal standard, wider consumer trends, and the entrance of big brands and manufactures into the halal market and their marketing strategies. Furthermore, it was suggested that second and third generations of Muslims would follow wider consumer and shopping trends: cooking less from scratch on a daily basis but eating out more or buying ready-made meals in supermarkets rather than fresh meat in ethnic shops. This forecast proved to be correct and, nowadays, it can be observed that a number of fast-food outlets such as McDonald's, KFC, Subway and major supermarkets (ASDA, Tesco) are entering the halal market and they are broadening the range of halal food that they offer, including ready-meals and processed foods (Mintel, 2002; Lever and Miele, 2012, p. 4).

Nearly a decade after the Mintel report, Lever et al. (2010) pointed to a significant growth of the UK's halal market – from 10 per cent to 30 per cent – in 2008 alone. Eblex, in *Halal Meat Market: Specialist Supply Chain Structures and Consumer Purchase and Consumption Profiles in England*, reports that in 2009 Muslims were consuming 20 per cent of all the lamb sold in England and they were increasing their consumption of beef (Eblex, 2010, p. 1).

This unprecedented growth might not be explained solely by looking at the size of the Muslim population, although the number of Muslim immigrants shows the fastest growth rate in the UK (Kerbaj, in Lever and Miele, 2012). A contributing factor is the growing number of non-Muslim consumers of halal meat, mostly due to the growth in the number of ethnic restaurants and the way in which the catering system (both public and private) works, buying all halal products in order to be able to say that 'halal' food is available. However, in the last 10 years this fast-growing market for halal food raised concerns among some Muslims about the 'authenticity' of the 'halal' claim, especially for halal meat (Lever and Miele, 2012). In 2002 Mintel estimated that 70–80 per cent of all halal meat in the UK was 'fake', whereas another survey revealed 'shocking' kebabs containing pork (BBC, 2009). The main debate on 'authenticity' of halal meat relates to practices of stunning before animal slaughter, because there is no agreement on a common 'halal slaughter standard'. An animated debate has taken place among all groups/stakeholders involved – Muslims, non-Muslims, animal welfare and animal rights' NGOs, and policymakers (see Miele, 2009). While one group regarded animal slaughter without stunning as 'authentic' and 'traditional halal' (the Halal Monitoring Committee; see Lever and Miele, 2012, p. 4), the other groups (such as the Farm Animal Welfare Committee, the BVA, and several NGOs) express concerns for animal welfare. Further complications arise due to the way in which the meat supply chains work and channel into the conventional market all those parts of the halal animals' carcasses that are not sold as halal. This is not causing real problems in the case of animals that have been stunned prior to the cut of the throat. However, the same happens to the carcasses of animals that are not stunned prior to the throat cut, and this led to a request by the main animal welfare organisations to identify these products by means of a label saying that they were obtained by animals 'non-stunned' before slaughter (see Miele, 2009). This issue has led the European Commission to explore the possibility of labelling meat in order to enable consumers to identify the meat that originates from non-stunned animals.

Additionally, a debate on stunned-halal versus non-stunned halal is very prominent and controversial among the halal certifying bodies. These two positions allow a segmentation of the halal market in the UK (Lever and Miele, 2012; Miele et al., 2005). Such a situation opens up a space for supplying to two halal markets, which is evident in a few retailing company's strategies nowadays:

> The supermarket chains ASDA and Tesco first started selling halal meat from pre-stunned animals in 2000; from 2007 to 2010 respectively they have also sold meat from non-stunned animals in a number of in-store halal butchers and specialist world food outlets.
>
> (Lever and Miele, 2012, p. 4)

There are many concerns about how to ensure a credible halal certification and how to reach these expanding markets (both domestic and export) but there is a paucity of studies about the relevance of the stunning/non-stunning in halal slaughter for this increasingly diverse British Muslim population, as well as the even more diverse global market. Henley (2013) has pointed out the lack of choice for the Muslim foodies or 'haloodies' who seem more interested in the lack of halal 'fine dining' options (where absence of pork and alcohol or other forbidden ingredients is guaranteed) or organic certification than in debates about technologies of stunning. And there are interesting trends that would suggest how the future development of the halal food market will be based on quality segmentation – organic-halal, sustainable-halal, convenience-halal (see for example Henley, 2013) – where other aspects of the farming system and processing techniques will be equally if not more relevant than the controversy around stunning. The expansion of the halal meat market seems to be linked to a growing acceptability of the practices of stunning and the big wholesalers are only offering halal meat from animals that have been stunned: DB Foods in Poole, Dorset, which recently opened a dedicated halal warehouse and is launching a new online home delivery business, Halal To Door, has seen halal meat sales grow from 1–2 per cent of its business to 9–10 per cent in recent years, spurred by demand from large food service companies supplying institutions such as schools, hospitals and airlines. The company spokesperson, whose halal meat is certified by the HFA, says he 'would not dream of touching' any meat that had not been pre-stunned.

> As a company, we're animal welfare-approved ... We would never compromise our business by handling meat from animals that had not been stunned before their throats were cut. But the point is, consumers need to know that. They have to know what they're getting. It needs to be clear.
>
> (Henley, 2013)

In Wales there is great potential especially in the market for lambs (most slaughterhouses have a much higher capacity than the current number of animals processed) but there is an issue of price and an unfavourable exchange rate (strong sterling pound). The interviews with the slaughterhouse managers have confirmed the general trends already identified by the Food Standards Agency 2008 report 'The future of abattoirs' (Palmer, 2008), which indicated that the decline in the number of animals reared in the UK would have led to a process of concentration of slaughterhouses and to a persistent overcapacity of the larger abattoirs which can only be run profitably at certain levels of throughput:

> Abattoir profitability has come under even greater pressure than in previous years from a combination of lower fifth quarter returns, higher costs of by-product disposal and the sourcing policies of the multiple retailers that have used their market power to control margins. The abattoir sector has become more concentrated. In 2006 the 10 largest companies slaughtering cattle, sheep and pigs respectively, accounted for 57%, 53% and 75% of total slaughtering for each of those species. By 2006 the number of operational abattoirs had fallen to 285, slaughtering about 5.3 million ELU, an average closure rate of about 21 plants a year.
>
> (Palmer, 2008, p.A2)

This report already pointed to the raise in the ethnic market (halal) and predicted that the scenario for 2010–2015 could therefore be one with 200–220 abattoirs with: a top tier of 40–50 large integrated operations controlled by 15–20 companies; a second tier of 60–70 medium/large independent abattoirs with a significant group looking to service the export/ethnic trade for sheep; some 100 or so 'artisanal' abattoirs with a better geographical spread to cater for local niche needs.

Our current study of the abattoirs in Wales has confirmed the rapid decline in the number of abattoirs and it underlined the difficulties in tapping into this growing halal meat market: a number of conventional operators are not aware that halal slaughter can be performed with stunning and are not interested in exploring this market. For small operators, already practising halal slaughter, the main issues are about establishing reliable business relationships with a number of partners both at national level and, more significantly, for the export market. Large operators have a much higher capacity of the current level of sales of certified halal carcasses of lambs/sheep. This is not a new trend and it was already identified by the FSA report (Palmer, 2008). The main issues are the current high prices of UK/Welsh lamb (due to the difficulties of selling the sheepskins and the competition from Spain and other EU producers) even in a context of oversupply. It is worth noting that even the large companies export to a limited number of countries and they do not reach the large markets in Asia.

A further complicating factor is the vagary of the current situation in which there are two ways of carrying out halal slaughter (with and without stunning), and the growing number of halal certifying bodies that promote different halal standards and compete on defining the 'authentic' halal slaughter practice. The discussion around a common halal standard is very difficult and it does not seem to be on the political agenda in the UK. This is actually causing a lack of transparency in the halal meat market in the UK/Wales and it might be a limiting factor for the expansion of the export towards East Asia and other growing markets.

The slaughterhouses in Wales remain in a fragile position even in a context of an expanding halal meat market. Concerns about animal welfare for the practices of stunning, financial issues and limited technological innovations are the emerging factors leading to this uncertainty and fragility in the market.

The focus on the controversy about stunning in halal practices is connected with a neglect of the broader set of concerns emerging from Muslim consumers, in the UK as well as worldwide: concerns about quality, about animal welfare, about environmental sustainability. It is interesting to see how this controversy about stunning methods is prominent and it is overshadowing all these emerging trends. Elsewhere, Lever and Miele (2012) have pointed out the active role of the halal certifying bodies in the UK to segment the halal meat market and for promoting 'non-stunned' halal as more authentic, but there is not indication that British Muslim consumers share this idea. For example there is so little debate about technological innovation and new stunning methods that would be acceptable even for the most traditional halal certifying bodies as well as Shechita boards for the production of kosher meat (see Miele, 2014). And given the scale of the demand for halal meat, it is surprising that there is so little attention or investment in this area of research. The recent call for a ban of 'non-stun' religious slaughter in the UK by the BVA (British Veterinary Association) does not seem to acknowledge the great progress made in terms of the acceptability of stunning methods by the British Muslim population, and it might only lead to a radicalization of anti-scientific reactions for a perceived islamophobia and antisemitism underpinning these positions, while an analysis of current market trends would suggest that investments in technological innovations and market transparency could be more effective means to change and improve the practices of religious slaughter.

Notes

1 In the UK as well there is a growing movement led by influential NGOs and the BVA for a ban on non-stun slaughter.
2 The derogation from stunning for religious slaughter is accepted/practised in all other EU countries; however, Germany imposes a strict control on the number of animals slaughtered without stunning, and it allows it only when the carcasses are destined to a local Muslim/Jewish community. In other countries religious slaughter without stunning is practised also for the export market (e.g. Ireland and Netherlands).
3 There is growing pressure from a minority of more radical certifying bodies in the UK to promote 'non-stunned' halal meat as more 'authentic' and traditional, e.g. the Halal Monitoring Committee. They claim that Muslim consumers are not correctly informed that other certifying bodies allow the practice of stunning for halal slaughter.
4 Apart from lambs under organic or Freedom Foods schemes.
5 In the UK the main certifying body is the HFA (Halal Food Authority). They accept stunning prior to the cut of the throat of the animals. The most important Halal certifying body that does not allow stunning before the cut of the throat of the animals is the HMC (Halal Monitoring Committee). The Halal Food Authority (HFA) currently certifies 12 abattoirs in the UK, three of which are in Wales. In all certified plants animals are stunned. There are in total five poultry slaughterhouses (zero in Wales); seven ovine slaughterhouses (three in Wales). The Halal Monitoring Committee (HMC), which requires the non-stunning of animals at the time of killing, currently certifies six poultry slaughterhouses (zero in Wales); five ovine slaughterhouses of which two also slaughter cattle (zero in Wales).
6 See www.ehda.co.uk.
7 Interestingly, HMC informs that testicles are Haram: www.Halalhmc.org/DefintionOfHalal.htm#Organs. Although the HMC does not certify this particular abattoir, it is just interesting to see the differences in what is considered Halal and what is not.

References

Anil, M. H. (2012) 'Religious slaughter: A current controversial animal welfare issue', *Animal Frontiers*, 2, pp. 64–67

Anil, H., Miele, M., Luy, J., Holleben K. von, Bergeaud-Beckler, F. and Velarde, A. (2009) *Religious Rules and Requirements – Halal Slaughter*, Dialrel report, Cardiff: School of Planning and Geography, Available at www.dialrel.eu/images/Halal-rules.pdf

Avasthy, D. (2014) 'Denmark bans ritual "halal" and "kosher" slaughter, stirs up animal vs religious rights debate', *International Business Times*, 22 February, www.ibtimes.co.uk/denmark-bans-ritual-halal-kosher-slaughter-stirs-animal-vs-religious-rights-debate-1437517, accessed 10 November 2014

BBC (2009) 'Study reveals "shocking" kebabs', *BBC News*, http://news.bbc.co.uk/1/hi/uk/7852168.stm, accessed 20 August 2014.

BBC (2012) 'Abattoir job loss concern of Caernarfon mayor', *BBC News*, www.bbc.co.uk/news/uk-wales-18025877, accessed 20 August 2014.

BBC Radio 4 (2012) 'The future is halal', *BBC Radio 4*, www.bbc.co.uk/programmes/ b01m0pq2, accessed 26 August 2014

Bergeaud-Blackler, F. (2004) 'Social definitions of halal quality: The case of Maghrebi muslims in France', in M. Harvey, A. McMeekin and A. Warde (eds), *Qualities of Food*, Manchester University Press, Manchester

Bergeaud-Blackler, F., (2007) 'New challenges for Islamic ritual slaughter: A European perspective', *Journal of Ethnic and Migration Studies*, vol 33, no 6, pp. 965–980

Bergeaud-Blackler, F., Zivotofsky, Z. A. and Miele, M. (2013) 'Knowledge and attitudes of the European kosher consumers as revealed through focus groups', *Society & Animals*, vol 21, no 5, pp. 425–442

Bonne, K. and Verbeke, W., (2007) 'Religious values informing halal meat production and the control and delivery of halal credence quality', *Agriculture and Human Values*, vol 25, pp. 35–47

Council Regulation (EC) No 1099/2009 of 24 September 2009, 18.11.2009 *Official Journal of the European Union* L 303/1 E, http://eurlex.europa.eu/LexUriServ/LexUriServ.do?u ri=OJ:L:2009:303:0001:0030:EN:PDF

DEFRA (2012) *Guidance Slaughter of Livestock: Welfare Regulations*, available at https://www. gov.uk/farm-animal-welfare-at-slaughter

Eblex (2010) *The Halal Meat Market*, www.eblex.org.uk/documents/content/ publications/p_cp_eblex_Halal_meat_final_111110.pdf

Eblex (2012) *Sheep Outlook May 2012*, www.eblex.org.uk/documents/content/ publications/p_smo_may_2012.pdf

EC Regulation No 853/2004 of the European Parliament and of the Council of 29 April 2004, 30.4.2004 *Official Journal of the European Union* L 139/55, http://eur-lex.europa. eu/LexUriServ/LexUriServ.do?uri=OJ:L:2004:139:0055:0205:EN:PDF

Evans, A. and Miele, M. (2012) 'Between food and flesh: How animals are made to matter (and not to matter) within food consumption practices' *Environment and Planning D-Society and Space*, vol 30, no 2, pp.298–314

FSA (2012a) *Approved Red, Poultry, and Game Meat Establishments*, www.food.gov.uk/ enforcement/sectorrules/meatplantsprems/meatpremlicence#.UJjoVbQxrnY

FSA (2012b) Results of the 2011 FSA animal welfare survey in Great Britain, published on 22 May 2012, www.food.gov.uk/sites/default/files/multimedia/pdfs/board/fsa120508. pdf, accessed 30 March 2015

Henley, J. (2013) 'Halal food: A market waiting to be tapped into?', *Guardian*, 25 September, www.theguardian.com/lifeandstyle/2013/sep/25/halal-food-why-hard-find-britain, accessed 25 September 2013

Lever, J. and Miele, M. (2012) 'The development of the Halal meat market in Europe: An exploration of the supply side theory of religion', *Journal of Rural Studies*, vol 28, no 4, pp. 528–537

Lever, J., Puig de la Bellacasa, M., Miele, M. and Higgin, M. (2010) *From the Slaughterhouse to the Consumer: Transparency and Information in the Distribution of Halal and Kosher Meat*, Dialrel Report, School of City and Regional Planning, Cardiff

Lowther, E. (2012) 'MPs want curbs on "unacceptable" religious slaughter', BBC News, www.bbc.co.uk/news/uk-politics-18187137, accessed 28 May 2012

Miele, M. (2009) 'Meat for a ritual', *New Scientist*, 204, pp. 35–36.

Miele, M. (2014) 'We already have the answer to humane religious slaughter', *The Conversation*, 18 March, http://theconversation.com/we-already-have-the-answers-to-humane-religious-slaughter-24428#comment_348246

Miele, M., Murdoch, J. and Roe, E. (2005) 'Animals and ambivalence, governing farm animal welfare in the European food sector' in Higgins, V. and Lawrence, G. (eds), *Agricultural Governance*, Routledge, Oxon, pp. 169–185

Miele, M. Rucinska, K. and Anil, H. (2013) *Halal Slaughter Practices in Wales*, end of project report for the Welsh Government, Cardiff University

Mintel (2002) *Halal Foods UK*, www.mintel.co.uk, accessed November 2012

Palmer, C.M. (2008) The future of abattoirs, annex to: Calvert, R., McGrath, S. and Hewson, P., *Future Delivery of Official Controls in Approved Premises*, FSA 14840.

Power, C. (2014) 'Ethical, organic, safe: The other side of halal food', *The Guardian*, 18 May, www.theguardian.com/lifeandstyle/2014/may/18/halal-food-uk-ethical-organic-safe

Velarde, A., Rodriguez, P., Dalmau, A., Fuentes, C., Llonch, P., von Holleben, K. V., Anil, M. H., Lambooij, J. B., Pleiter, H., Yesildere, T. and Cenci-Goga, B. T. (2014) 'Religious slaughter: Evaluation of current practices in selected countries', *Meat Science*, vol 96, no 1, 278–287.

Zivotofsky, A. Z., Anil, H. and Luy, J. (2009) *Judaism, Religious Rules and Requirements in Regard to Treatment and Slaughter of Animals*, Dialrel Factsheet, www.dialrel.eu/images/judaism-rules.pdf

16

ROUNDTABLE GOVERNANCE AND THE GREENING OF THE GLOBAL BEEF INDUSTRY

Lessons from the Roundtable on Sustainable Palm Oil

Adrienne Johnson

Introduction

This chapter presents an examination into the emergence of the 'green economy' and how this discursive regime is contributing to the popular rise of 'roundtables' – industry-led governing tools that are increasingly relied upon to manage and control the production of environmental resources. Lauded by the United Nations Environment Programme's (UNEP) Green Economy and Finance Initiatives, roundtables are significantly transforming the way human-environment relations are governed, resulting in uneven and unequal effects. On the one hand, more actors (especially marginalized ones) are presented with opportunities to become involved in decision-making processes, which theoretically yield more transparent, legitimate, and inclusive production decisions. On the other hand, through their industry-dominated nature, roundtables grant corporations far-reaching powers, shaping them into the ultimate authorities in the production, processing, and distribution of environmental resources. Roundtable governing arrangements have emerged in many commodity sectors involving palm oil, cotton, cacao, biomaterials, and most recently beef production. In this chapter, I compare the emergence and functioning of two roundtable arrangements: the well-established Roundtable on Sustainable Palm Oil (RSPO) and the up-and-coming Global Roundtable on Sustainable Beef (GRSB). I will use the more established RSPO as a lens through which the GRSB can be analyzed. This chapter analyzes the power relations within these fora, the actual principles and criteria and their effects, and finally, roundtable management approaches to the growing geographical presence of agricultural and livestock disease to demonstrate the creeping authority of capitalist roundtables in the governing futures of environmental resource production. The chapter argues that through roundtable governance initiatives, commercial actors appear to have become more accountable, transparent, and inclusive in their governing actions, but much of this appears to be symbolic; in many cases roundtable governance often reinforces power inequalities and unsustainable practices inherent to related capitalist industries. It is speculated that the GRSB and beef production may follow the same fate of the RSPO if some lessons are not properly gleaned from the RSPO experience.

The rise of the 'green economy'

In 2008, UNEP launched an initiative to build pathways to 'sustainable development' and poverty eradication through economic means. Known as the Green Economy Initiative, this project strives to promote the investment and growth of 'green' sectors while also promoting the 'greening' of environmentally unfriendly sectors. Working from the understanding that a green economy 'is one that results in improved well-being and social equity while significantly reducing environmental risks and ecological scarcities' (UNEP, 2014), the Green Economy Initiative anchors its transformative potential in the 'right' investment of capital in efforts that support green technologies, financial assets, agriculture and ecosystem protection, and land and water conservation. Overall, the Green Economy concept pushes for a world where economic growth can continue to expand but without the detrimental effects of pollution, environmental degradation, and persisting social inequality. Illustrating this new conceptualization of green growth is a report UNEP published in 2011 called *Towards a Green Economy: Pathways to Sustainable Development and Poverty Eradication*. This document provides a roadmap as to which sectors are most appropriate for companies, government and individuals to invest in. The report, which focuses on sectors such as agriculture, water, forests, manufacturing, waste, and finance details just how a transition to a 'green economy' might occur and pushes for policy reform and public-private partnerships to facilitate this transition.

Although UNEP's Green Economy Initiative is quite new, the idea of an economy that can achieve high profits, social inclusion, and, importantly, environmental sustainability is not. In fact, the idea first emerged through rhetoric surrounding sustainable development in the early 1990s and has since gained acceptance as a mainstream approach to environment–society issues in government and policy circles. The UN's notion of an economy that is 'green' is different from the typical green economy (which is defined by simply applying green requirements to the economy) or sustainable development. The UN notion is a more holistic approach where the shift towards more green ways of production is seen as possible through investments, both public and private, in innovation, technology, infrastructure and institutions so that economies shift their course or achieve fundamental structural change. Specifically, four key differences between the UN's green economy and previous versions can be identified: first, technology plays a large part in the UN's agenda to bring financial benefits and well-being to populations. Second, green investment is seen as a solution to economic crisis in that it will create jobs. This is where UNEP's support for roundtable governance is relevant. UNEP holds that green investment is one that is socially and environmentally responsible and as such, the organization has encouraged its international network of investor companies to participate in RSPO activities and follow its principles as well as other guidelines as established by similar roundtable arrangements (UNEP, 2014). Demonstrating the UN's commitment to spreading the ideals of the RSPO, in July 2014, the RSPO was granted 'special consultative status' within the United Nations Economic and Social Council which oversees issues related to national economic and social development (RSPO, 2014). In this role, the RSPO will increasingly participate in the work of the UN council and associated member states. Third, more power and authority are bestowed upon corporate entities in decision-making and governing resources. Finally, the idea of 'partnerships', particularly between transnational civil society actors and corporations, which was all but a novel idea in the 1990s, is now seen as the 'correct' way of managing agriculture and resources and this represents a major transformation in how authority is being shaped.

Through the implementation of the Green Economy Initiative and associated discourses, we are witnessing a set of major discursive and material shifts that have significant impacts for the future of environmental governance. First, we are seeing an alignment of logics that normalize certain understandings of the environment to dominate over others. In this case, nonhuman domains are increasingly being demarcated as fields for profit-generation through corporate management and control. Second, we are witnessing an enactment of these logics which sanction certain international actors (namely companies with the support of NGOs) as the top authorities in governing global commodity chains and human–environmental relations as a whole. Illustrating the green economy 'idea' in action is the emergence of 'green' roundtable initiatives that support the dual achievement of green profits and environmental sustainability.

Roundtables and the emergence of global private resource governance

'Roundtables' are fast emerging as important actors in governing agriculture, fisheries, and livestock sectors and they are outcomes of a wider trend in the neoliberalization of resource governance. Although newer examinations of neoliberalism's effects on the environment tend to emphasize its variegated patterns and often uneven processes (see Peck et al., 2010, for example), authors such as McCarthy and Prudham (2004) point to neoliberalism's consistent material practices and outcomes that characterize its uneven geographies (see also Bridge and Perreault, 2009). Along with its privatizing and commodifying tendencies, neoliberal governance projects feature the 'rolling back' of state functions and the 'rolling out' (Peck and Tickell, 2002) of new market-based regulatory frameworks through which social provisioning and environmental regulation gradually fall under the control of non-state actors such as NGOs and corporations. These new assemblages of authority are located in the global economy and are fixated on governing environmental sectors that have importance to international commodity networks. Recent scholarship has highlighted the significant role these actors play in shaping agendas, influencing policies in governance circles, and generally influencing the direction of discussion in international environmental affairs (Bulkeley and Mol, 2003; Lemos and Agrawal, 2006; Biermann and Pattberg, 2008). Another trend related to the neoliberalization of environmental resource sectors is the emergence of transnational 'push back' (Peck and Tickell, 2002; Falkner, 2003) directed towards corporations by activists and social movements (see McCarthy, 2004; Sawyer, 2004; Perreault, 2006, 2008; Bakker, 2007; Valdivia, 2008; McAfee and Shapiro, 2010 for examples). 'Sounding the alarm' on the destructive social and environmental actions of companies in community spaces, these actors have drawn global attention to the environmental injustices such as water contamination, privatization of common resources, and land-grabbing and have forced many organizations to make efforts to 'clean up' their acts.

The rise of new actors in environmental decision-making coupled with the growing transnational pressures against the destructive behaviors of corporate entities is the context in which voluntary environmental standards and codes of conduct emerge. Examples of current initiatives include, the International Organization for Standardization (ISO) guidelines (Clapp, 1998), and the Forest Stewardship Council (FSC) and Marine Stewardship Council (MSC) certification measures (Cummins, 2004; Cashore et al., 2005; Pattberg, 2005; Gulbrandsen, 2009; Klooster, 2010). Newer roundtable arrangements include the Roundtable on Sustainable Biomaterials (formally 'Biofuels'), Roundtable on Sustainable Soy, and the Roundtable on Sustainable Cacao. These initiatives are a means of governing a global supply chain in such a way that consumers (including retailers) are satisfied that the product was grown, fished or supplied according to some mutually agreed standards for 'sustainability'. McDonald's, for example, buys all of its fish from sources certified by the Marine Stewardship Council and has committed to using only RSPO-certified palm oil by 2015 and GRSB-certified beef by 2016.

Theoretically, roundtable governance outcomes are established in a manner that purportedly shapes a more equal playing field for conventionally marginalized actors like local farmers to negotiate and discuss with larger corporate powers. To many, the term 'roundtable' invokes the idea that all actors play an 'equal' role in making important decisions concerning the expansion and standards of involved sectors. Over the course of a typical roundtable meeting, various attendees are invited to participate in discussions and negotiations in order to establish or modify standards. These standards are the rules which govern all of the industry's actors. As some have argued, governance mechanisms such as roundtables and their associated meetings can be interpreted through the lens of governmentality (Djama et al., 2011; Johnson, 2014) in that they dictate 'the conduct of conduct' (Foucault, 1991) of involved actors, ultimately structuring the possible field of action so that negotiations and deliberations lead to predictable outcomes. This has major implications for environmental governance as roundtable arrangements are managed by corporate entities who favor capitalist, market-based production systems and who ultimately shape meeting activities so that capitalist outcomes are guaranteed.

Roundtables in context

The Roundtable on Sustainable Palm Oil (RSPO) was established in 2004 as part of an initiative set up by Unilever and the World Wildlife Fund (WWF). In the early 2000s, the WWF took great interest in improving the governance patterns of the palm oil industry since its largely negative effects of deforestation, loss of biodiversity, and land conflicts were increasingly being made public. Palm oil is an extremely common vegetable oil that is used in the production of processed foods, make-up, cleaning products, and biofuels (rainforest-rescue. org, 2014). According to Rainforest Rescue, 54 million tons of palm oil was produced in 2011, making it a versatile, low-cost, and essential ingredient. With the continuation of current consumption trends, it is estimated that palm oil production will jump to 70 million tons by 2025 (Kongsager and Reenberg, 2012). About 85 percent of the world's palm oil palm comes from Indonesia and Malaysia but global demand is driving the expansion of the palm oil frontier in African and Latin American countries. Intensified production is also augmenting social and environmental problems, therefore, many countries are looking towards the RSPO and its certification as a way to forge sustainable production pathways. The overall aim of the multi-stakeholder initiative is to advance global production standards that monitor and evaluate the economic, environmental, and social impacts of large-scale palm oil production. This is achieved through the method of stakeholder involvement in consultation activities at the national and international level. The RSPO is a members-only international non-profit organization composed of various global actors. The general assembly includes palm oil producers, buyers, processors and extractors, manufacturers, social and environmental NGOs, retailers, and banks/investors – all of whom are considered either ordinary members (with voting rights) or affiliate members (without voting rights) (see Figure 16.1 of the RSPO structure).

The RSPO board of governors, an elected body, oversees the functioning of the roundtable. Additionally, there is a secretariat which acts as the administrative branch of the RSPO as well as several working groups who investigate issues of relevance to palm oil governance. The RSPO is guided by the 'Principles & Criteria' (P&Cs) of the RSPO – a set of eight principles which lay out the official guidelines of certification (see Box 16.1 showing the RSPO's eight principles). Once a country decides that it would like to establish a national RSPO certification program, it initiates its own national interpretation of the P&Cs. Many of the findings in this chapter that are related to the RSPO are gleaned from Ecuador's national interpretation process that took place in 2013.

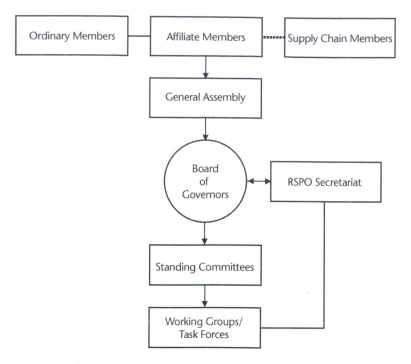

FIGURE 16.1 The RSPO structure.

Source: adapted from www.rspo.org/en/who_is_rspo

Box 16.1 The RSPO's eight principles

1 Commitment to transparency
2 Compliance with applicable laws and regulations
3 Commitment to long-term economic and financial viability
4 Use of appropriate practices by growers and millers
5 Environmental responsibility and conservation of natural resources and biodiversity
6 Responsible consideration of employees, and of individuals and communities affected by growers and mills
7 Responsible development of new plantings
8 Commitment to continuous improvement in key areas of activity

Source: '8 Principles for growers to be RSPO certified', www.rspo.org/en/who_is_rspo

The Global Roundtable on Sustainable Beef is a much newer governance regime which operates with a structure similar to the RSPO. Formally launched in 2012, it took shape after a 2010 meeting initiated by the WWF and other global actors in the global beef industry who gathered with the goal of formulating ways to reduce the social, environmental, and economic impacts of beef production. The founding corporate members of the GRSB are Cargill, Elanco, JBS, McDonald's, Merck Animal Health, Walmart/Sam's Club along with civil society organizations Solidaridad, Rainforest Alliance, The Nature Conservancy, and WWF. The roundtable has a board of directors that is constituted by 11 individuals from the roundtable's general assembly (see Figure 16.2 of the GRSB structure).

An executive committee is formed from the general assembly and is constituted by a president, secretary, treasurer, and two vice-presidents. The general assembly is composed of five constituencies: producer, commerce and processing, retail, civil society, and the Roundtable. Each member is allocated voting privileges while observing members are not. Presently, the GRSB has 65 members from Canada, USA, Europe, Namibia, Indonesia, Australia, Argentina, Paraguay, Uruguay, and Brazil. The GRSB also has several 'standing committees' formed by the general

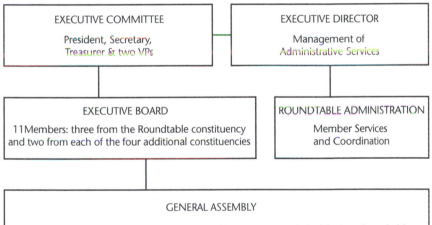

FIGURE 16.2 The GRSB structure.

Source: adapted from http://grsbeef.org/page-1565045

assembly dedicated to such issues such as budget, grievances, education, and future meeting planning. The GRSB has multiple technical working groups arranged by the executive board on topics such as: supplier guidelines, beef life-cycle assessments, and beef sustainability issues. In terms of governing documents, the GRSB is in the process of devising its own set of P&Cs that will govern the production (and definition) of sustainable beef in the future. At the present time, the GRSB has a draft version of their P&Cs as put together by the General Assembly (see Box 2 of the GRSB's five principles). The GRSB initiated a public consultation period over a 60-day period for comments beginning in March 2014 and at the time of writing is in the process of gathering the comments for a second draft.

Box 16.2 The GRSB's five principles

1 The global beef value chain manages natural resources responsibly and enhances ecosystem health
2 Global sustainable beef stakeholders protect and respect human rights and, and recognize the critical roles that all participants within the beef value chain play in their community regarding culture, heritage, employment, land rights and health
3 Global sustainable beef producers and processors respect and manage animals to ensure their health and welfare
4 Global sustainable beef stakeholders ensure safety and quality of beer products and utilize information-sharing systems that promote beef sustainability
5 Global beef stakeholders encourage innovation, optimize production, reduce waste and add to economic viability

Source: Principles and Criteria for Global Sustainable Beef, http://grsbeef.org/ DRAFTprinciples

---

Participation, 'public consultation', and roundtable meeting culture

As corporate-NGO partnerships and roundtable arrangements slowly become the ultimate authorities in governing environmental resources and agro-commodity networks, it becomes increasingly important to study how such fora define 'participation' and how participation is enacted within roundtables. Such information will provide a better understanding as to what roundtable governance 'in action' looks like as well as whom exactly is allowed to dictate such conditions of governance. I will discuss how the RSPO has enacted 'participation' in the context of Ecuador and then compare how the GRSB has handled the same issue.

In 2007, the RSPO launched its first set of P&Cs as a way to establish standardized production of sustainable palm oil around the world. The document consists of principles and indicators which state ways to measure things like transparency, laws and regulations, long-term and economic viability, technical 'best practices', environmental responsibility, company responsibility towards employees and communities affected by plantations and mills, awareness about new plantings, and a continuous commitment to improvement of key areas of activity. Before companies can officially implement the P&Cs into their production chain, a national interpretation of the document must take place to ensure that the P&Cs do not conflict with any existing national laws or regulations. A national interpretation is also a way in which local actors can voice their opinions about the shaping of production standards. Ecuador is the country that most recently went through the process of devising a national interpretation of the P&CS. But the 'participatory' way in which various actors have been included or excluded from the criteria devising process has generated controversy.

To begin, the interpretation process was completely handled online and took place during a 60-day period from July to September 2013. To participate in the interpretation process, participants were directed to the national palm oil cultivators' association of Ecuador's (ANCUPA) website and then were instructed to click on a link that would take them to the commentary process. Following this, participants were made to input their *cédula* or national identification information into the system. Participants were then taken to a screen which instructed them to read the official draft of Ecuador's National Interpretation of the P&Cs and were then required to type their comments into a textbox. These comments were then automatically sent to ANCUPA for review and possible incorporation into the final P&Cs for Ecuador. The creation of the GRSB's P&Cs also followed a similar route. For one year beginning in April 2013, various members and working groups of the GRSB spent time devising and refining principles that could be used as the GRSB's official criteria for sustainable beef production. The public consultation process took place between March 17 to May 16, 2014 and members of the public were invited to read the online draft copy of the Principles and Criteria for Sustainable Beef located on the GRSB's website and leave comments. The idea is that the comments will be gathered and reviewed by GRSB members and considered for inclusion in the next draft of P&Cs, to be released sometime in the second half of 2014.

Although appearing to be an inclusive process of involvement for various stakeholders involved in both the palm oil and beef industries, the public consultation process can be interpreted as quite exclusionary. Firstly, roundtable arrangements such as the RSPO and GRSB are almost completely reliant on online platforms for feedback to be given on potential governing criteria. As a result, many individuals, especially people who do not have access to a computer and internet are left out of the process. The GRSB has stated in their official document outlining the P&Cs Process Summary, once comments on the P&Cs are gathered, considerations must be made to have this material accessible, however no details are given on how the actual commentary process will be made accessible to people without internet access. Another questionable practice relating to the public consultation process of the RSPO is the inputting of a personal identification number in order to access the P&C document online. This requirement does two things: it prevents people, particularly those who do not have official personal identification (an extremely common reality in Latin America and the global south more broadly), from participating in the consultation process. Additionally, it requires participants to divulge their personal identities, which may prevent people from taking part in the process, in the first place. The lack of anonymity throughout the process is an issue for some as they may be less likely to express their thoughts, particularly ones that are in disagreement with the RSPO. A final issue regarding the consultation has to do with the socialization of the public consultation process. In terms of the RSPO National Interpretation of Ecuador, about 20 people submitted feedback on the P&Cs (personal communication). This seems quite a small number if one considers that ANCUPA has about 6000 smallholder members (ANCUPA, 2011). Members of ANCUPA told the author that the RSPO national interpretation process was promoted to various parties mainly through email and telephone. Potential commentators were selected by forming a map of stakeholders of the 'most important' actors in the palm oil industry. This map was created by a third-party consultant and not by an individual that has intimate knowledge of the industry. A simple glance at the map reveals a list of primarily government representatives, sustainability directors of palm oil companies, and smallholders who are active members of ANCUPA and are located in Quinindé, a city in the coastal province of Esmeraldas. Very few actors of the stakeholders' map were representatives from Ecuador's lesser-known palm-growing regions or organizations from the Amazon region.

Another problematic way the RSPO process was promoted in Ecuador relates to the third annual RSPO meeting in Latin America, held in Ecuador in 2012. The purpose of this meeting was to generate regional awareness of the RSPO mechanism among smallholders and companies. Leading up to the meeting, the RSPO national interpretation was promoted among various pro-capitalist civil society organizations such as SNV (Netherlands Development Organization) and Conservation International. Several NGOs and development organizations were invited to give presentations during the meeting in order to promote the work they do on palm-related issues. Interestingly absent from the group of participants was Ecuador's most outspoken NGO known as Acción Ecológica, an NGO that speaks out against monoculture agriculture, among other things. Other problems associated with the meeting were that it took place in the center of Quito – far from any of the palm-growing regions of the country. There were also high registration costs associated with attending. Fees started at US$200 which meant that many smallholders would not be able to attend.

While looking at the way in which roundtable governance is conducted in both palm oil and beef production realms, several trends become problematically apparent: first, the term 'public consultation' is becoming increasingly defined in

roundtable arrangements by online means. Not only does this mode of acquiring the opinions and comments of the public severely limit the number of people who can partake in such an endeavor (to people who only have access to a computer and internet), but it also reshapes how the act of consultation in resource debates is carried out. In the respective experiences of the palm oil and beef roundtables, 'consultation' is limited to providing opportunities to people to leave comments on wording or to make minor suggestions regarding the inclusion of certain ideas or concepts on text that *has already been written*. This consultation process does not provide room for participants to challenge the fundamental ideas on which the roundtable is built on. Another related pointed is that in the case of the RSPO in Ecuador, participants were required to input their identification information into the consultation system. This requirement can potentially prevent people from 'speaking their minds' due to the lack of anonymity as their responses can be traced back to their identity. Second, another critique directed towards roundtable arrangements centers on who exactly is a 'participant' in making governance decisions. In the case of the RSPO in Ecuador, although invited to take part, several outspoken actors such as the well-known NGO Acción Ecológica did not, arguing that their participation would legitimize an initiative that wrongly reinforces corporate control of the agro-industry (author's observations). Rather than triggering the RSPO to re-evaluate its position on supporting the expansion of palm oil plantations, it simply carried on with national interpretation activities within the country. Other actors who have been invited to take part in the RSPO process in Ecuador are pro-capitalist organizations such as SNV and Conservation International along with palm oil companies. This instance raises the issue regarding what an 'acceptable' RSPO 'participant' looks like. It appears that most participants are in favor of augmenting profit derived from palm oil production. The same can be said about the members of the GRSB; all members seek to drive up capitalist profits. By reviewing the RSPO Ecuador and the GRSB member's list, one can conclude that all members favor capitalist agro-development, including the NGOs. Devising the list of members in such a way ensures that the actor's 'possible field of action' is limited to predictable pro-industry outcomes. This in turn ensures that the results of any 'public consultation' will be shaped (Foucault, 1991) and predicated on the further growth of the industry and silences any opposition that may come about.

Roundtable principles and criteria and their effects

The notion of 'sustainability' is a contentious one, especially when it comes the production of consumer goods. Many scholars have critiqued the concep being one that is very elusive and unspecific in terms of what it promotes (Dob 1996; McManus, 1996; Seghezzo, 2009). The problem lies in the fact that the no one definition of 'sustainability' and it remains open for interpretation. W the RSPO and the GRSB, the definition of sustainability and how both the oil and beef roundtables are deploying the term in their P&Cs has been a of criticism. Specifically, many people are concerned over what the P&Cs

endorsing, concealing, or glossing over as they are implemented in the production chain. For instance the RSPO makes it mandatory for all parties who are interested in gaining certification to implement the P&Cs in their production practices. Criterion 2 is perhaps one of the most important sustainability standards as it promotes the general compliance of applicable laws and regulations of the home country in efforts to build a sustainable palm production system. Specifically, it notes that certification will be granted if, 'The right to use the land can be demonstrated, and is not legitimately contested by local communities with demonstrable rights' (RSPO, 2013). Within the RSPO sphere, holding land title is the acceptable form through which land claims can be verified. Land titles are also promoted during RSPO meetings as being a key way to preempt land conflicts before they start. But the belief that land titles are a key way *to prevent* land conflicts from arising is questionable, as evidence from Ecuador suggests that land-titling processes, particularly involving titles owned by local communities, can act as little defense against the interests of large companies (Johnson, 2014). This is mainly due to the few resources communities have to defend their territory and the overlapping legal systems of land recognition. Furthermore, the marking and delineation of customary or traditional tracts of land can speed up their commodification as they are made more 'legible' to market forces. Given this information, the adherence to the RSPO's criterion 2 leads to questionable outcomes in terms of the 'sustainability' of community land ownership and in fact, endorses and perpetuates the commercial ownership and monopoly of land.

In terms of the GRSB, the roundtable has been criticized for 'not going far enough' in terms of its approach to sustainability (Liebelson, 2014). Opposition has emerged because the GRSB does not aim to produce a global set of universal certification standards like the RSPO, but rather aims to generate a 'high level' outline of what 'sustainability' should look like. This is because, as GRSB personnel state, beef can be raised in various environments and ecosystems which makes a 'one-size-fits-all' approach unreasonable and unrealistic (Makower, 2014). The idea is to come up with a general set of guidelines relating to sustainability and to leave the actual implementation of these guidelines up to each company so that they can interpret them individually at a local level. The president of the GRSB has been noted as stating that it is not the roundtable's intention to label 'what is sustainable and what is not' but rather to establish a broad set of criteria that can be implemented with consideration to the nuances of any ecosystem (ibid.).

The proposed P&Cs of the GRSB center on five specific core areas, they are: natural resources, people and the community, animal health and welfare, food, and efficiency and innovation. According to the GRSB, these areas rest on three important pillars of social responsibility, environmentally soundness, and economic viability which ensure the sustainability of the industry. But many believe these areas and their related P&Cs contain enormous gaps in terms of creating any sort of sustainability guidelines. In a joint statement released by the Natural Resources Defense Council, Rainforest Alliance, Food Alliance, and Friends of the Earth US, the organizations criticized the GRSB for not thoroughly addressing issues such

as climate change, land conversion, fresh water conservation, sustainable feed, and manure management. For example, according to the organizations, the GRSB does not contain any plan for reducing or eliminating methane emissions. Considering that ruminants from livestock are the primary source of methane gas in the US, this is a major shortcoming. The GRSB also falls short in terms of stating plans to prevent land conversion or contamination of fresh water sources. Although the GRSB discusses plans to prevent deforestation for livestock production, it fails to acknowledge that land conversion is also driven by the need for monoculture crops such as corn or soybeans, which are usually used as feed for cows. Additionally, the GRSB falls short in recognizing that water contamination as linked to beef production does not only affect surface water sources, but also groundwater sources as well. The P&Cs also do not address issues of water quantity when used in beef production. This is a major issue of concern as linked to sustainability, particularly in production areas that are located in drought-prone locations or where water sources are limited.

Disease management and roundtable governance

The success of any agro-industry relies not only on the smooth production processes associated with various products, but also on the management and containment of natural causes that can disrupt and prevent governance systems from being fully implemented. One such barrier to governance implementation is the onset of disease, both in livestock systems and in plantation environments. Disease should be of major concern to roundtable initiatives due to the spatial effects disease has in commodity production chains and environments. Due to the current global nature of palm oil and beef production networks, diseases are able to rapidly travel to different global spaces, and are thus considered a major threat to commodity production. Surprisingly though, the geographies of disease among mono crops and livestock production have been given little consideration in the definitions of 'sustainability' by roundtable arrangements like the RSPO and the GRSB. This does not mean that livestock and palm oil are not vulnerable to threats of spreading pathogens; in fact, the situation is quite the contrary. Livestock and monocultures are particularly vulnerable to infection. Diseases such as bovine tuberculousis and infectious bovine rhinotracheitis (IBR) are primarily spread by contact with other infected livestock. The factors driving the spread of pudrición del cogollo (or bud rot disease) in palm plants has not entirely been identified but the lack of genetic diversity in monoculture plantations make the spread of infections a major issue for plantations.

The spread of agriculture-related diseases is an alarming problem for beef and palm industries because they are disrupting and in some cases 'undoing' the governance work of some of the roundtables. In the case of Ecuador, bud rot disease has wiped out hundreds of hectares of palm plantations located in the Province of Esmeraldas as well as the Amazon region. It is estimated that out of the country's 280,000 hectares of planted palm, approximately 5 percent of the crop has been lost due to bud rot (El Productor, 2013). In some cases, palm companies and farmers have lost 70 percent of their total plantations. No official cause of the spread of bud rot has been named but general theories blame factors such as a particular strain of fungi or bacteria, humid temperatures, excessive humidity, lack of soil drainage, or low quality of soil (ANCUPA, 2013). Many palm-producing companies have expressed their concern with how to manage and contain the spread. In several cases, palm companies have stated that the rapid pace of the spread of the disease has prevented them from implementing the RSPO's P&Cs due to the toll of bud rot (personal communication). To more effectively tackle the disease within Ecuador, ANCUPA is merging bud rot treatment and prevention practices with the implementation of RSPO standards across the country. The organization is encouraging individual farmers to 'take care' of the problem themselves by implementing 'correct' technical practices in palm oil cultivation. These practices heavily rely on the purchasing of special technical inputs such as fertilizers, special hybrid seeds, and disease-free palm seedlings from private organizations such as ANCUPA. While appearing to address the problem of bud rot, these measures further entrench farmers' reliance on ANCUPA and further fuel the neoliberal approach to disease management, as the only solution that is being offered is one that is tied to private certification.

The GRSB has not developed a systemized approach to dealing with disease among livestock, which has raised concerns for some (Liebelson, 2014). The absence, however, of any plans to address important issues regarding animal health in the GRSB is indicative of its approach. For example, the GRSB's P&Cs lack any mention of the beef industry's use of antibiotics. A common yet controversial practice in commercial livestock farming is the use of antibiotics to treat as well as prevent disease among animals. The idea is that such quick preventative treatment will reduce the chances of cattle developing sicknesses later on, therefore saving time and money for the company. Additionally, other non-medical uses of antibiotics have been noted for example, to promote the growth and fattening of animals (Harris, 2010). But such unrestricted use of antibiotics has led to an overuse of antibiotics in livestock production. According to figures gathered from the Centre for Disease Control, 70 percent of all antibiotics used in the United States are used for non-therapeutic purposes among livestock. The over usage of antibiotics has triggered the growth of resistant strains of bacteria, which has major impacts for public health because disease-resistant bacteria can be transmitted to humans by the food supply chain. By failing to challenge the dominant practices of corporate entities when it comes to antibiotic use, the GRSB is reinforcing the profit-driven objectives of commercial members at the expense of human and nonhuman health. This is because factory-farmed animals tend to be sicker than livestock raised in non-factory environments. Furthermore, the GRSB is sending the message that irresponsible antibiotic use is the way to address the threat of disease rather than more localized but likely more costly responses. These all contribute to the further neoliberalization of animal health (see Enticott, 2014).

Conclusion and further discussion points

Roundtable fora for cotton, fisheries, and, as this paper has indicated, beef and palm oil, have emerged as top authorities in governing environmental resources. Roundtables are the most recent manifestation of the ideals of effective and efficient resource governance as promoted by the UN's Green Economy Initiative and by the international neoliberal push for corporate social responsibility. Roundtable arrangements are seen by many as establishing a 'fairer' resource-based economy. But rather than simply being considered a 'new way' to manage and control resources, roundtables should be analyzed in terms of the impacts they have on our ontological ways of seeing resources and the material effects of this reimagining in practice. For example, the act of public consultation is increasingly being reimagined as something that is only to be carried out online; the material effects of this is extreme exclusion when it comes to reaching typically marginalized actors in the palm oil or beef industries. This transformation in what is considered 'participation' and 'consultation' in resource debates will continue to have major implications as roundtables continue to grow in popularity. Another important point that requires future analysis is the effectiveness of roundtable principles and criteria (P&Cs) and how they shape and enact definitions of 'sustainability'. As the above example concerning the RSPO and land titles shows, even the most well-intentioned criteria can have adverse effects 'on-the-ground'. At a broader level, more attention must be directed to thinking about what is the most appropriate way to handle voluntary approaches to resource governance. For example, the RSPO aims to establish production standards that, if followed, will result in a verifiable certification stamp. The GRSB, on the other hand, strategically aims to create a high-level outline of what sustainable beef looks like, ultimately leaving the operationalization of 'sustainability' up to the beef producers and processors themselves. Given the criticism the RSPO has endured regarding the difficulties it will have in implementing its voluntary guidelines through audit procedures, it appears that the GRSB may be setting itself up for an even larger failure since it is establishing a much more flexible, open-ended system for sustainable commodity production without an exact definition of sustainability. In the same vein, the absence of a certification stamp or an auditing process may trigger producers to promote their beef as 'sustainable' and there would be no way to verify their production practices. Finally the ways in which the RSPO and the GRSB are addressing disease management and prevention is inadequate. For example, the RSPO promotes an individualized, entrepreneurial approach to managing bud rot disease which further intensifies farmers' reliance on the inputs provided to them by companies. In the context of the GRSB, the beef roundtable's P&Cs fail to question and address the blatant overuse of antibiotics particularly in commercial factory farm environments, thereby perpetuating dominant capitalist practices or 'business as usual'. Taken together, it can be concluded that roundtable governance arrangements in agricultural resource sectors do very little to disrupt and restructure current beef and palm oil production systems. What such arrangements do, in reality, is obscure the environmental and social effects of resource production while reinforcing and justifying the perpetuation of the capitalist agro-production chain.

Acknowledgements

The author would like to thank all the individuals and groups, both in North America and Ecuador that made this work possible. Special thanks to Jody Emel and Harvey Neo for the invitation to contribute to this book. Many thanks go to Sascha Darius Mojtahedi for graphic design assistance. I am grateful to Jody Emel for encouraging my interest in roundtable governance and for dedicating much time and effort to helping me conceptualize and think through many of the concepts covered in this chapter. Funding for this research was made possible by the Social Sciences and Humanities Research Council of Canada, the Land Politics Deal Initiative, and the Geller Endowed Research Award from Clark University.

References

ANCUPA (2011) 'ANCUPA: Sirviendo al palmicultor', Powerpoint presentation, July

ANCUPA (2013) *Guia de Campo sobre la Pudricion de Cogollo*, Ecuador

Bakker, K. (2007) 'The "commons" versus the "commodity": Alter-globalization, anti-privatization and the human right to water in the global south', *Antipode*, vol 39, no 3, pp. 430–455

Biermann, F. and Pattberg, P. (2008) 'Global environmental governance: Taking stock, moving forward', *Annual Review of Environment and Resources*, 33(1), 277–294.

Bridge, G., and Perreault, T. (2009) 'Environmental Governance', in N. Castree, D. Demeritt, D. Liverman and B. Rhoads (eds), *A Companion to Environmental Geography*, Blackwell, Oxford

Bulkeley, H. and Mol, A. P. J. (2003) 'Participation and Environmental Governance: Consensus, Ambivalence and Debate', *Environmental Values*, vol 12, no 2, pp. 143–154

Cashore, B., van Kooten, G. C., Vertinsky, I., Auld, G. and Affolderbach, J. (2005) 'Private or self-regulation? A comparative study of forest certification choices in Canada, the United States and Germany', *Forest Policy and Economics*, vol 7, no 1, pp. 53–69

Clapp, J. (1998) 'The privatization of global environmental governance: ISO 14000 and the developing world', *Global Governance*, 4(3), 295–316.

Cummins, A. (2004) 'The Marine Stewardship Council: A multi-stakeholder approach to sustainable fishing', *Corporate Social Responsibility and Environmental Management*, vol 11, no 2, pp. 85–94

Djama, M., Fouilleux, E. and Vagneron, I. (2011) 'Standard-setting, certifying and benchmarking: A governmentality approach to sustainability standards in the agro-food sector', in S. Ponte, P. Gibbon and J. Vestergaard (eds), *Governing through Standards: Origins, Drivers and Limitations*, Palgrave Macmillan, New York

Dobson, A. (1996) 'Environment sustainabilities: An analysis and a typology', *Environmental Politics*, vol 5, no 3, pp. 401–428

El Productor (2013) 'Alternativas a la pudrición de la palma', http://elproductor.com/2013/07/21/alternativas-a-la-pudricion-de-la-palma/, accessed on October 9 2014

Enticott, G. (2014) 'Relational distance, neoliberalism and the regulation of animal health', *Geoforum*, vol 52, pp. 42–50

Falkner, R. (2003) 'Private environmental governance and international relations: Exploring the links', *Global Environmental Politics*, vol 3, no 2, pp. 72–87

Foucault, M. (1991) 'Governmentality' in G. Burchell, C. Gordon and P. Miller (ed.), *The Foucault Effect: Studies in Governmentality*, University of Chicago Press, Chicago, pp. 87–104

Gulbrandsen, L. H. (2009) 'The emergence and effectiveness of the Marine Stewardship Council', *Marine Policy*, vol 33, no 4, pp. 654–660

Harris, G. (2010) 'Antibiotics in animals need limits, FDA says', *New York Times*, www.nytimes.com/2010/06/29/health/policy/29fda.html?_r=0, accessed on October 3 2014

Johnson, A. (2014) 'Ecuador's national interpretation of the Roundtable on Sustainable Palm Oil (RSPO): Green-grabbing through green certification?', *Journal of Latin American Geography*, vol 13, no 3, pp. 183–204.

Klooster, D. (2010) 'Standardizing sustainable development? The Forest Stewardship Council's plantation policy review process as neoliberal environmental governance', *Geoforum*, vol 41, no 1, pp. 117–129

Kongsager, R. and Reenberg, A. (2012) 'Contemporary land-use transitions: The global oil palm expansion', GLP International Project Office, no 4, GLP Report

Lemos, M. C. and Agrawal, A. (2006) 'Environmental governance', *Annual Review of Environment and Resources*, vol 31 no 1, pp. 297–325

Liebelson, D. (2014). 'McDonald's definition of "sustainable": Brought to you by the beef industry', www.motherjones.com/blue-marble/2014/03/mcdonalds-sustainable-beef, accessed on October 9 2014

Makower, J. (2014) 'Can the beef industry collaborate its way to sustainability?', *GreenBiz*, www.greenbiz.com/blog/2014/01/09/can-beef-industry-collaborate-its-way-sustainability, accessed on October 10 2014

McAfee, K. and Shapiro, E. N. (2010) 'Payments for ecosystem services in Mexico. Nature, neoliberalism, social movements, and the state', *Annals of the Association of American Geographers*, vol 100, no 3, pp. 579–599

McCarthy, J. (2004) 'Privatizing conditions of production: Trade agreements as neoliberal environmental governance', *Geoforum*, vol 35, no 3, pp. 327–341

McCarthy, J. and Prudham, S. (2004) 'Neoliberal nature and the nature of neoliberalism', *Geoforum*, vol 35, no 3, pp. 275–283

McManus, P. (1996) 'Contested terrains: Politics, stories and discourses of sustainability', *Environmental Politics*, vol 5 no 1, pp. 48–73

Pattberg, P. (2005) 'What role for private rule-making in global environmental governance? Analysing the Forest Stewardship Council (FSC)', *International Environmental Agreements: Politics, Law and Economics*, vol 5 no 2, pp. 175–189

Peck, J. and Tickell, A. (2002) 'Neoliberalizing space', *Antipode*, vol 34 no 3, pp. 380–404.

Peck, J., Theodore, N. and Brenner, N. (2010) 'Postneoliberalism and its malcontents', *Antipode*, vol 41, pp. 94–116

Perreault, T. (2006) 'From the Guerra Del Agua to the Guerra Del Gas: Resource governance, neoliberalism and popular protest in Bolivia', *Antipode*, vol 38, no 1, pp. 150–172

Perreault, T. (2008) 'Custom and contradiction: Rural water governance and the politics of Usos y Costumbres in Bolivia's irrigators' movement', *Annals of the Association of American Geographers*, vol 98, no 4, pp. 834–854

Rainforest Rescue (undated) 'Facts about palm oil and rainforests', www.rainforest-rescue.org/topics/palm-oil, accessed on October 14 2014

RSPO (2013) 'Principles and criteria', www.rspo.org/file/revisedPandC2013.pdf, accessed on October 12 2014

RSPO (2014) 'United Nations grants "special consultative status" to RSPO', www.rspo.org/news_details.php?nid=209, accessed on October 3 2014

Sawyer, S. (2004) *Crude Chronicles: Indigenous Politics, Multinational Oil, and Neoliberalism in Ecuador*, Duke University Press, Durham, NC

Seghezzo, L. (2009) 'The five dimensions of sustainability', *Environmental Politics*, vol 18, no 4, 539–556

UNEP (2014) 'Online Guide to Banking and Sustainability', main page, www.unepfi.org, accessed on October 3 2014

Valdivia, G. (2008) 'Governing relations between people and things: Citizenship, territory, and the political economy of petroleum in Ecuador', *Political Geography*, vol 27, no 4, pp. 456–477

17

CONTESTING URBAN AGRICULTURE

The politics of meat production in the License-Buy-Back Scheme (2006–2007) in Hong Kong

Kin Wing Chan

Rarely do people associate pig farming with the cityscape of Hong Kong. Hong Kong, however, has a long history of agricultural development since the British ruled the area after the First Opium War in 1842. Controlling the food supply was a crucial political maneuver for the British government to safeguard the colony's stability and security. During the British rule, farming subsidies, technological extension services, and animal donations became the governing tactics to boost the production of vegetables, fisheries, and pigs (Chan, 2011). In 1978, China implemented an open-door policy and negotiated with the British government to export fresh food to Hong Kong. Since then, Hong Kong has depended heavily on Chinese imports of fresh vegetables, fish, and pork. This led to a dramatic decline in local food production. Recently, the desire to consume local products has increased because the public is concerned about food safety issues in China, ranging from milk powder contaminated with melamine, to recycled oil, and toxic chemical usage in the food production system. The rise and decline of agricultural activities in Hong Kong provides an opportunity to evaluate the conflicts over urban agriculture in specific time and space. There is a paucity of studies to examine why a higher value is assigned to certain forms of urban agriculture over others.[1] For instance, urban vegetable farming presents a more positive aesthetic image; urban pig farming differs from other types of agriculture because of associated sanitary risks, the need for manure management, and odor issues. This study employs a political ecology perspective informed by animal geographies to examine how the meat politics in the License-Buy-Back Scheme (LBBS) has become a tactic to reduce and control the pig farming industry in Hong Kong.

In order to eradicate the transmission of pig-to-human diseases and sanitary risks, governing institutions introduced the LBBS to discipline and regulate pig farming practices in 2006. A new system of sanitary norms and normative behaviors were produced to regulate farm spaces and farmers. The articulations of farm management, record system, standardization, and animal waste treatment knowledge became the tactics to transform pig farm spaces and produce normative sanitary pig farming behaviours. The LBBS was portrayed in a government document as a program voluntarily adopted by pig farmers. This chapter argues that the sanitary discourse created a cloak to disguise the intervention of the governing institutions and produced a marginalized pig-raising environment to force farmers to relinquish their licenses. The concept of voluntarily surrendering pig farmers' licenses should be critically revisited.

To understand better the politics of the LBBS, an archival investigation was conducted during 2009–2012 to understand the social and biophysical factors which tend to restrict the pig farming industry. To engage with pig farmers in this research, the author interviewed 19 pig farmers (out of 43 operating pig farms) to understand their perceptions on the LBBS, and conducted ethnographical studies of two pig farms to triangulate archival documents with farmers' daily practices (Shrum, 2004). This chapter begins by introducing the concept of political ecology and discusses the rationale for the governing institutions to implement the LBBS. Then the paper turns to illustrate the disciplinary techniques and political tactics in LBBS, highlighting how different stakeholders perceive these techniques. Finally, this chapter concludes by highlighting how the sanitary discourse constructs the pig farming industry as problematic and naturalizes the intervention of the governing institutions.

Political ecology and animal studies

Political ecology brings politics into consideration to understand society and environment interactions. According to Blaikie and Brookfield (1987, p17), political ecology concerns both ecology and political economy. The term 'political ecology' was first coined by anthropologist Eric Wolf in a research article titled *Ownership and Political Ecology* (Watts, 2003). Piers Blaikie's oeuvre further contributed to this field in three major ways. It:

1   integrated political economy perspectives in environmental science (Robbins and Bishop, 2008);
2   bridged the structuralist and post-structuralist debates with material ecologies, reflexivity, and network synthesis (Grove, 2009); and
3   adopted a multidisciplinary approach to address local knowledge and practical alternatives to the developmental issues (Simon, 2008).

Paulson et al. (2003) and Robbins (2004) provide succinct reviews of the intellectual genealogies of political ecology. The mid-twentieth century scholars, theorizing on political ecology, diverged from environmental and cultural determinism, which claimed that climatic factors influenced civilizations. The determinists' approach naturalized the domination of the powerful group and justified the process of colonization. By assuming inevitability, the practice of colonialism comes to appear apolitical (Robbins, 2004, p19). Combining political economy approaches with ecological studies opened up opportunities for research on opaque actors such as farmers and yielded more research on colonial and post-colonial systems, power and discourses, environmental justice, global and regional governance as well as the marginal groups in developing countries (Bryant and Bailey, 1997; Fairhead and Leach, 1995; Robbins and Sharp, 2003; Scott 1985; Swyngedouw, 2008). Concerning the themes of political ecology from geographical perspectives, Zimmerer and Bassett (2003) elucidate the understanding of social-environment interactions and production of scale. Yet, Bryant and Bailey (1997, p30) argue that the goals of political ecology in geography are to examine 'marginality, vulnerability, and risk' of the vulnerable groups in everyday and episodic bases.

Recent debates on political ecology emphasize four major aspects:

1   the social construction of scale and reproduction of scale from below (Bulkeley, 2005; Nielsen and Simonsen, 2003);
2   the call to combine both structuralist and post-structuralist perspectives in order to examine the biophysical and bio-economical changes in rural-urban, industrial, and global north and south settings (Swyngedouw and Heynen, 2003; Zimmerer and Bassett, 2003);
3   the discussion of gender and the household's power relationships in multiple scales (Paulson and Gezon, 2004); and
4   the engagement of traditional sciences, material ecologies, and complexity theories to look for practical solutions and ponder alternatives (Rocheleau, 2008).

The scope of political ecology not only addresses different levels of politics on vulnerable biophysical environment but also engages with science and social science to ponder alternatives to development paths for vulnerable groups. However, few political ecology studies address why certain forms of agriculture are viewed more positively than others. Particularly, why is pig farming less desirable than other types of urban agriculture?

Integrating animal geographies with the political ecology literature helps to answer the above questions two major ways: (1) it examines how 'the animal problematizes the power relationship' between governing institutions and farmers (Neo 2012, p951); and (2) it questions human–pig relationships and use of spatial tactics to control animal-human transmitted diseases (Emel and Urbanik, 2010; Enticott, 2008). Animal studies provide insightful angles to understand how humans perceive pigs in different spatial and temporal settings. Serpell (2004) argues that affection and utility determined human's perceptions toward pigs. Holloway and Morris (2014) explain that aesthetic evaluations and judgments transform human perceptions on pigs. For instance, humans evaluate pig odors and wastes as social nuisances (Vukina et al., 1996). In fact, images of pigs are constructed discursively to inform societal norms of urbanity, determining whether pigs are in place or out of place in the city (Cresswell, 1996). For example, Cronon (1992, p228) depicts how the city of Cincinnati in the nineteenth century constructed itself as the 'Porkopolis' because millions of pigs provided huge economic value. However, the Smithfield Meat Market in London was vilified because urban imagination of pigs in the city of London evolved to consider them unsanitary and filthy, leading to their removal in 1852 (Dodd, 1856). To illustrate how the perceptions of pigs changed over time and space, Stibbe (2003) examines the use of the word 'pig' in the British National Corpus and points out that presuppositions concerning pigs became constructed negatively, especially, during the outbreaks of animal–human transmitted diseases such as H1N1, foot and mouth disease, and avian flu (Convery et al., 2005; Davis, 2006; Perdue and Swayne, 2005). Pigs were perceived as the hosts of pathogens, which led governing institutions to develop a set of practices to increase biosecurity measures (Donaldson, 2008; Law and Miele, 2011). The above studies provide insightful direction to consider how the pig farming industry can become less desirable than other types of urban agriculture under the gaze of the stakeholders and governing institutions.

The context of the meat politics in the LBBS (2006–2007)

The rationale for implementing the License-Buy-Back Scheme (LBBS) was to reduce the 'risk of avian influenza outbreaks' because with 'rapid urbanization of the New Territories, pig farming has brought about public health and pollution concerns' (LCFC, 2006, p2). Pigs became a host for spreading the pathogenic H5N1, H1N1, Japanese encephalitis, and *Streptococcus suis* (Auewarakul, 2004; Menon, 2011). Both human and nonhuman actors, who came into contact with pigs, became possible carriers of these pathogens. This sanitary consideration drove governing institutions to control the whole pig farming industry in Hong Kong including pig farmers, workers, retailers, and live pig transporters.

After the 9/11 terrorist attacks, biosecurity became a major concern of numerous countries (Smart and Smart, 2008). Different levels of politics and governance were shaping the production, distribution, and consumption of livestock products, from global organizations such as the Food and Agriculture Organization (FAO), the World Organization for Animal Health (OIE), and the World Health Organization (WHO) to local government departments such as the Food and Environmental Hygiene Department, the Health Department, and the Center for Health Protection Services. Hong Kong's economy was hit hard by severe acute respiratory syndrome (SARS) in 2003; the gross domestic product (GDP) of Hong Kong decreased by 3.7 percent in one quarter and the government reminded the public to 'never forget the painful lesson from SARS' (AFCD, 2003–2008, 41st Livestock Subcommittee Meeting, 2005, p6). To control the spread of pig-to-human diseases at the local level, governing institutions produced new norms of sanitary practices on the territory, street, farm, and personal levels.[2]

The need for biosecurity reproduced the production relationships among governing institutions such as the Agricultural, Fisheries and Conservation Department

(AFCD), Food and Environmental Hygiene Department (FEHD), Legislative Council Financial Committee (LCFC) and pig farmers. Pig-to-human disease transmission became a problem for governing institutions, which had to consider the whole live pig industry (pig farmers, workers, retailers, and live pig transporters) in their political agendas. The *prima facie* reasons of the governing institutions for buying back the whole industry's licenses were:

1   pig-raising was perceived high sanitary and public health risks (AFCD 2003–2008, 2005);
2   pig farms became identified as mosquito breeding grounds (LCFC, 2006); and
3   reducing pig-human contact was deemed essential (FAO and WOAH, 2005).

In 2005, the governing institutions aimed to eradicate the whole industry by providing nine million Hong Kong dollars to attract operators, retailers, wholesalers, and transporters to return their licenses to the government. As a result, 222 out of 265 pig farmers gave up their licenses and ceased their operations. This study argues that the LBBS was depoliticized and neutralized by rhetorically emphasizing the pig farmers' willingness. The Legislative Council Finance Committee documented a debatable statement, that:

> the proposal to buy back pig farming licenses *was first raised by local pig farmers* ... [the] Health, Welfare and Food Bureau received over 190 written submissions, representing nearly half of all pig farms, *urging the early launch of the voluntary surrender scheme.*
>
> (LCFC, 2006, p9, emphasis added)

By arguing that pig farming created potential threats and risks to Hong Kong, the governing institutions could technically claim a neutral position by disguising the underlying political agenda as a conflict between the general public and pig farmers. The sanitary argument was highlighted when it was discovered that pigs were a host for the SARS virus. According to a survey undertaken by the Legislative Council, the public weighed health and safety concerns over the livelihoods of farmers and livestock, and the pig farming industry itself. The survey was anthropocentric[3] and did not consider animal ethics or human–pig relationships. Launching the LBBS was purportedly to reduce pig-to-human transmitted disease; however, the underlying reason to implement the LBBS was to lessen the political risk and reduce sanitary risks that hampered tertiary industry growth. For instance, the mishandling of SARS patients, the unnecessary delay of warnings, and bureaucratic inertia created extensive social discontent. On July 1, 2003, 500,000 Hong Kong citizens demonstrated to express their frustrations and distrust toward the government's enactment of security bills, mismanagement of the SARS crisis, and economic depression. Finally, the chief executive Tung Chee-Hwa was forced to resign. This political lesson illustrated that public health crises played a role in triggering political crises.

In addition, the conclusion of the report titled *Ex-Gratia Payments to Pig Farmers* highlighted the 'urgency' of buying back pig farmers' licenses so that the purchases could be made 'before the high risk summer season of Japanese encephalitis (JE) outbreak' (LCFC, 2006, p9). Two major reasons were given: (1) pig farms accumulate stagnant water and produce a breeding ground for mosquitoes; (2) the pig is one of the transmission hosts of JE. However, the Finance Committee rhetorically exaggerated the severity of JE although there were no supporting data to show the number of reported cases of infections from pig farmers, workers, retailers, and live pig transporters. Interestingly, the *Hong Kong Medical Journal* noted that the reported cases of JE in Hong Kong from 1967 to 2004 were sporadic. According to this report, 'Hong Kong sees only a few sporadic cases of JE, thus it is unwise and perhaps not necessary to advocate a universal vaccination programme' (Lam et al., 2005, p186). Furthermore, between 1967 and 2003, of the 45 cases of JE reported (including local and imported cases) only two cases were reported by the residents within 2.6 km of the abattoirs and pig farms, and 'in the remaining cases neither abattoirs nor pigsties existed nearby' (ibid., p185). The report makes four important points:

1   pigsties were not necessarily the breeding ground of JE;
2   according to the report, there was no reported case about the infections from pig farmers and live pork retailers and wholesalers (ibid.);
3   the medical doctors didn't argue that infected cases were directly related to pig farms or abattoirs areas. Their findings did not absolutely accuse pig farms as the breeding grounds of JE;
4   apart from pigs, domestic or wild animals were also a potential host of JE (ibid.).

Additionally, the medical doctors in this paper suggested providing a vaccination of the pigs as an effective way to solve the problem.

> The pig farming industry in Hong Kong has been shrinking over the last few years, so vaccination of a small and diminishing pig population may be the most efficacious, sustainable, and cost-effective measure to prevent the spread of JE.
>
> (Lam et al., 2005, p186)

Based on the mentioned arguments, JE became an imaginary enemy for the governing institutions. The government produced different sanitary monitoring schemes to discipline pig farmers, to depoliticize the License-Buy-Back Scheme and to mystify how the governing institution made a very tough environment for pig farmers to survive.

The LBBS (2006–2007)

In 2005, the Hong Kong Legislative Council's Finance Committee accepted the ex-gratia payment through the License-Buy-Back Scheme (LBBS) to buy back the pig farmers, retailers, and transport workers' licenses to operate. According to the Legislative Council Finance Committee (LCFC), there were three major reasons to buy back the whole industry licenses.

First, pig farming caused a serious pollution problem. The justification of the Finance Committee's actions was linked to the quantity of the pig excrement: in 2006, there were 265 farms raising about 330,000 pigs which generated 520 metric tons of excrement each day (LCFC, 2006, p2). But, if pig farmers participated in the Livestock Waste Control Scheme (1987–1997), they had to install pig waste treatment facilities and treat pig waste prior to discharging it into rivers. The amount of pig excrement was only a number used by the governing institutions to illustrate the impacts of pig waste. If the governing institutions wanted to accuse pig farmers of indiscriminately discharging pig waste, they should have provided the number of prosecutions and amount of indiscriminately discharged pig waste instead of merely relating that '330,000 pigs generated 520 metric tons of excrement each day' (ibid.). This statement accentuated the a priori linkages between number of pigs and direct impacts of excrement but ignored the fact that the majority of pig farmers had properly treated the pig waste.

Second, pig raising was argued to be unsuitable for Hong Kong because it caused public health problems.

> With the rapid urbanization of Hong Kong, particularly in the New Territories (N.T.), sustainable pig farming in Hong Kong is no longer a realistic long-term policy option in view of the public health and pollution problems arising from it. The Administration should therefore freeze the number of pig farms, by stopping the issue of new pig farm licenses and freezing the current rearing capacity to restrict the number of pigs in Hong Kong.
>
> (LCFC, 2006, p2)

Owing to the urbanization process in the New Territories (NT), pig farming became a sanitary and pollution problem. To reduce the risk to public health, the governing institutions decided to restrict the number of pig farms, stop issuing new pig farm licenses, and freeze the pig raising capacity as a means to control the pig farming industry.

Third, the urgency to eradicate the hosts of Japanese encephalitis and *Streptococcus suis* was cited as a reason to buy back licenses. These diseases create serious threats for the people in Hong Kong. An Agriculture, Fisheries and Conservation Department veterinarian said that the reason to implement the LBBS was to remove the health risk posed by pigs, which are hosts for the pathogen *Streptococcus suis* because it can cause serious illnesses. The bacterium can enter the human body through skin wounds. In order to prevent infection, people should avoid contact with pigs (AFCD, 2003–2008, 48th Livestock Subcommittee minutes, 2007). As aforementioned, Japanese encephalitis can be spread through pigs; eradicating pig-related businesses became a major tool for controlling the spread of Japanese Encephalitis and *Streptococcus suis* in Hong Kong.

The above reasons provide opportunities and justifications for the governing institutions to buy back the whole industry's licenses and tighten the pig farms' regulations. Those human and non-human actors[4] who interact with pigs came to be regarded as problematic as well. The 'curse' of pigs is diffused from their problematic body to pig farms, live pig handling vehicles, and abattoirs. Pig farm workers, live pig retailers, and transporters became problematic bodies themselves as their bodies assist virus transmission. Under the gaze of the governing institutions, the pig farming network had become a series of problematic spaces and moving bodies. These problematic spaces were targeted for eradication through the two major governing technologies by: (1) using ex-gratia payments to buy back the industry's licenses and (2) proposing the Codes of Practices to further regulate the pig farming spaces.

Ex-gratia payment

In 2004, the Health, Welfare and Food Bureau in Hong Kong proposed the ex-gratia payment for live pig farmers, workers, retailers, and transporters.[5] Meanwhile, the Agriculture, Fisheries and Conservation Department proposed the new Codes of Practices for the pig farmers. In fact, these two new policies are complementary: either an ex-gratia payment or stringent control is appropriate for pig farmers. The Health, Welfare and Food Bureau drafted a proposal:

> The Government should *tighten up the existing livestock licensing regulatory regime* by ensuring strict compliance with the licensing conditions. Under the circumstances, it is considered appropriate that a *voluntary surrender scheme* for pig farmers should be introduced for those who do not wish to continue to operate under an increasingly stringent regulatory regime.
>
> (LCFC, 2006, p3, emphasis added)

From the above statement, the meaning of 'voluntary surrender' was contradictory. First, the governing institutions only provided two choices and did not consult[6] with the pig farming industry beforehand. Second, the governing institutions increased stringent controls on pig farming, creating lots of stress, fear, and unsettling feelings among farmers (Tao, 2008). Pig farmers were involuntarily presented with a turbulent business environment; the only realistic option was to give up their licenses in return for financial compensation. Finally, it caused 222 pig farmers to give up their licenses and only 43 farms still continue pig farming (see Table 17.1).

To reduce the chance of human–pig contact, the governing institutions not only removed pig farm space, but also reduced the number of live pig workers, retailers, and transporters. The governing institutions aimed at providing ex-gratia payments for 800 workers and offered loans to 130 live pig transporters to convert their vehicles into frozen meat carriers.

TABLE 17.1 Change in the pig farming industry after 2006 LBBS.

Indicator	2006–2007	2007–2008
Pig farms	265	43
Number of licenses bought back	171	222 (accumulative total)
Number of local live pigs	426,000	75,000

Source: The data are summarized from the Agriculture Fisheries, and Conservation Department (AFCD), Livestock Subcommittee minutes (48th AFCD Livestock Subcommittee Meeting, September 2007; 49th meeting, January 2008; minutes, 50th meeting, February 2008)

> To assist those local workers of the live pig farming/transport industry who become unemployed as a result of their employers ceasing operation under the proposed voluntary surrender scheme, we propose to provide a one-off grant of $18,000 to each worker ... the livelihood of the live pig transporters whose sole business is to transport live pigs from local farms to slaughterhouses ... to assist these live pig transporters, we propose to provide an unsecured loan of up to $50,000 per vehicle for them to upgrade/convert their vehicles for conveying chilled/frozen products or for other business operations.
>
> (LCFC, 2006, p3)

The fates of local workers and live pig transporters were similar to pig farmers, since they were a derivative industry dependent on live pig supply from local pig farms. Buying back pig farmers' licenses affected the jobs of local workers and live pig transporters because the live pig businesses were shrinking. Local workers and live pig transporters might become unemployed or have to convert to other business operations. Surrendering their live pig handling rights and accepting ex-gratia payments were the plausible options for them.

Codes of practices – spatial controls on remaining 43 pig farms

In 2007, the AFCD announced the Codes of Practices in order to further monitor and regulate the remaining 43 pig farms. The experts from the Centre for Health Protection (CHP), Department of Health, in Hong Kong worried that these pig farms created health risks because of their proximity to 'human habitation' (Alberta Government, Hong Kong office, 2007). In 2007, the Food and Health Bureau, Environment Bureau (FHBEB) and Agriculture, Fisheries and Conservation Department (AFCD) proposed 43 codes to local pig farmers. The Codes of Practices was designed to remove Japanese encephalitis, increase farm efficiency, and improve the quality of live pig supply in Hong Kong. Here is the quote from the Legislative Council:

The emergence of Japanese encephalitis in recent years which is endemic among pigs, has also drawn public attention to the management and hygiene of local pig farms ... The Code of Practice (COP) aims at enhancing management efficiency of pig farms and reducing the risk of disease outbreaks, so as to ensure a more stable supply of fresh pork with better quality assurance. The health of farm workers and people on farm can also be better safeguarded.

(Legislative Council, 2008b, p1)

The governing institutions aimed to produce new rules and regulations to imbue pig farmers with new standards and practices as a means to reduce public health risks. These 43 rules were proposed to be incorporated into the Livestock Keeping License. These rules monitor five major pig-raising practices, including husbandry and farm management; movement control; disease monitoring and control; and waste management and hygiene. The marking scheme[7] identifies 43 prohibited pig-farming practices; they are grouped under categories 1, 2, 3. Category 1 includes minor misdeeds causing minor sanitary and hygienic threats. Items in category 2 are more serious and cause medium threats, while category 3 includes serious threats, which will cause the Director of AFCD to revoke a pig farmer's license immediately. In fact, the Codes of Practices impose more regulations and controls on pig farmers and imbue the new concept of sanitary management (See Table 17.2).

Rule 1 required pig farmers to draw out the production and non-production boundaries on their farms. Within each bounded area, there are different sets of values, norms, and orders appropriate for the normative farming practices. For instance, the visibilities of the painted lines between the production and non-production zones remind farmers that they have different practices in handling pig and waste treatment. The new spatial order enhances separation and control of pigs because boundaries delineate appropriate behaviors and confine normative practices. Boundary delineation, knowledge of hygiene, farm management, and biosecurity are articulated in the new spatial order.

Rule 7 is a self-regulating rule, which monitors farmers' work. Farmers must supervise themselves in the removal of rodents, pests, and mosquitoes that can become the host to spread diseases. Since the pig is seen as the host of Japanese encephalitis, regulating farmers to remove static standing water and cut down weeds are the ways to reduce the threats of Japanese encephalitis. Farmer representatives commented that rarely 'can pig farms eliminate rodents because the storage of fodder crops attracts them' (AFCD, 2008, LS 1/08, Annex, p1). If the governing institutions would like to reduce the rodent problems on pig farms, they should provide more financial and technological assistance to pig farmers.

Rule 39 (including rules 31 and 33) requires the provision of precise waste treatment floor plans and waste treatment records. Precise waste treatment procedures are produced to promote standardized sanitization behavior, self-regulation, and surveillance. This facilitates the monitoring agencies' waste sampling and the

TABLE 17.2 Proposed Codes of Practices to be imposed on pig farmers

Descriptions	Codes of Practices	Governing institution's explanations
(1) Spatial control and sanitary management of pig farms	Rule 1	There is clear delineation of boundary. The licensee must declare the boundaries, quarantine facilities, isolation facilities, production areas and non-production areas of his/her farm on a map that precisely indicates the geographic location of the farm structures (AFCD, 2008, LS 1/08, Annex, p1).
(2) Construction of normative pest control behavior in pig farm space	Rule 7	Licensee shall incorporate an active, effective rodent, pest and mosquito control system into management practice ... eliminate all accumulation of stagnant water in the farm, trim the vegetation, and clear the surface channels and sand traps especially during the time of the year when there is aggregation of migratory birds. The updated operation protocol for the aforesaid system shall be submitted to this Department (AFCD, 2008, LS 1/08, Annex, p1).
(3) Normative waste treatment and hygiene practices in pig farm space	Rule 39	No discharge of liquid livestock waste shall bypass the waste treatment system, the Sampling Point or the Discharge Point unless it is unavoidable to prevent loss of life, personal injury or severe property damage or no feasible alternative exist. Any pipe works that can be used for bypass discharge of liquid livestock waste, no matter permanently installed or temporarily connected, are prohibited (AFCD, 2008, LS 1/08, Annex, p7).

Source: AFCD (2008)

farmers' adherence to norms. Regarding farmers' perceptions on this normative waste treatment practice, pig farmers strongly disagree with these rules for three major reasons:

1 it is not necessary for farmers to resubmit another farm plan because the AFCD already has the farmers' farm plans;
2 it is nonsensical to put signs or notices to indicate the discharge outlets in a private farm space;
3 it is difficult to remove obstacles such as grass nearby the discharge outlets (AFCD, 2003–2008, 47th Livestock Subcommittee, 2007, p3).

Pig farmers who break rule 39 will have their licenses revoked by the AFCD directors if they are found to be directly discharging animal wastes into the river, due to the high risk to public health. This is a direct command to inform farmers that they must follow the uniform rules and regulations. This command develops a new conception of order to confine waste management in designated farm premises with appropriate hygenic norms. Pig farmers fiercely object for two major reasons: (1) current environmental ordinances provide adequate legal power for the monitoring agencies to penalize offending farmers; farmers argue that the ulterior intention of this rule is to force pig farmers to surrender their licenses; (2) pig farmers argue that revoking their licenses is directly meant to estrange their businesses and create entensive economic hardship to their entire family. In this situation, farmers would choose prison confinement over revocation of their licenses (AFCD, 2003–2008, 50th Livestock Subcommittee meeting, 2008, pp2–3).

In short, the Codes of Practices imbue the new knowledge of precision, sanitarization, farm management, biosecurity monitoring, and survelliance of farmers' waste treatment practices. New spatial order and normative practices are produced through boundary delination and animal quarantine. A system of hygenic and santiary rules transform pig farming space into a hygenic and sanitary space. In this new spatial order, farmers are expected to have appropriate waste treatment behaviors and normative sanitary practices. The author argues that the Code of Practices will further strangle the pig farming industry and force farmers to give up their licenses.

Perceptions of crucial players in the Hong Kong pig farming industry

In the following section, the perceptions of the Deputy Director and veterinarians of the Agriculture, Fisheries and Conservation Department, legislative council members, and the general public of the License-Buy-Back Scheme will be presented.

The perceptions of deputy director and veterinarians of the AFCD

The AFCD perceived the License-Buy-Back Scheme as an 'emergency exit for pig farmers' because there is no possibility for long-term development of pig farming in Hong Kong and the control will be tightened and strengthened (author's translation from the representative of the AFCD in the 52nd Livestock Subcommittee, 2008). The attitudes of the AFCD on Hong Kong pig farming are pessimistic and negative for four reasons:

1   pig farming causes serious sanitary and pollution problems especially regarding the threats of pig-to-human disease transmissions;
2   the urbanization process increases the proximity of human habitation and pig farms, which presents a public health risk;
3   the impossibility of relocating all livestock and pig farming to one special farming zone involves adding a huge financial cost of buying land; and

4   Hong Kong doesn't have sufficient land for long-term development of the pig
     farming industry.

The perceptions of the Legislative Council members

In the Legislative Council discussions of the ex-gratia payment and codes of
practices for the pig farming industry, most of the legislative council members supported the LBBS and the Codes of Practices for five reasons:

1   reducing public health and environmental problems (e.g. the 520 metric tons
     per year of pig excrement);
2   the provision of the ex-gratia payment is a way to help pig farmers and their
     workers change to other occupations;
3   pig farmers can operate their businesses in Mainland China, for example, by
     relocating pig farms into the Guandong Province as it is close to Hong Kong;
4   Hong Kong cannot provide enough land for the long term development of
     the pig-farming industry;
5   the only contribution of the pig-farming industry is to stabilize food produc-
     tion and provide fresh meat (Legislative Council, 2008a; 2008b).

The view of the general public

The views of the general public toward the pig farming industry are speculative
and fluctuate with the occurrence of the animal-human transmission diseases. For
instance, the Prevention of H5N1: Reduction of the Risk of Human Infection
of H5N1 Survey (Prevention of H5N1 Survey in short) was conducted by the
governing insistutions in 2005 suggested that the general public was worried
about H5N1 effects on the health of citizens and the economy in Hong Kong.
The survey also suggested that public safety and health is the first priority of citizens. However, another survey, Opinion Survey on the Incident of the H5N1
Bird Flu (Opinion Survey in short), which was conducted by the University of
Hong Kong in 1999 had different interpretations. This survey suggested that the
'perception of the citizens toward H5N1 threats is inflated,' reflecting tempo-
rary fears of H5N1 and even '90 percent of the interviewees said they were not
worried that they might be infected with the H5N1' (Opinion Survey, 1998,
pp14–15). When comparing the Opinion Survey with the governing institutions'
survey – Prevention Survey of H5N1 – these two surveys presented two different outcomes. These results show that public opinion of the livestock industry
is dependent on the number of animal-human transmission cases at any point in
time. Fear and distrust over the local pig farming industry becomes exaggerated
whenever there is a disease outbreak. According to the *South China Morning Post*
(2003), the mass media amplifies the threats of the pig diseases by grossly exaggerating a general disease such as foot and mouth disease into epidemic level.
There is no doubt that the general public is concerned about how H5N1 poses

threats to livelihoods because of the reports of the mass media and the discourses constructed by the governing institutions.

The perception of the Federation of Pig Raising Co-operative Societies

The Federation of Pig Raising Co-operative Societies in Hong Kong opposed the new regulations on the pig farming industry because it is skeptical that the government wants to restore its credibility, retain goodwill from the general public, and fairly regulate the pig farming industry. Pig farmers commented in letters published in the FPRCS's magazine:

> The government portrays a negative image of the pig farming industry by accusing the pig farming industry of causing the outbreaks of H5N1 and Japanese Encephalitis. This is a tactic for the government officials to restore their credibility from the general public by strengthening the controls of live pig production, retailing, and logistics. We are treading on thin ice because farmers can easily violate the Waste Disposal Ordinance, Public Health Safety Ordinance etc. Once farmers violate these ordinances three times within 18 months, their licenses will be revoked and their whole family will be put in jeopardy. The government mobilized numerous resources, like recruiting many officers to monitor pig farmers and devising lots of regulations to discipline farmers to follow the new rules. The underlying intentions are to strangle the whole industry and create a process of attrition. Then pig farmers will unintentionally perish in smoke and ashes. The government is happy to see this scenario because pig farms then will not hamper the economic development.
>
> (Federation of Pig Raising Co-operative Societies, 2001 pp51–53,
> author's translation).

Pig farmers' perceptions

In order to understand farmers' perspectives on LBBS, 21 in-depth interviews were conducted with pig farmers from September 2010 to October 2010. Pig farmers expressed their difficulties and opinions of the future development of the pig farming industry and new proposed Codes of Practices.

Mr Chan[8] commented that the Codes of Practices

> are impossible to follow because the rules are too strict for us. In fact, farmers already had an agreement in place with the government in the Livestock Waste Control Scheme since the 1980s. Without a doubt pig farmers had installed waste treatment facilities and treated animal wastes prior to any discharge. There is no reason to accuse us of being the major polluters of Hong Kong.

Mr Leung[9] commented that the consultations organized by the AFCD 'are just a window-dressing to legitimize the number of farmers who participate in the consultations. The AFCD officials always promise farmers verbally; however, the suggestions from farmers are yet to materialize.'

Mr Yuen[10] argued that

> almost every government department visits my farm. I don't know why the Housing Department also came to my farm. You know that the visits of government officials create pressure and psychological anxiety for me. Not only do I face the internal farm issues and hectic pig farming routines, but I face the frequent visits from the government officials. Why can't they allow me to raise my pigs peacefully?

From the above comments, one can see that pig farmers were worried about the proposed Codes of Practices, and the tightening controls on the pig raising industry. In fact, the AFCD is also responsible for the sanitary problems and the marginality of the pig farming industry. Reviewing AFCD's policies, free vaccinations and veterinary services were provided for pig farmers from the 1960s to the mid-1980s. However, the AFCD stopped providing free vaccination services in the late 1980s. At the 47th AFCD Livestock Subcommittee meeting, pig farmers had a debate with the government's veterinarians over the issue of veterinary service provision. A pig farmer representative argued that local pig farmers are unable to hire a veterinarian and 'this caused pig farmers to test different drugs on pig bodies and find out the right remedies for pigs' (AFCD, 2003–2008, 47th Livestock Subcommittee, 2007, p3). Inappropriate veterinary drug practice not only reduces pigs' resistance to diseases, but it also reduces the effectiveness of drugs. Facing this situation, a government veterinarian replied that the AFCD only provides 'verbal opinions on veterinary drugs usages, quarantine, and sterilization methods' (ibid.) because 'the suggestion of drug usage involves commercial considerations' (ibid.), which are not suitable for a veterinarian to be involved in. This veterinarian suggested the farmers' representative set up a drug record system and write down their animal drug usage experiences on their own. Facing the lack of veterinary services and support in Hong Kong, farmers should figure out different self-help tactics in order to sustain their businesses. The AFCD emphasised the control and monitoring of the pig farming industry but was unwilling to train husbandry veterinarians to help pig farmers combat pig diseases. Therefore, the governing institutions restricted veterinary services and produced a self-help mentality among pig farmers, which becomes a tactic to marginalize the pig farming industry. Even worse, the LBBS in 2006–2007 did not offer any capital grants to help pig farmers upgrade their waste treatment and sanitary management facilities. Therefore, on the one hand, the marginality of the pig farming industry drives pig farmers to give up their licenses. on the other hand, receiving the ex-gratia payment becomes the alternative for the pig farmers. Faced with the increasing precariousness of their marginalized situation, pig farmers reluctantly chose to give up their businesses in return for the ex-gratia payment. As a result, more than 222 pig farmers gave up their licenses in 2007.

Conclusion

To reduce the transmission of pig-to-human diseases and sanitary risks, the LBBS was launched to buy back the whole industry's licenses and the new Codes of Practices were proposed to standardize spatial configurations to change farmers' sanitary and pest control practices in pig farms. In the LBBS, the governing institutions problematized and constructed pigs as the hosts of contagious pig-to-human diseases. The sanitary discourse not only produced an uncertain pig-raising environment to coerce farmers to return their licenses but also highlighted the environmental conflicts (e.g. odor, risks of disease transmission, and pollution) between the pig farming industry and the general public. These conflicts produce political opportunities for the governing institutions to regulate the sanitary and environmental problems of the pig farming industry and to justify the LBBS. This research exposes the defects in a dominant sanitary discourse that favored governing institutions in their efforts to reduce political risks in the domain of public health. The function of the sanitary discourse naturalized the active role of governing institutions to further regulate farm spaces through the proposed new Codes of Practices; farmers are imbued with the concepts of farm management, sanitation, and standardized spatial configuration. Additionally, the pig farming industry was further constructed as undesirable and problematic because of the perceived filth (e.g. manure management), sanitary concerns (e.g. sewage discharge) and the flows of problematic bodies of pig farmers, live pig handlers and transporters who assist virus transmission (e.g. Japanese encephalitis). In light of these developments, the majority of pig farmers (222 farmers) chose to give up their business in return for the ex-gratia payment. After the LBBS in 2008, there are only 43 pig farms still operating in Hong Kong. Through the lens of political ecology, this study critically rethinks the phenomenon of 'voluntary surrender' of pig farmers' licenses and shows how the image of the voluntary is prejudicially constructed by governing institutions. Pig farmers were simultaneously dangled with the carrot of ex-gratia payments to give up pig farming or hit with the stick of stricter regulations under the proposed Codes of Practices, the latter of which may ultimately lead to a revoke of their license without compensation. It is hence arguable whether pig farmers have indeed 'volunteered' to surrender their licenses.

Acknowledgements

Writing this paper has been a rewarding experience for me. I am very thankful to my supervisors; Dr Byron Miller and Prof. Alan Smart commented on my earlier drafts and provided directions to amend the introduction of this paper. I am grateful for Prof. Jody Emel, Dr Harvey Neo, and Dr Martha Cook's comments and editorial work of this paper. Special thanks go to Prof. Maria Lam for her encouragement and guidance.

Notes

1 The author had a discussion with Prof. Alan Smart on 21st October 2013 and he would like to acknowledge Prof. Smart's suggestion to use the comparison between vegetable and pig farming as an example to illustrate the rise and fall of the H.K. agricultural activities.

2 After the outbreak of the severe acute respiratory syndrome (SARS) in March 2003, the Chief Executive in Hong Kong established the Team Clean in May 2003 to formulate and implement policies in order to improve hygiene and provide environmental recommendations. For instance, the Food and Environmental Hygiene Department launched the Cleaning Hong Kong program to wash and clean up different streets in Hong Kong in 2001. Biosecurity measures and codes of practices were introduced to livestock and pig farming level in 2005 and 2007 respectively. The Public health monitoring network was activated on March 1, 2005 in order to provide an updated report of H5, H7 and H9 diseases. At the same time, the Center for Health Protection provided a leaflet to introduce hand-washing methods and other hygiene measures to the personal level.

3 This survey concerned the public views on the government measures to reduce the outbreak of H5N1 diseases and considered how citizens perceived (1) the health of Hong Kong people, (2) the impact of H5N1 on Hong Kong's economy, (3) the livelihoods of people engaged in live animal trade, (4) the culinary tradition of Hong Kong people and the reputation of Hong Kong as 'gourmet paradise' (Legislative Council, 2005, Paper No. CB (2) 566/04-05(03), pp. 8–12).

4 Human actors who interact with pigs include pig farmers, retailers, and transport workers and non-human actors include materiality such as pig farming spaces, vehicles, and abattoirs.

5 The ex-gratia payment is a financial compensation from the government to those farmers who would like to give up their licenses.

6 The governing institutions explained that, owing to time constraints, they could not consult on the Scheme with farmers. In this sense, the choices were created by the governing institutions without farmers' participation.

7 The mentality behind the use of the marking scheme is borrowed from the 'Marking Scheme for Tenancy Enforcement in Public Housing Estates' in 2003. This marking scheme is to control 28 misdeeds which affect public estate's cleanliness and hygiene conditions under Category A (3 points), B (5 points), C (7 points) and D (7 points). If tenant offences of public health issues reach 16 points within two years, the tenancy will be terminated.

8 In-depth interview H.K. 001, Hong Kong, September, 2010. An in-depth interview was conducted with a pig farmer who is still engaged in pig farming in Hong Kong. To protect the interviewee's privacy, I use Mr Chan as his pseudonym.

9 In-depth interview H.K. 004, Hong Kong, September 2010. This in-depth interview is conducted with a former member of the AFCD's Livestock Subcommittee. To protect the interviewee's privacy, I use Mr Leung as his pseudonym.

10 In-depth interview H.K. 007, Hong Kong, September 2010. This in-depth interview is conducted with a pig farmer. To protect the interviewee's privacy, I use Mr Yuen as his pseudonym.

References

AFCD (2008) The Codes of Practices, File No: LS 1/08 Annex: 1–16

Alberta Government, Hong Kong Office (2007) *Rearing Capacity of Pig Farms Further Diminished in Hong Kong*, http://alberta.design97.com/market-news/rearing-capacity-of-pig-farms furtherdiminished-in-hong-kong/, accessed 30 May 2007

Auewarakul, P. (2004). Harvard Public Health Review, www.hsph.harvard.edu/review/

rvw_winter06/rvwwinter06_flucatchers.html, accessed 11May 2011

Blaikie, P. M. and Brookfield, H. (1987) *Land Degradation and Society*, Methuen, London

Bryant, R. L. and Bailey, S. (1997) *Third World Political Ecology*, Routledge, London

Bulkeley, H. (2005) 'Reconfiguring environmental governance: Towards a politics of scales and networks', *Political Geography*, vol 24, no 8, pp. 875–902

Chan, K. W. (2011) 'Government regulation and governmentality in the Hong Kong pig farming industry, 1950–2008', ProQuest, UMI Dissertations Publishing

Convery, I., Bailey, C., Mort, M. and Baxter, J. (2005) 'Death in the wrong place? Emotional geographies of the UK 2001 foot and mouth disease epidemic', *Journal of Rural Studies*, vol 21, no 1, pp. 99–109

Cresswell, T. (1996) *In Place/Out of Place: Geography, Ideology, and Transgression*, University of Minnesota Press, Minneapolis

Cronon, W. (1992) *Nature's Metropolis: Chicago and the Great West*, WW Norton & Company, New York

Davis, M. (2006). *The Monster at Our Door: The Global Threat of Avian Flu*, Henry Holt, New York

Dodd, G. (1856) *The Food of London: A Sketch of The Chief Varieties, Sources of Supply, Probable Quantities, Modes of Arrival, Processes of Manufacture, Suspected Adulteration, and Machinery of Distribution, of the Food for a Community of Two Millions and a Half*, Longman, Brown, Green and Longmans, London

Donaldson, A. (2008) 'Biosecurity after the event: Risk politics and animal disease', *Environment and Planning A*, vol 40, no 7, pp. 1552

Emel, J. and Urbanik, J. (2010) 'Animal geographies: Exploring the spaces', in M. Demello (eds), *Teaching the Animal: Human-Animal Studies Across the Disciplines*, Lantern, New York

Enticott, G. (2008) 'The spaces of biosecurity: Prescribing and negotiating solutions to bovine tuberculosis', *Environment and Planning A*, vol 40, no 7, pp. 1568

Fairhead, J. and Leach, M. (1995) 'False forest history, complicit social analysis: Rethinking some West African environmental narratives', *World Development*, vol 23, pp. 1023–1035

FAO and WOAH (2005) *A Global Strategy for the Progressive Control of Highly Pathogenic Avian Influenza (HPAI)*. WHO, Geneva, www.fao.org/avianflu/documents/HPAIGlobalStrategy31Oct05.pdf, accessed 10 June 2011]

Federation of Pig Raising Co-operative Societies (2001) Letters to the Pig Raising Co-operative Societies in The Annual Magazine of the Federation of Pig Raising Co-operative Societies, 51–53, 21st Mile Castle Peak Road, Hong Kong

Food and Environment Hygiene Department (2005). *The Prevention of H5N1: Reduction the Risk of Human Infection of H5N1 Survey*, FEHD, Hong Kong

Grove, K. (2009) 'Rethinking the nature of urban environmental politics: Security, subjectivity, and the non-human', *Geoforum*, vol 40, no 1, pp. 207–216

Holloway L. and Morris, C. (2014) 'Viewing animal bodies: Truths, practical aesthetics andethical considerability in UK livestock breeding', *Social and Cultural Geography*, vol 15, no 1, pp. 1–22

Lam, K., Tsang, O. T. Y., Yung, R. W. H. and Lau, K. K. (2006) 'Japanese Encephalitis in Hong Kong', *Hong Kong Medical Journal*, vol 11, pp. 182–188

Law, J. and Miele, M. (2011) 'Animal practices', in B. Carter and N. Charles (eds), *Human and Other Animals: Critical Perspectives*, Palgrave Macmillan, Basingstoke, pp. 50–65

LCFC (2006), FCR (2006–07) 5, titled – New Item 'Ex Gratia Payments to pig farm licensees'/ New Item 'One-off grants to assist affected pig farm and live pig transport workers', pp. 1–16

Legislative Council (2005) The *Food Safety and Environment Hygiene Committee*, LC Paper No. CB (2) 566/04-05(03), 'Prevention of avian influenza – consultation on long-term direction to minimize the risk of human infection', pp. 8–12

Legislative Council (2008a) FC104/05-06, CB1/F/1/2 titled the '"Ex-gratia payment" proposal to buy back pig farmers licenses', pp. 1–13

Legislative Council (2008b) *Panel on Food Safety and Environmental Hygiene*, LC Paper No. CB (2)1486/07-08). Hong Kong: The Legislative Council of Hong Kong

Menon, K. U. (2011) *Pigs, People and a Pandemic: Communicating Risk in a City-State*, Nanyang Technological University Working Paper Series No. 6

Neo, H (2012) 'They hate pigs, Chinese farmers … everything!': Beastly racialization in multiethnic Malaysia', *Antipode*, vol 44, no 3, pp. 950–970

Nielsen, E. H. and Simonsen, K. (2003) 'Scaling from "below": Practices, strategies and urban spaces', *European Planning Studies*, vol 11, no 8, pp. 911–927

Opinion Survey (1999) *The Opinion Survey on the Incident of the H5N1 Bird Flu*. Hong Kong: The University of Hong Kong

Paulson, S. and Gezon, L. L. (2004) *Political Ecology across Spaces Scales and Social Groups*, Rutgers University Press, New Brunswick

Paulson, S., Gezon, L. L. and Watts, M. (2003) 'Locating the political in the political ecology: An introduction', *Human Organization*, vol 62, no 3, pp. 205–217

Perdue, M. L. and Swayne, D. E. (2005) 'Public health risk from avian influenza viruses', *Avian Diseases*, vol 49, no 3, pp. 317–327

Robbins, P. (2004) *Political Ecology: A Critical Introduction*, Blackwell Publishing Ltd

Robbins, P. and Bishop, K. M. (2008) 'There and back again: Epiphany, disillusionment, and rediscovery in political ecology', *Geoforum*, vol 39, no 2, pp. 747–755

Robbins, P. and Sharp, J. (2003) 'The lawn-chemical economy and its discontents', *Antipode*, vol 35, no 5, pp. 955–979

Rocheleau, D. (2008) 'Political ecology in the key of policy: From chains of explanations to webs of relation', *Geoforum*, vol 39, no 2, pp. 716–727

Rose, N. and Miller, P. (1992) 'Political Power beyond the State: Problematics of Government', *British Journal of Sociology*, vol 43, no 2, pp. 173–205

Scott, J. C. (1985) *Weapons of the Weak: Everyday Forms of Peasant Resistance*, Yale University Press, New Haven, CT

Serpell, J. A. (2004) 'Factors influencing human attitudes to animals and their welfare', *Animal Welfare*, vol 13, S145–S152

Shrum, W. (2004) 'Science and the committee process: The presentation of the scientific self', *Social Studies of Science*, vol 34, pp. 472–432

Simon, D. (2008) 'Political ecology and development: Intersections, explorations and challenges arising from the work of Piers Blaikie', *Geoforum*, vol 39, no 2, pp. 698–707

Smart, A. and Smart. J. (2008) 'Time-Space Punctuation: Hong Kong's border regime and limits on mobility', *Pacific Affairs*, vol 81, no 2

South China Morning Post (2003) 'Pig Disease "not epidemic"', written by May Fung, Collected from the World Poultry Science Association (Hong Kong Branch) Newspaper Archive

Stibbe, A. (2003) 'As charming as a pig: The discursive construction of the relationship between pigs and humans', *Society and Animal*, vol 11, no 4, pp. 375–392

Swyngedouw, E. (2008) 'Scaled Geographies: Nature, Place, and the Politics of Scale', in E. Sheppard and R. B. McMaster (eds), *Scale and Geographic Inquiry: Nature, Society, and Method*, Wiley-Blackwell, Boston

Swyngedouw, E. and Heynen, N. (2003) 'Urban Political Ecology, justice, and the politics of scale', *Antipode*, vol 35, no 5, pp. 898–918

Tao, K. C. (2008, April 8). [Pig Farmers' Letter to the Legislative Council]. The Legislative Council Archive (LC Paper No. CB (2) 1514/07–08(02)), Hong Kong

The 41st Livestock Sub-Committee meeting's minutes (2005: 1–10), Ref No: (61) in AF AGD 05/9/2/2 Pt.5, Agricultural, Fisheries, and Conservation Department, Hong Kong

The 42nd Livestock Sub-Committee meeting's minutes (2005: 1–11), Ref No: (69) in AF AGD 05/9/2/2 Pt.5, Agricultural, Fisheries, and Conservation Department, Hong Kong

The 45th Livestock Sub-Committee meeting's minutes (2005: 1–7), Ref No: (17) in AF AGD 05/9/2/2 Pt.2, Agricultural, Fisheries, and Conservation Department, Hong Kong

The 47th Livestock Sub-Committee Meeting's minutes (2007: 1–8), Ref No: (7) in AF AGD 05/9/2/2 Pt.6, Agricultural, Fisheries, and Conservation Department, Hong Kong

The 48th Livestock Sub-Committee meeting's minutes (2007: 1–10), Ref No: (7) in AF AGD 05/9/2/2 Pt6, Agricultural, Fisheries, and Conservation Department, Hong Kong

The 49th Livestock Sub-Committee meeting's minutes (2008: 1–6), Ref No: (9) in AF AGD 05/9/2/2 Pt.6, Agricultural, Fisheries, and Conservation Department, Hong Kong

The 50th Livestock Sub-Committee meeting's minutes (2008: 1–3) Ref No: (15) in AF AGD 05/9/2/2 Pt.6, Agricultural, Fisheries, and Conservation Department, Hong Kong

The 52nd Livestock Sub-Committee meeting's minutes (2008: 1–9), Ref No: (18) in AF AGD 05/9/2/2 Pt.6, Agricultural, Fisheries, and Conservation Department, Hong Kong

Vukina, T., Roka, F. and Palmquist, R. B. (1996) 'Swine odor nuisance', *Voluntary Quarter*, pp. 26–29

Watts, M. (2003) 'Development and governmentality', *Singapore Journal of Tropical Geography*, vol 24, pp. 6–34

Zimmerer, K. S. and Bassett, T. J. (2003) *Political Ecology: An Integrative Approach to Geography and Environment-Development Studies*, Guilford Press, New York

18

MITIGATING GREENHOUSE GAS EMISSIONS FROM LIVESTOCK

Complications, implication and new political ecologies

Christopher Rosin and Mark H. Cooper

Introduction

That human-induced climate change will result in a reconfiguration of livestock production systems and their social, economic, and environmental effects over coming decades is beyond doubt. Increasing climatic variability and more pronounced climatic extremes will alter existing systems of livestock management as farmers and pastoralists learn to adapt to the changing accessibility of water and feed and occurrence of disease. In the process, political relationships and human–environment interactions will change and adapt to these new patterns as well. Because the provision of meat and milk products from livestock has become a globalized activity, these changes will reverberate beyond the local contexts of adaptation; responses in one region of the globe will inevitably impact practices elsewhere.

In addition to the more widely acknowledged challenges associated with adapting to climate change, livestock production has also been identified as a significant source of greenhouse gases (GHGs) and faces calls to mitigate these emissions. Despite being the source of between 10–15 percent of total anthropogenic GHG emissions and the largest single source of anthropogenic methane emissions, livestock production has largely evaded the scrutiny and attempts at regulation applied to stationary electricity generation, industrial production and transportation (Gerber et al., 2013; Havlik et al., 2014; Ripple et al., 2014).[1] Industrial sources of emissions have attracted more attention as sites of GHG mitigation, at least in part, because they represent a larger proportion of emissions in most industrialized economies and there is greater technological potential for mitigation by substituting non-GHG-emitting sources of energy or improving production efficiency. However, a growing global appetite for animal proteins (especially those from ruminant animals) demands serious engagement with the mitigation of GHGs from livestock production (Cooper et al., 2013; Ripple et al., 2014).

In this chapter, we examine some nascent and tentative steps taken to mitigate GHGs from livestock production and the potential implications of these actions on the social and environmental systems within which livestock production occurs. To date, the mitigation of GHGs from livestock production has been directed toward establishing measurement and reporting frameworks for livestock-derived emissions and the fitful use of emissions trading as a regulatory instrument. These mitigation efforts direct farmers and pastoralists to incorporate a new matter of environmental concern – the direct and indirect production of GHGs from livestock – into the existing cognitive frameworks and regimes of practice that structure livestock production. Two challenges emerge from the growing concerns regarding GHGs from livestock for New Zealand. The first involves the social value of livestock production within New Zealand's culture and the New Zealand economy's reliance on the commodity production of meat and dairy products since the mid-nineteenth century. The second relates to the potential impact of efforts to mitigate GHGs upon wider social, economic, and ecological systems.

The introduction of this new matter of concern, and the means by which farmers and pastoralists engage with the mitigation of GHGs from livestock, may unsettle existing political ecologies of livestock production. Within New Zealand, this political ecology is frequently described through reference to a few dominant features, including: extensive pasture-based grazing (with supplemental feeding of dairy cows), continued production increases arising from intensification and land-use conversion (sheep and beef to dairy; forestry to dairy), global supply chain development for both bulk commodity and high value products, the significance of livestock farming in the country's history, culture, and economy (Gray and Le Heron, 2010; Jay, 2007; Le Heron, 2011, 2013; MacLeod and Moller, 2006; Rosin and Campbell, 2012). The implications of attempts to measure and manage livestock emissions of methane and nitrous oxide have, until recently, been invisible to or ignored by political ecologists. It is our contention that, given New Zealand's attempt to include agricultural emissions in its national GHG mitigation program, the county's meat and dairy sectors provide an exemplary case study for investigating the political ecology of livestock production in the context of climate change. Based on our observations of the introduction of the New Zealand Emissions Trading Scheme (ETS), the response of both farmers and industry representatives, and subsequent amendments to the agriculture sector's involvement with the ETS, we argue that the emergence of GHGs as a factor in livestock production makes for 'strange' political ecologies. By this, we mean that the introduction of GHGs as something to be measured, valued, and managed does not follow the typical or model pathways of human–environment interaction and power relations within political ecology (Jay, 2007). Rather, the primary relevance of this case for political ecology in other contexts is how the introduction of a new matter of concern and the unsettling of existing social, economic, and ecological relationships that ensue can open potential spaces for the reassertion and a reordering of what and who society values.

We frame our argument by first reviewing the emergence and historical context of livestock production in New Zealand. We then review the attempt to regulate GHG emissions through the ETS and argue that both technical challenges inherent to GHG accounting in livestock production and political opposition from powerful sector interests impeded implementation of the ETS's coverage of livestock emissions. Following this, we evaluate the potential effects of attempts to mitigate GHGs as an unsettling force in the political ecology of livestock production with reference to political interests within the sector and potential second-order environmental implications. We conclude by discussing the relevance of the New Zealand case for other contexts.

Livestock farming in New Zealand's culture, economy, and politics

The political ecology of pastoral farming in New Zealand developed during the early colonial period following the signing of the Treaty of Waitangi in 1840. Prior to European settlement, there was little management of livestock, as the indigenous Maori largely relied on hunting, fishing and shellfish gathering to supplement cultivated and gathered botanical foods. The early English settlers, however, were quick to overlay their idyllic perceptions of productive pastures on both open and forested landscapes of the islands (Brooking and Pawson, 2007). Recent environmental history research refers, in fact, to New Zealand as an important part of Britain's Empires of Grass (Pawson and Brooking, 2002), due to the role of grass in transforming the 'native' ecology into a colonized one. The process of re-creating the country as a grassed landscape has continued to the extent that relatively treeless countrysides in many formerly forested regions are now considered natural and iconic.

The value of pasture-based production of meat, milk and wool was reinforced by New Zealand's position within the British Empire. The underlying rationale for production was oriented toward fulfilling an allegiance to the mother country, while also developing a viable economy for an isolated and relatively small colony (Brooking and Pawson, 2007). This strong emphasis on exports led to the normalization of excess production in New Zealand, which has evolved to the current situation in which over 90 percent of its meat and dairy products are consumed in other countries. The shipment of first wool and eventually (following the development of refrigerated shipping) frozen animal carcasses and processed dairy products (e.g. cheese) was a 'niche' in colonial markets that was more easily exploited than competing with geographically more favored grain producers such as North America or Australia (Galbreath, 1998). The lack of a large local labor pool also encouraged more extensive livestock production on open grasslands which required only occasional labor for mustering the flock to facilitate shearing or butchering. Both official and unofficial assessments of the colony's progress recognized and promoted the potential for and value of pastoral production in the country (Winder, 2009). The result was the emergence of the iconic pastoral farmer in New Zealand whose contribution to the country's identity underlay the social value placed on livestock production. For individual farmers, their profession lent a widely accepted social prestige with livestock seen as a key source of value creation, while also being a prominent source of support for the empire, especially in periods of need. Thus they were recognized not only for their farming skills but also as good and productive citizens, a position which imparted legitimacy in social and political arenas.

The social value of livestock production in New Zealand also influenced the ways in which the country represented itself to the rest of the empire and world. Until the United Kingdom joined the European Union in 1973 and terminated its favored trade relation status, the New Zealand livestock sector relied on its reputation for low-cost production and innovation to maintain export returns (Le Heron, 1989). As a result, in part, of its unique situation of a plenitude of pasture and minimal competition from horticultural or crop production, New Zealand became a world leader in innovation related to electric fencing and pasture management and utilization, including rotational grazing (Galbreath, 1998). The combined effects of increasing exposure to competition and the growing concerns about the environmental impacts of food production led to a subsequent repositioning of New Zealand pastoral farming as environmentally friendly (Wildblood-Crawford, 2006). This representation relied on more extensive management practices which required fewer chemical inputs and left a more dispersed ecological footprint on the landscape. Among farmers, this led to the perception of their practice as being more 'natural' and reinforced their contribution to the country's branding as 'clean and green'. The apparent legitimacy of these claims was solidified by the sector's success in international markets (especially for dairy products since the start of the twenty-first century), which suggested global recognition and acceptance of the imaginary of New Zealand livestock production. Within this context, both farmers and associated processing industries became convinced of their pivotal role as leaders in the production of meat and dairy products and as essential suppliers to a hungry world (Cooper and Rosin, 2014; Rosin, 2013). Thus, despite the continuing urbanization of New Zealand, livestock farmers continued to retain an honored social position.

Concern about climate change, and specifically the recognition of livestock production as a significant source of GHGs, has begun to disturb both the imaginary of New Zealand livestock production and the social ordering that evolved with the sector. In recent years livestock farmers have been increasingly exposed to public criticism, a situation that is exacerbated by the impact of more intensive livestock management on water quality. Acknowledgement of the imperative to mitigate GHG emissions both within New Zealand and internationallly has introduced a competing and often contradictory measure of good practice for farming. In particular, there is a noticeable discursive shift toward considering not only the quantity of food produced, but also the relative quantity of GHGs associated with that production relative to other countries (Saunders and Barber, 2008). Because there is, at present, no means to reduce emissions without reducing either livestock numbers or the volume of meat and milk produced, strict restrictions on the growth of GHGs from livestock would impose limits upon ongoing pastoral intensification. The attempt to mitigate GHGs therefore runs counter to the dominant focus within New Zealand's livestock sector on increasing production through nutrient inputs such as nitrogen fertilizers or animal feeds sourced off-farm or internationally. As a challenge to the traditional metrics of good farming, the shift threatens to undermine the established social value of farmers and agricultural products in New Zealand. Substantially reducing New Zealand's gross emissions could require realignment of the nation's economy toward a reduced emphasis on livestock production and the simultaneous development of competitive advantages in other agricultural products and other economic sectors.

Emissions trading and the mitigation of greenhouse gas emissions from livestock

Seeking a role as a 'responsible global citizen' with regard to the mitigation of GHG emissions, the New Zealand government was faced with the task of 'allocating' emission permits among sectors and firms in a politically acceptable manner. Following an aborted attempt at establishing a carbon tax and levy on agricultural emissions (intended to support research on developing technological mitigation options), the government introduced an emissions trading program with the intention of achieving mitigation at 'least cost' to the aggregate economy. Despite the Kyoto Protocol's binding emissions reductions targets for developed countries and non-binding progress commitments for all UN Framework Convention on Climate Change signatories, only two mandatory national emissions reductions programs exist at present: the New Zealand Emissions Trading Scheme and the European Union Emissions Trading Scheme.[2] The EU ETS does not include emissions from agriculture, making the New Zealand ETS the world's only attempt – to date – at establishing mandatory regulation of GHG emissions arising from livestock production (Cooper et al., 2013).[3] According to the Labour-led government that developed the ETS, the inclusion of agricultural emissions in the scheme was necessary due to their significance within New Zealand's emissions profile (almost of half of New Zealand's GHG emissions are attributable to agriculture) and out of a desire to avoid exemptions that would inhibit the putative efficiency of the emissions market or privilege some sectors of the economy (Ward, 2006; Moyes, 2008).

The development of the ETS, and especially the Labour government's intention to include emissions from livestock, was politically contentious (Cooper and Rosin, 2014). Many members of the agriculture sector, and the lobby group Federated Farmers in particular, expressed strident and vocal opposition (Bullock, 2012). Recognizing that there was limited potential for the sector to reduce its emissions or pass on the cost of emissions liabilities to consumers in other countries, the Labour government agreed to give the agriculture sector a free allocation of emissions units equivalent to 90 percent of its emissions (using 2005 as a baseline), meaning that the sector's financial liability was a tenth of the 'full cost' of the emissions that it generated. The ETS was established in legislation in September 2008 and called for staggered entry of economic sectors into the scheme; agriculture was to be the last sector, entering the scheme in 2012. Elections held in November 2008, however, resulted in a new government formed by the National Party with parliamentary support from the ACT, United Future, and Māori parties. The first act of this new government was an announcement that it would delay implementation of the ETS and establish a parliamentary committee to review the scheme. Since 2008, a number of significant changes to the ETS have reduced the financial liabilities for emitters of GHGs; particularly notable among these changes is the exclusion of agricultural emissions from the scheme until at least 2015. In late 2014, the National Party government was elected to a third term (with continued support from the same minor parties). As a result, regardless of the original intent to regulate GHGs from New Zealand's livestock through the ETS, it appears unlikely that this will materialize in the near future.

Despite perpetual delays to the inclusion of livestock emissions in the ETS, regulations detailing how the program would function remain in place. The alignment of the 'cost' of emissions to a specific point in the production chain was a significant issue in the design of the scheme (Ministry of Agriculture and Forestry, 2009). The government ultimately favored having processing firms participate in the scheme – instead of individual farms – due to concerns about cost and compliance issues associated with administering the scheme across thousands of farms. Consequently, meat and milk processors serve as the point-of-obligation for reporting their emissions-related activity to the government. Under an ETS that included agricultural emissions, firms would be required to purchase emissions units based on the GHGs produced by their supplying farms and would then pass the cost of these units back to their suppliers. Equally important for the design of the government's scheme was the belief that accounting methodologies for livestock emissions were not precise enough to recognize mitigation activities undertaken at the farm-scale (Cooper et al., 2013). Differences in feed intake, soil type, breed characteristics, and the metabolism of individual animals all affect the volume of emissions from livestock (Clark, 2006). Within existing regulations however, the volume of GHG emissions from livestock is calculated based only on the number and type of animals involved in production and the volume of meat or milk produced. Therefore, while emissions from livestock and actions that would mitigate these emissions both occur on the farm, farmers are not directly involved in the ETS. Based on ETS regulations as they now stand, it is not possible to differentiate the volume of emissions between two otherwise identical farms where one farm undertakes actions to mitigate livestock emissions and the other farm does not. This inability to account for mitigation activities that might be undertaken represents a significant impediment in using emissions trading as a means to regulate GHG emissions from livestock.

The connection of GHG emissions to livestock production raises many issues that extend beyond the simple juxtaposition of increasing production (through continued intensification) and mitigating emissions (through some form of de-intensification or yet to be developed technological interventions). The attempt to attach value to GHGs – both in the form of normative concern and through pricing an economic externality – in order to more effectively regulate them has had implications that go beyond the narrow intent of providing a more 'objective' or 'neutral' basis for distributing emissions allowances across economic activities. For the livestock sector, and especially for farmers, the move toward regulating GHGs arising from livestock production has been interpreted as an attack on their integrity, on their hard-won identity as good farmers, and good citizens of New Zealand and the world (Cooper and Rosin, 2014; Rosin, 2013). It is in this light that their largely skeptical response should be understood. The livestock sector's challenges to the scientific findings and the 'fairness' of the relative responsibility assumed by other economic sectors and social groups are fuelled by a defensive reaction to this perceived attack. In short, New Zealand pastoral farmers have largely rejected the legitimacy of calls to reduce the volume of GHG emissions produced by their livestock as doing so would require reducing the volume of their production, their net revenue, or both – and in the process evicerating their position in New Zealand society.

Strange political ecologies and the mitigation of greenhouse gases from livestock

Predicting what changes might arise in the political ecology of New Zealand livestock production under future GHG mitigation policies is beset by complications arising from the apparent inevitability of livestock's production of 'biological' GHGs and the spatial, temporal, and causal distance between GHG emissions and their effect on global climate change. These complications call into question the appropriateness of a more traditional political ecology analysis that follows power relations and economic structures to examine the resulting distribution of benefits, harms, and environmental outcomes (Watts, 2003; Liverman, 2004). While the attempt to regulate agricultural GHGs has some similarities with other forms of environmental management associated with agriculture, the matter of mitigating GHGs in livestock production makes for some strange political ecologies. In this section we attempt to untangle the knot of the various ways that mitigating livestock emissions might affect political relationships within New Zealand's livestock production system and examine some of the potential second-order effects of pursing GHG mitigation in livestock production.

The challenge for understanding the political implications of mitigating GHG emissions in livestock production arises from the potential of these regulations to affect multiple interest groups at a variety of scales. Acceptance of the necessity of mitigating GHGs in livestock production at a level equivalent to other economic sectors would appear to require a reconfiguration of established orders of social value regarding the place of farmers and pastoral farming in New Zealand's society and economy. It is unsurprising that concerns about GHG emissions and other environmental problems arising from livestock production in New Zealand have been insufficient to instigate such changes – such resistance is common across industrialized countries. However, the demand for reductions in GHG emissions – and the persistence of environmental concerns more generally – will require the whole of the livestock commodity system to either accommodate more moderate rates of growth or largely ignore the climatic implications of their production.

Despite this general contradiction between increased livestock production and the imperative to mitigate GHGs from livestock, the specific ways in which farmers, firms, and the state's interests are translated through markets which are demanding increased supply of livestock products could yield instances of both emissions mitigation and further intensification. Globally, consumers exert their economic power in diverse ways with some demanding a more GHG-efficient food supply, including reduced consumption of animal proteins, while a much larger segment is expressing a preference for increased consumption of protein-rich meat and dairy products (McCluskey and Loureiro, 2003; Tait et al., 2013). Retailers have responded to these differentiated consumer demands by carving out niches: selling either higher value environmentally friendly products to a smaller number of discriminating consumers, or continuing to pressure producers for inexpensive, undifferentiated commodities (Carolan, 2011). In the absence of prices or other regulatory measures on GHGs from livestock, it is unclear how retailer-driven interventions premised on lower-emissions production would affect particular actors within New Zealand's livestock production system. In the New Zealand domestic context, environmental and recreation NGOs have challenged further intensification of livestock production principally out of concern for impacts on water quality, rather than increased GHG emissions (or other issues such as animal welfare), a stance that is largely mimicked by subnational government bodies with directives to monitor and regulate environmental impact.

When seeking to adapt to the disruption caused by GHGs as a new and largely uncontrollable matter of concern, existing interests within the political ecology of livestock production in New Zealand are often unable to consistently draw on their traditional modes of power. For example, despite efforts to develop technologies that would reduce the production of GHGs by ruminant livestock while increasing per animal production volumes, current expectations are that technological innovations are most likely to result in low levels of mitigation through more efficient management (Vermont and DeCara, 2010). This lack of available technological solutions likely precludes the possibility of significant technology-driven shifts in production practices; however, it also limits the ability of large private-sector actors to monopolize access and generate excess profits from such fixes. Similarly, meat and dairy processing firms would prefer to shift the costs and risks of GHG reporting to suppliers and farmers, but this desire has so far been thwarted by government insistance that current GHG accounting capabilities make this option more costly and more prone to compliance issues. This issue of where the responsibility for GHG reporting should be sited within the production chain is not merely technical, it is an attempt by the government to manage the multiple and competing interests of farmers as political constituents, processing and exporting firms as drivers of national economic growth, global environmental responsibilities, and international political relations.

Attempts to regulate GHGs from livestock exhibit several important differences from other environmental issues. As an environmental problem, the defining characteristic of GHGs is their broad spatial extent and the temporal and causal distance between discrete emissions sources and aggregate changes in the global atmosphere. This is a notable difference from the traditional scales of political ecology in which social-ecological systems are linked at the community or regional level and ecological effects are more proximate to related socio-economic processes (Rangan and Kull, 2009; Haarstad, 2014). The effect of GHGs from livestock on the global atmosphere would be difficult, if not impossible, to disaggregate from the effect of GHGs from other sources. Likewise, the effect of livestock emissions – or of the mitigation of these emissions – on the atmosphere is unlikely to be felt for decades. The implications of this for a political ecology of GHG mitigation are important and complex.

Both the political ecology of livestock production and how we, as scholars, investigate this political ecology are shaped by climate change science at local, national, and international levels. Scientific and technical networks play a critical role in understanding and attributing the consequences of GHG emissions and mitigation; the knowledge that these networks produce and the role of this knowledge in governance is an essential part of any political ecology of GHG mitigation. Due to the distinctive materialities of GHGs as an environmental issue, calls to action and programs to mitigate emissions from livestock are predicated on abstract norms and broad spheres of political and ethical concern. Such concern is most often expressed by national governments as part of international GHG mitigation commitments, and by national and international NGOs. The translation of such concerns into environmental programs, however, is likely to rely on the imposition of financial costs or regulatory controls on livestock producers. While some portion of producers may share these norms or concerns about the effects of GHG emissions, political opposition to programs that raise the costs of production or reduce the volume of production is to be expected (Gerber et al., 2010). For farmers, the experience of climate change as an environmental phenomenon is inherently mediated by abstract representations of scientific knowledge, rather than any direct experiential feedback. Within New Zealand, farmers experience climate as annual and seasonal variations in weather rather than regional expressions of anthropogenic climate change. Moreover, when farmers voice the perception that they have experienced climate change, they typically attribute such changes to natural cycles or express that the relationship of GHGs to climate change is beyond their ken. The spatial, temporal and causal distance between livestock emissions and climate change precludes local environmental feedbacks or contradictions from being felt by livestock producers.

While the ultimate goal of emissions mitigation is to reduce the volume of GHGs, both New Zealand livestock producers and the New Zealand government have favored improving the efficiency of production per unit of emission rather than pursuing an absolute reduction in GHGs from livestock. Both the livestock sector and the government have argued that increased production is necessary in order to meet the rising demand for protein in the developing world and for high-quality products in the developed world. The pursuit of efficiency gains rather than a reduction in the volume of emissions is in keeping with these aims for the continued growth of production and exports of milk and meat. If the growing demand for livestock products is genuinely immutable, then improving efficiency while increasing production is seen by producers as the only reasonable strategy (Garnett, 2014). Within New Zealand, producer interest groups and the government have both argued that, since global livestock production must inevitably increase along with rising demand, it would be better that production increase in New Zealand, which has relatively higher production per unit of emissions than in less efficient countries. This same argument has been made in justifying the exclusion of livestock emissions from the ETS: production discouraged in New Zealand by a price on emissions would simply take place in other countries where production is less efficient, thus leading to even more emissions than would occur in the absence of regulation.

The diversity of strategies that offer some potential to reduce the emission of methane and nitrous oxide from livestock gives rise to a number of potential trade-offs and co-benefits (Verspecht et al., 2012). Due to the significant variation among livestock production systems, particular mitigation strategies may generate trade-offs and co-benefits in some situations but not others (Garnett, 2009). Adding a novel element – GHGs – to the political economy of livestock production will have repercussions – potentially positive and negative – through associated social, environmental and animal systems. For example, a number of studies have found that diets for ruminant livestock rich in cereals and oilseeds reduce the volume of methane output per unit of milk or meat produced. However, if such inputs are used to replace grass-fed diets on a significant scale it could incentivize land clearing to meet new demand or displace crop production for direct human consumption; this could yield a reduction in emissions directly from livestock but a net increase in emissions attributable to the livestock production system. Similarly, controlling GHGs from outputs such as effluent is more readily attainable in confined or partially confined livestock rearing systems (Garnett, 2011). Increasing animal confinement for the purpose of effluent control or non-pasture feeding could in many cases yield GHG reductions, but may prompt new concerns for animal welfare. Given the complexity and diversity of livestock production systems, attempts to mitigate GHGs from livestock will have consequences which reverberate throughout animal and land use systems. As calls to improve the emissions efficiency of livestock production and to generate overall reductions in emissions continue to grow, it will become increasingly important to investigate and understand how moves to control GHGs from livestock reconfigure the wider political ecologies of livestock production.

Conclusions

The New Zealand experience with attempts to introduce GHG mitigation policies into the agriculture sector, and more specifically to influence emissions trajectories from livestock production, indicates that such efforts are likely (at least initially) to create 'strange' political ecologies. It is apparent from the New Zealand case that the social interactions at play will involve a diverse set of interests, expressed at a multitude of scales that reverberate through the global commodity system. These diverse interest groups will also implicate a variety of 'winners' and 'losers', with opportunities and threats for all participants. It is also evident that the introduction of emissions trading or other attempts to regulate emissions in livestock production will need to overcome existing subjectivities and social orderings that frequently rely on justifications that contradict the constraints placed on emissions. The potential for GHG mitigation to disrupt established power relations in livestock production is tempered, however, by the overarching threat of global climate change. Whereas persistent negotiation and contestation of an unsettled political ecology opens space for agency, something concrete needs to be done to reduce the impact of livestock on the global climate.

Attempts to mitigate GHGs from livestock production may also yield surprising social, political and environmental changes based on the distinctive attributes of GHGs as an environmental issue and the connectedness of livestock production to other agricultural and land use systems. Explaining the political ecology of mitigating emissions from livestock requires attention to the role of scientific networks as knowledge producers and the role of scientific knowledge in emissions governance, but also reflexive attention to how our analysis of social and environmental systems is premised upon particular scientific understandings of climate science and emissions attribution. The complexity and connectedness of livestock production to other social, animal and environmental concerns means that both mitigating emissions and the politics of mitigating emissions may generate second and third-order consequences the require consideration of activities occurring across a range of social and environmental scales. Political ecology's attention to complexity and diversity is a strength relative to other analytical approaches making it well suited for recognizing and analyzing these difficult issues.

Neither the complexities of an increasingly interdependent global commodity system for livestock products nor the elusiveness of GHG emissions as a newly acknowledged participant facilitate the elaboration of a typical political ecology. This may simply reflect the early stage in the insertion of GHG mitigation into the livestock production framework. We would argue, however, that any assessment of the political ecology of livestock production in the context of the mitigation of GHG emissions must account for a broader set of actors than multi-national corporations and small-scale pastoralists, or states, economic elites and family farmers. It must also be prepared to acknowledge the potentially brief temporal coalescence of a given political ecology given the continued elusiveness of GHG emissions within the negotiation of the emerging social and human–environment relations of which it is composed. The challenge for the academic employing a political ecology framework is to contribute to a fairer allocation of the benefits and costs of such change.

Notes

1 Figures on the contribution of livestock to total emissions are based on 100-year global warming potentials consistent with UNFCCC methodologies and embodied in the Kyoto Protocol.

2 The European Union Emissions Trading Scheme includes 31 EU member countries as well as Iceland, Liechtenstein, and Norway. Australia established a carbon tax in 2012 which was repealed in 2014. During its operational period Australia's carbon tax did not apply to livestock emissions.

3 Livestock GHG mitigation in other jurisdictions includes information provision, subsidies, grants, and tax incentives, and earned emissions offsets, all of which are voluntary – rather than compliance-based – programs.

References

Brooking, T. and Pawson, E. (2007) 'Silences of grass: Retrieving the role of pasture plants in the development of New Zealand and the British Empire', *Journal of Imperial and Commonwealth History*, vol 35, no 4, pp. 417–435

Bullock, D. (2012) 'Emissions trading in New Zealand: Development, challenges and design', *Environmental Politics*, vol 21, pp. 657–675

Carolan, M. (2011) *The Real Cost of Cheap Food*, Routledge, London

Clark, H. (2006) 'Methane emissions from New Zealand ruminants', in R. Chapman, J. Boston and M. Schwass (eds), *Confronting Climate Change: Critical Issues for New Zealand*, Victoria University Press, Wellington

Cooper, M. H. and Rosin, C. (2014) 'Absolving the sins of emission: The politics of regulating agricultural greenhouse gas emissions in New Zealand', *Journal of Rural Studies*

Cooper, M. H., Boston, J. and Bright, J. (2013) 'Policy challenges for livestock emissions abatement: Lessons from New Zealand', *Climate Policy*, vol 13, pp. 110–133.

Galbreath, R. (1998) 'A grassland utopia? Pastoral farming and grassland research in New Zealand', in *DSIR: Making Science Work for New Zealand*, Victoria University Press, Wellington

Garnett, T. (2009) 'Livestock-related greenhouse gas emissions: Impacts and options for policy makers', *Environmental Science and Policy*, vol 12, pp. 491–503

Garnett, T. (2011) 'Where are the best opportunities for reducing greenhouse gas emissions in the food system (including the food chain)?', *Food Policy*, vol 26, pp. S23–S32

Garnett, T. (2014) 'Three perspectives on sustainable food security: Efficiency, demand restraint, food system transformation. What role for life cycle assessment?', *Journal of Cleaner Production*, vol 73, pp. 10–18

Gerber, P., Key, N., Portet, F. and Steinfeld, H. (2010) 'Policy options in addressing livestock's contribution to climate change', *Animal*, vol 4, pp. 393–406

Gerber, P. J., Steinfeld, H., Henderson, B., Mottet, A., Opio, C., Dijkman, J., Falcucci, A. and Tempio, G. (2013) *Tackling Climate Change through Livestock: A Global Assessment of Emissions and Mitiation Opportunities*, FAO, Rome.

Gray, S. and Le Heron, R. (2010) 'Globalising New Zealand: Fonterra Co-operative Group, and the future', *New Zealand Geographer*, vol 66, pp. 1–13

Haarstad, H. (2014) 'Climate change, environmental governance and the scale problem', *Geography Compass*, vol 8, pp. 87–97

Havlik, P., Valin, H., Herrero, M., Obersteiner, M., Schmid, E., Rufino, M. C., Mosnier, A., Thornton, P. K., Böttcher, H., Conant, R. T., Frank, S., Fritz, S., Fuss, S., Kraxner, F. and Notenbaert, A. (2014) 'Climate change mitigation through livestock system transitions', *Proceedings of the National Academy of Sciences*, vol 111, pp. 3709–3714

Jay, M. (2007) 'The political economy of a productivist agriculture: New Zealand dairy discourses', *Food Policy*, vol 32, pp. 266–279

Le Heron, R. (1989) 'A political economy perspective on the expansion of New Zealand livestock farming, 1960–1984: Part I. Agricultural policy', *Journal of Rural Studies*, vol 5, pp. 17–32

Le Heron, R. (2011) 'Market-making and livelihood challenges in contemporary New Zealand's dairy and sheep pastoral economies', in J. Gertel and R. Le Heron (eds), *Economic Spaces of Pastoral Production and Commodity Systems: Markets and Livelihoods*, Ashgate, Farnham

Le Heron, R. (2013) 'Emerging neo-liberalising processes in New Zealand's land-based sector: A post-structural political economy framing using emergence diagrams', *Applied Geography*, vol 45, pp. 392–401

Liverman, D. (2004) 'Who governs, at what scale, and at what price? Geography, environmental governance, and the commodification of nature', *Annals of the Association of American Geographers*, vol 94, pp. 734–738

MacLeod, C. and Moller, H. (2006) 'Intensification and diversification of New Zealand agriculture since 1960: An evaluation of current indicators of land use change', *Agriculture, Ecosystems, and Environment*, vol 115, pp. 201–218

McCluskey, J. J. and Loureiro, M. L. (2003) 'Consumer preferences and willingness to pay for food labeling: a discussion of empirical studies', *Journal of Food Distribution Research*, vol 34, no 3, pp. 95–102

Ministry of Agriculture and Forestry (2009) 'Point of obligation designs and allocation methodologies for agriculture and the New Zealand emissions trading scheme', Report for the Ministry of Agriculture and Forestry by the Agriculture Technical Advisory Group, New Zealand Government, Wellington

Moyes, T. E. (2008) 'Greenhouse gas emissions trading in New Zealand: Trailblazing comprehensive cap and trade', *Ecology Law Quarterly*, vol 35, pp. 911–965

Pawson, E. and Brooking, T. (eds) (2002) *Environmental Histories of New Zealand*, Oxford University Press, Melbourne

Rangan, H. and Kull, C. A. (2009) 'Rethinking "scale" in political ecology', *Progress in Human Geography*, vol 31, pp. 28–45

Ripple, W. J., Smith, P., Haberl, H., Montzka, S. A., McAlpine, C. and Boucher, D. H. (2014) 'Ruminants, climate change and climate policy', *Nature Climate Change*, vol 4, pp. 2–5.

Rosin, C. (2013) 'Food security and the justification of productivism in New Zealand', *Journal of Rural Studies*, vol 29, pp. 50–58

Rosin, C. and Campbell, H. (2012) 'The complex outcomes of neoliberalization in New Zealand: Productivism, audit and the challenge of future energy and climate shocks', in R. Almås and H. Campbell (eds), *Rethinking Agricultural Policy Regimes: Food Security, Climate Change and the Future Resilience of Global Agriculture*, Emerald Group Publishing, Bingley, UK

Saunders, C. and Barber, A. (2008) 'Carbon footprints, life cycle analysis, food miles: Global trade trends and market issues', *Political Science*, vol 60, pp. 73–88.

Tait, P. R., Saunders, C., Rutherford, P. and Guenther, M. (2013) 'Valuation of sustainability attributes of food products in India and China: Decomposing the value of New Zealand's "Clean-Green" brand', Paper presented at the European Association of Environmental and Resource Economists Annual Conference, Toulouse, France, June 26–29

Vermont, B. and De Cara, S. (2010) 'How costly is mitigation of non-CO_2 greenhouse gas emissions from agriculture? A meta-analysis', *Ecological Economics*, vol 69, pp. 1,373–1,386

Verspecht, A., Vandermeulen, V., Ter Avest, E. and Van Huylenbroeck, G. (2012) 'Review of trade-offs and co-benefits from greenhouse gas mitigation measures in agricultural production', *Journal of Integrative Environmental Sciences*, vol 9, pp. 147–157

Ward, M. (2006) 'The role of economic instruments in New Zealand's domestic climate change policy', Briefing Paper Commissioned by WWF New Zealand, Worldwide Fund for Nature, Wellington

Watts, M. (2003) 'Political ecology', in E. S. Sheppard and T. J. Barnes (eds), *A Companion to Economic Geography*, Blackwell, Oxford

Wildblood-Crawford, B. (2006) 'Grassland utopia and *Silent Spring*: Rereading the agricultural revolution in New Zealand', *New Zealand Geographer*, vol 62, pp. 65–72

Winder, G. M. (2009) 'Grassland revolutions in New Zealand: Disaggregating a national story', *New Zealand Geographer*, vol 65, pp. 187–200

19

DOMESTIC FARMED FISH PRODUCTION

An overview of governance and oversight in the US aquaculture industry

Paula Daniels and Colleen McKinney

It is well recognized that the political, governmental and societal interactions of capture and production of fish are as complex and diverse as its myriad inherent types; deriving, also, from the very nature of our interaction with the animal. We recreationally and nostalgically catch fish in lakes and rivers; we hunt them down in the ocean in massive quantities; we farm them. There are over 25,000 species of fish, most of them still roaming wild in the yet untamed ocean. Many species have been domesticated for farm production, and while the number of farmed species is limited by consumer preferences and the constraints of farming methods, consumption of not only seafood, but farmed seafood, is on the rise. In 2012, worldwide consumption of farmed fish surpassed that of beef (Larsen and Roney, 2013) as well as wild caught fish (FAO, 2012), for the first time in modern history. As the *New York Times* put it: 'Fishing is the only part of global food production in which the tillers and breeders of the world are not dominant, and [in 2013], the last stronghold of the hunter-gatherers will be eclipsed' (Leisher, 2013). In other words, aquaculture (fish farming) has taken its place on the world food production stage. The trend is projected to continue and our consumption of fish is projected to increase (OECD/FAO, 2014).

Given that over 85 percent of the world's fisheries are classified as exploited, and 32 percent as overexploited or depleted (FAO, 2012), the rise of aquaculture is notable for many reasons. We are already seeing the impacts of climate change on our food system: changes in temperatures impact the ability to grow some conventional crops, and invasive pests – linked by some to climate change – threaten others. In the coming decades, regions will struggle with food security on a new level, beyond the chronic question of equitable distribution and affordable access; in other words, the question may become one of whether we can even meet the current level of supply. Farmed fish has potential as a climate-resilient protein source, because of the flexibility of production methods and the comparatively lower use of resources for its production. According to the US National Oceanic and Atmospheric Administration (NOAA):

> Aquaculture is one of the most resource-efficient ways to produce protein. Fish come out well because, in general, they convert more of the food they eat into body mass than land animals … [Even] salmon – the most feed-intensive farmed fish – is still far more efficient than other forms of protein production.
> (National Marine Fisheries Service, 2014)

Several types of farming methods have developed in three distinctly managed farming areas: in the ocean, the tidal zones, and on land. Land-based farming practices include ponds and tanks, the latter of increasing interest for its potential use in urban areas, and the ability to better manage inputs and effluent.

In fisheries management, '[d]iversity is a characteristic of the entities that form fisheries systems and it points to the nature and degree by which they vary' (Kooiman et al., 2005, 13). Fisheries 'are among the most regulated resources in the United States' (Andreatta and Parlier, 2010, 180) and weak trade restrictions have given foreign competitors an advantage in the US market, threatening the livelihood of a number of local commercial fisheries as well as the economic viability of locally produced farmed fish (Hanson and Sites, 2011).

Production of farmed fish is dominated by China, which in 2012 produced over 60 percent of farmed fish, showing indisputable world dominance in the area (with the US trailing in thirteenth position, producing less than 1 percent) (FAO, 2012). The US imports seafood in significant quantity – according to recent data, about 90 percent by weight. The majority of those imports are farmed fish, and most of that is shrimp (USDA ERS, 2013). Recent reports of slave labor practices and environmental destruction of mangroves in the shrimp farming industries of Asia raise the question of why we are importing such negative externalities at the expense of supporting environmentally sound farmed fish production in the US.

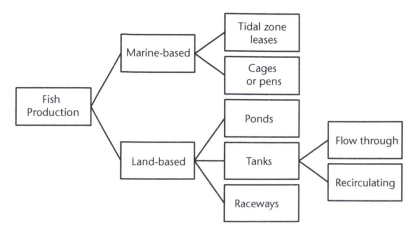

FIGURE 19.1 Methods for aquaculture production.

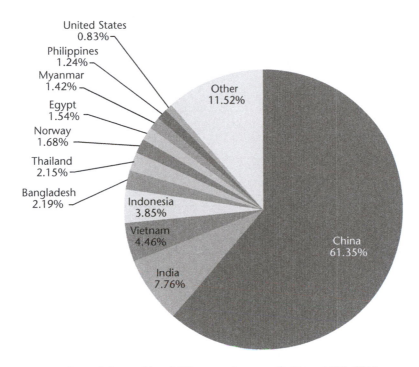

FIGURE 19.2 Growth in world and US aquaculture production, 1980–2011.

Despite an apparent recognition of the importance of developing a strong domestic aquaculture industry, as evidenced by the development of a national aquaculture plan in the 1980s, growth in farmed fish production in the United States lags far behind the rest of the world (see Figure 19.2), and as mentioned, overall production is significantly less than leaders China, India, and Vietnam (see Figure 19.3).

Recognizing that '[f]isheries and aquaculture have considerable potential as vectors for the green economy' (FAO, 2012), the Food and Agriculture Organization of the United Nations called for effective governance of modern aquaculture, which 'must reconcile ecological and human well-being so that the industry is sustainable over time' (Hishamunda et al., 2014, 59). A comprehensive management system should 'provide incentives for wider ecosystem stewardship. The greening of fisheries and aquaculture requires recognition of their wider societal roles within a comprehensive governance framework' (FAO, 2012).

The food policy council model is a policy and governance innovation that attempts to operate in a holistic, ecosystem-oriented framework. Food policy councils by definition bring together diverse stakeholders to advance policy change within a local food system. Food system issues typically selected for local policy action address obesity and diet-related illnesses, food insecurity and hunger, limited access to health care and affordable food, the performance of the local food economy, agriculture, and the natural resources necessary to produce food.

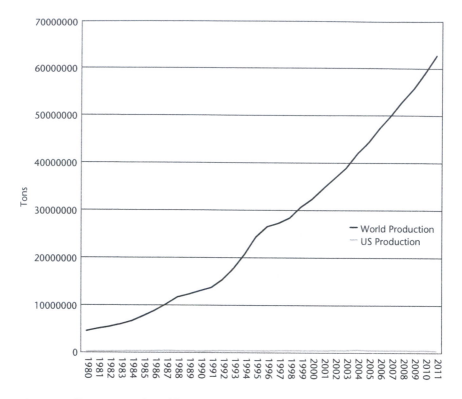

FIGURE 19.3 Percentage of world aquaculture production, top 10 countries and US, 2012 (tons).

Source: FAO (2012).

There are over 250 food policy councils in the United States and Canada, each with their unique needs, resources, configurations, and objectives. What they have in common is an effort to bring together leaders from across sectors, geographies, and socio-economic communities to build new relationships to strengthen, facilitate, and coordinate decision-making for systemic change, and to overcome the widely recognized fragmentation and specialization of the food system, with its resulting silos.

There is an increasing call for the creation of these types of food policy councils. Oliver De Schutter (2014), the United Nations Special Rapporteur on the right to food from 2008–2014, recommended to the United Nations that rebuilding local food systems is a key strategy in democratizing food security policies, and further that:

> Local initiatives informed by social participation will be better informed and therefore more effective in reaching their objectives, and they will result in a more transparent and accountable use of resources. The establishment of local food councils formally linked to municipalities can be one way of achieving this.

Food policy councils were recently characterized as potentially 'the next new government trend' by Mary Beth Albright (2014), writing for National Geographic as part of their Future of Food series.

Typically, food policy councils are focused on the regional production and availability of fruits and vegetables. Recently, the Los Angeles Food Policy Council (considered the largest and most sophisticated in the country with the most extensive reach) formed a Sustainable Seafood Working Group, which has been organizing educational events, in partnership with educational institutions and aquaria, to raise awareness about the various issues pertaining to fisheries and aquaculture (including governance-related issues), and to incorporate a local fish effort into the local food organizing principle.

While there are many ways forward on that path toward a coordinated and comprehensive political ecosystem that will advance sustainable production of aquaculture, the purpose of this chapter is to provide an overview of the existing United States regulatory and oversight governance structures for aquaculture, which may serve as background information foundational to developing a responsible, ecosystem-based approach relevant to the modern political ecology of fish as farmed food.

As complex as governance is for fisheries, it is arguably even more so for aquaculture. In contrast to countries that have a more centralized focus on aquaculture production, such as in Norway, Chile and China, there is a greater regulatory palimpsest in the United States, possibly derived from the dominant production of beef, chicken and pork. This may well be a function of the contrast between fish and other forms of livestock production, with the monolithic singularity of cattle (of which there are many breeds but only two modern bovine species) and the mono-specific chicken. It is also more complicated than that of other livestock, due to the unique animal diaspora which it inhabits. Fish are not fowl. In other words, because it is still a wild species for which we forage and hunt commercially, because it typically grows in protected natural resource areas (rivers, oceans), but because it can also be a domesticated and farmed species – it invokes many jurisdictional layers in the United States.

Federal aquaculture governance

Domesticated livestock species raised on farms or ranches for human consumption – such as cattle, pork and poultry – fall within the jurisdiction of multiple agencies, including the United States Department of Agriculture (USDA), the Food and Drug Administration (FDA), and the Environmental Protection Agency (EPA). These agencies' roles are somewhat distinct based on the stage of production. For example, the USDA has primary oversight during the animal production phases, while the FDA has primary oversight of meat processing as products make their way to consumers, in addition to drug use in animals. The EPA has jurisdiction over air and water quality and chemical uses, at the farm production level.

Within the aquaculture industry, regulation and oversight are also dispersed among many agencies with an even greater variety of responsibilities, missions, and functions (USDA ERS, 2012). The oversight structure is made more complex, by the diversity of the industry, including the variety of species, production methods, and environments in which fish are raised necessitating involvement by the agencies which oversee agriculture, coastal management, wastewater runoff, food safety, and endangered species protection.

The relationships of each relevant federal agency to aquaculture oversight and research are formalized under the auspices of the Joint Subcommittee on

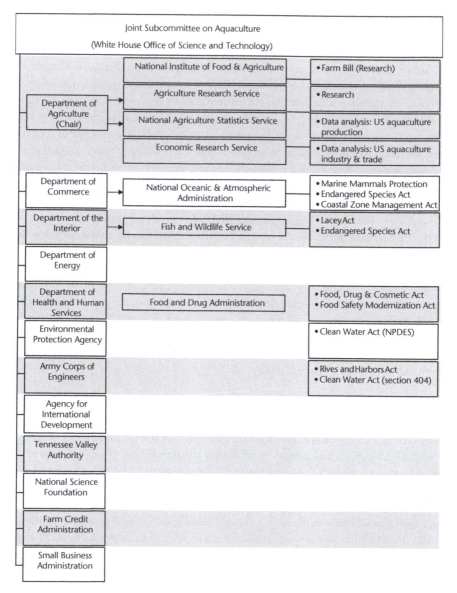

FIGURE 19.4 Composition of Joint Subcommittee on Aquaculture.

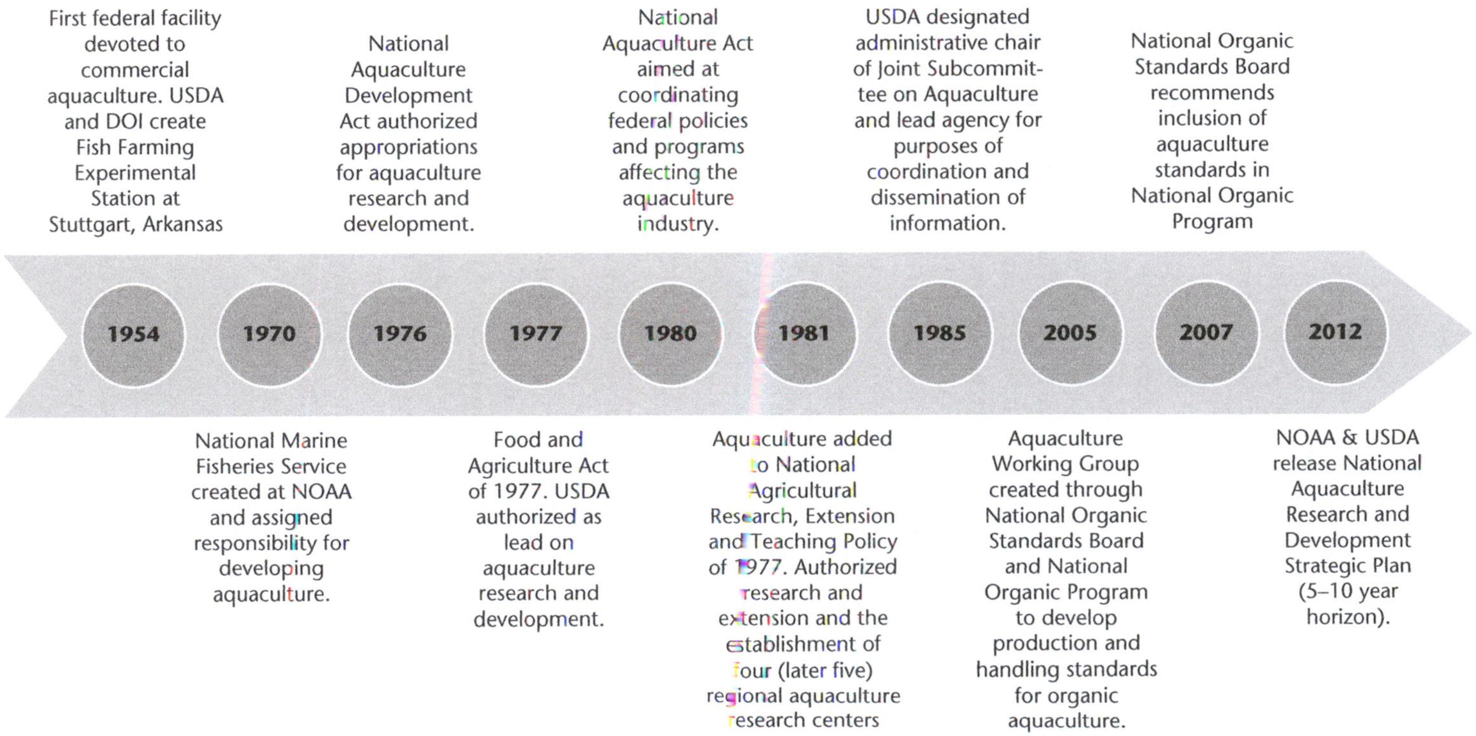

FIGURE 19.5 Critical aquaculture governance actions and milestones.

Timeline (above):

- **1954**: First federal facility devoted to commercial aquaculture. USDA and DOI create Fish Farming Experimental Station at Stuttgart, Arkansas
- **1970**: National Aquaculture Development Act authorized appropriations for aquaculture research and development.
- **1980**: National Aquaculture Act aimed at coordinating federal policies and programs affecting the aquaculture industry.
- **1981**: USDA designated administrative chair of Joint Subcommittee on Aquaculture and lead agency for purposes of coordination and dissemination of information.
- **2007**: National Organic Standards Board recommends inclusion of aquaculture standards in National Organic Program

Timeline (below):

- **1970**: National Marine Fisheries Service created at NOAA and assigned responsibility for developing aquaculture.
- **1977**: Food and Agriculture Act of 1977. USDA authorized as lead on aquaculture research and development.
- **1981**: Aquaculture added to National Agricultural Research, Extension and Teaching Policy of 1977. Authorized research and extension and the establishment of four (later five) regional aquaculture research centers
- **2005**: Aquaculture Working Group created through National Organic Standards Board and National Organic Program to develop production and handling standards for organic aquaculture.
- **2012**: NOAA & USDA release National Aquaculture Research and Development Strategic Plan (5–10 year horizon).

Nodes: 1954, 1970, 1976, 1977, 1980, 1981, 1985, 2005, 2007, 2012

Aquaculture (JSA), as defined by the National Aquaculture Act of 1980. The Act created the JSA and designated it the body responsible for the development and implementation of an overarching National Aquaculture Development Plan. The JSA continues to be the committee primarily responsible for coordinating national policies and programs related to aquaculture development, and its composition reflects the various agencies with a role in aquaculture governance (Jensen, 2007). Figure 19.4 provides a scan of the agencies represented on the JSA and their responsibilities related to aquaculture.

The United States Departments of Agriculture (USDA), Commerce (DOC) and Interior (DOI) are the primary agencies with specific jurisdiction over the aquaculture industry, although Dr Gary Jensen, former National Program Leader for Aquaculture at the USDA and chair of the JSA (recently retired) notes that the role of the DOI has decreased relative to the USDA and the DOC (ibid.). As established by the Food and Agriculture Act of 1977, the USDA is the lead agency for matters related to aquaculture, and its representative is the permanent chair of the JSA. Despite attempted coordination through the JSA over time, the USDA and DOC have maintained independent plans for aquaculture development, and inter-agency efforts have proven difficult to navigate through the bureaucratic process, such as a failed effort in 1995 to update the National Aquaculture Development Plan (ibid.). Instead, the agencies most central to aquaculture oversight have traditionally updated their aquaculture plans independently. The timeline in Figure 19.5 summarizes the history of federal actions related to aquaculture.

NOAA

As recently as 2011, the National Oceanic and Atmospheric Administration (NOAA - part of the DOC) updated their Marine Aquaculture Policy (NOAA, 2011). Their jurisdiction is defined by the Magnuson-Stevens Fishery Conservation and Management Act, the Marine Mammal Protection Act, the Endangered Species Act, and the Coastal Zone Management Act, among others. The strategic goals of NOAA have historically reflected its mission-driven emphasis on maintenance of coastal waters and protection of endangered species. In the past, this focus and emphasis of the department has been on aquaculture regulation, to manage the impact of the industry on wild stocks and coastal habitats (Jensen, 2007). In the recent decade, there has been a renewed focus by NOAA on the development of the aquaculture industry to expand sustainable coastal aquaculture initiatives and to:

> encourage and foster sustainable aquaculture development ... that is in harmony with healthy, productive, and resilient marine ecosystems, compatible with other uses of the marine environment, and consistent with the National Policy for the Stewardship of the Ocean, our Coasts, and the Great Lakes.
>
> (NOAA, 2011)

USDA

The USDA has also maintained an independent set of initiatives to support the development of a thriving domestic industry, and it funds aquaculture research through several departmental agencies. Funding priorities reflect an emphasis on improved efficiency and performance in farmed fish populations, in contrast to NOAA's emphasis on protecting wild species from the influence of farming and animal domestication. The National Institute for Food and Agriculture (NIFA – an entity within the USDA) funds grants for projects related to aquaculture research and development, while the Agricultural Research Service (ARS – also a USDA entity) has an active research action plan focused on genetics, animal performance, nutrition, and production systems.

Box 19.1 Funding of aquaculture at the USDA

According to the USDA, that department has consistently funded and supported aquaculture since the 1970s, and is currently funding aquaculture research more strongly than ever, in strong coordination with its other agricultural programs. An attempt to catalogue recent USDA funding found that funding for aquaculture research across agencies may be around $50 million in 2011: the ARS funding for aquaculture in that year was about $32 million and NIFA grant funded research was approximately another $18.6 million. Aquaculture funding is only 0.4 percent of the USDA Research and Development budget.

The regularly updated omnibus farm legislation has consistently authorized funding for aquaculture. In 2014, the total authorization in the Agriculture Act of 2014 (informally known as the Farm Bill) was $8 million. Specifically, it authorizes $1 million to each of the Department of Agriculture, the Department of Commerce, and the Department of the Interior for aquaculture; however, these authorized funds have historically never been appropriated so they have never been available for use by the departments. The Agriculture Act of 2014 also authorizes up to $5 million to fund the USDA Regional Aquaculture Research Centers (a decrease from the previous authorization of $7.5 million in the 2008 Food, Energy and Conservation Act). For the past 25 years, only $4 million of those funds have been appropriated annually.

Sources: USDA ARS (2011); Jensen (2007); USDA National Institute of Food and Agriculture (2009), total value compiled by authors.

Various other federal agencies maintain responsibility for aspects of aquaculture oversight. The Fish and Wildlife Services (an agency of the DOI) enforces the Lacey Act, which pertains to interstate shipment and sale of wildlife. The Food and Drug Administration of the Department of Health and Human

Services regulates food safety (particularly as it pertains to the inspection of imported goods), and the Environmental Protection Agency and Army Corps of Engineers both oversee issues related to aquaculture discharge into rivers and coastal waters. After previous challenges at coordinating interagency strategy around aquaculture development, such as the abandoned 1995 attempt to update the National Aquaculture Development Plan, in the summer of 2012, the JSA (operating as the Interagency Working Group on Aquaculture, or IWGA) released a draft Research & Development Strategic Plan aimed at shaping the goals and focus of the IWGA to encourage aquaculture development over the next five to ten years (USDA ARS, 2012). The plan lays out nine strategic goals with a strong orientation toward research and development – investing public dollars in both public and private efforts to develop better technologies so that the industry can expand while maintaining a high level of commitment to environmental sustainability. Focus areas identified for research and development include integration of aquaculture development and conservation efforts, animal health and feed requirements, production efficiency and innovative systems, and workforce development, among other areas. It remains to be seen whether this new attempt at coordination influences overall industry growth.

This renewed energy around coordination of efforts by agencies within the JSA has been cited by former USDA aquaculture representative, Gary Jensen, as a critical element of sharing information and creating synergy around funding priorities that can lead to more efficient investment in research and development (Jensen, 2007). At the same time, Jensen asserts that the strengths of each program and agency should be recognized and integrated more fully into collaborative aquaculture planning. One such opportunity is the ability to use the characteristics of the various types of aquaculture to differentiate and market products in ways that resonate with consumers. For example, recent efforts at the USDA to establish organic standards for aquaculture products are one case in which land-based tank aquaculture – largely the purview of the agriculture-oriented USDA – can be distinguished from marine-based net pen aquaculture by the ability to control all inputs into the product (USDA AMS, 2013). The awareness of US consumers of the organic label and rigor around its enforcement creates a market opportunity for organic-certified American-raised fish. Organic certification of marine-based aquaculture may be more challenging due to more limited ability to ascertain inputs and control the marine environment.

In addition to the critical role federal governance plays in supporting aquaculture monitoring, research, and development, each state also plays an important role in the oversight and development of the aquaculture industry. The next section of this chapter examines various ways in which states situate aquaculture within their own regulatory environments.

State aquaculture governance

Wide variation exists within the states in the extent to which aquaculture is regulated, the way in which oversight is conducted and permitting occurs, and the types and number of agencies involved. Often, the variations in jurisdiction and laws between states create a tangle of regulations which may challenge and even discourage coordination of the industry across state lines. Table 19.1 provides an overview of the primary governance bodies for aquaculture in each state, showing that jurisdiction may fall to departments of agriculture, fish and wildlife, natural resources or ecology, coastal management, or a separately established aquaculture office/bureau. It demonstrates that among states, there is little consensus around what type of activity aquaculture is and which department should be responsible for regulating its practice and ensuring its growth. The Department of Agriculture has jurisdiction most commonly, in 24 total states, while Fish and Game has jurisdiction in 12 states and the Department of Natural Resources/Ecology in nine states (departmental jurisdiction could not be identified for five states).

TABLE 19.1 State-by-state governance of aquaculture.

State	Governing Department	Aquaculture Definition
Alabama	Department of Agriculture and Industries, Marketing and Economics Division	No information available online.
Alaska	Department of Fish and Game	Shellfish only. Marine finfish aquaculture prohibited. Land-based aquaculture regulations and permitting for hatcheries only.
Arizona	Department of Agriculture, Animal Services Division (No information on website)	'Aquaculture' or 'aquaculture facility' means the controlled propagation, growth and harvest of aquatic animals or plants, including fish, amphibians, shellfish, mollusks, crustaceans, algae and vascular plants.
Arkansas	Agriculture Department, Aquaculture Division	More than 20 species of fish and crustaceans … supply food-fish markets, recreational fishing markets and waters, retail pet markets, gardening supply markets, and markets for aquatic weed and snail control. (No detailed information available online.)
California	Department of Fish & Wildlife	Marine: Finfish, plants, and shellfish. Inland: plants and animals for food, bait and stocking.
Colorado	Department of Agriculture, Division of Animal Industry	Permit required for all facilities that broker, propagate, sell, trade or transport live native or nonnative fish or viable gametes.

Continued

State	Governing Department	Aquaculture Definition
Connecticut	Department of Agriculture, Bureau of Aquaculture	Aquaculture is the cultivation of aquatic plants and animals. In Connecticut aquaculture operations include a diverse range of operations such as growing shellfish on underwater leases in Long Island Sound and raising fish in inland freshwater tank farms.
Delaware	Department of Natural Resources (tidal-based finfish and shellfish aquaculture on a case by case basis)	Formal rules for non-tidal aquaculture have not been implemented by the Department of Agriculture.
Florida	Department of Agriculture and Consumer Services, Division of Aquaculture	Florida aquafarms culture products for food and non-food markets that include seafood (fish and shellfish), freshwater and marine aquarium hobbyists, high-fashion leather, water gardening, bait, biological control, biofuels, or as 'seed' for national and international aquaculturists.
Georgia	Department of Natural Resources, Wildlife Resources Division	Aquaculture permit is for aquaculturists producing and selling or retailers/wholesalers reselling domestic fish. Game fish and non-domestic fish (including tilapia), are not covered under aquaculture regulations, and may be permitted under a Wild Animal License.
Hawaii	Department of Agriculture, Animal Industry Division	2011 Hawaii total aquaculture sales were valued at $40 million, increasing $10 million from 2010. Algae sales accounted for 63% of the value, ornamental category 6%, finfish 4%, Shellfish 1%, and the rest 26% includes seedstock, broodstock and fingerlings.
Idaho	Department of Agriculture, Division of Animal Industry	Anyone obtaining, possessing, preserving or propagating fish to sell must first secure a commercial fish-rearing license from the Director of the IDA.
Illinois	Department of Natural Resources	No definition available online.
Indiana	Department of Natural Resources, Division of Fish and Wildlife	No definition available online; fish for stocking and human consumption permitted, per permit application.

State	Governing Department	Aquaculture Definition
Iowa	Department of Natural Resources	A holder of an aquaculture unit license may possess, propagate, buy, sell, deal in, and transport the aquatic organisms produced from breeding stock legally acquired, including minnows. Also, a license holder may be an owner or operator of a pond where guests or customers are allowed to fish for a fee, or allowed to take fish without regard to angling licenses, seasons, gear restrictions, or bag limits.
Kansas	No information available online.	
Kentucky	Department of Agriculture (marketing); Department of Fish and Wildlife (Permitting)	Propagation, sale and transport permitted for food, stock, and bait (per permit).
Louisiana	Department of Wildlife and Fisheries	Permit required for 'domestic aquatic organism culture' and culture of exotic species (i.e. tilapia and triploid carp).
Maine	Department of Marine Resources	Primarily leases in coastal waters.
Maryland	Department of Natural Resources, Fisheries Service	Commercial bottom leases for shellfish; hatcheries division for finfish is only for stockers.
Massachusetts	Department of Agricultural Resources	Commercial cultivation of aquatic plants and animals
Michigan	Department of Agriculture and Rural Development, Animal Industry Division	Need an Aquaculture Facility Registration if you will be commercially culturing, producing, growing, using, propagating, harvesting, transporting, importing, exporting, or marketing approved aquaculture species under the Michigan Aquaculture Act.
Minnesota	Department of Natural Resources	There are four type of commercial aquaculture licenses available: (1) aquatic farm; (2) private fish hatchery with sales over $200; (3) private fish hatchery with sales less than $200; and (4) aquarium facility. An aquatic farm license can include ponds, vats, tanks, raceways, and other indoor or outdoor facilities that an aquatic farmer owns or has the right to use.

Continued

State	Governing Department	Aquaculture Definition
Mississippi	Department of Agriculture and Commerce	Permit required for non-native fish, game fish, endangered species, genetically modified plants and animals. Permit not required for native fish, including catfish.
Missouri	Department of Agriculture	Missouri fish production includes warm and cold-water species, bait, ornamental, food fish, and fish for stocking.
Montana	Nebraska, New York, New Hampshire	No information available online.
Nebraska		No formal regulation info.
Nevada	Department of Wildlife	Must register commercial possession of live wildlife for all species.
New Hampshire		No information available online.
New Jersey	Department of Agriculture, Division of Agricultural and Animal Resources	Primarily mollusks; some finfish for food, bait, and sport.
New Mexico	Department of Game and Fish	No information available online.
New York		No formal regulation info.
North Carolina	Department of Agriculture and Consumer Services, Division of Marketing	Aquaculture is the business of farming aquatic plants and animals. In North Carolina, farmers grow trout, catfish, hybrid striped bass, prawn, crawfish, ornamental fish, baitfish, clams and oysters.
North Dakota	Game and Fish Department, Fisheries Division	No formal regulation info.
Ohio	Department of Agriculture; permits issued by Department of Natural Resources	'Aquaculture' means a form of agriculture that involves the propagation and rearing of aquatic species in controlled environments under private control, including but not limited to, for the purpose of sale for consumption as food.
Oklahoma	Department of Agriculture, Food and Forestry, Division of Animal Industry	Aquaculture operation means a private commercial producer of catfish, minnows, fingerlings, fish, frogs, or other aquatic species.
Oregon	Department of Fish and Wildlife	Stocking, human consumption.

State	Governing Department	Aquaculture Definition
Pennsylvania	Department of Agriculture	The Pennsylvania Department of Agriculture licenses parties propagating and dealing species that live on or in the water, including but not limited to all game fish, fish bait, baitfish, amphibians, reptiles and aquatic organisms.
Rhode Island	Coastal Resources Management Council	Currently all of the farms in the state's waters grow shellfish with the vast majority being oysters. There is a marine ornamental fish farm but it is on land in tanks, not in the state's waters. Additionally the state cultures fish for stocking freshwater fisheries and for restoring coastal habitats.
South Carolina	Department of Agriculture	Aquaculture permitted through Aquaculture Permitting Assistance Office (established in law, but not in practice?); no information available online.
South Dakota	Department of Game, Fish and Parks	This license authorizes the licensee to sell, possess, transport, propagate, rear, or produce live fish or any fish reproductive product for commercial purposes in all facilities, man-made waters and natural waters approved by the Department.
Tennessee		No information available online.
Texas	Department of Agriculture	A business that produces and sells cultured species raised in a private facility must obtain an aquaculture license from TDA. A private facility is a pond, tank, cage or other structure capable of holding cultured species in confinement wholly within or on private land or water or on permitted public land or water.
Utah	Department of Agriculture and Food, Fish Health Program	The program registers commercial aquaculture and fee fishing facilities, conducts fish health inspections for those operators wishing to sell live products, issues entry permits for all imports of live fish or eggs into Utah, performs export inspections of brine shrimp, maintains a current listing of those facilities determined to be fish health approved for movement of live fish or eggs, offers limited diagnostic services for operators, and provides advice and information on aquaculture and fish health.

Continued

State	Governing Department	Aquaculture Definition
Vermont	Department of Agriculture	Stocking only.
Virginia	Molluscs: Marine Fisheries Commission; Other fish: Department of Game and Inland Fisheries	Primarily molluscs in tidal waters; certain regulated breeds, including crayfish, tilapia, perch, and catfish may be propagated and sold for human consumption.
Washington	Department of Fish and Wildlife and Department of Ecology (Shoreline Master Programs)	Aquatic Farm Registration authorizes an individual to commercially manage and farm cultured aquatic products on privately owned lands.
West Virginia	Department of Agriculture and Division of Natural Resources	Propagation, rearing, and/or use of aquatic species in controlled or selected environments for private and or commercial purposes related to food production, recreation, research, importation, exportation, marketing, transportation and science.
Wisconsin	Department of Agriculture, Trade and Consumer Protection and Department of Natural Resources (for environmental permitting)	'Fish farm' means a facility or group of facilities, all located on a single parcel of land or on two or more contiguous parcels, at which a person hatches fish eggs, rears live fish or holds live fish for the purpose of introduction into the waters of the state, human or animal consumption, fishing, use as bait or fertilizer, or for sale to another person to rear for one of those purposes.
Wyoming	Game and Fish Department	Regulations on sale of hatchery fish for human consumption unclear.

Sources: State agency websites, accessed 2013.

In reviewing each state's approach to aquaculture governance, three distinct models are apparent. In order to illustrate these different approaches, we present three case studies for aquaculture governance across different states. In each model, primary jurisdiction falls under a different department, illuminating strengths of the various models that could be considered across states to encourage cohesion and facilitate interstate cooperation in the sustainable development of the domestic aquaculture industries. The three states are California, North Carolina, and Washington. These states represent a diversity of types of aquaculture, governance structures, and industry sizes. Washington's aquaculture industry is primarily made of marine shellfish and net-pen production; California has a relatively even mix of offshore and land-based production, and North Carolina's production is largely land-based (USDA NASS, 2005b).

California, North Carolina, and Washington represent states with relatively high aquaculture sales that have also shown recent growth in the aquaculture sector. North Carolina exhibited particularly strong growth compared to most states between 1998 and 2005 (the most recent year for which data is available), with a 115 percent increase in overall sales, while California saw a 60 percent increase in sales and Washington a 65 percent increase in overall sales. The United States aquaculture industry as a whole has seen just a 12 percent increase in sales, indicating that the three states selected, in addition to representing a diversity of production methods and oversight models, are also representative of states that are growing their aquaculture industries more successfully than average (see Figure 19.6). Overall, aquaculture comprises a small portion of overall agricultural sales in each state. In California, it makes up about 0.07 percent of sales, in North Carolina, about 0.68 percent, and in Washington, about 1.4 percent of overall sales, so despite stronger than average growth, the industries in each state are small compared to other types of agricultural production (USDA NASS, 2005a, 2007). Other states with high aquaculture sales and recent growth were not selected for study due to relative similarity in governance structure or production types to the three cases selected; diversity of cases was prioritized in final selection.

California

Jurisdiction over aquaculture in California is primarily with the Natural Resources Agency houses the Department of Fish and Wildlife, which is the agency with jurisdiction over the regulating and permitting of aquaculture activities. Within the department, distinct processes exist for marine-based and land-based aquaculture (see Figure 19.7).

In California, both land and marine-based aquaculture facilities must be registered annually. The expense associated with registering an aquaculture facility in California can be significant (over $1,000 per year for facilities with revenues greater than $25,000) (California Natural Resources Agency, 2013). It has been noted that the fee structure may discourage some operators using land-based recirculating aquaponic systems from registering as an aquaculture facility so that they are able to sell the fish they cultivate (aquaponic farm operator, personal communication, 2013). Additionally, there are a number of permits, including multiple types of importation and stocking permits which one must navigate when registering an aquaculture facility.

The fee structure for marine-based aquaculture in California is the same as for land-based aquaculture, but the applicable regulations and permits are distinct and governed by a wide variety of state agencies. For instance, the California Department of Public Health regulates issues related to shellfish health and sanitation, the Regional Water Quality Control Boards oversee discharge and benthic habitat monitoring, and the Coastal Commission regulates land and water use in the coastal zone. State-sponsored marketing of aquaculture products in California

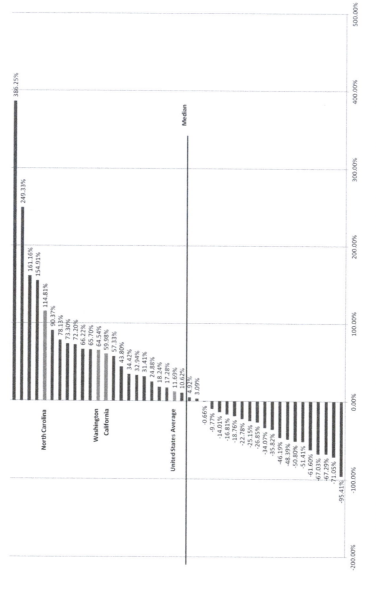

FIGURE 19.6 Percentage change in aquaculture production by state (with sales over $20 million), 1998 to 2005.

Sources: USDA NASS (2005a), calculations by author, data not available for seven states.

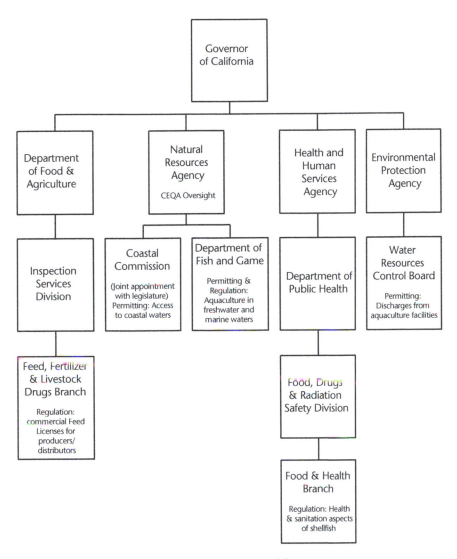

FIGURE 19.7 California aquaculture governance model.

is limited. The state does not have a strong public campaign for aquaculture products and producers in the state (which is a typical function of an agriculture department), and searching the public database for state aquaculturists is difficult to navigate for a public consumer seeking a specific product (California Natural Resources Agency, Department of Fish and Game, 2013). Marketing and promotional support for the aquaculture industry seems to be concentrated instead in the independent, membership-based California Aquaculture Association.

North Carolina

Figure 19.8 demonstrates North Carolina's oversight structure. In contrast to California, in North Carolina, an operator can obtain a free license through the Agricultural Commissioner's Office for land-based aquaculture in North Carolina that lasts up to five years (though additional permits may be required, such as a permit to transport stock or to cultivate a non-approved species). The state's simplified, streamlined permit and fee structure is concentrated under the jurisdiction of the Department of Agriculture. The streamlined process and concentrated oversight model may be one contributing factor to North Carolina's strong aquaculture growth.

The presence of strong marketing and technical support for the state's aquaculture industry by the North Carolina Department of Agriculture and Consumer Services seems to be another contributing factor to growth in the state's industry. Seafood and aquaculture products are incorporated within the Department's broader 'Got to Be NC Agriculture' marketing campaign (www.gottobenc.com;), and the Department's website includes a public list by species of sources for North Carolina aquaculture products (North Carolina Department of Agriculture and Consumer Services, n.d.). Additionally, the Department has a Seafood Marketing

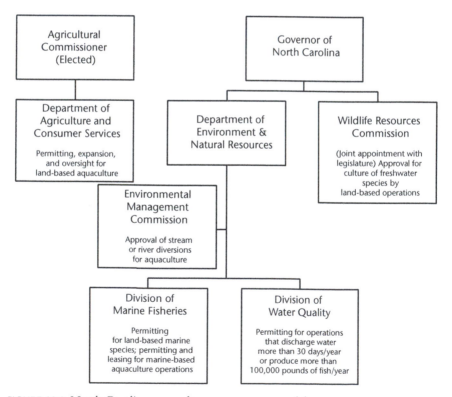

FIGURE 19.8 North Carolina aquaculture governance model.

Office which promotes both catch fisheries and aquaculture in the state; it also advertises the services of NC Extension agents who provide technical support for aquaculture farmers in the state.

Washington

Similarly to California, Washington defines aquaculture as primarily a natural resources concern, concentrating jurisdiction over aquaculture within the Department of Ecology (see Figure 19.9). This is reflective of the strong marine aquaculture presence (both net-pen and shellfish) in that state. Marine aquaculture is defined as a preferred shoreline activity that is beneficial to the state in the short- and long-term if properly managed, and local governments are instructed to allow it if there is no evidence of the net loss of ecological functions (Washington State Department of Ecology, 2012).

The Department of Ecology's role is instructive to local governments in making decisions about where and when net-pen and shellfish aquaculture activities are to be allowed. The Department also manages point source pollution permitting and works closely with net-pen operators to monitor escapement plans, fish feed, biomass and chemical usage on a monthly basis (Washington State Department of Ecology, n.d.).

Careful monitoring of the shellfish and net-pen aquaculture industries and the prioritization of aquaculture as an activity that benefits the state, supported by a science-based process for monitoring ecological impacts has allowed the Washington State aquaculture industry to grow over time. However, the Washington model

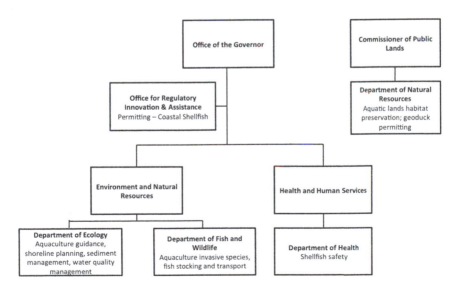

FIGURE 19.9 Washington aquaculture governance model.

has limited applicability in most states without long stretches of shoreline, and may not provide a strong model for overall federal governance, especially given the challenges experienced at the federal level in balancing ecological protection with industry growth. Washington's success may also be attributable to the relatively small amount of coastline it must monitor, relative to the broader diversity of coastal habitats that must be managed nationwide.

While Washington has been successful in growing its shellfish and net-pen industries compared to many states, continued growth over time may also be limited by the capacity of the coastline. While inland space is relatively unlimited and can handle increased capacity without environmental detriment in many cases, states such as Washington with a strong emphasis on marine-based aquaculture may need to turn toward land-based aquaculture to continue experiencing industry growth.

Summary

The case studies presented in this section highlight different approaches to governance that states have taken to support and regulate the aquaculture industry. Two main lessons can be drawn from the comparisons that are suggestive of approaches that administrators and policymakers could take to encourage future growth in the industry.

1   Centralized regulation and oversight appear to contribute to a successful aquaculture industry within a given state. While North Carolina and Washington house aquaculture oversight in different types of departments, North Carolina's industry has experienced strong growth under its agriculture department and Washington's aquaculture industry comprises a strong percentage of its overall agriculture compared to the other two states. This centralized governance also allows for a streamlined permitting process through one department, which may make it easier for aquaculture operators in North Carolina to navigate the permitting process than is the case in California, where permits must be renewed frequently from several departments.
2   State-sponsored marketing support may be a critical component of the growth of the aquaculture industry in that state, and departments of agriculture are traditionally responsible for marketing of agricultural commodities in ways that a science-based monitoring body such as a department of ecology or natural resources may not be as well funded to handle.

Conclusions

United States aquaculture governance is comprised of a diversity of regulatory environments, reflecting the unique nature of the industry at the intersection of species management, environmental protection, and agricultural production. This is apparent from the range of agencies involved in aquaculture regulation and oversight at the federal level and reinforced by the variety of governance structures across states. Some argue that a lack of consensus over where to best situate the industry for the purposes of providing centralized oversight and minimizing the inefficiencies that result from the necessary involvement of many agencies has contributed to the overall lack of growth in the US aquaculture industry compared with growth in other countries. This raises the question, then – one prime for consideration by economists, scientists, and policymakers – of whether oversight of aquaculture should be more centralized, to encourage innovation and investment in the industry while maintaining the relatively high standards for environmental sustainability and food safety that are important to US production practices.

While the involvement of many agencies in aquaculture oversight is necessary given the overlap in jurisdictions that arise from the unique nature of aquaculture as compared to other forms of agriculture, the multi-agency Joint Subcommittee on Aquaculture [JSA] at the federal level appears to have been limited in its ability to create a cohesive national aquaculture agenda which promotes industry growth. The success of the cattle and poultry industries under the auspices of the USDA suggest that more centralized responsibility may be a key to growth. While the involvement of each agency represented on the JSA is critical, an important question for continued consideration is whether responsibility for aquaculture has been too widely dispersed to effectively manage and grow the industry. And if so, how can governance be concentrated more effectively within one agency while retaining the critical benefits that come from the involvement of a multitude of agencies?

The three case studies demonstrate that aquaculture growth can thrive under the primary oversight of a variety of different agencies. However, the strength of the North Carolina industry suggests that categorizing land-based aquaculture as primarily an agricultural activity may allow for greater promotional and development opportunities which can draw attention to the relative benefits of aquaculture and help grow the land-based industry. This is reinforced by findings from federal aquaculture oversight. NOAA has traditionally had to balance its mandate for coastal preservation with industry expansion within marine-based aquaculture oversight. The USDA has demonstrated that it can successfully grow and market livestock commodities such as cattle and poultry, so this agency could have a particularly critical role in supporting the growth of land-based aquaculture, using a model similar to that of North Carolina's.

It is also easier to control inputs, effluent, and species protection in land-based aquaculture than marine aquaculture, such that land-based aquaculture presents an opportunity for growth in the aquaculture industry nationwide which can be pursued sustainably and with minimal negative consequences for natural ecosystems and wild stocks. For this reason, the North Carolina model of regulating aquaculture as agriculture holds promise. While the Washington state model has worked well given the particular characteristics of that state, it may not be an effective and replicable framework for most states without expansive coastlines.

While the case study model used here helps illustrate a variety of issues related to regulation and oversight in the US aquaculture industry, further investigation into the successes and limitations of a complete analysis of governance structures in all 50 states, the influence of governance in each state on industry growth, and analysis of the influence on growth of factors besides governance structure is critical for informing decisions made by policymakers and governmental entities.

References

Albright, M. (2014). 'Food czars and food policy councils', *The Plate*, 14 August, http://theplate.nationalgeographic.com/2014/08/14/food-czars-and-food-policy-councils/

Andreatta, S. and Parlier, A. (2010) 'The political ecology of small-scale commercial fishermen in Carteret County, North Carolina', *Human Organization*, vol 69, no 2

California Resources Agency, Department of Fish and Game (2013) '2013 registered aquaculturists', https://nrm.dfg.ca.gov/FileHandler.ashx?DocumentID=3265&inline=true

California Natural Resources Agency (2013), '2013 Aquaculture Registration Application', California Natural Resources Agency, Sacramento, CA, https://nrm.dfg.ca.gov/FileHandler.ashx?DocumentID=35115&inline=true

De Schutter, Oliver (2014) *Report of the Special Rapporteur on the Right to Food*, United Nations Human Rights Council, 24 January

FAO (2012) *The State of World Fisheries and Aquaculture*, Food and Agriculture Organization of the United Nations, Rome

Hanson, T. and Sites, D. (2011) *U.S. Farm-raised Catfish Industry, 2010 Review and 2011 Outlook*. Auburn University, Auburn, AL

Hishamunda, N., Ridler, N. and Martone, E. (2014) 'Policy and governance in aquaculture: Lessons learned and way forward', *FAO Fisheries and Aquaculture Technical Paper*, no 577

Jensen, G. L. (2007) 'Evolutionary role of federal policies and actions to support the sustainable development of aquaculture in the United States', in P. S. Lueng, L. Cheng-Sheng and P. J. O'Bryen (eds), *Species and System Selection for Sustainable Aquaculture*, pp. 179–208

Kooiman, J., Jentoft, S., Pullin, R. and Bavinck, M. (2005) *Fish for Life: Interactive Governance for Fisheries*, p. 13, Amsterdam University Press, Amsterdam

Larsen, J. and Roney, J. M. (2013) *Plan B Updates: Farmed Fish Production Overtakes Beef*, Earth Policy Institute, Washington, DC

Leisher, C. (2013) 'Milestone Looms for Farm-Raised Fish', *New York Times*, 24 January

National Marine Fisheries Service (2014) 'Aquaculture FAQ', www.nmfs.noaa.gov/aquaculture/faqs/faq_aq_101.html, accessed 18 August 2014

NOAA (2011) *Marine Aquaculture Policy*, NOAA, Washington, DC

North Carolina Department of Agriculture and Consumer Services (n.d.) 'Marketing-aquaculture', www.ncagr.gov/markets/aquaculture/product.htm

OECD/FAO (2014) *OECD-FAO Agricultural Outlook 2014*, OECD Publishing

USDA AMS (2013) 'National Organic Standards Board (NOSB) – Subcommittee meeting notes', www.ams.usda.gov/AMSv1.0/NOSB

USDA ARS (2011) Aquaculture (NP 106) Annual Report for 2011, USDA Agriculture Research Service, Washington, DC, www.ars.usda.gov/SP2UserFiles/Program/106/AnnualReports/NP106%20Ann%20Rep%202011%20Final.pdf

USDA ARS (2012) *National Aquaculture Research and Development Strategic Plan*, USDA Agriculture Research Service, Washington, DC, www.ars.usda.gov/SP2UserFiles/Program/106/JSA%20AQUA%20RD%20PLAN%20DRAFT%208JUN2012.pdf

USDA ERS (2012) 'Animal production and marketing issues – policy and regulatory issues', www.ers.usda.gov/topics/animal-products/animal-production-marketing-issues/policy-regulatory-issues.aspx#.UdMq5TsipIE

USDA ERS (2013) 'Aquaculture data', www.ers.usda.gov/data-products/aquaculture-data.aspx#.VDGhIPldXHQ

USDA NASS (2005a) 'Table 1: Value of aquaculture products sold by type, by state and United States', *Census of Aquaculture*, United States Department of Agriculture,

USDA NASS (2005b) 'Table 4: Freshwater and Saltwater Acres Used for Aquaculture Production, by State and United States: 2005 and 1998', *Census of Aquaculture*, United States Department of Agriculture, Washington, DC

USDA NASS (2007) 'Census of Agriculture', www.agcensus.usda.gov/Publications/2007/Online_Highlights/Desktop_Application Washington, DC, www.agcensus.usda.gov/Publications/2002/Aquaculture/aquacen2005_01.pdf

USDA National Institute of Food and Agriculture (2009) 'Aquaculture', http://nifa.usda.gov/program/aquaculture

Washington State Department of Ecology (2012) 'Shoreline Master Program Updates: Aquaculture Interim Guidance', www.ecy.wa.gov/programs/sea/shorelines/smp/handbook/aquaculture_guidance.pdf

Washington State Department of Ecology (n.d.) 'Shoreline Planning and Commercial Net Pens', www.ecy.wa.gov/programs/sea/aquaculture/planning_netpens.html

20

CONCLUSION

Affect and attribution

Jody Emel and Harvey Neo

Researching the industrial livestock sector is like watching the Luis Buñuel film, *Los Olvidados* (The Forgotten Ones). Set in Mexico City's slums, the film depicts a number of events in the lives of a neighborhood stricken by poverty and despair. It's difficult to find the good guys because everyone but the animals is somewhat maleficent. Yet there are explanations for much of violence and neglect: Pedro, one of the lost youths who is complicit in the murder of another, has a mother who doesn't or can't love him. She refuses to feed him and treats her other children (by other fathers) with preference. You despise her until you find out later that Pedro is the result of a rape. The circumstances afford some empathy then even though you can't entirely forgive her for her cruelty. You feel sorry for the young people in these miserable conditions; but then they attack and rob a blind man and break his musical instruments. You despise them for it but find out later that the blind man is a miser, a seducer of young girls in the neighborhood, and an informant who tells the police where Jaibo (the leader of the group) is, resulting in his death. Yet the blind man also helps a sick woman and takes in a small boy whose parents have deserted him. The youth also torment a legless man and, again, you can't help but abhor them. But then, with more insight, we viewers are led again to feel sorry for the violent youths who are unloved, unfed, and unseen by the rest of society. Indeed, the film begins with a narrator stating that the film has no answers and leaves the amelioration of the problems of exploitation and brutality to the 'progressive forces of society', which will be shown as 'well-intentioned but ultimately feckless'. Buñuel, a contemporary of Salvador Allende and Pablo Neruda, was an anarcho-Marxist (although at times, disavowing both) with a marked orientation toward surrealist nihilism.

The same kind of rolling blame and shifting empathy happens when evaluating the industrial animal production sector. You feel bad for the 'producers' (or 'farmers') because of their oppression and exploitation by the 'processors' (or slaughterers) until you realize that they (the producers) are responsible for the exploitation and torture of the animals and for the non-transparency of the 'growing' process. You feel terrible for the animals but you realize that the animal welfare groups who provide some of the descriptions are accused by the industry of adulterating some of their narratives. But when you read what has been done to silence those who want to make visible the exploitation of animals and workers, you despise the producers all over again – not to mention the politicians who support this just to get votes and financing for their elections. And finally, as several commentators on the whole supply chain observe, what about the consumers? Certainly they (we) are not innocent bystanders!

Los Olvidados is recognized as a social critique, as an indictment of contemporary urban society through its depiction of overcrowded slums, domestic abuse, incest, child abuse, the arbitrary nature of crime and punishment, poverty, and the ineptness of public social services. One could easily argue that a similar depiction of industrial animal production is quite plausible, full of worker exploitation, animal abuse, farmer abuse, inept regulatory policies and efforts, and the overall fault of an economic system that focuses, inexorably, on wealth maximization for those with access to capital. Let us take a brief look at some of the actors involved.

The producers/farmers

Producers may range in size from those with a few animals to those managing hundreds of thousands. For example, one of the largest individually owned poultry 'farms' in the world (Al Watania in Saudi Arabia) maintains over 26 million broiler chickens and 245 million hatching eggs (Bal, 2011). A Ukrainian 'farm' hosts 1.5 million chickens. Anna Creek Station in southern Australia is a ranch of 6 million acres hosting up to 17,000 cattle. One of the massive pig farms in China hosts 6,500 breeding sows and their offspring – far bigger than anything in Europe. So do we call all of these people or systems farmers or farms? We wouldn't call Tyson Foods or Seaboard Farms farmers. Do we consider feedlot operators farmers? And what if the difference is between a so-called small feedlot of 10,000 head and one of over 100,000 head? In the poultry model which developed in the southeastern US (Boyd and Watts, 1997), the farmer/producer is essentially at the mercy of the processor or integrator. The integrator controls every phase of production and even owns the chickens or turkeys. Much hog production also takes place under these sorts of conditions. This model whereby the farmer becomes a serf on his or her own land is widely accepted as a product of industrialized agriculture (Watts and Goodman, 1997). But as Ashwood et al. (2014) argue, this is not always the case; in fact the proliferation of limited liability corporations (LLCs) yields a somewhat different pattern, albeit not without problems for the rural communities nearby. Hog farmers, investors, and management companies can use overlapping LLCs to reduce risk and make it impossible for rural communities to gain compensation from pollution, disease, property devaluation, or other hazards generated by concentrated animal feeding operations (CAFOs).

Despite this fuzziness and confusion regarding who is a farmer, it is difficult to read the hearings from the US Department of Justice's antitrust tour in 2010, especially in the southeastern US, without feeling sympathy for the poultry 'farmers'. So many families who invested (and borrowed) heavily in poultry buildings and land testified about their difficulties with big processors like Tyson and Purdue. Contracts which were supposed to last ten years, allowing for the payoff of the loans, were shorted to three, then one, then just one growing cycle. Producers who couldn't or wouldn't invest in new technology and upgrades were just cut off, denied new contracts, and with no other processors in their area, were forced to bankruptcy. Producers/farmers were paid very little per chicken, a portion of the pay being dependent upon what is called the 'tournament' system which pits producer against producer (and sometimes neighbor against neighbor). The best, judged non-transparently by the processor or integrator, gets a bit more per chicken, the worst, a bit less. Yet all are given the same genetics, feed, medications and so forth — allegedly. The system is supposed to induce innovation and good management, yet it seems most people who testified believe it rewards the newest buildings and those who don't quibble. Many people who testified also complained about the lack of transparency throughout the system — particularly the poultry production system. With no spot (cash) markets left for chickens, the producers get just what the integrators want to pay. The hog spot market is only about 4 per cent of the traded value so the transparency there is waning as well. Even cattle producers or ranchers complain about the lack of transparency in the pricing process involved in the market.

The animal rights people and the animals

Yet, just as we start feeling bad for the 'farmers', we have to look at what these folks, their corporations and their public relations councils do to reduce transparency as to how the animals are treated. First of all, there is no animal that is 'happy' with industrialized, intensive production. We might argue that the lambs and cows on a cow-calf ranch are best off because they are out grazing for some of their relatively short lives. But the pigs and birds that live their short lives inside buildings with very little exercise, and standing in their own excrement day after day (as do feedlot sheep and cattle), are pretty much miserable creatures who must be mutilated in order not to attack each other in their boredom and forced proximity. To bring the pictures of these poor animals to the consumer or to society (as in the case of Buñuel's film which shows the viewer the miserable plight of children in Mexico City slums in the 1950s), animal groups must pose as workers and go undercover to reveal the situation. Individuals within these groups, like People for the Ethical Treatment of Animals, the Human Society of the United States, Mercy for Animals, have gotten hired as workers and filmed all kinds of horrors that have led to some changes in retailer supply chains and public knowledge of animal production. But several states have recently passed ag-gag laws to make this a crime.

In the US, and spreading to other countries like Australia, there is a battle ongoing to prohibit the undercover filming of factory farm practices. A Utah law invents the crime of 'agricultural operation interference'. The basic idea is that no sound or image can be recorded without the owner's permission. Now in court, the plaintiffs contesting the law argue it prohibits a form of political speech which is 'of great public interest'. They also claim that the law violates the protection of whistle-blowers. Kentucky House Bill 222 was recently created to make euthanasia methods on factory farms less inhumane, but state senators inserted a clause that would prohibit people from gaining 'access to an agricultural operation through misrepresentation,' thus making it unlawful for activist undercover investigators to seek employment at factory farms. Ag-gag proponents claim that animal cruelty can be fought without secret exposés, but covert investigations have been the most effective method of revealing the cruel practices of the animal agriculture industry. For example, in late February 2014, footage taken at the Iron Maiden Hog Farm in Owensboro, KY, showed sows being kept in extremely confining cages while being fed the intestines of their piglets who had died from a diarrheal disease.

A catalyst for the prohibition of unauthorized transparency was the 2010 video filmed by an undercover worker on behalf of the United States Humane Society at a Hallmark Meat Packing plant where a slaughter plant worker is shown attempting to force a 'downed' cow onto its feet by ramming it with the blades of a forklift in Chino, California. The battle between producer organizations and animal rights activists over laws prohibiting secretly filmed documentation of animal abuse has moved to federal courts as ag-gag laws in Utah and Idaho face constitutional challenges. Opponents of the law point to the Chino video and the investigation that followed, which led to the largest meat recall in US history, saying the secrecy puts consumers at higher risk of food safety problems and animals at higher risk of abuse. During the past few years, criminal charges were brought against numerous factory farming operations. Charges were brought against the North Carolina Butterball facility after a recording showed turkeys being violently kicked and thrown and having their wings pulled by employees. A hidden camera revealed abuses towards laying hens at Sparboe Farms in Iowa, Minnesota, and Colorado, including workers maliciously torturing animals, dead birds in cages along with live laying hens, and employees throwing live birds into plastic bags to suffocate. A hidden video at Central Valley Meat Co., a slaughterhouse in Hanford, California, that supplies meat for the USDA's National School Lunch Program and other federal food initiatives, documented deeply objectionable animal treatment, improper slaughter methods, and intentional cruelty to sick and injured cows. The violations at this facility were so serious that it was temporarily shut down by the US Department of Agriculture. Workers at a Seaboard Farms facility in Oklahoma were charged and convicted of cruelty to pigs because of the torture that was captured on film by an undercover worker.

Europol reports that 'animal rights extremists' are a rising problem and that they use disinformation to malign their 'targets' and that 'images of sick and abused animals are embedded in video footage and made public' (Europol, 2011). The industry and their political allies agree. State Senator Jim Patrick, a lead sponsor of the Idaho legislation and a farmer himself, explained the rationale behind his bill: 'It's not designed to cover up animal cruelty, but we have to defend ourselves.' And they see themselves defending against 'terrorism'; conflating groups like Mercy for Animals with more extreme groups like the Earth Liberation Front known for property damage.

Interestingly, the American Legislation Exchange (ALEC) provided the template for the state legislation in the US. ALEC is a right-wing organization that is attempting to change the course of US politics, one state at a time. Known as the 'corporate bill mill' by its critics, this group also provided legislative models for voter identification laws, 'stand your ground' gun laws, and the teaching of climate change denial in public schools (under the rubric of 'environmental literacy').

The workers

The issues of workers in slaughterhouses have been examined by numerous authors, including most recently, Tim Pachirat's exemplary *Every Twelve Seconds: Industrialized Slaughter and the Politics of Sight* (see also Stull and Broadway, 2012; Fink, 1998). And not only do the workers face the problems of line speed, hazardous chemicals and machinery, monotony, and temperature extremes, they also have to live in the communities nearby these facilities as Part II of this volume portrays. They suffer from a largely non-union, underpaid employment system, but they also end up, in some cases, performing acts of cruelty toward the animals (see Pachirat, 2013; Eisnitz, 2006; Neo and Emel, forthcoming). Should we blame them? Mark Bittman wrote, when commenting upon the animal rights movement in 2011, blaming individual farms or ranches and their employees is like blaming Lynddie England for Abu Ghraib. The problem is the system. Although Bittman goes on to charge the lack of laws to protect farm animals (there are no federal laws except for humane slaughter), we must also raise the specter of capitalism and the mission to accumulate at any cost.

> The biggest problem of all is that we've created a system in which *standard* factory-farming practices are inhumane, and the kinds of abuses documented at E6 [a cattle company in Texas] are really just reminders of that. If you're raising and killing 10 billion animals every year, some abuse is pretty much guaranteed.
>
> (Bittman, 2011)

Such an analysis is echoed by Cynthia Enloe, being interviewed by Doug Henwood about Abu Ghraib and Ms England:

> What we've all learned from Tailhook and from the Air Force Academy rape revelations and from Watergate and from My Lai, what we've learned but what we need to keep relearning is: always ask about the entire organizational decision-making process, the entire institutional culture. What is considered normal?

What's considered trivial? What's considered allowable? What's considered outrageous? Feminists have become very smart about this because they have had to learn all these skills to find out how sexual harassment happens in a law firm or in an automobile manufacturer, or in the military. At the top and in the middle of an organization, the directives that cumulatively make up the culture look either benign or bland or 'civilized', 'rational', 'modern', if you will, 'suited.'

(Enloe, 2004)

As Tony Weis (2013) has pointed out in his wonderful book on the ecological hoofprint, the gross externalities of the large operations (both producers and processors) make them seem efficient compared to smaller, mixed crop-livestock operations (or even pastoral systems for that matter). These large industries require public subsidies in terms of cheap grains and other feedstocks and free receptacles for waste disposal. They also require cheap labor – often immigrants without papers who have to work in sub-par conditions for low wages. Then there is the terrible exploitation of the animals themselves in order to mass produce at low cost.

And our response?

Sight is an important theme in the Buñuel film – the sightlessness of society is partly what creates *Los Olvidados* – a trope purveyed by Timothy Pachirat in his book about the invisibility of animal slaughter and human exploitation. Seeing or moving toward, or sensing as Kathryn Yusoff (2013) writes about following Jean-Luc Nancy, encourages or elicits a response. This is the impetus in John Berger's *Why Look at Animals*, encouraging the reader to 'see' animals as subjects and to see them differently. The eye – the seeing – is critical to feeling and responding. But this cannot be done in a postdomestic setting where there is such spatial distance between people and their living meat. The importance of seeing is underscored in the research, writing and organizing of workers as well. In Buñuel's movie, seeing and the eye are hyperemphasized because those who watch the film are spatially segregated from those subjects of the film. Sensing produces the possibility of a response, but what response?

As those who promote the 'livestock revolution' argue, people need to be fed what they want and cheaply. The argument is premised upon food security and a version of sustainability that requires GHG emissions be reduced through genetics and intensive confinement of animals. Workers on farms and in slaughterhouses will presumably continue to work at cut-throat speeds for low wages. Discursively, this path might be considered one of security and stability. The blind man in the film has nostalgia for the time of Don Porfirio. Porfirio Diaz ruled Mexico from 1876 to 1911 and while some associate him with modernization, internal stability, and economic development, others consider his regime repressive and stagnating. Similarly, the farmer/producers who testified at the US antitrust hearings in 2010 divided themselves between those who like the security and efficiency of the contract system and those who find it repressive and exploitative.

Berger (2009) reminds us that cattle had magical functions before they became meat and hide. In many cultures, animals still have these spiritual and cultural meanings. Not all people separate themselves from other animals through Western-developed taxonomies or 'species' categories. Some imagine their relatives married to particular animals, or sisters and brothers of particular animals. These ontologies are quite different from western European or so-called modernist conceptualizations of people and nonhuman meat animals. The reduction of animals with many capacities to eaters and breeders is primarily a post-Second World War phenomena. The presence of animals (hens and donkeys) in *Los Olvidados* as emotional markers and indicators of innocent helplessness, reminds us of the commonalities between all animals – human and nonhuman. A hen suddenly appears by the fallen blind man after the children attack him. Pedro is seen in his house embracing a hen (but later kills one in a frustrated rage). The little boy who cries for his parents sucks milk from a cow with whom he shares a barn. The animals are as defenseless as the blind man and Pedro – they are in the same position in life. Violence and exploitation seem to be part of life, at least at the bottom of the animal hierarchy. Buñuel sees humans as animals, and animals must do what they can to survive. Yet like the farm animals in the film, many humans are at the mercy of others for sustenance: bodies that must eat, sleep, and find shelter – but not always with the means to do so. An example is the overt exploitation seen at the fairgrounds where all the rides are powered by child labor. The leader of the children insists that the boss pay them their wages but the boss knocks him around. Systematic exploitation is founded upon implicit violence on the part of owners and policymakers. Similarly, in industrial animal production, the workers are exploited and they in turn exploit the animals … all under the hand of the owners and policymakers.

But it isn't just the commonalities that bind us and encourage us toward a more just response; it is also the relationships or the relationality. Whether we acknowledge it or not, we are already in relationships with the farmers, the workers, and the nonhuman animals. We are produced by the particular configurations of these relationships; we are part of the meat system phenomena (after Barad, 2007). We are already in cohabitation and under co-obligation to the others in this entanglement (Yusoff, 2013). Surely we can find ways and means to make these entanglements more just.

References

Ashwood, L., Diamond, D. and Thu, K. (2014) 'Where's the farmer? Limiting liability in Midwestern industrial hog production', *Rural Sociology*, vol 79, no 1, pp. 2–27

Bal, A. (2011) 'Al Watania, Saudi Arabia: Poultry professionals in the Saudi desert', *World Poultry*, 20 September 2011, www.worldpoultry.net/Home/General/2011/9/Al-Watania-Saudi-Arabia-Poultry-professionals-in-the-Saudi-desert-WP009338W/, accessed 28 October 2014

Barad, K. (2007) *Meeting the Universe Halfway: Quantum Physics and the Entanglement of Matter and Meaning*, Duke University Press, Durham, NC

Berger, J. (2009) *Why Look at Animals?*, Penguin, New York

Bittman, M. (2011) 'Who protects the animals?, http://opinionator.blogs.nytimes.com/2011/04/26/who-protects-the-animals/?, accessed 23 October 2014

Boyd, W. and Watts M. (1997) 'Agro-industrial just-in-time: The chicken industry and postwar American capitalism', in D. Goodman and M. J. Watts (eds), *Globalising Food: Agrarian Questions and Global Restructuring*, Routledge, London

Eisnitz, G. (2006) *Slaughterhouse: The Shocking Story of Greed, Neglect and Inhumane Treatment Inside the U.S. Meat Industry*, Prometheus Books, New York

Enloe, C. (2004) 'Masculinity, oil, water, torture', interview with Doug Henwood, www.leftbusinessobserver.com/Enloe.html

Europol (2011) 'EU terrorism situation and trend report', *TE-SAT 2011*, https://www.europol.europa.eu/sites/default/files/publications/te-sat2011.pdf, accessed 24 October 2014

Fink, D. (1998) *Cutting into the Meatpacking Line: Workers and Change in the Rural Midwest*, University of North Carolina Press, Chapel Hill, NC

Neo, H. and Emel, J. (forthcoming) *Geographies of Meat*, Ashgate, Farnham

Pachirat, T. (2013) *Every Twelve Seconds: Industrialized Slaughter and the Politics of Sight*, Yale University Press, New Haven, CT

Stull, D. and Broadway, M. (2012) *Slaughterhouse Blues: The Meat and Poultry Industry in North America*, Cengage Learning, Independence, KY

Watts, M. J. and Goodman, D. (1997) 'Agrarian questions: Global appetite, local metabolism: Nature, culture, and industry in fin de siècle agro-food systems', in D. Goodman and M. J. Watts (eds), *Globalising Food: Agrarian Questions and Global Restructuring*, Routledge, London

Weis, T. (2013) *The Ecological Hoofprint: The Global Burden of Industrial Livestock*, Zed Books, London and New York

Yusoff, K. (2013) 'Insensible worlds: Postrelational ethics, indeterminacy, and the (k)nots of Relating', *Society and Space*, vol 31, pp. 201–236

INDEX

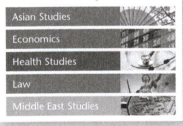
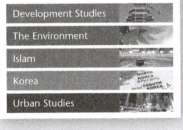